Emerging India in Asia-Pacific

Emerging India in Asia-Pacific

Edited by
Y. Yagama Reddy
Director, Centre for Southeast Asian & Pacific Studies
Sri Venkateswara University, Tirupati

New Century Publications
New Delhi, India

NEW CENTURY PUBLICATIONS
4800/24, Bharat Ram Road,
Ansari Road, Daryaganj,
New Delhi-110 002

Tel.: 23247798, 65396605
Telefax: 011-41017798
E-mail: indiatax@vsnl.com
www.newcenturypublications.com

Editorial office:
34, Gujranwala Town, Part-2,
Delhi - 110 009
Tel.: 27247805, 27464774

First Published 2007

ISBN: 81-7708-129-2

Published by New Century Publications and printed in India at Singhal Print Media, New Delhi, India.

The Book

After Independence in 1947, India was found to be more inward-looking than showing concern for its eastern neighbours. Its indifference to the ASEAN process and inclination towards the Soviet Union only widened the gulf between India and the ASEAN members. The termination of Cold War brought in a radical change in the perceptions and approaches of the regional powers towards regional cooperation. India's gradual integration with ASEAN, the enlargement of ASEAN into a full-fledged regional grouping, ASEAN's Summit level dialogues with China, Japan and Korea, (ASEAN+3), and India (ASEAN+1), have all kept the spirit of regional cooperation high.

Having steered its Look East Policy as a means of getting integrated with East Asia, India is now committed to consolidating the partnerships at various levels. India is not only being projected as a counter-balance to China, but also considered as a bridge to the markets of other Asian Countries. The historic East Asia Summit held in December 2005 at Kuala Lumpur, clearly demonstrated that the concept of *Asian-ness* is at last translated into reality.

This book contains 23 articles on the subject authored by eminent scholars in their respective field of specialization. The multidisciplinary character of the contents and treatment in this volume is obvious. The wide range of papers, delving deep into economic, cultural, political and strategic aspects at bilateral and multilateral levels, has shed light on the inherent potentialities and strengths of India to broaden and consolidate its prospects in Asian affairs. The facts and figures provided in various articles of this volume are a valuable source of information for the scholars who would be involved in research on India's multilateral relationships in Asia-Pacific region. In short, the book is useful for all those concerned with India's sustained engagement with its eastern neighbours.

The Editor

Y. Yagama Reddy (born in 1952) has been a faculty member since 1985 and is currently the Director of the Centre for Southeast Asian & Pacific Studies, a UGC sponsored Area Studies Centre established in 1976 at Sri Venkateswara University, Tirupati. Besides associating himself with the teaching programme on regional geography and geopolitics of Southeast Asia and South Pacific, he is involved in multidisciplinary research encompassing strategic, security, economic and demographic aspects of Southeast Asia and Australia. He has to his credit 5 books and 27 papers published in national and international journals. He has also presented 37 research papers at various national and international conferences/seminars and delivered lectures at the Refresher Courses on Southeast Asia and Australia as well as during his visit to Australia in 2005, on the topics concerning India-Australia bilateral relations.

Professor Reddy has also served as the Chairman of the Board of Studies in Southeast Asian and Pacific Studies at S.V. University (2001-2004) and is currently a member of Board of South and Southeast Asian Studies, University of Madras, Chennai. He was also a member of the UGC Standing Advisory Committee on Area Studies Programme, New Delhi (2002-2005). He is a Life Member of various professional bodies including the Indian Association for the Study of Australia, the Indian Congress for Asia and Pacific Studies, the Indian Association for American Studies, the South Indian American Studies Network, and International Association of Asian and European Studies as well as a Member of Indian Association for Asia and Pacific Studies.

Editor's Note on the Book

Phrases such as "One Asia", "Asian Century", "Asian Community", "Asian Identify" and "Asian-ness", have almost become household expressions, being on the lips of many, of late, thanks to the rapid strides the Asian nations have been making since the end of the Second World War particularly, since the termination of the Cold War. The idea of Asian solidarity as the sine qua non of the advent of Asian century, has been gaining ground, gathering momentum in recent years, as if in fulfilment of the prophetic hints at the emergence of Asia by the politically sagacious and far-sighted statesmen like, say, a Burke or a Churchill, in the years of the past. But these words and phrases are not altogether new, especially to those, who have had the benefit of the history of India's freedom struggle and formative years of independence.

The Indian National Congress, which had resolutely demanded independence for the colonies and extended an overtly staunch support to the nationalist movement in Asia, at its Annual Session in 1946, held the view that "India and the countries of Southeast Asia must hang together...". In the context of the vulnerability of the Indian defense during the Japanese occupation of Southeast Asia, the noted Indian historian, K.M. Panikkar, advocated a regional security system for Southeast Asia, with India to assume responsibility in that endeavour. Nehru explained the Asian identity in a nutshell, when he said: "we are of Asia and the people of Asia are nearer and closer to us than others". While welcoming the Australian and New Zealand observers to the Asian Relations Conference at New Delhi in March-April 1947, Nehru candidly observed: "we have many problems in common, especially in the Pacific and in the southeast region of Asia, and we have to cooperate together to find solutions".

Having been cognizant of India's pivotal position in the Indian Ocean region with which Australia's security issues were linked, Australia had also begun to collaborate with India on the issues of regional and international importance. Later, at the 18-

nation Conference on Indonesia in New Delhi in January 1949, India felt obliged to assure Australia and New Zealand that the "Indian concept of Asian Cooperation was not directed against any non-Asian Power and had no racial overtones". Again, on the eve of Bandung Conference, Nehru exalted Australia and New Zealand as being nearer to Asia and thereby in the region (Australasia).

Lord Casey, the then Australian External Affairs Minister who had endeavoured to promote an understanding of the mutual interests of India and Australia, concurred with Nehru when he noted in his foreword to the 'Special Number: Modern India', Australian Journal of Politics & History (Vol. XII, No.2, August 1966, pp.125-126): "Australia and India....have a common interest ... in that region (Southeast Asian) and in the evolution of our huge neighbour China....We have a common concern to raise standards of living for all people..." Another Australian External Affairs Minister Paul Hasluck, made a case for Australia's contribution to the 'rebuilding of Asia', while Kim Beazley of the opposition Australian Labour Party felt the need for Australia's realization of India as being 'crucial in Asia'. It was with this awareness, that many Australian foreign policy makers expected India's benign role in the affairs of Southeast Asia.

For all the impressions and expectations of India, its image began to wane and India was found to be of more inward looking than one, showing little or no concern for its eastern neighbours. Its indifference to the ASEAN process and inclination towards the Soviet Union had only widened the gulf between India and the ASEAN members. The termination of Cold War tension had brought in a radical change in the perceptions and approaches of the regional powers towards regional cooperation. India's gradual integration with ASEAN, the enlargement of ASEAN into a full-fledged regional grouping, ASEAN's Summit level dialogues with China, Japan and Korea, (ASEAN+3), and India (ASEAN+1), had all kept the spirit of regional cooperation in a better stead. It was about the same time that the ASEAN Regional Forum (ARF), with the participation of several regional and extra-regional powers, had been contemplating the confidence-building measures and cooperation paradigms. The multifarious activities resting on the edifice of cooperation rather partnership for peace and prosperity extending beyond neighbouring countries, would no doubt, testify to an emerging Asian Community. This community of nations, as envisioned by the Indian Prime Minister Manmohan Singh, would constitute an 'arc of advantage' across which, there would be large scale movement of people, capital, ideas and creativity.

The feeling of 'One Asia' invariably generated the need for economic integration through interdependence as well as the requirement of developing security partnerships. The process of cohesion expedited by ASEAN, led to the implementation of ASEAN Free Trade Area and the launch of several other regional initiatives including the integration of economies of major Asian countries – JACIK (Japan, ASEAN, China, India and Korea) – into East Asian Free Trade Area (EAFTA), so as to emerge as a potential third pole of world economy. This East Asian Community as an inclusive group of JACIK, is destined to evolve into a Pan-Asia framework, so as to ensure equitable distribution of gains. This process of Asian Solidarity has never been in a state of isolation but on the other hand, it has acted as a stimulus to extract response from many a country in the Asia-Pacific region, involved in the building up of the increased cooperation to mutual advantage. Australia and New Zealand, which have for long been identified with Eurocentric approach, realized that their future and prosperity are inextricably linked with its immediate Asian neighbours. Despite their initial reluctance to sign the Treaty of Amity and Cooperation, these two nations too joined the East Asia Summit (EAS) in which, India's participation was very much sought after by ASEAN.

Having steered its Look East Policy as a means of getting integrated with East Asia, India is now committed to consolidating the partnerships at various levels, by taking advantage of the complementary strengths in economy and demography as well as its shared experience of historical and cultural ties with Asian neighbours, in addition to its geographical proximity in the form of common land and maritime boundaries with some of the ASEAN members-states. Besides being the littoral states of Indian Ocean, India and Australia have shared commonalties based on colonial heritage and advantages of complementarities to sustain the partnership. India is not only being projected as a counter-balance to China, but also considered as a bridge to the markets of other Asian Countries. The historic East Asia Summit held in December 2005 at Kuala Lumpur, clearly demonstrated that the concept of Asian-ness is at last translated into reality.

Nehru, who had exalted the spirit and purpose of Asian-ness, was definitely far ahead of the present day accomplishment of the Asian Solidarity, which obviously fructified thus, only after a lapse of 5 decades, since the Asian Relation Conference in 1947. Though Cold War geopolitical equations shattered the hopes of prophetic vision of Pandit Nehru, the imperatives of geo-economics as a logical corollary of globalization and the revolutionary changes in information technology, have forced the nations to shed their demur caused by inward looking. In the context of inevitable interdependence of nations either for raw materials or for marketing the manufactured goods, the nations are found to pursue the policy of open-regionalism. India's proven capabilities and inherent potentialities have conferred on it, the distinction of one in possession of the key to the Asian balance of power and prosperity.

This book contains 23 articles presented at a Seminar organized by the Centre for Southeast Asian & Pacific Studies, Sri Venkateswara University, Tirupati in February 2006. The authors of these articles are eminent scholars in their respective field of specialisation

The organisation of the Seminar and the publication of this work would not have been possible but for the financial support of the UGC, timely response from the participants, cooperation of my colleagues and the sustained interest of New Century Publications, New Delhi. I feel it my bounden duty to express my thanks to Professor Richard who spared his time and energy to offer advice and assistance to get all these papers edited.

I am confident that this work, which is fairly replete with inspiring and enlightening matter, will commend itself to all categories of readers, particularly academicians, researchers, policy makers, students of international relations and all those interested in India's foreign policy.

Y.Yagama Reddy

Tirupati
February 2007

List of Contributors

Amit Singh	Research Scholar, Centre for South, Central, South East Asia & South West Pacific Studies, School of International Studies, JNU, New Delhi.
Chandrakant Yatanoor	Department of Political Science, Gulbarga University, Gulbarga, Karnataka.
Ganganath Jha	Associate Professor, Centre for South, Central, South East Asia and South West Pacific Studies, School of International Studies, JNU, New Delhi.
Gautam Murthy	Associate Professor of Economics, Centre for Indian Ocean Studies, Osmania University, Hyderabad.
R.G. Gidadhubli	Formerly Director, Centre for Central Eurasian Studies, University of Mumbai, Mumbai.
D. Gopal	Department of Political Science, School of Social Sciences, IGNOU, New Delhi.
S. Gopal	Special Secretary (Retd.), Cabinet Secretariat, Government of India, New Delhi.
Jayachandra Reddy	Assistant Professor, Department of Geography and Environmental Studies, Mekelle University, Ethiopia.
P. Krishna Mohan Reddy	Post-doctoral Researcher, Department. of Classics and Religion, Carleton University, Ottawa, Canada.

A. Lakshmana Chetty	Formerly Director, Centre for Southeast Asian and Pacific Studies, Sri Venkateswara University, Tirupati.
Man Mohini Kaul	Associate Professor, Centre for South, Central, South East Asia and South West Pacific Studies, School of International Studies, JNU, New Delhi.
P. Munirathnam Reddy	Associate Professor, Centre for Southeast Asian and Pacific Studies, Sri Venkateswara University, Tirupati.
G.V.C. Naidu	Senior Fellow, Institute for Defence Studies and Analyses, New Delhi.
Nirmala Devi	Director, Centre for SAARC Studies, Andhra University, Visakhapatnam.
M. Prayaga	Senior Technical Assistant, Centre for Southeast Asian & Pacific Studies, Sri Venkateswara University, Tirupati.
K. Raja Reddy	Centre for Southeast Asian & Pacific Studies, Sri Venkateswara University, Tirupati.
C. Ravindranatha Reddy	Associate Professor, Centre for Southeast Asian and Pacific Studies, Sri Venkateswara University, Tirupati
Sailaja Gullapalli	Consultant, School of Social Sciences, IGNOU, New Delhi.
V. Suryanarayan	Senior Professor and Director (Retd), Centre for South and Southeast Asian Studies, University of Madras, Chennai.

K. Syamalamma	Academic Consultant, Centre for Southeast Asian and Pacific Studies, Sri Venkateswara University, Tirupati.
Tridib Chakraborti	Department of International Relations, Jadavpur University, Kolkata.
S. Utham Kumar Jamadhagni	Lecturer, Department of Defence and Strategic Studies, University of Madras, Chennai.
G. Vijaya Kumar Reddy	Research Associate, Centre for Southeast Asian & Pacific Studies, Sri Venkateswara University, Tirupati.
Y. Yagama Reddy	Director, Centre for Southeast Asian and Pacific Studies, Sri Venkateswara University, Tirupati.

Contents

Contents

1

Towards Asian Century

Professor (Dr.) S. Jayarama Reddy
Vice-Chancellor
Sri Venkateswara University, Tirupati

In the context of India's Look East policy leading to India-ASEAN partnership, BIMSTEC and East Asia Summit (EAS), India's commitment to ASEAN is reflected in the bilateral trade with ASEAN, which galloped from US$ 1.3 billion in 1992 to US$ 18 Billion in 2004, and is poised enough to reach the US$ 30 billion in 2007.

The fact that 'Asia is in sharper focus today', is vindicated by Jeffrey Sachs, a distinguished economist, currently a professor at the University of Columbia, New York, in a thought-provoking article, "Welcome to the Asian Century," published in *Fortune* (January 26, 2004). An assiduous student of global trends, Jeffrey arrived at a not altogether provocative conclusion that the age of American dominance in the world economy, is coming fast to an end. The idea of "Asia Shining" on the whole, seems to be the core of his message. The logic of Professor Jeffrey Sachs' conclusion is built on two arithmetical facts, namely, the higher rate of growth of per capita incomes of the Asian economies, particularly those of India and China and their higher population, compared to that of the US. China has been growing on an average of 10 per cent since 1970 and India, around 6 per cent per year since the 1991 reforms. This invites a comparison with the US annual economic growth of 3.5 per cent.

The combined effect of both these factors tends to drive down the margin between the US on one hand, and India and China on the other, thanks to the continued effect of the faster growth of per capita GDP and the higher population of Asian

Countries. The per capita GNP is growing in China at around 4.6 per cent per year. Given the current rates of growth by China and India, China, whose current per capita income accounts for around 13 per cent of that of the USA, would reach the US' per capita income levels by 2050. At this point, China's GNP would be about 75 per cent larger than that of the US. India's per capita income would reach a little more than 25 per cent of that of the US' by 2050. Therefore, India's overall economy would be about the same size as that of the US, by 2050.

Together with India and China, the entire South-East Asian region as well as Northeast Asia, will also be growing as an integrated economy. The Asian economy with 60 per cent of the population, would rise to about half of the world's GNP, up from the current one-third. The US will have only about 5 per cent of the world's population with its economic weight, sliding from more than the current 20 per cent of the global GNP to 10 per cent, by 2050.

It is pointed out, that the higher differential in economic rates of growth of developing Asia, is itself a function of the ability with which poorer countries will continue to access "capital" and technology from the US. Of course, the FDI flows from the US to the Asian economies are in a sense, a mirror image of the forex flows, which currently go out of Asia towards the US. The FDI in its present form from the US, does carry with it the new technologies as well as the new marketing and management skills. But this may not sustain. Asia must also increase its R&D expenditure and start honing its human resource skills, in order to catch up with the US. The very fact, that the US itself is continuously scurrying for Asia's technical brain-power to strengthen its R&D armoury shows, that the gap will not be difficult to fill, in the two-way traffic.

The rise of Japan, Korea and Taiwan in the cutting edge of industries of semi-conductors and bio-technology indicates that India and China also can make it, provided there is a will and a conscious plan to exploit the countries' pool of technical man power. China and India have an abundance of skilled manpower. However, it is necessary to motivate this vast stock of intellectual capital adequately through incentives. Korea and Japan have shown remarkable ability to adapt and to promote the technical innovations independently. China and India have to demonstrate that they are as capable as Japan and Korea of bridging the emerging technology gap, in which case, the US would find its dominance, threatened.

This requires much more than mere investment in terms of buildings and equipment. India's institutions of scientific instruction are mostly driven by a pursuit of "rote" methods of learning. They should opt for a shift of emphasis to a rewarding enquiry and a technical and scientific innovation. The examination system itself, which has been emphasizing rote-learning over years, has to be changed to the extent of accommodating an emphasis on innovation. The task is difficult, but is both achievable and indispensable. It has to be at the centre of governmental attention for the Asian century forecast to become a reality, instead of Asia being a copycat of the developed West. This requires a change, not only in the approach of the educational institutions, but also in that of the corporates, which has to encourage the generic R&D, in a truly pioneering spirit.

This analysis is primarily built on the fact that there is at present, a significant difference in the rates of growth between Asia and America. But to depend on the difference would be tricky because, much depends on the continued willingness of the US to transfer R&D and Asia's ability to adapt. Some hopeful signs are discernible in the area of biogenetic research, dealing with stem cells. However, while the US ideological inhibitions tend to block further research, Asia, with its freedom from such a restriction, can score a march. This is already evident from Korea's recent advances in this area. So too, the wealth of herbal medicine available in the traditional societies like China and India, gives room for spectacular advances in pharmaceutical research. These are only two of the promising areas worth mentioning.

The issue whether Asia will dominate the 21st century and the US will decline in relative terms, will however, depend on how successfully the political leaderships manage to avoid settling down in a morass of regional conflict or war and mis-governance. Asia's advances of the last two decades, are reflective of relative peace and good governance in Asia. Asia has, above all, to stay clear of conflicts and Asians also have to avoid problems inflicted by the unforeseen pestilences, such as SARS. This involves a massive upgrading of health services and environmental conditions. Barring these unforeseen and unfortunate developments, the prospects of Asia shining are indeed bright, as Sachs forecasts. As a result, the US will necessarily have to shed its imperial ambitions. It will no longer be the sole monarch of all its surveys. It will no longer be in a position to tell the rest of the world, how to behave.

All this will call for a radical transformation of global financial and political management. Once Asian dominance arrives, the international financial institutions will no longer be the monopoly of the US and Europe with Japan being allowed to peep in, as it is, at present. The lesser mortals from Asia will also have to be given a higher voice in governing these institutions. There will be changes in the functioning of WTO, which will have to reflect in its governance, its procedures and policies, the dominance of Asia rather than that of the US.

"We got a small glimpse of the coming US eclipse in the fall of 2004, when President Bush traveled to Asia for an Asia-Pacific economic meeting. The US tried to find Asian allies to bash China over its exchange-rate policies but found no takers, as the other Asian countries sided with China. China's economic diplomacy has already trumped that of the US, since China's Asian neighbors clearly understand that China is their engine of growth." Asia will soon be shining and the US' sheen will be less, at least by comparison. Asia's dominance will change the world's power equations. Hence, I consider it the sacred duty of each and every nation of Asia, to make this great continent a pre-eminent region endowed with stability and prosperity which alone will make the 21st Century, an Asian Century.

I am really delighted to inaugurate the seminar, as eminent academics and analysts have come from different parts of the country and abroad, to participate in it. I fervently hope, that your deliberations on this topic of contemporary relevance, would serve the national interests. Much in tune with the sustained research activities undertaken by the Area Studies Centre of our University, I feel very much privileged to inform that our Centre would bring out a bi-annual, *Journal of Area Studies*, which would serve as a mode of dissemination of expert knowledge on all the areas of the world for the benefit of not merely the academic community and policy-makers but the general public too.

2

India in 21st Century Asia-Pacific

Nagesh Kumar

I consider it an honour to have this opportunity to address this conference on a very topical theme *India in the 21st Century Asia-Pacific*. Asia in the 21st Century is well on its way to reclaim its place as a centre of gravity of the world economy with the rapid emergence of large economies of China and India, with the recovery of Japan from a decade long recession and growing regional economic integration. I congratulate the Centre for Southeast Asian and Pacific Studies of Sri Venkateswara University, for taking the initiative to organize the seminar attended by a galaxy of eminent scholars. This is also a theme that receives a great deal of attention in our work at RIS and hence I would like to use this opportunity to share with you some of our work on the subject.

Emergent India and its Place in Asia

Recent performance of Indian economy is attracting a lot of attention worldwide for its dynamism and long-term prospects. There has been a progressive acceleration in the growth performance of Indian economy over the past five decades. In the first 30 years of Independence, India's growth rate averaged 3.5 per cent which was derisively called 'Hindu Rate of growth'. Since 1980, however, there has been a marked acceleration in growth rates and average annual real growth rate of GDP over the 1980s, 1990s and first three years of the new millennium has been close to 6 per cent. There has been a further acceleration in the growth trajectory since 2003 and the average growth rate over the past three years has been higher than 8 per cent per annum. Furthermore, as the growth rate of population has declined over time from 2.3 per cent to 1.6 per cent, per capita GDP has been rising much faster than before. The average rate of per capita income therefore has moved up from just 1.2 per cent during the first three decades in the post-Independence period to nearly 4 during the 1990s and to 6.6 per cent in the last few years.

India's potential to sustain rapid growth rates in the future is widely shared. A Goldman Sachs' study has remarked that 'India has the potential to show the fastest growth over the next 30 and 50 years'. An IMF study projects India's growth rate to 2025 at 7 per cent 'with more upside potential than downside risks'. In sustaining high growth rates, India will also be able to benefit from the demographic transition that will see a rising proportion of working age population in the coming years.

The present dynamism of the Indian economy seen in consonance with that of another highly populous economy viz. China's, has implications for the world economy and for the place of Asia in it. According to IMF, already India is contributing to 10 per cent of growth of GDP of the world economy and 20 per cent of Asian growth. China and India together have become major growth drivers of global growth and are helping Asia's re-emergence as the centre of gravity of the world economy that it was in the eighteenth century. An OECD study by Angus Maddison shows that by 1500AD, China and India alone accounted for 50 per cent of world GDP with each sharing roughly 25 per cent. Because of rising incomes of Western Europe, by 1820 AD Asia's share in world GDP had come down but was still substantial at 56 per cent. Asian incomes stagnated during the period 1820 to 1950 bringing its share in world GDP. The Goldman Sachs study shows that Asia is now on its way to regain its lost share in the world economy by 2050. According to these estimations share of China, India and Japan in world GDP is expected to reach 57 per cent by 2050. They expect that led by rapid growth, 'India's economy, for instance, could be larger than Japan's by 2032, and China's larger than the US by 2041'. India's economy could be larger than all but the US and China in 30 years'.

India and Asian Economic Integration

Let me now turn to the other notable trend in Asia viz. that of growing economic integration of Asia in the 21st century. Asian developing countries had made a number of attempts at regional economic cooperation in the 1970s with UN-ESCAP's initiative. These include the Bangkok Agreement established in 1975 which covered exchange of tariff concessions between five member governments viz. Bangladesh, India, Lao PDR, South Korea and Sri Lanka. The Asian Clearing Union with seven members in the region viz. Bangladesh, India, Iran, Myanmar, Nepal, Pakistan and Sri Lanka, came into being in 1974. However, these early experiences have not been very successful because of their limited scope and coverage.

Successful experiences with regional economic integration in the industrialized countries since the mid-1980s in Europe and North America have also prompted Southeast and South Asian countries to adopt economic integration strategies. ASEAN had limited co-operation in economic areas until 1992 when it decided to set up the ASEAN Free Trade Area (AFTA). Similarly SAARC adopted a SAARC Preferential Trading Arrangement (SAPTA) in 1995 upgraded into a SAARC Free Trade Agreement (SAFTA) in 2004. Another notable initiative in Asia is BIMSTEC (Bay of Bengal Initiative for Multisectoral Techno-economic Cooperation) involving five South Asian countries viz. Bangladesh, Bhutan, India, Nepal, and Sri Lanka and two Southeast Asian countries viz. Myanmar and Thailand as a bridge between South and Southeast Asia.

The East Asian Crisis of 1997 also highlighted the importance of regional economic cooperation. The ASEAN countries expedited the programme of implementation of ASEAN Free Trade Area (AFTA) and moved on to further deepen the economic integration. The crisis also led to launch of several regional initiatives such as the Chiang-Mai Initiative which involves ASEAN+3 (Japan, China, and South Korea) countries. Besides this the ASEAN's policy of engaging key Asian countries namely Japan, China, India and South Korea as dialogue partners have provided much needed cohesion in the Asian region as is clear from the numerous schemes of regional and bilateral free trade arrangements that are at different levels of implementation. China, Japan, India, and South Korea are all engaged in negotiations of free trade arrangements with ASEAN.

However, it can be argued that the sub-regional or bilateral attempts at regional co-operation that have been initiated such as those under the framework of ASEAN and SAARC or the dialogue partners while desirable are unlikely to exploit the full potential of the regional economic integration in Asia and hence are sub-optimal. This is because the extent of complementarities are limited at the sub-regional levels because of similar factor endowments and economic structures within a neighbourhood. It is clear from the fact that trade of ASEAN or SAARC countries with the East Asian countries is much larger than their intra-subregional trade. It is for this reason that the success achieved so far from the sub-regional or bilateral attempts at cooperation have so far been meagre. At the broader Asian level, on the other hand, the diversities in the levels of economic development and capabilities are quite wide thus providing for more extensive and mutually beneficial linkages. Hence, Asia needs an overarching Asia-wide scheme of economic integration to fully exploit the full potential of efficiency-seeking industrial restructuring or to exploit the synergies that exist in the region.

It was in this context that RIS developed the proposal of an Asian Economic Community as an approach towards pan-Asian economic integration. Keeping in mind the experiences of regional economic integration from other regions, a practical approach to regionalization in Asia had to be a phased one. ASEAN has helped to bring together four major economies of Asia as its annual Summit-level dialogues partners viz. Japan, China, South Korea and India. ASEAN and these four dialogue partners namely **J**apan, **A**sean, **C**hina, **I**ndia and **K**orea (**JACIK**) countries are all engaged in evolving FTAs between their different pairs. Through this complex web of FTAs a virtual JACIK FTA is emerging. Hence a vision for the Asian economic integration is to begin by coalescing these multiple FTAs between JACIK countries into an overarching regional trading arrangement. A broader overarching framework alone will allow optimal utilization of Asia's resources and synergies for their mutual common benefit by creating a seamless market.

Combining fourteen of the largest and fastest growing economies of Asia with vast complementarities, JACIK could be a potential third pole of the world economy. JACIK countries combine between them a population of 3 billion or a half of the world population and a GNP of over $7.2 trillion comparable to that of EU in 2000. In terms of purchasing power parity, the JACIK grouping will have the gross national income of $ 13 trillion, much larger than either NAFTA or EU. JACIK's exports will add up to $1.37 trillion compared to $1.2 trillion of NAFTA. The combined official reserves of the JACIK economies at $2 trillion in 2004 are much larger than those of the US and the EU put together. Therefore, the region would have sufficiently large market and financial resources to support and sustain expedited development of the region's economies.

RIS studies conducted in computable general equilibrium (CGE) model framework have shown that a trade liberalization in the framework of an RTA in JACIK could produce efficiency gains worth US$ 210 billion representing more than 3 per cent of combined GDP of JACIK economies. What is more, all the JACIK countries benefit from integration. Interestingly the welfare of even the rest of the world also improves by US$ 109 billion suggesting that Asian economic integration will be Pareto optimal. Similar findings have been reached by an ADB study which suggested that regional integration could promote Asian economic convergence, raising average growth rates and benefiting poorer countries. In particular, greater regional integration will propagate commercial linkages and transfer the stimulus of Asia's rapid growth economies, particularly China and India, to their neighbours. The Asian economic integration increases trade and incomes for the rest of the world. Hence it is a win-win for the region and the world! The idea of an Asian

Economic Community as a roadmap for broader regional cooperation in Asia was first presented and discussed by RIS at its High Level Conference on Asian Economic Community at New Delhi in March 2003.

The proposal of an Asian Economic Community was first officially made by the Prime Minister of India at the Bali Summit of ASEAN in October 2003. Subsequently the concept has been further refined and Prime Minister Dr Manmohan Singh has championed the vision of an Asian Economic Community at various forums. He has argued that an Asian Economic Community as an approach to pan-Asian economic cooperation and integration could serve as 'an arc of advantage, peace and shared prosperity in Asia' across which there will be large scale movement of people, capital, ideas and creativity. Subsequently a number of Asian leaders have endorsed the vision of an Asian Economic Community including Prime Minister Koizumi of Japan during his visit to India in April 2005.

Asia had lacked a forum for dialogue for giving effect to such a broader cooperation. The first East Asia Summit (EAS) held in Kuala Lumpur in December 2005 provided to the region a forum for such a dialogue. The Summit was attended by the leaders of ASEAN10, Japan, China, South Korea and India and also of Australia and New Zealand. Combining all the JACIK economies and also Australia and New Zealand at a single forum, EAS is widely believed to be a forum for pursuing a scheme of broader regional economic integration in Asia. The East Asia Summit provides an opportunity for Asia to take initial first step in the long journey towards broader regional economic integration in Asia by first building an East Asian Community (EAC) which could be later expanded into an Asian Economic Community (AEC) with the inclusion of other Asian countries. Besides trade and investment cooperation the EAC could provide a framework for monetary and financial cooperation, cooperation for energy security, development of transport infrastructure and connectivity, and for harnessing the fruits of new core technologies for addressing the digital divide and nutritional and health related issues as well as global governance, peace and security.

The formation of an Asian Economic Community could thus be viewed as the culmination of India's Look East policy. As a part of this policy, India has consciously integrated its economy with East Asia since the early 1990s. With this, the share of East Asia in India's trade is approaching nearly a third thus making it a more important trade partner compared to the EU or the United States. India's trade with China grew by nearly 57 per cent in 2005 to surpass US$ 17 billion. Her trade with South Korea grew by 48 per cent in 2004. ASEAN-India trade has grown by over 30 per cent over the past couple of years and is projected to cross US$ 30 billion by 2007. To further strengthen her economic links with East Asian countries India is evolving FTAs with ASEAN and is studying FTAs with China, Japan, and Korea. This is complemented by bilateral agreements signed with Thailand and Singapore. With FTAs either under negotiation or under study with ASEAN, Japan, China, and Korea, it is very much part of the growing web of FTAs linking the East Asian countries.

India's strengths in software and services fruitfully complement the hardware and manufacturing prowess of East Asia and together could produce a formidable strategic combination. With the growing recognition of these complementary strengths by corporations, India is increasingly getting linked with the East Asian production networks. These links may not be very substantial in value terms as yet but are certainly critical as they generally relate to more knowledge intensive parts of the value-chain such as software development, R&D, engineering and designing, and high quality manufacturing. The trend is likely to be more firmly entrenched as the emerging free trade arrangements between India and East Asian countries come into effect.

India shares land boundaries with China and Myanmar and maritime boundaries with Thailand and Indonesia. India's geographical contiguity with East Asia was highlighted vividly by the ASEAN-India Car Rally organized in November 2004 in conjunction with the ASEAN Summit. India has deep age-old civilizational links with a number of East Asian countries. With its excellent trading and transport links and emerging preferential trading arrangements with South Asian countries, GCC and West Asian countries India could act as a bridge for East Asia for the markets in South, West and Central Asian countries. Furthermore, it can be argued that India's participation in the grouping will make it more balanced and less susceptible to domination by any particular large country.

I may now conclude my remarks by recapitulating that the 21st Century Asia will not only be a dynamic region but also highly integrated one and able to exploit the synergies for mutual benefit. It will serve as a centre of gravity of the world economy and will increasingly sustain global growth as a source of final demand with its growing middle class. And an emergent India, the second largest economy in Asia, will be an important pillar of the new dynamic and integrated Asia-Pacific.

3

Indo-Thai Relations: Misplaced Rhythm of Cooperation

Ganganath Jha

Thailand, which is strategically located in Southeast Asia, used to be considered India's gateway to Far East during the colonial era. [1] The location advantage brought geo-political importance to it and Thai diplomats understood and used it meticulously to escape the yoke of Western colonial masters. Thailand remained the only country in Southeast Asia, which was not colonized. France and Great Britain treated Thailand as a buffer zone between French Indochina and British Burma. Whenever serious threat to its sovereignty arose in the 19th Century, attempts were made to resolve them through negotiated means. When France demanded territories on the eastern side of the Mekong River or when Great Britain claimed jurisdiction over Kedah, Perlis, Kelantan and Trengganu, there was resentment in Thailand. But the King of Thailand avoided going to war. He pleaded compromise with France and Great Britain in order to protect the sovereignty of the country. It was meaningless to fight a battle, if the adversary was very strong and also when the alternatives of battles were available.

In 1893, the French navy had attacked Thai positions at Paknam. It was meant to provoke Thailand to retaliate, but the king dissuaded its forces from retaliating. They understood that it was a meticulously laid French trap to colonize the area. Thailand agreed to vacate the areas on eastern side of the Mekong River as demanded by the French colonial masters. [2] Burmese on the other hand did not understand the meaning of British provocation. They decided to fight war against the British and ultimately lost the sovereignty of the country. On the other hand, Thailand was ready to concede, cooperate and compromise with the Western powers in order to maintain and preserve the sovereignty of the country. They projected it by saying that "Like a bamboo, we bend with the wind". The astute conduct of Thai foreign policy established the wisdom and foresight of Thai rulers. It was successful in projecting that Thailand was peaceful and friendly towards Western powers and ready to cooperate with Western world. Its image as a friendly and cooperative Kingdom remained unalterable in Europe and thus the country was not colonized.

It was only during the Second World War that Thailand's role became adverse to the Western World. Thailand signed offensive defensive pact with Japan and supported the slogan of "Asia for Asians". It was also during that period that a strong foundation for Indo-Thai relations was laid. Thailand supported Netaji Subhas Chandra Bose and India's freedom struggle. It supported Indian National Army (INA) by providing facilities for base propaganda channels, aid and assistance. The INA volunteers were kept in high esteem even after the end of the World War. Although Great Britain projected INA volunteers as war criminals and wanted their repatriation to India, Thailand did not oblige them.

When the Second World War was over, the international power equation was in favour of the US which had emerged the most powerful force in the region. Thailand understood this reality at a time when it was facing lot of internal and external problems, like anti-Chinese riots, the threat of communist subversion and the issues of economic reconstruction and to address them, Thailand decided to cultivate relations with the United States. [3] Americans on the other hand, had already started a containment drive and had evolved a grand strategic design for Southeast Asian region. They responded appropriately to Thai overtures and influenced Thailand to be a strategic partner. As Thailand was always independent and had not fought war against colonial powers, it kept herself open to the Western World. Thailand agreed to be the headquarters of SEATO and strongly supported the containment policy of the US. Thus, the partnership with the US facilitated Thailand's building of the infrastructure, transportation network, port and airport in the country. The development of the country in terms of human resource development and external profile was impressive. Although Thai territories were used extensively in Vietnam War, in that process, Americans also built an advanced infrastructure in the country. The US spent billions of dollars in establishing military and naval bases and all of them are now under the control of Thailand.

Although Thailand was on the opposite side of India during cold war years, it did not ignore India but attached importance to it as the cultural and spiritual center. When ASEAN was born in 1967, Thailand wanted India also to be associated with it. India was not enthused to join it as the new organization was viewed pro-American. The ASEAN countries again tried to bring India into their fold in 1978-79, but again there were indecisiveness and debates about colonialism, anti-colonialism, idealism, etc and India missed the opportunity. India began to attach due importance to the ASEAN region only after the termination of cold war in 1991. Thailand was very happy to note the transformation in Indian policy perspectives towards eastern neighbors. It had been trying to cultivate India seriously ever since the visit of the Thai Prime Minister Chatchai Choonhavan to New Delhi in 1989, but the termination of the Cambodian conflict and cold war in 1991, offered new opportunities in regional politics. Thailand, then was enthusiastic in turning Indo-China from battleground to market place in the east but it was keen to explore markets and cooperation with India in the West, where it envisaged immense opportunities for business and trade.

Thailand while evolving new areas of cooperation, thought of involving India in establishing growth areas in Andaman's on the pattern of Bantam and Johore. India was not keen to explore Thai proposals instantly, as the intelligence report suggested that the smugglers and drug peddlers would get a free hand if government control of the area is relaxed. Moreover, government of India did not find the proposal fine-tuned to be suitably responded. But there was a new development in the post -1995 eras that both

Thailand and India began to attach importance to the opinion and proposals of one another seriously. The proposals for bilateral and multilateral collaboration were mooted and the two also agreed to establish BIMST-EC, the sub-regional grouping, to link South Asian countries with ASEAN for trade, investments and tourism.

BIMST-EC has proved an important instrument to understand culture and to promote socio-economic interaction and confidence building, but it has to attend to every delicate issue with caution. But before analyzing the achievements of BIMST-EC, it is necessary to examine Indo-Thai relations in retrospect.

Indo-Thai bilateral relations have witnessed different phases, of ups and down ever since 1947 and they have not always been pleasant. However, in order to understand relations from proper perspective, it is necessary to analyze some of the major developments that shaped the foundation of our relations in the past and which very often influence the mindset of our decision makers in the present.

During 1947-86, neither the King nor the Prime Minister of Thailand ever came to India on a State visit. In 1972, after twenty-five years of independence, President V.V. Giri of India visited Thailand. There were many reasons for the absence of warmth in Indo-Thai relations. First, there was a difference in the international outlook of the two countries. India became an ardent advocate of non-alignment and peaceful co-existence after getting independence from the British rule. On the other hand, Thailand strongly supported the US military presence in the region, especially, after 1950. It also provided bases and manpower to the United States to put down the Communist movements. From 1948 to 1973, Thailand remained under the dictatorship of three military strongmen namely Field Marshal Phibun Songgram, Field Marshal Sarit Thanarat, and Field Marshal Thanom Kittikachorn. It became a founder member of the South-East Asia Treaty Organization (SEATO) in 1954. It even allowed Bangkok to be the headquarters of the SEATO. Although the developments in the region and especially in Thailand were not positive for India, our diplomats worked hard to cultivate friendship.

India attached geo-strategic importance to Thailand and showed friendly gestures, on the eve of its independence. In February 1947, India's interim government extended a loan to Thailand, which was the first of its kind, given to a foreign country. The loan was Rs. 50 million, to be paid in installments. India on its part, adopted a very sympathetic attitude towards Thailand on the question of payment of reparation, which had been dictated by the British government. The war claims were $5,224,220 to be paid to Great Britain of which, India's share was one-fifth $104,484. On the other hand, Thailand adopted a very sympathetic attitude towards INA volunteers who preferred to stay back in Thailand, which facilitated their rehabilitation.

In December 1946, India appointed a consul general meant for Bangkok and one B. Dayal was deputed to go there. Thailand reciprocated this gesture by deputing Dr. Thanat Khoman to work as first charged affairs in New Delhi. Luang Pimitaksorn, as the first Thai Minister in New Delhi, succeeded Dr. Thanat, who later became the Foreign Minister of Thailand, and B. Dayal became his counterpart in Bangkok. Both the governments decided soon to upgrade diplomatic relations to ambassadorial level in 1951, when Thailand appointed Luang Wichitwadhakarn, as the first ambassador. Though the diplomatic interactions were exchanged, the regional environment and the domestic developments in Thailand were not complimentary enough to boost Indo-Thai relations.

Thailand in the post-Second World War era, was witnessing the civil unrest. Thailand's ethnic Chinese were unhappy because of the communal riots in Bangkok and communist movements were picking up momentum. The communist take-over of power in China and their open support to Chinese population in Thailand, had created a hostile atmosphere. The Chinese had accelerated propaganda drives against military rule of Field marshal Phibun Songgram in Thailand. On the other hand, there were disturbances in Patani, and the national security was a matter of prime concern for Thai decision makers.

The United States well knew about the strategic importance of Thailand in the containment drive and they had started showing common concern for Thailand. The US had appointed Edwin F. Stanton as an ambassador to Thailand, who astutely cultivated relations with military elites and thus, the two countries came closer to each other. Thailand and the US, signed military assistance agreement in 1950 and they founded SEATO in 1954 and became allies. Thailand became the headquarters of SEATO and thus, contributed in terms of contingents of armed forces in Vietnam War. Thailand gave its air and naval bases to the US and American air force regularly used those bases to bomb the communist belts in Vietnam. When the war finally came to an end in 1975, Thailand became a frontline state to prevent Vietnam from expanding and consolidating its influence in the region.

However, a number of economic reforms (Doi Moi) in Vietnam since 1986, the signing of the Cambodian peace accord (1991) and the disappearance of the Soviet Union (1991) changed the global security and economic environment. The Uruguay Round of talks, WTO, human rights issues and the rise of radicalism, generated new challenges and this diverted the opinion of the countries in the region to attend to the issues of regional concern.

In retrospect, we find that the cold war of the two super powers had intensified the disputes in the region, wherein the ideological and strategic issues predominated the deliberations at the regional and global level. The China factor and Cambodian crisis were the preoccupations of nations in the Asia-Pacific. The end of the Cold War in 1991, although offered some new opportunities, some new challenges also emerged. Accordingly, the countries of the region began to review their old policies and alignments. Indo-Thai relations, who had been marginalized as a consequence of the cold war, got new life and meaningful dimension in the post-cold war era. Both understood the importance of one another and took initiatives to make the relations more vibrant and beneficial.

Indian Premier, Rajiv Gandhi had done some necessary homework when he had gone to Thailand on an official visit in October 1986. This was surprisingly, the first visit of an Indian Premier to Thailand, after independence in 1947. Prime Minister Rajiv Gandhi tried to provide economic dimensions to existing relations and thus the Indo-Thai Joint Business Committee (JBC) was established to explore the possibilities of promoting trade, cultural and educational interaction. This committee suggested some measures to promote bilateral trade and both sides showed keenness to implement them.

Thai Premier Chatichai Choonhavan, later took an initiative to strengthen ties. He reciprocated the visit of Indian Premier and came on a state visit to India in 1989. Being an astute businessman, he admired the role of JBC and wished to upgrade it. Hence the JBC was renamed as Indo-Thai Joint Business Council/Indo-Thai Joint Trade Commission and entrusted with the task to promote trade on the lines suggested earlier by the JBC. Premier Chatichai took personal interests in the success of the JBC and so, the business targets for 1990-92 were fixed in New Delhi. The bilateral trade picked up momentum, and both sides felt happy about the satisfactory progress.

It is interesting to know that the trade turnover was quite encouraging. According to Joint Trade Commission spokesman, the trade plan projected for 1990-92, had been achieved in 1991 itself. The target of US$ 1 billion was reached within 18 months and there were prospects of boom. India exported gems and precious stones, cotton and fabric, machinery and parts, urea and fertilizers to Thailand, while imported pulses (Moong and Urad), rubber, machinery, synthetic fibres and inorganic chemicals. The export of gems during 1989-91, rose from 10 per cent to 75 per cent and earned India about $600 million, cotton and fabric about $60 million, and leather and fodder about $40 million in 1991. Joint Trade Commission in the meanwhile explored avenues of trade in other sectors like textiles, machinery, pumps, diesel engines, vehicle parts, organic and inorganic chemicals, dyes and hand tools.

India's investment relations with Thailand also started growing. Being ranked as the 13th largest investor in Thailand, India involved itself in 20 Joint venture projects in the fields of textiles, rayon, chemicals, dyestuffs, iron and steel products. India and Thailand agreed to expand collaboration in fishing, including joint ventures in deep-sea fishing, fresh water and brackish water prawn farming, fish processing and study of tuna in the Andaman Sea.

In retrospect, we find that Two- way trade between India and the ASEAN countries has grown at a fast rate in the post-1991 period. India's exports to ASEAN-9 (excluding Cambodia) had grown from US$ 1.77 billion in 1990 to US$ 4.31 billion, in 1996. On the other hand, India's imports from ASEAN-9 had grown from US$ 1.38 billion in 1990 to US$ 3.97 billion in 1996. The two-way trade between India and ASEAN as per Indian official data, has grown more rapidly in the period 1993-94 to 1996-97. The relevant trade turnover has been more than doubled from just over US$ 2.5 billion in 1993-94 to 1996-97. This reflects 8 per cent of India's global trade in 1996-97 (up from 6 per cent share in 1993 94) Considering this healthy trend, India has set an ambitious target of US$ 15 billion trade with the ASEAN countries for the year 2000-2001. [4]

The major exports from India to ASEAN countries currently comprise of agro-based products such as oil meals; edible nuts (ground nuts); sesame seeds; meat and meat products; textiles including cotton yarn, fabrics and ready-made garments; drugs and pharmaceuticals; chemicals including inorganic, organic and agro-chemicals; primary and semi-finished iron and steel; machinery (including textile machinery) and transport equipment; and processed minerals. Apart from expanding India's exports of the above major items of ongoing exports, the following goods and services have tremendous potential for giving further push to India's exports to the ASEAN countries. These include sugar processing machinery; railway rolling stock; electrical equipments and machinery; gem and jewellery; automotive components; and above all, information technology including software development consultancy and training in both hardware and software; construction; health and educational services, and processed fruits and vegetables.

Apart from bulk imports of palm oil and other metals, minerals and primary articles, India can profitably expand its imports from ASEAN countries of electronic items, computer hardware, electrical equipment, and most importantly services for the construction, maintenance and upgrading of ports, airports, telecommunications centers, roads, bridges, and power stations.

Despite the satisfactory incremental growth of India's growth of two-way trade with the ASEAN countries during the post-1991 period, the basic asymmetrical nature of this two-way trade has not yet materially changed. Thus, viewed from the ASEAN perspective, India still accounted for only 1.17 per cent of ASEAN's worldwide exports in 1996. Similarly exports from India had amounted to just 1.05 per cent of total imports of ASEAN in 1996. Clearly, ASEAN's trade relations with India are still much below their potential, commensurate with their economic strengths (comparative advantage) and considering the areas still untapped. [5]

Mr. P.V. Narasimha Rao gave a new thrust to India's "Look East" policy and incidentally attached great importance to partnership with the ASEAN. [6] He was also interested in improving the investment climate and thought that Thailand could play a key role in this respect. He therefore, decided to pay a state visit to Thailand coinciding with the meeting of Indo-Thai Joint Commission in Bangkok in April 1993. He eloquently underlined the significance of a new orientation in India's foreign policy, in which Thailand occupied a key position as a close and contiguous maritime neighbor. Thailand was indeed regarded as one of the gateways to the expanding trade, investment and tourism ties with the ASEAN. It had been admired as India's major trade partner and Mr. Rao showed his eagerness for further cooperation and collaboration.

Indo-Thai Joint Commission which was scheduled to meet for setting up the target for 1993-95 tried to turn Thailand as one of the largest trade partners of India. New areas of cooperation were being explored and suggestions were given. Thailand has already emerged as the sixth largest foreign investor in India. In 1993, Thailand had approved of the investments worth \$120 million in areas like fisheries, chemicals, air-conditioning systems, hotel and tourism. Thai companies have also signed agreements with Indian companies for joint ventures in the telecom sector.

As Thailand attached importance to growing relations with India, it sent its Foreign Minister, Prasong Soonsiri to India in November 1993. Besides meeting the business people, he met Prime Minister Rao. He discussed the issues of cooperation in the area of nuclear energy, business exchanges, fisheries and agriculture. Thailand also accepted India's offer of technology transfer of areas like fibre optics electronics including computer software and hardware.

Innovative ideas were evolved to boost the investment ties and in this connection, the proposal of a "growth triangle", is quite interesting. In October 1994, Mr. Surin Pitsuwan, Thai Deputy Foreign Minister, visited India and proposed "growth triangle" amongst Sri Lanka, Thailand and India for business and trade. Such a tie is expected to augment the supply of raw materials, financial goods and high technology. India, however, was not enthusiastic enough to respond.

Thailand reinforced its suggestions for "growth triangle", when Supachai Panitchpakdi, Deputy Prime Minister of Thailand, visited India in January 1995. He discussed the proposal with Indian businessmen and exposed the idea in detail at Secretary level talks. This proposal envisions the building of a four-lane highway between Andaman Sea and the Gulf of Thailand. The projection is to construct deep-sea ports, refineries and industrial ventures, alongside the highway.

In fact, India is unable to take a decisive step in the direction of establishing a "growth triangle". When Prasong Soonsiri had met Rao in November 1993, he had himself suggested that India and Thailand should cooperate in business ventures in third countries, such as Vietnam. This proposal, later known as

"Troika", could involve partnership of India with various partners of the ASEAN and could produce items required outside the region, but this is yet to be taken up seriously.

In fact, India has suggested troika to Singapore also for collaborative efforts and business in Vietnam. Though they have welcomed Indian proposals they involved India in business ventures in the SAARC region, namely, Sri Lanka, Bangladesh and Nepal.

"Growth Triangle", or "Troika", both aimed at the collaboration involving three countries of the region but "growth triangle," has assumed some meaning in the ASEAN countries. They have established this at Johore and Bantam and the three countries – Singapore, Malaysia and Indonesia – have been benefited with this venture. However, the meaning and scope of troika is yet to be explored.

Indonesia, the biggest country of the ASEAN, has also expressed its intentions to be a partner in the "growth triangle" in the Andaman regions with India and Thailand. They emphasized the importance of our collaboration through meetings of the India-Indonesia Friendship Association. India is an important dialogue partner of ASEAN, in which Thailand is a member. The relations with ASEAN countries are improving and Thailand has facilitated India's playing its legitimate role, in the region.

Dr. Surin Pitsuwan, Foreign Minister, led a delegation including senior officials and representatives from the private sector to visit India during 8-10 July 2000. Members of the private sector accompanying the Thai Foreign Minister were representatives from the Thai Chamber of Commerce, the Thai Bankers Association, Fishery Association, Thai Computer Association and the Thai businessmen with Indian origin. The Thai delegation held talks with Indian leaders such as the President, Prime Minster, Foreign Minister, Agriculture Minister. Foreign Minister Surin also took the opportunity to meet Indian businessmen and delivered an address at the Confederation of Indian Industry.

During his talks with Indian officials, both the sides explored the opportunity to increase the amount of two-way trade. At the moment, the average annual trade volume is only US$ 846 million. The Thai side also proposed to the Indian side, its plans for enhancing cooperation in the area of fishery, investment, education, information technology, and culture, and will review the progress in cooperation every 3 years. Thailand expressed its particular interest in investing in the Indian infrastructure projects and invited Indian companies in the information technology (IT) and food sectors to invest in Thailand.

The Thai side also proposed to enhance cooperation with India in international and regional organizations such as UN, BIMST-EC, IOR/ARC and ASEAN. And, Thailand being the chairperson of ASEAN Standing Committee, the Foreign Minister Surin invited India to increase its participation in ASEAN, especially in IT, human resources development, Mekong development, and the "Great Wonders of Suwannaphumi" project.

On behalf of the Royal Thai Government, Foreign Minister Surin Pitsuwan concluded two agreements with the Indian Government, which were; the Agreement on the Promotion and Protection of Investment and the Agreement on Joint Cooperation for the Peaceful Use of Energy.

Members of the private sector accompanying the Foreign Minister Surin had an opportunity to meet their Indian counterparts at Indian Chamber of Commerce and Industry, the Federation of Indian Industry, and importers, to explore business opportunity in areas such as computer, banking and finance, IT, automotive parts, and agro-industry.

Bilateral trade between India and Thailand amounted to US$ 248 million in 1991, rising to US$ 644 in 1995-9 and remained the same in 1996-97. Indian exports to Thailand have gone up steadily in the 1990s, as have Thai exports to India. Exports to Thailand rose to 58.6 per cent in 1993, went up by 18 per cent in 1995 and registered a growth of 16.2 per cent in the first half of 1996. Thai exports increased 12.6 per cent in 1993, went up phenomenally by 159 per cent in 1994, rose to 49.3 per cent in

1995 but dropped by 16 per cent in the first six months of 1996. The decline was in keeping with the general decline in Thai exports. The major items of Indian exports to Thailand are diamonds and stones, primary and semi-finished steel, plant solvent extracts, chemicals, dyes, raw and finished cotton, drugs and pharmaceuticals and machinery. Thai exports to India comprised pulses, rubber products, electrical machinery, tools & metal scrap and gems & ores, including rice at certain times.

Investment proposals from Thailand in the fields of fisheries, chemicals, air conditioning systems, hotel and tourism, were approved of, in 1994-95. Indian investment of US$ 25 million in Thailand was registered in the same period. At present, there are 27 Indian joint ventures in Thailand involving about US$ 16.5 million. Total approved investment from Thailand for the 1991-98 period was, Rs. 24517.21 million.

However, Thailand and other ASEAN partners are presently interested in economic relations and in exploring South Asian market. They may like to expand their economic influence through India in South Asia and treat India as the gateway to enter into the SAARC market.

Thailand is a key regional actor. It has been taking landmark steps in the promotion of business and trade. It tried to turn Indo-China into a market Place and facilitated the construction of Lao-Thai Friendship Bridge. Now it is giving new thrusts to Look West policy and in that connection, they attach prime importance to India for its success.

Thailand has evolved "Look West" policy to complement India's "Look East" policy. Thailand's Foreign Affairs newsletter stated that 'the conceptual basis of the Look West policy for Thailand is to cope effectively and efficiently with the rapid changes in the international political and economic environment in accordance with the reality of the post cold war era. The Look West policy is also derived from the fact that Thailand recognizes promising economic potential of other regions beyond Southeast Asia. The main objectives of the Look West policy as they summed up are, as follows:

- to strengthen the existing bilateral relations with the target states, and;
- to seek potential markets and investment opportunities overseas, and to promote foreign investment in Thailand.

Target states are countries in South Asia, Middle East & Africa. But South Asia is a gateway to the Middle East and Africa. In that connection, there is special reference to India, where they find promising economic environment, vast economic potential, cheap labor and an abundance of natural resources. "Look West" policy of Thailand, as explained by Pitak Intrawitya nunt, Deputy Minister of Foreign Affairs, on 27 May 1997, in New Delhi, was to strengthen and expand the economic, political and cultural cooperation between India and Thailand. The ministerial visit to India was projected as part of the Look West policy, and both the sides agreed to expand trade from $900 million to $2 billion by 1998. Thai products with high market potentials in India, were electronic devices and plastic goods and Thailand assured to explore ways and means of increasing her investment in India. It was during this visit that India agreed to consider the issues of expanding of cooperation in fishery around the Andaman and Nicobar Islands and the release of the 16 Thai fishermen who had been detained. [7]

In fact, Thailand had taken an initiative in 1995, to establish a sub-regional grouping involving India for greater cooperation in the name of BIMST-EC, and this evoked a positive response. On June 6, 1997, this sub-regional grouping was formally launched and the main areas of cooperation included cooperation in trade, investment industry, transportation, infrastructure, science and technology, human resources development, energy fisheries, agriculture, natural resources and tourism.

A special meeting of the BIMST-EC took place in Bangkok in December 1997, where Myanmar too was admitted into the grouping. Hence, BIST-EC was renamed as BIMST-EC and it decided to establish an Economic Forum with both private and public sector participation, from member countries.

Again Economic and Trade Ministers of BIMST-EC met at Bangkok on August 7, 1998, where India was represented by commerce Minister R.K. Hegde. This meeting underlined BIMST-EC's substantive economic agenda and marked a significant step towards further institutionalizing BIMSTEC cooperation. A BIMST-EC Senior Economic Officials Committee (SEOC) was established and the responsibilities for the various sectors identified for cooperation were delegated amongst the five countries, as follows:

Bangladesh	Trade and investment
India	Technology
Thailand	Transport and Communication
Myanmar	Energy
Sri Lanka	Tourism and Fisheries

Although the "Look West policy" of Thailand, is meant for promoting the relations with India in cultural, political and economic areas, the cooperation in strategic/security areas are important. There is convergence of interests between India and Thailand in strategic areas, which had not been properly understood in the past. There are non-traditional security threats such as terrorism & spread of small arms, drug trafficking, maritime piracy, money laundering, illegal migration, environmental degradation, growing scarcity of energy resources and spread of infectious diseases. These matters are of great concern in South and Southeast Asian region. Therefore, both Thailand and India have been struggling to evolve policies to ward off the non-traditional security threats, but both have failed in that attempt. An effective coordinated action plan is needed to address various issues and Thailand and India can contribute significantly especially to controlling drug trafficking, maritime piracy and terrorism.

Drug trafficking is a serious problem and both India and Thailand are interested in curbing it. The golden triangle, which includes the territory of Laos, Myanmar and Thailand, is the largest producer of opium. The opium producers have their transit points through India or China and through them it is illegally transported in the outside world. Drug trafficking generates narco-terrorism, crimes, Aids and other infectious diseases. A large number of people in Thailand and India are the victims of drug abuse and drug trafficking. Both Thailand and India can coordinate their activities in the Gulf of Thailand and Andaman Seas to contain the activities of drug lords and smugglers. As far as maritime piracy is concerned, there are reports of attacks by the pirates in Malacca and Sunda straits. The pirates are always violent and unscrupulous and they target only small local vessels, tugs, supply ships and fishing trawlers, and attack their targets for stealing the cargo or kidnapping the crews for ransom. [8] However, the most disturbing issue for both India and Thailand is the rise of terrorist outfits in the region. Islamic fanatics are engaged in violent activities and Muslim fanatics in Patani (Thailand) have definite links with Jemmah Islamiyah. On the other hand, India is witnessing violent activities in northeastern states, especially in Nagaland, Mizoram and Manipur, which have impinging impacts on broader issues of regional cooperation.

Again, terror attacks in the US on 9/11, serial bomb blasts in London on 7/7, and bombing attacks in Bali, Jakarta, New Delhi, Patani and Mindanao, have disturbed the security environment. India and Thailand, sharing common maritime borders, are cooperating under the framework of ARF and have signed several agreements against terrorism in the region. However, it can be stated, that terrorism and other issues of non-traditional security matters are sensitive issues and demand utmost care and urgent attention to handle. It is a complex exercise and demands a dynamic approach. The western panacea as witnessed in Iraq and Afghanistan are counterproductive. A regional consensus and solution are required and as a Centre of Buddhist learning and civilization, Thailand is expected to play an enlightened role in that direction.

There is scope for cooperation and coordination in security and defense matters in the present dispensation and the ARF is exploring them. The cooperation in strategic areas between Thailand and India, was dismal before 1991. Both were patrolling their maritime frontiers individually and in isolation of each other. However, they were arresting fishermen trespassing into each other's territory. Thailand was the strategic partner of the US and so was the case of India vis-à-vis the Soviet Union. The smugglers and pirates were active in the region and they were treating Andaman as an important channel for narcotics and drug supplies. The smugglers exploited the differences in the attitudes of the two countries and branded both India and Thailand as soft vis-à-vis drug mafias. But now the situation has changed. India and Thailand are associated with ARF and they discuss their problems and policies. Again, China's strategic presence in Myanmar, especially in Coco Island and Hainggi, was a matter of concern for all of us. The countries in the ASEAN region, disliked China's sovereignty claims over the Spratlys and incidents of skirmishes at Mischief Reef. Hence Thailand also began to review its strategic perspective and found Indian opinion sharing Thai concerns.

Kavi Chongkittavorn who has been writing about Thai strategic thinking in the Nation, noted that the opinion of Thai Armed Forces towards India started changing after 1992, which became clear after the exchange of visits by senior army officers and defence personnel to India. Thus, the army officers from India also reciprocated and the growing interaction showed areas of cooperation. India and Thailand are the only two Asian countries, which possess aircraft carriers. Thailand has Spanish built Chakri Naruebej aircraft carrier based at Phuket. India has its naval presence at Andamans. India has missile technology and potentials to assist Thai navy's modernization plans. [9] India has conducted nuclear tests and its missile technologies are advanced. If Thailand and India will coordinate their strategies in the region, it will prove beneficial for both. Thailand and India through their joint exercises, joint patrolling and coordination, can ensure the safely of the international waters, especially in the Gulf of Thailand and Andaman regions from maritime piracy, illegal poaching of fish, and unauthorized extraction of various types of marine resources. Thailand shares 10,000 nautical miles of common maritime boundary with India in the Andamans. [10] If the two agree to have joint patrolling and surveillance, it will prove useful for both the countries. If they ensure cooperation in that area, they will significantly and substantially contribute to the safety of the international sea-lanes of communication in the straits of Malacca, Lombok and Sunda.

Thus we find that Indo-Thai relations are on the right track. In economic or security matters, both of them have similar views. They are evolving common stand in WTO and on free trade. However, it can be found that all these matters are constantly in a flux and the business is much below the target. What binds India with Thailand on permanent basis, is culture and Buddhism and therefore, we must attach importance to cultural interaction, and use that feedback for regional cooperation.

To sum up, it can be stated that the status of relations with Thailand is a decisive factor in promoting our ties with Asia-Pacific. Thailand continues to remain an important gateway to promote our partnership with ASEAN and East Asian countries. Thailand had played a key role in promoting the bonds of regionalism in the past. The idea of establishing ASEAN had emanated in Thailand. Thai foreign Minister, Thanat Khoman, had played a pivotal role in bringing Indonesia and Malaysia on a common platform to work for regional cooperation and forget the policy of confrontation. The confabulation amongst Thailand, Malaysia and Indonesia paved the path for cooperation and thus, ASEAN had been evolved. Although ASEAN had a slow progress in due course of time, it substantially contributed to the boom of the region.

Thailand has been given credit for evolving the policy of changing Indo-China from battleground to marketplace. It has given its own interpretation of democracy and human rights, free trade and fight against terror as an alternative to Western views. Its support of regional cooperation especially in the post-Cold War period, is appreciated. But the attitudes and mindset of the leaders cannot be changed abruptly. It takes time to evolve a common vision and strategies. We understand that India and

Thailand have immense scope of cooperation in mining, fishing, IT, BT, science and technologies. The economic thrust in relations is indeed rewarding, but in our assessment, the relations with Thailand are symbolic of our friendship with Southeast Asia. Whenever Thailand solidly supported India in any regional trials, it was successful. Whether it was the subject of spread of Buddhism in the ancient past, INA struggle against colonial rule in India or the establishment of BIMST-EC in the recent past, Thai support proved to be crucial. If India is willing to contribute to Asian resurgence, and if it believes that Asia-Pacific must be given a priority in trade and investments, it has to give attention to clearing India's gateway to Asia- pacific. In that attempt, it can be stated that with Thai support, cooperation and coordination, we can handle the situation effectively. Although the support of Myanmar and Bangladesh is important, they are tough bargainers. If Thailand is in the forefront, the making of cooperative environment is possible.

India has been pursuing "Look East Policy" and has attached priority to the ASEAN region for economic and strategic partnership. It has cultivated strategic partnership with Indonesia and Singapore. It has helped in reviving nuclear plant in Ho Chi Minh City under international supervision. Its credentials as a responsible important power in the region are recognized. However, geo-politics of the region suggest that Indians can achieve their objectives in the Asia-Pacific, if there is peace in the northeast, coordination with Bangladesh, and complete solidarity with Myanmar. Thailand is the only country in the region, which can act as a facilitator in that process, to provide new thrusts to regional cooperation and integration.

Thailand finds convergence of interests with India and "Look West Policy" is intended to create conditions for better relations. It is aimed at evolving a new mindset, new environment and new incentives conducive to promote relations. [11] India is slowly framing suitable rules and regulations to exploit growing opportunities. The "Look West Policy" explored avenues to establish contacts for mutual benefit and regional prosperity and

India reciprocated them by actively supporting their proposals both for strategic and economic cooperation. Both sides have exchanged high-level visits for complete understanding and solidarity and ASEAN partnership facilitated these exercises.

However, the trade and investment figures indicate that it is far less than its potentials. There is lot of scope for improvement. Various issues like the .cold war mind-sets, standards of production, business environment and bureaucratic loopholes etc very often come in the way of cooperation. Those issues spoil the rhythm of cooperation and various elements to promote cooperation get "misplaced". It is the need of the hour that all the elements of cooperation are fine-tuned with sincerity, understanding and urgency. The respective Prime Ministers of Thailand from Chatichai Choonhavan (He was the first Prime Minister of Thailand to come to India on a State visit in 1989) to present Prime Minister Thaksin Shinawatra are highlighting the importance of India in the contemporary world and their views are suitably reciprocated by India. Indian Prime Ministers from Rajiv Gandhi (He was the first Indian Prime Minister to visit Thailand on a state visit in 1986) to the present Prime Minister, Manmohan Singh, have tried to remove negative mindsets persisting in both the countries, but the transformation is gradual. Both India and Thailand are trying to expand areas of cooperation in economic, cultural and strategic areas. Thai perspective of India can be understood in the words of Field Marshal Phibun Songgram, the architect of modern Thailand, who spoke the following words, years ago: "India is the mother country of religion, culture, arts and sciences, as she has been the world teacher from olden times. The light of Indian soul has therefore never been extinguished, but henceforth shine gloriously brighter, fanned by the unity, endeavor and perseverance of all of us." [12]

Notes

1. For an understanding of Thailand's Strategic importance, See K.M. Panikkar, *The Future of Southeast Asia: An Indian View*, New York, 1943 and Donald E. Nuechterlein, *Thailand and the Struggle for*

Southeast Asia, New York, 1965 and Ganganath Jha, *Foreign Policy of Thailand*, New Delhi, 1979.

2. Prince Chula Chakrabongse, *Lords of Life: A History of the Kings of Thailand*, London, 1960, pp.197-2001

3. To know in detail, about this aspect, see Frank C. Darling, *Thailand and the United States*, Washington, D.C. 1965, and Ronald W. Pruessen, "John Foster Dulles and Decolonisation in Southeast Asia", in Marc Frey & others (ed.) *The Transformation of Southeast Asia*, New Delhi 2004, pp 226-40.

4. S. Pushpanathan, "ASEAN and India: A Partnership for Success", Jakarta, *ASEAN secretariat*, 2003, pp.32-34.

5. *MEA Annual Reports, 1995 to 2005*, New Delhi.

6. A.N. Ram, "India's 'Look East' Policy" in Raja Reddy (ed.) *India and ASEAN: Foreign Policy Dimensions for the 21st century*, New Delhi, 2005, pp.1-11.

7. Outcome of Deputy Foreign Minister's visit to India, crystal Lotus, Bangkok, Information Department, *Ministry of Foreign Affairs*, April-June 1997, p.16

8. For a better understanding of this aspect, see P. Chalk, Grey-area Phenomena in *Southeast Asia: Piracy, Drug Trafficking and Political Terrorism*, Canberra papers on Strategy and Defence, no.123, Canberra 1997. (Prime Minister, P.V. Narasimha Rao in his famous Singapore Lecture on September 8, 1994 had spoken about security threats in the following words, "India has in fact been subjected to considerable burdens on account of migrations of populations, terrorist attacks and smuggling. Our interests lie in peace and harmony which will enable us to improve our standards of living".)

9. *The Nation*, Bangkok, 1 August 1997

10. Kavi Chong Kittavorn, Thai-Indo a Security ties enjoy peace dividend," *The Nation*, 1 August 1997

11. Rita Patiyasevi, "Video-Conference Opens India Link", *The Nation*, 1 August 1997.

12. Quoted by Ranjit Gupta, "Indo-Thai Relations", *The Nation*, August 1, 1997.

4

India and Singapore: Economic Partnership

Gautam Murthy

India's links with Southeast Asia go back to centuries when India had left an indelible impression of its potent culture all over the region, especially in matters, relating to religion, art, architecture, language, literature, folklore, music, dance and drama. However, during the first four decades following India's independence, these historic linkages became weakened, when India turned inwards. Today, India, in the context of globalization, is determined to rediscover the Southeast Asia region, having realized fully that it is a resource rich region with a market potential of 300 million people. India's "Look East" strategy and the economic liberalization efforts, have provided a common valid ground for cooperation with Southeast Asia. India's economic potential and its geostrategic importance for Southeast Asia's security in the post-Cold War world, are today recognized as a significant aspect of the international diplomacy.

India Reinventing its Ties with Southeast Asia

India has moved purposefully progressively, in developing a broad economic and strategic partnership with the dynamic countries of the Southeast Asia. Yet, India chooses to have a distinct "Focus" and even a lucid "Vision" with regard to its ties with Southeast Asia. In pursuance of India's "Look East" policy, the dialogue with the Association of Southeast Asian Nations (ASEAN) has moved from a limited sectoral partnership (1992) to a full dialogue partnership (1995) and the membership of the high-profile strategic forum ARF (ASEAN Regional Forum) in 1996, culminating in ASEAN+India summits which had begun since 2002. A fruitful FTA (Free Trade Agreement) between India and ASEAN, would come into being in 10 years, and India is committed to aligning its peak tariff to East Asian levels by 2007. [1] There is much scope for further expanding and deepening India's our cooperative agenda for synergizing its economies as well as ASEAN's and for exploring new avenues for diplomatic complementarities.

India-ASEAN cooperation has progressed substantially in many spheres – mainly in science and technology, IT and electronics, HRD, transport and infrastructure, space technology, tourism and trade and investment. These initiatives are however not adequately reflected in trade figures. The Indo-ASEAN two-way trade grew by 30 per cent from U.S$ 7.6 billion in 1999 to $ 16 billion in 2005. ASEAN-India trade is still at a very low level, accounting for only 1 per cent of ASEAN's global trade in 2005, while India's trade with ASEAN countries still hovers around 9 per cent of its global trade. The volume of trade continues to be tiny, considering the vast potential for trade; and it is hoped that the target of $30 billion, will be reached by 2010. The list of goods for which duties are brought down to zero by 2007, include a host of petrochemicals and polyesters, apart from other items like marine foods, white goods, electrical machinery, precious stones, office equipment, printed circuits and key auto-components like gear box and petrol engines.

By all means, a trade pact with ASEAN, makes the best beginning, since India has been traditionally enjoying many links-economic and strategic- with the region, although there remains still, a lot of untapped potential. However, there are major differences in regard to "tariff rates," between India and the big five of ASEAN. Indian customs duties are on an average, at least double and in many cases, triple the rates of ASEAN. Thus, the tariff equalization and rationalization, will not be possible for a free and facile trade in near future. Moreover, changes in domestic tariff and commercial policy, will be, more often than not, detrimental to the interests of the domestic producers.

India's merchandise exports to ASEAN, have more than tripled from about US$ 1.0 billion (5.7 per cent of its world exports) to US$ 3.4 billion in 2001-02(7.7 per cent of its world exports). The overall trend has been upwards, except during the Asian crisis period of 1997-99.The rising trend of merchandise exports from India to ASEAN, has been accompanied by a shift in the share of the individual countries in India's total exports to ASEAN, during this period. ASEAN countries are more important for India as import sources than as export markets. Among ASEAN-members, Singapore and Malaysia have been India's prominent trading partners and India's trade with Laos has been the least, in value terms. In general, growth in India's exports to ASEAN in recent years has been much higher, in comparison with other important destinations. ASEAN's position in India's total trade, relative to EU and North America, has improved between 1991-92 and 2001-02. The shares of EU and North America in India's exports have been declining, whereas that of ASEAN has been on the rise.

India's aggregate balance of trade with ASEAN-5 shows, that India posted deficits in every year since 1994, which became more pronounced in the last five years (Table 4.1). This trend is attributed to the pattern of the relatively higher deficits with Singapore and Malaysia, and correspondingly, India's inability to generate matching surplus elsewhere in the region, even when the balance-of-trade is in its favour.

The level of investment that flows on both the sides has a lot of untapped potential and can easily rise to $ 2 billion by 2007, provided there are sustained efforts by both the sides. The redeeming fact is that there are substantial investments by both India and ASEAN in each other's countries but the investment relations between ASEAN and India, have remained rather limited because of the fact that while Singapore, and to some extent, Malaysia have significant investments to their credit in India, Indian companies have been showing the limited capacity to invest abroad until recently. The share of ASEAN-6 in India's total approved FDI inflows increased, nearly fourfold from 2 per cent to about 8 per cent between 1996 and 1998. Malaysia has made substantial investments in expanding capacities in selected infrastructural areas such as logistics and highways in India. It has also been cooperating in assisting India by providing infrastructure expertise and investments in the energy sector, particularly for oil and gas exploration and in downstream processing activities.

Table 4.1: Share of ASEAN-5 in India's Global Exports and Imports (per cent)

Share in India's Global Exports	1991	1996	2001
Indonesia	1.3	2.7	1.2
Malaysia	1.6	2.3	1.7
Singapore	2.3	3.1	2.5
Philippines	0.4	2.5	0.5
Thailand	5.2	2.0	1.5
Share in India's Global Imports			
Indonesia	0.3	1.5	2.5
Malaysia	1.6	3.4	3.2
Singapore	5.1	5.7	5.6
Philippines	0.1	0.5	0.1
Thailand	0.3	0.7	1.0

Source: *ASEAN Statistical Yearbooks*, ASEAN Secretariat.

The motivation for the current and future Indian investments abroad, is economic efficiency and profitability criteria (pull factors), rather than to escape the restrictive business environment at home (push factors).This is indicated by the fact that over the past few years, over 150 firms from India have been identified in Singapore, as contributing factors to its economy and to employment generation. Indian companies are also poised enough to invest in Thailand (auto components sector), in Indonesia and Vietnam (motor vehicles and energy sector), and in the Philippines (ICT sector). These opportunities arise from substantial complementarities that exist between India and

ASEAN in factor endowments, economic structure, skills and capabilities. The experience and competencies of Malaysia and Singapore in the infrastructure development, complements India's needs for physical infrastructure, particularly in the area of roads, industrial parks and housing estates.

Possibilities for the functional cooperation are limitless, and enthusiasm should get translated into tangible gains. India also needs to get her links deepened with MGC (Mekong Ganga Cooperative forum) - a new co-operative forum floated by India with five of its eastern neighbours- Myanmar, Thailand, Cambodia, Vietnam and Laos. Tourism, culture and education are given precedence. The terms of India-ASEAN engagement needs to be taken much more seriously. Transport, communications and infrastructure will be prioritised in the next phase. The MGC also provides immense opportunities for India's private sector to create a niche in the region so that India can make amends for its past mistakes. Indo-ASEAN cooperation in tourism, culture and education, can also be strengthened in Indonesia and Malaysia.

ASEAN also faces the problem of disparity in development, as the new entrants – Cambodia, Laos, Myanmar and Vietnam (CLMV countries) – are able to show only lower levels of performance compared to the other members and thus, require time to integrate fully into the ASEAN framework, India can offer its help here as well, by providing interest-free credit facilities for speedier development of these CLMV countries, and get benefited by cashing in on the tremendous good-will that existed for her in the Cold War days.

Other measures to promote greater India-ASEAN interaction should include the relaxation of visa restrictions by ASEAN countries, an opening up of the financial and banking sector, a reduction of non-tariff barriers, a sustained improvement in the delivery system of the Indian bureaucracy, and continuing to give explicit economic orientation to foreign policy.

While India's membership of the ARF enables it to participate in regional security issues, India would seriously undermine its long term strategic and economic interests, if it does not take into account China's rapidly expanding economic and strategic profile in its eastern neighbourhood. While India's trade with ASEAN is currently around $16 billion annually, China's trade with ASEAN economies is multi-layered and currently stands at $ 60 billion.

India-Singapore Growing Bilateral Relationship

Singapore is located at the heart of Southeast Asia which is a resource rich region with a market potential of some 300 million people. The city-state of Singapore is also strategically located at a critical intersection of international commerce, and in the geo-strategic vicinity of India and China. Singapore commands attention on the international stage as a dynamic economy, and according to Michael Leifer as an "exceptional state". Singapore is a natural gateway for India to engage the other Southeast Asian countries, because of its historical ties and a special kind of intimate friendship with India.

Thus, Singapore is well placed to serve the fast growing markets of this region. Singapore's unique location and sophisticated telecommunications network, allow the financial institutions and other companies in the country, to transact business with any part of the world within the same working day. The other added advantages of Singapore include: the capability of the handling international trade (the country being divided into 7 Free Trade Zones), the Economic Development Board to promote foreign investment, the business-friendly and transparent regulatory environment, an open investment regime, being conducive to attract foreign investment in various sectors and the incentives of Singaporean government to the capital-investors.

The increasingly close relations between India and Singapore in recent years have been underpinned by a dramatic growth in the bilateral trade and investment links. Singapore's economy complements India's economy, and does not pose any kind of threat to India's sensitive sectors, if the commodity composition of trade is of any indication. [2] The recently concluded CECA (Comprehensive Economic Cooperation Agreement) between

India and Singapore, creates the necessary congenial environment for a strong bilateral relationship, and wider cooperation between India and Southeast Asia..[3]

With an investment of $1.29 billion, Singapore has emerged as the third largest foreign investor in India. The major investments in India from Singapore, are channelised through three major agencies-Government of Singapore Investment Corporation, Monetary Authority of Singapore and Temasak Holdings. Many Indian companies, mainly trading and software companies, have set up joint ventures and subsidiaries in Singapore, to promote their business activities in the region, covering diverse product areas such as automobile ancillaries, precision tooling, palm kernel processing, micro and mini computers.

In the tourism sector, opportunities are emerging rapidly for Singapore as Indian tourists have become the highest spenders of all the tourists to Singapore which became the fourth largest revenue generating market, corresponding to the growing affluence among the Indian middle class. In the logistics sector, the Port of Singapore Authority (PSA) has been involved in port development and management in Tuticorin in Tamil Nadu and Piparav in Gujarat. These developments have the potential to lead to major investment opportunities for other Singapore firms in the logistics sector.

Defence-related research, could be an area of future cooperation. Incremental interactions have taken place across a wide spectrum, ranging from education and culture. Singapore is also keen that India plays an appropriate role in a "creative fashion" in the maintenance of security along the Straits of Malacca.

Singapore also played a leading role in India, by becoming a member of the ARF (ASEAN Regional Forum) and the ASEAN+1 Summit. It was the country coordinator for the ASEAN-India dialogue. Among the ASEAN states, Singapore has gone farthest, to improve both the bilateral and the associational ties. India's former Prime Minister, P.V Narasimha Rao, in his path-breaking Singapore lecture of September 1994, which set in motion India's "Look East" policy, said, "The Asia-Pacific could be the spring board for our leap into the global market place. I am happy to have had this opportunity to enunciate my belief in this vision of a new relationship between India and the Asia-Pacific from Singapore, which I consider the geographic and symbolic centre of the Asia-Pacific." Since then, Singapore has been the key country for India's engagement with Southeast Asia. Singapore's exertions on behalf of India are openly acknowledged by the Indian policy making community.

During his visit to Singapore in August 2003, the then Indian External Affairs Minister candidly noted: "... in the development of our ties with ASEAN, few countries have been as creative and pro-active as Singapore. We are grateful to our many friends here, in particular, (then) Prime Minister Goh Chok Tong, for his vision and leadership in bringing India and ASEAN closer. This has been made possible by virtue of the strong bilateral relationship that India and Singapore have built over the years".

Singapore Prime Minister Lee Hsien Loong, in a recent speech in New Delhi in July 2005, noted:"... India's influence is being felt all over Southeast Asia. In Singapore alone, there are more than 1,500 Indian companies. Many are regional headquarters, some even overseeing operations in the Indian market. Thousands of Indian professionals work in Singapore in IT, financial services and other fields. Bollywood movies enjoy a strong following ...the stage has been set for a burgeoning bilateral relationship between Singapore and India, and wider and deeper cooperation between India and Southeast Asia. With greater collaboration and integration between the people of both sides, and continued reforms by those in Government, we can look forward to a vibrant and dynamic future for Asia".

India-Singapore Trade

Singapore is the largest market in ASEAN for India's merchandise exports, and is followed by Malaysia, Thailand, Indonesia, and the Philippines in the order of precedence.

Singapore is India's largest trading and investment partner in ASEAN. A dramatic growth in the bilateral trade and investment linkages reinforced close relations between India and Singapore in recent years. India is looking for infrastructure investments, critical technologies and export markets. Singapore has surplus capital and could be a useful partner in the infrastructure development in India as well as in the investment, in Indian companies.

Total trade between India and Singapore has been steadily increasing since 1999. The trade between India and Singapore increased by 3.22 per cent (in 2001), to S$6.88 billion, and decreased by 1.16 per cent (in 2002). On comparing the trade figures of 2003 with 2002, it is seen that the total trade has gone up by 16.20 per cent. India's Imports from Singapore, have increased by 14.22 per cent and exports to Singapore, by 21.25 per cent. Over a period of 5 years, India's imports from Singapore have increased by 26.88 per cent, whereas, during the same period, India's exports to Singapore have increased by 100.8 per cent. Moreover, it may be noted, that most of Singapore's exports to India, consists of re-exports, which constitute slightly over 50 per cent of Singapore's exports to India (Table 4.2).

Table 4.2: India-Singapore Trade

Year	Singapore's Exports to India		Of Which Re-exports		Singapore's Imports from India		Total Trade	
	(S$ bln)	(US$ bln)	(S$ bln)	(US$ bln)	(S$ bln)	(US$ bln)	(S$ bln)	(US$ bln)
1999	4.24	2.50	2.28	1.35	1.25	0.74	5.49	3.23
2000	4.80	2.74	2.71	1.54	1.86	1.06	6.66	3.81
2001	4.87	2.76	2.87	1.63	2.00	1.13	6.87	3.90
2002	4.71	2.67	2.79	1.58	2.08	1.18	6.79	3.85
2003	5.38	3.16	2.89	1.70	2.51	1.48	7.89	4.64

The balance of trade, as can be noted from Table 4.3, has remained in favour of Singapore since 1999. However, despite growth in bilateral trade, the balance of trade in favour of Singapore, has more or less remained the same for the last five years in value terms (in S $). Indian exports to Singapore have been steadily increasing, growing in S$ terms by 48.8 per cent (2000), 7.52 per cent (2001) and 3.5 per cent (2002), and 21.25 per cent (2003).

Table 4.3: Comparison of Trade Balance between India and Singapore (Value in S$ billion)

	1999	2000	2001	2002	2003
India's Import from Singapore	4.24	4.80	4.84	4.72	5.38
India's Export to Singapore	1.25	1.86	2.00	2.07	2.51
Balance of Trade	-2.99	-2.94	-2.84	-2.65	-2.87

Bilateral trade between the two countries is surging, rising over 50 per cent in the fiscal year 2004/05 (April-March) to US$6.38bn, according to India's Ministry of Commerce and Industry. India's imports from Singapore were worth US$2.58bn in 2004/05, consisting principally of electronic goods (39 per cent of its total imports from Singapore), organic chemicals (14 per cent) and transport equipment (9 per cent). India's exports to Singapore totalled US$ 3.80bn, consisting largely of crude oil and petroleum products (46 per cent of its total exports to India), gems and jewellery (15 per cent), and machinery and instruments (5 per cent). India's bilateral trade surplus with Singapore in the last fiscal year was US$ 1.21bn.

Given the diversity of products and services that make up the trade between India and Singapore, there is ample potential for the CECA to boost bilateral commerce significantly. India has been granted more or less complete duty-free access to Singapore, which is positioning itself (primarily through the negotiation of bilateral free-trade agreements, or FTAs) as Asia's trade hub. Singapore has signed FTAs with six other countries (including Japan, Australia and the US) and is negotiating with a further a deal with South Korea, which is due to be concluded soon.

Thanks to Singapore's FTA network, India's exporters will have greater access to eastern Asian markets, thanks to the CECA. Singapore is already India's largest trading partner in the Association of South-East Asian Nations (ASEAN), accounting for 37.5 per cent of its trade with ASEAN members, but this is likely to grow. The CECA's provisions, establishing common measures and standards for Singaporean and Indian goods, will enable the traders in Singapore to push Indian products more easily through the region.

However, India's trade policy is less clear cut than that of Singapore's. A broader strategy for establishing bilateral deals worldwide is hampered by the domestic concerns about the increased competition. Acknowledging the complaints from the Indian manufacturers about the threat of foreign competition, the CECA is hardly generous in terms of import liberalisation. As well as keeping tariffs unchanged on over 6,500 Singaporean products, India has negotiated the application of the stringent rules-of-origin safeguards, to prevent the third-party goods from reaching the Indian market via Singapore. A minimum of 40 per cent of value must be added in Singapore for the products to qualify themselves for an access under the CECA's tariff schedule, a stipulation similar to that which has caused a friction in India's FTA negotiations with Thailand.

Despite its limitations, the deal with Singapore does mark a watershed in India's broader strategy of encouraging the domestic economic growth through promoting export-oriented industries. It was significant that India's cabinet approved of the deal just three days after the first meeting of the revamped Board of Trade, a collaborative government/industry forum in charge of developing a coherent national trade strategy. At this meeting, the commerce and industry minister, Kamal Nath, exhorted the body to come up with the required ways to boost India's total trade to US$ 500bn in the next four years. (By comparison, India's trade in goods in 2004/05 was of an estimated US$ 173bn.) With most of the rest of Asia committed to establishing free-trade networks, rather than relying on the WTO, Mr. Nath presumably, had deals like the CECA in mind as a first step to achieving this goal.

Investment Patterns

Singapore has emerged amongst the top foreign investors in India. During the period from January 1991 to May 2003, approvals for Foreign Direct Investment from Singapore to India (excluding NRI and euro issues/portfolio investment) amounted to Rs. 53 billion (approx USD 1.2 billion,) making Singapore among the largest foreign investors in India. The annual break-up since 1995, of Singapore's investment, and the share of total FDI (excluding NRI and portfolio investment) in India, is given in Table 4.4.

Table 4.4: Approvals for FDI in India (Rs. million)

Year	Total World FDI*	Singapore FDI	Singapore FDI as % of Total
1995	301725	9910	3.28
1996	286923	3198	1.11
1997	485720	8619	1.77
1998	268392	7673	2.86
1999	246855	8259	3.35
2000	156183	3232	2.07
2001	203319	3799	1.87
2002	111398	3722	3.34
2003 (up to May)	17436	1254	7.2
Total (since 1991)	2,280399*	53604	2.35

*Excluding NRI/ Euro issues

Source: SIA Newsletter, June 2003

Singapore investments: Some of the Government-Linked Corporations (GLCs) of Singapore's projects include, Ascendas' Information Technology Park in Bangalore, the participation of the Port of Singapore Authority (PSA) in both equity (40 per cent) and management of Piparav Port, Gujarat, PSA's 30-year contract for operation and management of the Tuticorin Port, Singtel's joint venture with Bharati Telecom and Singapore Technologies Telemedia's JV with Modi Corp. The Government of Singapore Investment Corporation (GIC) has registered itself in India as Financial Institutional Investors, and has committed Rs. 119 million to HDFC Ltd., apart from investing in other stocks and equities.

The GIC along with other investors, has invested Rs.11 billion (S$407 million) for a 13.6 percent stake in India's ICICI Bank as its strategic partners. In December 2003, Temasek holdings has acquired a 5.2 per cent stake, costing around S$ 342.2million in ICICI Bank. In January 04, Temasek Holdings, Singapore Government's investment arm, bought a stake in Matrix laboratories, Hyderabad for S$ 114.7million, thus getting a 14 per cent equity stake, in the company.

Singapore-based MNCs and Singapore's government-linked-companies (GLCs) such as Singapore Telecom, Port of Singapore Authority and Singapore Technologies, have also made investments in India. Singapore's private sector companies have made small-scale investments in health care, real estate, and tourism.Favourable experience and profitability of Singapore's technology park in Bangalore, created a positive environment for investments by Singapore in India.

Singapore, through its government holding company, government of Singapore Investment Corporation (SGIC), is also one of the largest Foreign Institutional Investors in India. The majority of the MNCs in Singapore, have used Mauritius to route investments to India because of its favourable double taxation treaty with India. Thus, the official figures of inflows of FDI from Singapore to India, is understated as they exclude all those investments, routed via Mauritius.

Temasek and Stanchart Bank formed the Merlion - India Fund of US$ 100 million towards investing in mid to late stage of the Indian Companies. The fund does not cover investment in infra - structure, real estate and trading. This fund was set up for the purpose of Singapore companies investing in Indian companies expanding in India and abroad. The fund has been invested (in December 03), S$ 35 million to a 5.46 per cent stake in Aurobindo Pharma, Hyderabad.

The Singapore Business Federation (SBF), which is the government-guided amalgamation of different chambers of commerce and industry, is also likely to open an office in India. Individual chambers of commerce associated with SBF such as the Chinese, Malay and Indian chambers, might also open their own separate offices in due course.

While Singapore's manufacturing base, centering on electronics and petrochemicals, and its role as an entrepot will continue to sustain the merchandise trade, the emerging opportunities are largely in the services sector, particularly in the Information and Communication Technology (ICT), logistics services, business and financial services, tourism, and health services This is more so, as Singapore plans to develop itself into a service hub and to improve its capabilities in areas in which, complementarities with India abound. The opportunities are not only in trade in services transactions (such as used by Singapore Airlines of India as a base for some of its IT-enabled services) but also in the investments (presence of Indian ICT, Pharmaceutical, and trading companies in Singapore, and Singapore's investments in India's ICT, tourism and health services, besides in port development and logistics). The probable involvement of Singapore's polytechnics in technical education in Tamil Nadu, and perhaps other states, could further strengthen bilateral linkages.

The Info-Comm. Development Authority of Singapore (IDA) has signed an MoU with India's premier IT training company, National Institute of Information Technology (NIIT), to persuade IT professionals to locate in Singapore, from anywhere in the world. As Indian professionals are internationally competitive and culturally compatible, India is among the largest sources of IT manpower in the world and a significant proportion is likely to be sourced from India. This could create a dynamic Indian Diaspora with positive externalities for both the countries. The investments by Singapore Telecom (SingTel) in India's telecom sector in partnership with India's Bharti Televentures to take advantage of India's huge potential domestic telecom and Internet market also form another example in this sector.

Opportunities are emerging rapidly for Singapore in the tourism sector, as Indian tourists have become the highest spenders among the tourists to Singapore which thus became the fourth largest revenue generating market, in view of the growing affluence among the Indian middle class. Singapore tourism authorities have also been actively involved in promoting select areas in India as a tourism destination for Singaporeans, through a joint marketing by the Government of India tourism office already established in Singapore.

Indeed, Singapore's two airlines, Singapore Airlines and Silk Air, have quite liberal rights to fly to several destinations in India. They could however, take greater advantage of India's open sky policies concerning air cargo. In the logistics sector, the Port of Singapore Authority (PSA) has been involved in port development and management in Tuticorin in Tamil Nadu and Piparav in Gujarat. These have the potential to lead to major investment opportunities for other Singapore firms in the logistics sector. Negotiations between Singapore's largest supermarket operator, NTUC Fairprice which has close links with the government, and India's Apollo Group, one of Asia's largest hospital and health-care management companies to set up a pharmacy and retail chain of convenience stores numbering in the hundreds in the petrol stations run by the Indian oil corporation, also hold promise for greater economic linkages. It would contribute to Singapore's food security, and to its supply chain for other essential household goods. Indian IT companies have recognized the importance of Singapore as a marketing and development center, and their presence is growing. As Indian business has been given much greater freedom to invest abroad, the presence of Indian companies from other sectors in Singapore, is also increasing. This should also have a positive impact on Singapore's importance as a business hub, and on trade in business services.

Singapore intends to increasingly rely at the margin on the investment income from abroad. Its rather large reserves, conservatively estimated to be about US $ 90 billion, are mostly invested abroad through holding companies of the Singapore government. It is suggested that these holding companies, consider the passive investments in infrastructure projects in India. The issue of setting up of a physical presence in India by the Singapore Government Investment Corporation (SGIC), and other Singapore government investment companies of the kind, merits serious consideration. Currently, these holding companies do act in a limited way as the venture capitalists for Indian IT companies. However, there is much greater scope not only in the IT sector, but also in the biotechnology, life sciences, and other areas. For these purposes also, the physical presence in India would be beneficial.

Investment Implications

The provisions of the CECA related to investment, are equally significant for India. As of December last year, Singapore had invested US$6.41bn in India, which made it the ninth-largest investor in the country. (According to the Indian commerce ministry, Singapore's investments in India grew 114 per cent in fiscal 2004/05 from 2003/04.) The CECA is expected to boost this considerably. Singaporean institutional investments in Indian technology, manufacturing, financial services and aviation, are to rise to US$ 5bn within the first year of the CECA's implementation, while Singaporean investment in India's infrastructure, would top US$2bn.

Certainly, there are measures in the deal that will promote the investment. For example, it revamps a bilateral double-taxation-avoidance treaty that was first signed in 1994, to give Singapore the same status as that of Mauritius (which had hitherto been unique in that its companies could invest in India without paying the capital gains tax on profits, earned there). The CECA provisions liberalising trade in financial and other services--paving the way for an air-services deal and an open-skies agreement, for example, are also likely to boost the business between the two.

The CECA contains some important specific provisions regarding Singaporean investment. It allows the government-linked investment agencies Temasek Holdings and the Government of Singapore Investment Corp, each to invest 10 per cent stakes in Indian companies, whereas previously they had been restricted to acquiring 10 per cent between them. Temasek alone, has invested almost US$ 1.5bn in India in the past 18 months, with stakes in India's largest bank (ICICI), its largest healthcare firm (Apollo Hospitals Enterprises), Tata Consultancy Services, and an automotive firm, Mahindra & Mahindra. It is also, one of India's foremost private equity investors.

The CECA also, opens up India's financial services sector to Singaporean investment, allowing three banks from the city-state--DBS Holdings, Oversea-Chinese Banking Corp and United Overseas Banking, to set up branch operations in India. The three may either set up wholly owned subsidiaries (in which case they will be subject to local regulations) or set up regional branches, in which case, they will be limited to opening

India-Singapore CECA

On June 29, 2005, India and Singapore signed a Comprehensive Economic Co-operation Agreement (CECA), the first of its kind for India, concluding two years of intensive negotiations. Its distinctive feature is that it is indeed 'comprehensive' and covers trade in goods and services, investment flows and encompasses a double taxation avoidance agreement (DTAA).Such wide-ranging agreements are, in a sense, the next logical step in a world economy, increasingly driven by the flows of trade in goods, services and the movement of capital.

For India, it seems, the gains driving the partnership with Singapore, would be in the area of services exports and in-bound FDI. Singapore accounted for approximately 2.5 per cent of India's FDI inflows, from 1991 to 2005 and has been investing especially in Indian infrastructure industries such as ports, telecommunications and banks, in the last few years. The Singapore government has in the past indicated its willingness to set up a $1 billion fund, to invest in India after the CECA comes into force. Since the island-nation is a free-trading port, most of the duties on its tariff lines are zero and there is much it can offer by way of tariff concessions, though the hope is that the synergies in Indian manufacturing and Singaporean branding expertise can be tapped to profit in the ASEAN market. One of the difficult aspects of the negotiations was that of determining the rules of origin (ROO)-by which the nationality of goods is determined to ensure that only the citizens of the contracting country avail themselves of the trade concessions and thereby to alleviate the concern in India, that the exporters from the third countries, could use the Singapore route, to dump cheap goods in the country.

The Prime Minister of Singapore, Lee Hsien Loong, believes that the main advantage for Singapore from the agreement is the tariff less access to the Indian market, for a large number of goods. Besides, some banks will have an access to the Indian market. For the Indian side, the big gain from the agreement is, on the movement of the professionals. Also, an inward investment into India from Singapore has become very much attractive.

The CECA with Singapore is "a free trade agreement (FTA) plus", that covers the trade in goods as also services, besides investment flows and "mutual recognition" clauses and is expected to help Singapore, widen its frontiers of international commerce. Singapore has close economic linkages with the US, Japan and China among others. The business communities in both the countries could now "leverage" across this win-win development.

In the services sector, Indian companies stand to benefit through increased market access in the distribution services, including retail trading, business services, market research, legal, environmental management, management consultancy, tourism, real estate, consultancy and advertising, engineering, architecture and computer-related services.

India was Singapore's 14th largest trading partner in 2004/05 and the bilateral trade has nearly tripled within the past decade, from S$4 billion in 1995 to S$ 11.8 billion in 2004/05. Over the last year, while negotiations were ongoing, the bilateral trade with India increased by almost half, from S$7.8 billion in 2003, making India the fastest growing trading partner among the major economies. The provisions of the CECA are broad, aiming not only at liberalizing the bilateral trade in goods and services but also at increasing the investment and the ease visa regulations. The CECA is likely to enhance Singapore's position as Asia's trade hub, boost Indian trade with East Asia, and encourage more foreign investment in India.

Under the provisions of the CECA, Singapore will cut all duties on goods made in India (excepting tobacco and automobiles), while India will remove or reduce duties on a range of Singaporean products, covering around four-fifths of its exports. As a first step, India will scrap duties on 506 items immediately (from August 1st) and will phase out tariffs on a further 2,202 items over the next four years, and also reduce duties on another 2,407 items by 2009. However, it will maintain the current level of duties on a list of 6,551 items from Singapore. The deal also includes agreements on trade in services and a commitment to liberalise visa requirements for professionals.

Key Provisions of the CECA

Improved Avoidance of Double Taxation Agreement: An Avoidance of Double Taxation Agreement ("DTA") provides for an avoidance of double taxation of income earned in one Contracting State by a resident of the other state and makes clear the taxing rights between the two Contracting States on all forms of income from cross-border economic activities between the two Contracting States. The DTA thus, helps to facilitate the flow of trade, investment, technical know-how and the expertise between the two Contracting States by eliminating double taxation of income.

Singapore and India have agreed on a protocol, to improve the existing DTA, which was signed in January 1994. The main improvement to the DTA is that the tax residents will enjoy capital gains tax exemption on investments in India. The capital gains tax exemption regime of a country is an important consideration for investors and this exemption, which was previously available only to Mauritius, will help promote greater investment flows between Singapore and India.

Trade in Goods: The Trade in Goods Chapter provides for tariff concessions that will make Singapore goods more competitive vis-à-vis other foreign imports into India. Tariffs on approximately 75 per cent of Singapore's domestic exports will be eliminated or substantially reduced within 5 years. The sectors benefiting, includes the electrical and electronics, instrumentation, pharmaceuticals, and plastics. For Singaporean goods entering India, those that qualify for tariff concessions, are classified into one of the following categories: immediate elimination, phased elimination and phased reduction. Goods in the immediate elimination category will have tariffs on them eliminated completely when CECA comes into effect. For goods in the phased elimination and phased reduction categories, the reduction to the final tariffs will be phased in over 5 years and the percentage reduction is expressed as a margin of preference, over the Most Favoured Nation (MFN) applied rates, as shown in Table 4.5.

To illustrate phased tariff concessions, we can use an Indian HS tariff line, as an example. If the tariff line has an MFN rate of 10 per cent in May 2009, a 50 per cent reduction under Phased Tariff Reduction means, that an import duty of 5 per cent would be imposed on the Singapore-originating goods entering India.

For Indian goods entering Singapore, Singapore is committed to grant a zero-tariff treatment for all imports from India. For example, tariffs on Indian beer, entering Singapore, will be eliminated.

Table 4.5: Timeline for the Phased Tariff Concessions

	Tariff reduction by date CECA enters into force (1.8.2005)	Tariff reduction by 1.4.2006	Tariff reduction by 1.4.2007	Tariff reduction by 1.4.2008	Tariff reduction by 1.4.2009
Goods qualifying for phased tariff elimination	10 per cent	25 per cent	50 per cent	75 per cent	100 per cent
Goods qualifying for phased tariff Reduction	5 per cent	10 per cent	20 per cent	35 per cent	50 per cent

Rules of Origin: Rules of Origin (ROO) readily identify the "nationality" of the goods and ensure the tariff concessions under CECA, to both Singaporean or Indian goods only.

The general rule of origin embraces a combination of 40 per cent local content and a change in tariff classification at the 4-digit level. CECA also takes into consideration, the unique production pattern of Singapore and accordingly provides, for a list of products that are exempt from the general rule. For each of these products, a specific rule of origin (e.g., change in tariff classification only) has been drafted.

Customs: Good customs procedures are indispensable to facilitate the movement of goods traded between both the countries. The lack of such procedures can affect an increase in the compliance costs and a corresponding diminution in the benefits that result from the tariff reduction.

Standards and Technical Regulations, Sanitary and Phytosanitary Measures: The potential benefits are a reduction in the cost, due to an elimination of the duplicative testing and reduction in time, to make these products enter the Indian or Singapore market. As most of these products have relatively short life cycles, the result is a reduction in the relative cost and an improved time, to-market competitiveness of Singapore certified products entering the Indian market and vice versa. India is expected to make the necessary amendments to its legislation, to implement these MRA arrangements. This may take another 12 – 18 months. Singapore will also be providing the required technical training conforming to Indian standard bodies, so as to enable them to implement the MRA.

Of immediate benefit, is the food sectoral annex, where Singapore has facilitated the import of egg products, dairy products and packaged drinking water, from India. This will widen the sources of supply for these food products, in Singapore.

Investment: The investment chapter aims to promote and protect investments from both the countries. Market access for investments is based on the principle of National Treatment, subject to the commitments or reservations, undertaken. The chapter contains a number of useful features, to protect investments. [4]

Trade in Services: The services chapter ensures that service suppliers in India and Singapore are guaranteed an access into each other's markets. [5]

Generally, the benefits of the CECA will be extended to the citizens, permanent residents, local companies as well as foreign MNCs that are constituted, or otherwise organized, in India or Singapore. Companies, wishing to supply audio-visual, educational, financial and telecommunication services through commercial presence in India or Singapore, would have to meet the ownership or the control criteria, in order to benefit from the CECA.

Both the countries are committed to liberalise various services sectors beyond its WTO commitments. The sectors in which Singapore gets preferential access, include business services, construction and related engineering services, financial services, telecommunication services, tourism and travel related services and transport services. [6]

Air Services: India and Singapore have reaffirmed their rights and obligations under previous agreements and recognise the importance of air connectivity, to support the expansion of tourism, trade and investments. Both the countries will review and enhance air services linkages through the bilateral Air Services Agreement, in future.

Movement of Natural Persons: The cross-border movement of natural persons plays a central role in initiating and supporting the trade and investments in goods and services. This chapter enhances the trade and investment flows by facilitating a temporary entry for 4 categories of business persons from India and Singapore. [7]

The Movement of Natural Persons chapter does not apply to measures regarding the citizenship, residence or employment on a permanent basis. It also does not apply to the immigration measures as long as these immigration measures do not nullify or impair the commitments made by either of the two countries. The chapter will grant the Singaporean and Indian Citizens and the Permanent Residents a guaranteed entry and a stay in each other's country as business visitors, short-term service suppliers, professionals and intra-corporate transferees.

Singapore companies will enjoy a sense of certainty, when they choose to deploy Singapore staff, to help manage their Indian operations. Skilled and qualified professionals and service suppliers from Singapore, would also gain easier access to the vast Indian market. Similarly, this would also apply to Indian companies when they deploy Indian staff, to manage their operations in Singapore. With freer movement of business persons between the countries, the bilateral trade and investment flows should be significantly enhanced. Hence, companies from both the countries can leverage on the chapter to drive greater economic integration between India and Singapore.

E-Commerce: Both India and Singapore reaffirm their commitment to promote a liberalised environment for electronic commerce. The chapter on electronic commerce, addresses fair treatment of digital products, such as software, e-books and e-movies, coming from Singapore.

The Agreement also prohibits any imposition of customs duties on digital products delivered electronically. In addition, both the sides commit to an ensuring transparency by making publicly available, all relevant laws and regulations, affecting the electronic commerce.

Intellectual Property: The Chapter on Intellectual Property (IP) Cooperation is focused on collaboration and cooperation between the Parties.

The Parties agreed to undertake and promote the mutually beneficial cooperation in the fields of IP and Plant Variety Rights. These forms of cooperation could include the joint organisation of training programs, and collaboration on projects, to promote an effective use and application of IP. The Parties have specifically identified their leading training centres: the IP Academy, Singapore, and the Intellectual Property Training Institute (Nagpur), as initial partners for cooperation.

The provisions on cooperation and collaboration in IP and training arrived at, under the Chapter, paves the way forward for collaboration between the Parties in the development of key IP programmes and IP infrastructure. Singapore and India benefit mutually, in terms of potential exchange on IP and IP-related training and education programmes. In addition, the mutual recognition of the importance of plant variety rights means, that both Singapore and India will be able to consider cooperation activities in this field.

Science & Technology: The Science and Technology cooperation chapter will allow of the fostering of closer collaboration in research and development and commercialisation of technologies between the scientific and research communities from the two countries based on an amplification of an earlier agreement on science and technology, signed in 1995.

The agreement is geared towards harnessing the complementary capabilities available in the two countries. The areas of focus that have been identified for possible cooperation are marine and agricultural biotechnology, space research, advance materials and information technology.

Education: The education cooperation chapter aima at combining the strengths of the education system in India and Singapore, to the mutual benefit of the two countries.

One of its key mandates is, to facilitate joint post-graduate programs between the world-renowned Indian Institutes of Technology (IIT) and the Institute of Science (IISc) with the Singapore universities. These programs will focus on research and education with clear industrial linkages to companies from both the countries. Arising from this, NUS and IIT Bombay have recently signed an MOU, to establish a joint graduate engineering programme. The NUS-IIT-B tie-up is the first significant alliance by any IIT with a foreign university. The programme will draw heavily on the existing NUS and the IIT-B infrastructure and course modules. Both the IIT-B and NUS professors, will participate in joint teaching and the supervision of projects. The partnership is expected to yield some 40 MS and eight PhD graduates, annually.

The chapter also provides that degrees specified by the University Grants Commission of India or an Institution of National Importance of India, and by the universities in Singapore, shall be recognised for the purposes of admission into the universities of both the countries. This is, in addition to all other admission criteria that must still be satisfied.

A Joint Committee on Education will be established to emphasise the key role that education will play in fostering the relationship between the two countries. Its members will be drawn not only from government but also from the private sector.

Media: The media cooperation chapter offers a platform for the regulatory agencies from both the sides to work closely together. This will allow a focus not only on regulatory issues of mutual concern, but also on promoting greater industry and private sector collaboration especially some of the areas of collaboration that could be looked into, are digital media and convergent services, intellectual property rights, education and training, co production of film and television content, distribution and marketing, and research and development.

Dispute Settlement: In any international agreement, whilst we do not anticipate any disputes between the Parties as to what the agreement means, it would nevertheless be prudent to prepare for such an eventuality. In this connection, Singapore and India have negotiated a comprehensive set of dispute settlement procedures. Disputes are subject to consultations, negotiations, conciliation and arbitration as in the WTO, and thus, the rule of law in international trade gets enhanced.

Review: The Ministers of India and Singapore, who are responsible for trade negotiations, will meet within a year of the date of entry, into the force of CECA, for a review. Subsequent reviews will be done biennially, or otherwise, as appropriate.

Conclusions

The intermeshing of Indian and Singaporean areas of concern in trade, augurs well for both the countries. Singapore is looking out for viable and lucrative destinations besides China and the US, and India is well placed both economically and diplomatically to forge an effective and mutually beneficial partnership.

Thus the increasing diplomatic complementarities and synergies of the two countries in trade and investment, will act as a stabilizing force, in the Asia-Pacific region.

Notes

1. The highlights of the framework agreement lays down, that negotiations on FTA in goods would begin in 2004, and be concluded by 2005. Talks on FTA in services as well as investments, would start in 2005 and be concluded by 2007. Areas of economic co-operation would include trade facilitation measures, sectors of co-operation and trade and

investment promotion measures. The framework agreement provides for exchange of tariff concessions on the "early harvest programme" (EHP).

2. Major items of India's Exports: The major items of India's exports to Singapore in 2005, were Crude petroleum, Refined Motor spirit, Petroleum oils, Polished diamonds for jewellery, Polished industrial diamonds, articles of Jewellery, Aluminum Unwrought, Aluminium sheets, Parts & accessories of computers, Synthetic fabrics, Silk fabrics, Embroidery/Table linen of Man Made Fibres, Combed cotton, Knitted T-shirts, Vests, Benzene, Dyes, Acids, Insecticides, Fungicides, Household articles of stainless steel, Corrugated products of iron and steel, Forged/stamped articles of iron and steel, Bars and Rods of iron steel, Parts of Boring or Sinking machinery, X-ray tubes, Medical Surgical Dental or Veterinary instruments/ appliances, Penicillin, Rice, Sugar, Cashew nuts, Essential oil, Crabs live/dried, Fish (fresh/chilled/dried), Titanium ore, Menthol, Diesel/semi-diesel generating sets, Static converters, Valves/Taps Cocks for Pipes, Boilers, tanks etc, Bus/lorry tyres, Tobacco. These items in value terms constitute over 70 per cent of India's exports to Singapore.

Major items of India's Imports: The major items of India's imports from Singapore in 2005, were parts and accessories of Computers and Computer peripherals, Integrated Circuits, Cellular phones, CD ROMs, Styrene, P-Xylene, O-Xylene, Polypropylene, Vinyl Acetate, Topped Crudes, and Parts of boring and sinking machinery. Nickel, Tin (unwrought), lead (unwrought) Aluminium (unwrought) Zinc (unwrought), Waste & scrap of Iron and steel, Photographic chemicals, Sewing Machines, Ball/Roller bearings, Parts for bulldozers, Parts of Aero planes/Helicopters, Parts for Audio/Video recorders, Medical instruments and appliances, parts of cellular phones, parts of motor vehicles, Cigarettes, pigments, Parts of Cathode Ray Tubes, Auto parts, parts for electrical Machines & apparatus. These items in value terms constitute over 60 per cent of India's imports from Singapore.

3. A (Comprehensive Economic Cooperation Agreement) combines liberalized commercial transactions in goods and services, with two-way investment flows in untapped areas. It is a very big psychological step for India, signifying a new direction in India's economic diplomacy. It is India's first overarching economic pact with any country. Integral to the CECA is a wide array of established practices and proposed initiatives, ranging from dispute settlement arrangements and a review mechanism to an updated avoidance of double-taxation and other measures. India through the CECA, has moved from the old policy of substantial self

sufficiency to one where it wants to link up and open up markets in a controlled sort of way, and encourage linkages and exchanges. The CECA lays the groundwork for agreements with many other countries.

4. Key features are highlighted as follows:

- **Beneficiaries:** Citizens and Enterprises based in Singapore or India. Indian investors are not required to seek foreign investment approval for coverage under the investment chapter.
- **Broad Range of Investment Instruments:** The chapter covers a broad range of investment instruments and assets, such as equity and debt instruments, Intellectual Property Rights (IPR) and, business licenses and permits. Investments in the nature of both Foreign Direct Investment (FDI) and portfolio investments, are covered.
- **National Treatment:** The chapter accords National Treatment to investors from both the countries. The market access feature of this provision is subject to the commitments and reservations, undertaken.
- **Expropriation and Compensation:** Both countries cannot expropriate investments, directly or indirectly, without proper legal safeguards. Expropriation must be premised on public purpose and compensation based on market value. Land expropriation will be governed by the domestic legislation of each country.
- **Investor to State dispute settlement:** To give investors greater confidence in investing in either country, both countries have committed to allowing investors, once the investment is established, to take a dispute relating to an obligation under the chapter to an international arbitration tribunal.
- **Free Transfers:** Both countries will allow the investors to freely transfer funds relating to their investments, such as capital, profits, dividends and royalties.
- **Joint-Ventures:** India has agreed to bind its recent liberalization measures regulating the ability of the current joint-ventures to enter into new joint-ventures (India's Press Note 1 of 2005).
- **Real Estate:** India has agreed to bind its new regulations governing investments in the real estate sector (India's Press Note 2 of 2005).
- **Others:** The Indian government has formally recognised Temasek and GIC as distinct entities. They are allowed to each own up to 10 per cent of a listed Indian company, similar to other Foreign Institutional Investors (FII), as stipulated under current Securities and Exchange Board of India (SEBI) regulations.

5. The following of the key features highlighted:

- **Market Access:** Both countries may not restrict access into their services market by imposing quantitative restrictions (e.g. numerical quotas on services suppliers that are allowed in the market).
- **National Treatment:** Services suppliers will be granted the same treatment like local service suppliers, leaving no room for discrimination.
- **Domestic Regulation:** The chapter ensures the reasonableness, impartiality and objective nature of the domestic regulations governing the provision of services.
- **Mutual Recognition Agreements (MRAs):** The chapter facilitates the movement of people. Professional bodies in the accounting and auditing, architecture, medical (doctors), dental and nursing services sectors in both countries will negotiate agreements, within a year of the signing of CECA, recognising each other's education and professional qualifications. This means that, upon the completion of these mutual recognition agreements, Indian and Singaporean professionals from these five professions would be able to practice in Singapore and India respectively. Professional bodies for services sectors not listed above, would also be encouraged to enter into negotiations, for MRAs.
- The services commitments made by each country, can be found in the Annexes to the Services Chapter. There are additional disciplines pertaining to Telecommunication Services and Financial Services in their respective Annexes to the Services Chapter.

6. India would be able to enjoy preferential treatment for sectors such as business services, distribution services, education services, environmental services and transportation services.

- For Financial Services, Singapore owned or controlled financial institutions have been given greater privileges to access the Indian market. In banking, DBS, UOB and OCBC can each set up a wholly owned subsidiary (WOS) in India, to enjoy treatment on par with Indian banks in branching the places of operations and prudential requirements. Alternatively, if they choose to set up as branches, they have been allocated a separate quota of 15 branches (for all 3 banks) over 4 years, over and above the quota for all foreign banks.
- For asset management, Singapore owned or controlled fund managers have the additional privilege of offering the Indian investors mutual funds and collective investment schemes (CIS) listed on the Singapore Exchange (SGX) as well as exchange traded

funds (ETF). These instruments offered by our asset managers, are free from the restriction that they must only invest in entities which have a stake in Indian companies. India has similarly lifted this limitation for India owned or controlled fund managers. Both Singapore and India owned or controlled fund managers can also invest an additional US$250m in equities and instruments listed on the SGX, including mutual funds, CIS and ETFs. This is, in addition to the US$1 billion cap that all asset managers can invest abroad.

- Indian banks and financial institutions can take advantage of CECA to expand their activities in Singapore. To this end, Indian banks that satisfy Singapore's admission criteria will be given Wholesale Bank licences and up to 3 bank licences with Qualifying Full Banks privileges. In addition, India insurers and capital market intermediaries that satisfy our admission criteria will have an open access to set up in Singapore.
- For Telecommunication Services, India will bind its foreign equity limit from 25 per cent to 49 per cent for most services including basic, cellular and long-distance services and 74 per cent for internet and infrastructure services. India will also ensure that the telecommunication providers from Singapore, are treated fairly, transparently, and allowed to obtain an access to the necessary public infrastructure in order to offer their services, thereby creating a fairly level playing field in India for our Singapore's telecom providers. On its part, Singapore has made the binding commitments for telecommunication services such as Basic Telecommunication Services (facilities-based), Mobile Services, and Value-Added Network (VAN) Services.

7. Business Visitors who are holders of five year multiple journey visa, will be permitted to enter and engage in business activities for a period of 2 months, which upon request, may further be extended by 1 month.

- Short-term service suppliers will be granted temporary entry to service their contracts for an initial period of 90 days in the first instance.
- Professionals employed in 127 specific occupations, will be allowed an entry and stay for 1 year or for the duration of contract, whichever is less.
- Intra-corporate transferees (i.e. managers, executives and specialists within organisations), will be permitted to stay and work in India and Singapore for an initial period of 2 years or the period of the

contract, whichever is less. The period of stay may be extended for a period of 3 years at a time for a total term, not exceeding 8 years.

Select Bibliography

1. *India-Singapore CECA-Information Kit*, Ministry of Trade and Industry, Government of Singapore, 2005.
2. *US Country Commercial Guides*, (Singapore, 2004).
3. *Singapore Economic Development Board-Reports*, 2003-2005.
4. *Country Studies-Singapore, 2005*, (Microsoft Internet Explorer).
5. Rajesh Mehta, *Economic Cooperation between India and Singapore: A Feasibility Study*, RIS-DP # 41/2003.
6. Margaret Liang, "Singapore's Trade Policies-Priorities and Options," *ASEAN Economic Bulletin*, Vol.22, No.1 (2005).
7. *Trade Policy Review*, (Singapore, WTO, Geneva, 2004).
8. Goh Chok Tong, "Anchored in Singapore, Connected to the World", Speech at the International Enterprise Forum, Singapore, February 2005.
9. *Foreign Equity Investments in Singapore*, (Department of Statistics, Singapore 2001-2002).
10. *Yearbook of Statistics*, (Department of Statistics, Singapore 2004).
11. S. Gaur, "ASEAN-India Ties Entering a New Phase," *Business Times*, (Singapore, 2004).
12. Nagesh Kumar, *Towards an Asian Economic Community: The Relevance of India*, RIS-DP #34/2002
13. A. Sarma, and P.K Mehta, *Exploring Indo-ASEAN Economic Partnership in a Globalising World*, (Bookwell, New Delhi, 2002).
14. Rahul Sen, M.G Asher, and R.S Rajan, "ASEAN-India Economic Relations-Current Status and Future Prospects," *Economic and Political Weekly*, 2004.
15. Lee Hsien Loong, Speech delivered at the CII, FICCI, ASSOCHEM, Joint Forum, New Delhi, 2005.
16. Bharat Jhunjhunwala, "Singapore FTA: Against Asian Unity?" *Business Line*, (New Delhi, 2005).
17. Frederic Gare and Mattoo, A., *India and ASEAN: The Politics of India's Look East Policy*, (Manohar Publishers, New Delhi, 2001).
18. P.K. Jha, "Reassessing India's Look East Policy," *World Focus*, Vol. 287-288, 2003.
19. T. Saywell, "Singapore's New India Play," *Far Eastern Economic Review*, (Hong Kong, 2001).

5

India's Diplomacy of Regional Trading Groups: A Case of India-ASEAN Free Trade Area and Sub-Regional Agreements

D. Gopal and Sailaja Gullapalli

During the first quarter of 2005-2006, India has been hailed as the second fastest growing economies of the world, with a gross domestic product of US $ 3.36 million and the fourth largest in terms of purchasing power parity. Of late, India has been engaged in sustained efforts and renewed concerns about forging stronger relations with the region and its neighbourhood and these efforts are based on the consciousness to proceed beyond the confines of the traditional approach. In this context, India's engagement with the Association of Southeast Asian Nations (ASEAN), particularly, has reached new heights. Taken in a historical perspective, India's association with the region is not anything new. The transformed approach towards this region needs to be recognised by taking into consideration India's growing economic prowess. ASEAN provides an enormous economic opportunity to India and the decision makers are quick to understand these untapped potentials. The economic diplomacy of India thus assumes an important role in the wider context of the global trend towards regionalism. With varied opinions on whether economic regionalism is a viable alternative or not, especially in the context of the globalisation of the world economy, India's efforts towards global and regional economic integration, have been highlighted in this paper.

Defining Globalisation

Globalisation, for the last two decades, has been gaining prominence at the backdrop of a changing economic scenario at the regional as well as international level. Globalisation is a process of interaction and integration among the people, companies, and governments of different nations, a process driven by international trade and investment and aided by information technology. This process has effects on the environment, on culture, on political systems, on economic development and prosperity, and on human physical well-being in societies around the world. Ruud Lubbers, a Dutch academician, defines it as a process in which geographic distance becomes a factor of diminishing importance in the establishment and maintenance of cross border economic, political and socio-cultural relations. David Held and Anthony McGrew, in their entry for Oxford Companion to Politics, define it as a process (or set of processes) which embodies a transformation in the spatial organization of social relations and transactions, expressed in transcontinental or interregional flows and networks of activity, interaction and power. [1] According to the wikipedia, in specifically economic contexts, the term refers almost exclusively to "the effects of trade, particularly trade liberalization or "free trade". More broadly, the term refers to the overall integration, and resulting increase in interdependence, among global actors (be they political, economic, or otherwise)".

The concept of globalisation has come to occupy a core position in the foreign policies of different nation states. People are no more confined to their communities or local areas. With rapid developments in communication, information technology and economic activity, the movement has now spanned distant miles. This has increasingly brought about an enhancement in economic transactions. While some of the nations associated themselves with their affluent neighbours and improved the state of their economies, many of their counterparts failed to initiate liberal economic policies, owing to apprehensions. Therefore, an uneven relative growth performance by individual countries and changing patterns of trade, investment and production has tilted the balance towards the formation of regional trading groups to withstand the shifts of balance of economic power.

The role of trans-national corporations (TNCs) has increased, mergers of companies across borders have multiplied and private finance have assured greater role in the world trade. The strength of this kind of economy depends greatly on how the various economies within the groups interact with the economies of other regional groups and subsequently with the global economy. In the context of a regional approach, the countries become really competent competitors in the global market. The developing countries, in particular, perceive the global financial integration as an indispensable factor for securing financial stability. The cross-border linkages have become the order of the day. For India, globalisation has brought about mixed results. India has been trying to cope with the changed economic circumstances in consonance with its regional engagements.

Why are Regional Trade Groups Important?

With the expansion of markets and the removal of trade barriers, the regional trading groups are no longer confined to a specific region than have extended across the globe. The growth of regional economic zones is characterised by new technologies in knowledge intensive areas like computers and electronics. The countries that invest in these areas have a higher advantage than others. Technology transfers, joint ventures, co-production, cross-licensing etc. call for a wider area of co-operation and the regional trade agreements have greatly facilitated these moves.

Regionalism is defined as an attempt by a group of states to order their relations amongst each other. Their purpose is to advance "commonly agreed aims, to avoid local conflict and to manage it, if it does break out, as much as possible, on a regional basis." [2] It is also viewed as the formation of interstate associations or groupings where 'a limited number of states are linked by a geographical relationship and by a degree of mutual dependence'. [3] It is aptly pointed out that the 'regional economic integration can be compared along various dimensions of the scope (the range of issues included), depth (the extent of policy harmonization), institutionalization (the extent of formal institutional building) and centralization (the degree to which effective authority is centralized)'. [4]

As the cold war ended, there arose much complex issues leading to new conflicts, tensions, local wars, decline of living standards, environmental degradation and so on. In order to achieve a more balanced development, the nation states converged their common interests to create compact regional groups to achieve common goals. This helped them manage their relations in a much more cordial manner which would have been otherwise difficult at a global level. They have thus become the dominant players in a "fragmented and unstable world characterised by free trade within each of the blocs and managed trade with them and other countries". [5]

The theoretical interpretations also significantly view this mode of cooperation from various dimensions. The neo-realists are of the view that the factors that dominate the formation of regional groups are politico-economic oriented rather than the welfare dominant schemes. According to them, "economic regionalism is a strategy in the game of neo-mercantilist competition". [6] In contrast, the theory of neo-liberal institutionalism stresses the increasing level of interdependence among the states as the prime reason for the nation states to enter into regional trade. It is the state that serves as an effective link between the domestic and international concerns. It requires the state to balance the collective management and facilitation of intra-regional linkages. [7] The *Convergence* theory studies the dynamics of regional co-operation in terms of 'converging domestic policy preferences among regional states'. The urge for integration results in 'focused national policies' rather than a 'broad international vision'. This focused approach envisages a strengthened role of the state, and enables it formulate economic policies that emphasise the liberalisation and deregulation resulting in deeper regional integration. [8] Thus, the regional trade agreements are seen as providing underpinnings to strategic alliances and implicitly forming security arrangement; for smaller countries, it is a way of obtaining more security through their access to large country markets.

With this at the backdrop, the growth of regional trading groups, henceforth, has become a regular feature in almost all the regions of the world. Towards the end of 2001, 239 regional agreements have been notified to the World Trade Organisation (WTO). Though the groups discriminate against non-members, their objective is to stimulate trade among the members and realise the benefits of trade liberalisation and investment and regulatory reforms. An overwhelming majority of the nations has been part of one regional trade group or other.

India's Role in Regional Trade

While different nations have been pursuing free trade agreements and reaping benefits, India's performance in these pursuits has been rather dismal. India is not part of any credible or meaningful trade bloc. While the Asia Pacific economic Co-operation (APEC) has not yet considered India's entry into the bloc, the South Asian Preferential trade Agreement (SAPTA) got engulfed in the Indo-Pak political tensions; efforts are now underway to enhance greater economic integration through South Asia Free Trade Agreement (SAFTA). India is leaving no stone unturned to become a part of the East Asian Economic grouping that would provide much more leverage which it desperately needs. It is projecting itself as one of the strategic partners in the scheme of a greater Asian Economic Community.

However, what ails the Indian foreign economic policy is the enthusiastic rhetoric it displays leaving much of the implementation component as a query. Though India had a late start on economic reforms, the acceleration of transition towards the market oriented and export led growth strategy has been significant. The opening up of the economy provided an immense scope to redefine India's relations with its neighbours. The inflow of the foreign investment, significant reduction of import tariffs, removal of quantitative restrictions, reforms and modernisation of financial sector, adjustments in government monetary fiscal policies, helped in stabilising the economy and made India have a comparative advantage over others in the region. A brief look into the profile of India's role in regional trade will help understand its economic activities vis-à-vis the region.

India and South Asia Free Trade Agreement (SAFTA)

South Asia, as is already recognized, is in fact, one of the regions plagued by poverty and lack of human development. It is home to a biggest number of populations that lives on less than a dollar as income per day and with an illiteracy rate of 45 per cent. The intra regional trade, accounts for less than 5 per cent, as compared to the 63 per cent of the intra ASEAN trade. Much of this can be marred if concrete steps are taken towards mitigating this state of affairs. The regional trade holds much promise in terms of the costs involved in transportation as well as geographical proximity that make it least expensive. Unfortunately, the India-Pakistan tussle over the Kashmir region has rendered the functioning of this trade group ineffective for a considerable length of time and made the possibility of cooperation painfully sluggish. This is in spite of the fact that the gains involved include, cultural similarities that make the interactive process all the more an easier one. For no region in the world presents a much better cultural amalgamation than South Asia. India's ties with Sri Lanka span several centuries and have resulted in meaningful trade with the conclusion of a bilateral free trade agreement in 1998. As of today, the bilateral trade stands at $ 1717 million and is expected to grow by 15-20% in 2006. Being the biggest cruiser in the region, it could have carried the region ahead in trade through consistent and co-ordinated efforts.

Almost two decades after the formation of the SAARC, the South Asia Free Trade Agreement (SAFTA), an updated version of South Asia Preferential Trade Agreement (SAPTA), came into force on 1st January, 2006. The concessional duty on sub-continent trade characterises this transformation and all the countries of the region, after prolonged deliberations, have agreed upon a framework that would require them to bring down the duties to 20% in the first phase of the two year period beginning with the year 2006. By the final phase, the duty would be brought down to zero through various annual cuts. While India, Pakistan and Sri Lanka agreed to bring down their customs duties to 0-5 per cent by 2013, the least developed nations such as Bangladesh, Maldives, Bhutan and Nepal will do so by the year 2018. [9] From the positive side, India's aggregate trade with the SAARC countries rose from $4,816.88 million in 2003-04 to $5,205.57 million in 2004-05, an increase of 8.07 per cent, with India's overall trade (export and import) coming to double-digit, making nearly 20 per cent. India's negotiation on the rules of origin and the sensitive list of items include the goods and products from agricultural sector, textile sector, chemicals and leathers and items from small scale industries. [10] India and Pakistan have also decided to steer clear of certain litigious issues before formalising the trade agreement. India needs to convince its neighbourhood on the subject of their apprehensions about its adopting a bullying attitude and also to assure them that the bloc will not be dominated by the Indian business circles.

SAFTA can follow the example of The Greater Mekong sub-region grouping in this regard. By bridging their long pending differences, this group facilitated the integration in customs, and other issues thereby enabling a freer movement of goods and people in the region. Their conflicts were more or less similar to those of South Asia's which, having aligned themselves with the opposite camps during cold war, were unable to establish trust for a long time. Later on they managed to overcome this Cold War Divide and if their sustained efforts have borne fruit today, it is due to regional cooperation. The South Asian leaders can take a clue from this extra ordinary illustration and set their egos aside to fulfil their pledges and commitments and translate their rhetoric into concrete action. [11] The foremost need of the hour is to step up confidence measures that would boost the economic dexterity of the region and a great deal of this depends on how India conducts its foreign economic policy with its neighbours.

India, criticised for giving too little to its trading partners in the region before, has been running a sizeable trade surplus on a low volume of trade with its neighbours. In 2004-05, its trade surplus was 65 per cent of a total trade of $5.2 billion with SAARC countries; in the two preceding years this figure was even higher at 72 per cent and 68 per cent, respectively. Though Bangladesh, and more recently, Sri Lanka have stepped up exports to India, Indian exports continue to drive intra-SAARC trade growth.

Source: *Economic and Political Weekly* Editorial, 7 January, 2006. http://www.epw.org.in/

India and Association of Southeast Asian Nations (ASEAN)

India's reorientation of its economic relations with its Asian neighbourhood, is a step towards accelerating the pace of its role in regional trade. India is yet to make the impact of its presence felt in the region, and also needs to adopt a persuasive approach to establish itself as a credible trading partner.

At the outset, one should not forget that there was a negligible linkage or co operation between the Asian countries. After years of disregard and doubts, the relations are being re-energised through the consolidation of the Asian solidarity via trade agreements. By virtue of its close historical and cultural linkage with the ASEAN region, it was widely perceived that India could play a significant role in mending the odds and in extending regional cooperation. While India realised the significance of the ASEAN members for attracting the FDI, the South East Asian nations were also proficient in utilising the opportunities offered by India. Consequently India became a sectoral dialogue partner in 1992, full dialogue partner in 1995 and a member of the ASEAN Regional Forums (ARF) in 1996. The process clearly reflected the interest exhibited by both the sides to tap mutual capabilities and resources, keeping in mind the possibilities and vulnerabilities.

The economic engagement between India and ASEAN has established a firm basis for wide-ranging programmes of co-operation. According to Raja Mohan, partnership with India has been conceived as an ongoing effort to create interdependence and linkage with a country with a large and liberalizing market as well as a democratic and pluralistic polity which could respond positively to ASEAN's aspirations. [12] India's proposal to initiate a free trade area with ASEAN (AFTA) reflects its desire towards deeper regional economic linkages by initiating bilateral and sub-regional dialogues. The strategic and economic imperatives have resulted in India's adoption of the Look East Policy. Through ASEAN and sub-regional arrangements like Bangladesh, India, Myanmar, Sri Lanka, Thailand Economic Co-operation (BIMSTEC), and India-Singapore Free Trade Area, India tends to forge closer economic relations with the region so as to make amends for the lost time and missed opportunities. During his visit to Laos, Prime Minister Manmohan Singh has called for an inclusive approach for a historic partnership agreement with South East Asia in the political, economic, science and technology, health, culture and other key areas. He has also reiterated India's commitment during the inaugural East Asian Summit and called for closer links through collaboration in education sector.

The India-ASEAN partnership is based on the politico-security, socio-cultural and economic co-operation. A free trade agreement in goods, services, trade and investment as envisaged in the Framework Agreement on Comprehensive Economic Co-operation in 2003, holds much promise, by forging significant ties between the countries of the region. India's trade target with ASEAN is aimed at $ 13 billion as of now and $ 15 billion for 2005 and $ 30 billion for 2007. According to the sources in Ministry of External Affairs, the target of US $ 30billion was reiterated by the Prime Minister at the 3rd ASEAN-India Summit held in Vientiane on 30th November, 2004. Moreover there is a likelihood of India's economic interaction with China, Japan and Korea which eventually would make it possible to forge an Asian Economic Community on the lines of European Union.

India's exports to ASEAN member countries consist of oil meals, gems and jewellery, meat and meat preparations, cotton yarn, fabrics, machinery, rice, drugs and pharmaceuticals, chemicals, etc. The imports mainly consist of artificial resins, plastic material, natural rubber, wood and wood products, electronic goods, organic chemicals, edible oils, fertilisers, etc. ASEAN countries, particularly, Malaysia, Singapore and Thailand, are also increasingly investing in India in sectors such as telecommunications, fuels, hotel and tourism services, heavy industry, chemicals, fertilizers, textiles, paper and pulp, and food processing. Singapore and Malaysia have been India's active trading partners so far with more than 70% share in trade. Nevertheless, it should be noted that India, in comparison to China, has not been able to reach anywhere near trade surplus with the region. Its trade percentage is still a minuscule one and needs to put in consistent labour to improve upon the existing scenario. For example, India's share with ASEAN totalled around 1%, China's share in the ASEAN-aggregates witnessed a steep rise in the 1990s. ASEAN's imports from China in 2001 were close to $21 billion (about 6% share) an unparalleled increase over the 1991-level of $6 billion (3% share). [13]

Sub-regional Arrangements with Southeast Asian Nations

India's role in sub-regional arrangements is important in the wider context of the whole gamut of regional trade with Southeast Asia. India entered into two important agreements in this connection: one is BIMSTEC and the other, India-Singapore Free Trade area. India considers this as a calculated move that would facilitate its cooperation at a much larger level with the region. The coming together of Bangladesh, India, Myanmar, Sri Lanka and Thailand into an economic agreement, popularly known a **BIMSTEC**, is one such example. The members set an ambitious target of forging cooperation in the areas of information technology, telecommunications, tourism, power and transport sectors that are very much essential to maintain their standard of living, to generate employment and to enhance respective GDP growth in the countries. As one of the key officials in the Ministry of External Affairs, India, pointed out, "the agenda included trade facilitation through harmonisation of customs procedures and practices, exchange of information on standards, strengthening of banking arrangements to facilitate trade and investment and tourism, promotion of transport and communication facilities and mobility of business people through facilitating "issue of visas to BIMSTEC businessmen undertaking commercial visits to member countries". [14] Similar sentiments were expressed by one of the business houses officials that BIMSTEC is a follow-up of the Look East Policy, has implications on geo-economic settings and acts as a medium of opening up their economies for trade enhancement.

The members also discussed the following areas of cooperation: energy, human resources development, agriculture, fisheries, public health, education, rural community development, small and medium scale enterprises, construction, environment, biotechnology, weather and climate research and technology, natural disaster mitigation and management, hydropower and hydrocarbon projects and natural gas grids, promoting traditional systems of medicine and facilitating an access to affordable drugs. The Joint Working Group on Counter Terrorism and International Crimes (JWG-CTTC) also agreed on member countries looking after the concerns of intelligence sharing, law and legal enforcement issues, funds to combat terrorism, prevention of illicit trafficking in narcotic drugs, psychotropic substances and precursor chemicals. [15]

The India-Singapore Comprehensive Economic Cooperation Agreement (CECA) that was signed in mid 2005 set the target of enhancing the two-way trade by $ 10 billion by the end of 2005-06 and to $ 50 billion by 2010. According to the ASSOCHAM estimates, Singapore's cumulative investment in India, which is around $3 billion as of now, would go up to $5 billion by 2010 and to $10 billion by 2015. Singapore's leverage in the areas of finance, manufacturing and marketing, IT and advanced electronic industry, is to be tapped by the Indian business. India is one of the important destinations for Singapore's exports, the total exports amounting to 2.5 billion dollars in 1999 as compared to 1.1 billion dollars in 1990. The import scenario is rather discouraging, with Singapore's imports from India amounting to one third of its exports. India's exports to Singapore are on an increase since 1995, whereas the imports account for less than 1 per cent. Around 44 per cent of Singapore's exports to India are in the sectors of machinery and transport equipment, mineral fuels, manufactured materials and chemicals. Singapore's trade surplus has been more than S $ 3000 million since 1998. A major share of Singapore's FDI is directed towards financial and insurance sectors, manufacturing and commerce. [16]

Significantly, India has more than 300 IT companies in Singapore, and the trend is towards an increase with around 150 companies setting up their operations every year. India was Singapore's 14th largest trading partner in 2004 and the bilateral trade has nearly tripled within the past decade, from S$4 billion in 1995 to S$11.8 billion in 2004. Over the last year, Singapore's bilateral trade with India increased by almost half, from S$7.8 billion in 2003, making India the fastest growing trading partner among the major economies. Indian statistics also show that in 2004-5, India's exports to Singapore grew faster than exports to India from any of the other trading partners (Table 5.1). [17]

Table 5.1: India - Singapore Trade

Year	Singapore's Exports to India		of which Re-exports		Singapore's Imports from India		Total Trade	
	(S$ bln)	(US$ bln)	(S$ bln)	(US$ bln)	(S$ bln)	(US$ bln)	(S$ bln)	(US$ bln)
1999	4.24	2.50	2.28	1.35	1.25	0.74	5.49	3.23
2000	4.80	2.74	2.71	1.54	1.86	1.06	6.66	3.81
2001	4.87	2.76	2.87	1.63	2.00	1.13	6.87	3.90
2002	4.71	2.67	2.79	1.58	2.08	1.18	6.79	3.85
2003	5.38	3.16	2.89	1.70	2.51	1.48	7.89	4.64

India-Thailand FTA

India and Thailand signed a Free Trade Agreement on October 09, 2003 for enhancing cooperation in agriculture, tourism and science. They also signed a Memorandum of Understanding (MoU) on agricultural cooperation, tourism cooperation, agreement on visa exemption for diplomatic and official passport holders and programme of cooperation in biotechnology. The areas of cooperation are agricultural and forestry research, biotechnology soil and water conservation, watershed management, land use planning and horticulture. The fifth agreement upon biotechnology envisages the establishment of an India-Thailand biotechnology panel for formulation, approval, monitoring and review of action plans.

The sub-regional agreements which India forged at the bilateral level with the nations of Southeast Asia, highlight the urgency of the mutual economic collaboration. An Emulation of these models for a wider network of cooperation would pave the way for an economic accord between India and ASEAN. India needs to further accelerate its efforts without which there will be long-term repercussions. Firstly, any degree of complacency will result in its isolation. Secondly, in spite of enormous potentials, it is likely to lose out on major benefits considering China's efforts to penetrate into the regional markets. China's ascendant role in the region has put India at considerable unease as the former is perceived as the principal source of insecurity and threat to its vital interests. By seeking renewed and strengthened ties with ASEAN, India hopes to balance the asymmetric equation of power in the region. The need of the hour is to redefine its collaboration modalities and overcome its past constraints and barriers to play a meaningful and fruitful role in the future course of action. Any failure in these efforts will be nothing short of its marginalisation in the post-cold war world economy.

So far, so good with this framework. But the modalities of implementation, particularly from India, needs to be examined considering the occasional lapses that sneak into such ambitious agreements. What are the sectors that need assistance in terms of foreign direct investment? What are the areas that need to be looked at from a humanitarian point of view rather than purely economic dimension? What are the cost effective ways of achieving these targets? What has India to proffer to its counterparts? What does it need to do, to extend its promises?

Look East via Northeast

As on today, India has a greater opportunity to enhance trade with its Southeast Asian counterparts via the North eastern region. This will help not only in making the trade transactions cost-effective but also in taking major developmental strides in the North eastern region. For long, these regions have been complaining of their not being included in the mainstream of India; this has resulted in a feeling of isolation and to a great extent, revulsion towards the governmental approach. The option of trade via Northeast is an opportunity not to be missed at any cost. India shares its borders with China, Bangladesh and Myanmar and this is a strategic location which India cannot afford to ignore. If India chooses to go via Northeast, it will develop the latter as a major hub of economic activity, by establishing the manufacturing and distribution locales and modes. For this to come true, the infrastructure facility and connectivity needs to be improved. This includes transport, rail links, improvement of highway connectivity and routes, telecommunication, easy transit route, and also a sea-link between India and Myanmar via Kolkata and Sittwe ports. There should also be wide operation of air links at a discounted amount for the transportation of goods. This would not only enhance the trade, involving fewer expenses, but also bring in a sense of being included into the mainstream, for the North-eastern states. There will be massive gains through generation of employment, infrastructure and effective capacity-building through real estate. Two most viable optional routes to the Southeast region are the Stilwell road that connects the Capital of China's Yunan province to Assam via Myanmar. Also, via Myanmar, India can establish road links between North-eastern region and Thailand through Manipur. All this would result in better market access, education, healthcare, commercial, financial, and business services and support. Tourism would be one of the sectors that will receive colossal gain through this scheme. India needs to dispel its fears through rigorous negotiations and therein lies its certified approach.

Towards a Greater Asian Economic Community

The plurality of economies can be assimilated if only there are willing efforts to achieve an Asian Economic Community. For this, India has to negotiate hard with its South-eastern counterparts along with China, Japan and South Korea. The frictions between China and Japan can be well attended to in a regional forum or with a third country acting as a facilitator. The aims need to be clearly defined and each member has to put forward its issues after weighing the pros and cons involved in forging a larger community. While divergences are common in any negotiation process, they should not cast a haze over the initiatives or ultimate goal. This, precisely, is the reality that should be borne by all the members and formulate policies accordingly. The political, economic and strategic magnitude should be systematically discussed so that the community moves are not clouded by apprehensions. The ASEAN + 4, which is being visualised by the members, should also decide upon the timeframe in which they would like to open up their region as a complete free trade area, and the issue of including more members into the grouping.

Is ASEAN +4 different from East Asian Community? Is there a leeway of merging the two together? What are the parallel tracks that are underway in the whole process? Most importantly, will there be an imminent presence of the United States in the region? Considering the division among the members regarding the inclusion of the US into the bloc, it would involve many more painstaking negotiations than mere imagining to make the superpower a part of the bloc. The known political differences between China and Japan and China and India will undoubtedly dominate the proceedings of the negotiations. But going by the adage, that the economic relations bury the most difficult differences, it is imperative that these countries should make concessions for forging better relations. When the European Union members could succeed in coming together in Europe and members of South East Asian nations in their region, it is definitely possible to repeat the miracle in forging a greater Asian economic community. All it needs is, an unswerving effort from the members towards moving in this direction.

India's Choices for Future

India's renewed initiation into Look East Policy and its attempts towards deeper economic integration with the region, did result in a positive development with the free trade agreement, to come into effect in the near future. India needs to send right signals to its trading partners regarding its sincere attempts to the betterment of its population. It needs to take several crucial measures for this pace to continue. Now that the ASEAN is responding positively, India needs to reiterate its commitments and dismantle the complacency on its part.

- A mere projection of a knowledge based economy is detrimental to India's interests. It should be able to tackle the most menacing issue of 'corruption' which is rampant throughout the governmental set up and elsewhere.
- Development of basic infrastructure and building the managerial competence, should be its priorities. Using IT and Communication as imminent tools, will benefit it enormously.
- In co-ordination with the regional neighbours, India should bridge the lacunae in the technical information and enlarge the horizons of the basic research and development facilities throughout the country.
- Intra-industrial collaboration and design and distribution of its commercially valued products form an excellent option that could facilitate cooperation in the set up of new industries.
- The merging of capital with entrepreneurial skills, can be undertaken to enhance R&D on a mutual basis.

- India should encourage the exchange programmes, by involving businessmen and technical experts to widen the knowledge in the industrial set up.
- India's performance towards human development is rather dismal. It should invite the regional partners to invest in health care sector so as to improve upon its maternal and child mortality rate. The cooperation should not confine itself to finances only; it should involve the roping in of the services of the expertise of its partners.
- Education is another sector where India can score good points by inviting foreign collaborations between educational institutions. It can also improve upon its primary and secondary education in rural areas, by providing better infrastructure to the pupils.
- Training in technical and self employment schemes can be facilitated by emulating the regional examples and learning from its partners the innovative methods of imparting knowledge.
- Tourism is another prospective sector where people to people contacts could become enriched through the discounted tour packages and affordable transport rates.
- Infrastructure development can be taken up on a large scale basis in the North-eastern region of India, to make it accessible to the mainstream. Promotion of tourism includes North-east, which is a vital linkage between India and South-east Asia.
- India should extend economic aid and support to the least developed economies of the region. It should also extend its IT services to make them technically competent and build wider networks through its expertise.

India has already articulated its options clearly; it needs to demonstrate seriousness in implementing these policies and programmes. India should also prove itself as a reliable and competent trading partner and this alone would earn for it a rightful place in the group. Through consensus and compromise,

India can make use of its opportunities and play a dominant role towards a common Asian Economic Community. Every step it takes, needs to be considered as a last chance to strive towards the desired end. Otherwise, it runs the risk of being left out or isolated which, in the long run, would prove detrimental to its economic growth.

Notes

1. http://www.globalisationguide.org/01.html
2. John Chimpman, *The New Regionalism: Avoiding Strategic Hurdles*, (London: MacMillan Press, 1997), p.22.
3. Joseph Nye, *International Regionalism*, (Boston: Little Brown and Company, 1968).
4. Peter H. Smith, The Challenge of Integration: Europe and the America, (New Jersey: New Brunswick, 1992), p.5.
5. Sandro Sideri, "Globalization and Regional Integration", The European Journal of Development Research, vol.9, no.1, June 97, p.49
6. Louise Fawcett and Andrew Hurrell, Regionalism in World Politics, London: Oxford University Press, 1995, p.48
7. Robert O. Keohane, "Institutionalist Theory and the Realist Challenge after the Cold War", in David A. Baldwin (ed.), Neo-realism and Neo-liberalism, New York: Columbia University Press, 1993, p.274. Also see Richard N. Cooper, 'Interdependence and Co-ordination of Policies' in Economic Policy in an Interdependent World: Essays in World Economics (Cambridge, MA: MIT Press, 1986)
8. Andrew Moravcsik, 'Introduction, Integrating International Domestic Theories of International Bargaining' in, Peter B. Evans, Harold K. Jacobson and Robert D. Putnam' (eds) Double Edged-Diplomacy: International Bargaining and Domestic Politics (Berkeley, LA: University of California press, 1993).
9. See http://www.saarc-sec.org/main.php?t=2.1.6. Also refer Grare, Frederic,and Amitabh Mattoo., Beyond the Rhetoric: The Economics of India's Look East Policy, New Delhi: Manohar Publications, 2003.
10. G. Srinivasan, SAFTA should lead by example, The Hindu Business Line, 5 January, 2006, Internet edition.
11. Can the South Asian Region do it too? The Hindu, 23 November, 2005.

12. C. Raja Mohan, Look East Policy: Phase Two, The Hindu,9 October, 2003.Also see Nathan, K.S., India and ASEAN: The Growing Partnership for the 21st Century, Kuala Lumpur: Institute of Diplomacy and Foreign Relations, 2000

13. Department of Commerce: Export Import Data Bank, Ministry of Commerce & Industry, Government of India. http://commin.nic.in/.

14. See http://meaindia.nic.in

15. See Regional Organizations, BIMSTEC, 2005, http://meaindia.nic.in/.

16. Rajesh Mehta, Economic Cooperation between India and Singapore: A Feasibility Study, RIS-DP # 41/2003. www.ris.org.in/dp41_pap.pdf

17. http://app.fta.gov.sg/asp/index.asp.

References

Books

Acharya, Amitav., The Quest for Identity: International Relations of Southeast Asia, Singapore: Oxford university Press, 2000.

Ayoob, Mohammed., India and Southeast Asia: Indian Perceptions and Policies, London: Routledge, 1990.

Broinowski, Alison (ed)., ASEAN into the 1990s, London, Macmillan, 1990.

Dixit, Ramesh., Southeast Asia in Indian Policy: Problems of Relationship with a Neighbouring Region 1966-77, New Delhi: Radha Publications, 1998.

Dosh, Joern and Christian Wagner, ASEAN and SAARC, Hamburg, London, 1999.

Dubey, Muchkund and Nancy Jetly (eds), South Asia and its Eastern Neighbours: Building a Relationship in the 21st Century, New Delhi: Konark, 1999.

Gordon, Sandy., India's Rise to Power: In the Twentieth Century and Beyond, London: Macmillan, 1995.

Leifer, Michael., The ASEAN Regional Forum: Extending ASEAN's Model of Regional Security , Adelphi Paper 302, London: IISS and Oxford University Press, 1996.

Sarma, Atul, and P.K. Mehta., Exploring Indo-ASEAN Economic Partnership in Globalizing World, New Delhi: Bookwell, 2002.

Suryanarayan, V., (ed) South and Southeast Asia in the 1990s: Indian and American Perspectives, New Delhi: Konark, 1992.

Articles

Acharya, Amitav., A Concert of Asia?, Survival, vol.41, no.3, Autumn, 1999.

Adams, John., India's Economic Growth: How fast? How wide? How deep? India Review, vol.1, no.2, April, 2002.

Ayoob, Mohammed., Southeast Asia in Indian Foreign Policy: Some Preliminary Observations, Contemporary South-East Asia, vol.9, no.3, June, 1987.

Baru, Sanjaya., The Problem, Seminar, no. 487, March, 2000.

Baruah, Amit., Looking East, Frontline, vol.17, no.24, Nov 25-Dec 8, 2000.

Braun, Dieter., Asian Power India: A New Equation, Aussen Politik, vol. 41, 2nd Quarter, 1990.

Dutta, Sujit., India and ASEAN: A Framework for Comprehensive Engagement, Strategic Analysis, vol. XX, no.3, June, 1997.

Gaur, Seema., Framework Agreement on Comprehensive Economic Co-operation between India and ASEAN: First step towards Economic Integration, ASEAN Economic Bulletin, vol.20, no.3, December, 2003, p.283.

Jha, Ganganath., ASEAN and India: Dawning of New Partnership, The Indonesian Quarterly, vol.25, no.2, 1997.

Khoo, How San, ASEAN as a Neighbourhood Watch Group, Contemporary Southeast Asia, vol.22, no.2, August, 2000.

Koopmann, Georg., Growing Regionalism- A Challenge to Multilateral Trading System, Intereconmics, vol.38, no.5, Sep/Oct, 2003.

Kumar, Nagesh., Towards an Asian Economic Community: Vision of Closer Economic Co-operation in Asia, An Overview, RIS Discussion Papers no. 32, Research and Information System for the Non-Aligned and other Developing Countries, New Delhi, 2002.

McDonald, Hamish., Joining up: India looks to strengthen ties with Asia, Far Eastern Economic Review, 22nd September, 1994.

Natraj, Geetanjali, and P.Sahoo., India- ASEAN FTA-Small step for a big stride in World trade, The Hindu Business Line, 22 September, 2004.

Ram, A.N., Historical Perspectives, Seminar, no. 487, March, 2000.

Ramesh, M., Regional Trade Agreements: The Right Way to go for India, Businessline, 9 October, 2003.

Ruland, Jurgen., India's New Interests in Southeast Asia, Aussen Politik, vol.46, n0.1, 1995.

Singh, Udai Bhanu., Outlook of the ARF: Relevance for India, Strategic Analysis, vol.23, no.6, September, 1999.

Suryanarayan, V., Looking Ahead: India and Southeast Asia in the 1990s: New Perspectives, New Challenges, in Baladas Ghoshal (ed), India and Southeast Asia, New Delhi: Konark, 1996

__________, Prospects for a Bay of Bengal Community, Seminar, no. 487, March, 2000.

Urata, Shujiro., Globalization and the Growth in Free Trade Agreements, Asia-Pacific Review, vol.9, no.1, 2002.

Vajpayee, A.B., The India-ASEAN Partnership and Beyond, Speech delivered by India's Prime Minister A.B.Vajpayee at ASEAN Business and Investment Summit, Bali, 8 October, 2003.

Websites

http://dgft.delhi.nic.in/

commerce.nic.in/annual2003_04/html/lesson-3.htm

www.wto.org/

http://www.gunung.com/seasiaweb/

http://www.iseas.edu.sg/

http://iias.leidenuniv.nl/wwwvl/southeast.html

http://www.arts.monash.edu.au/mai/cseas/

http://www.lib.duke.edu/ias/SEAsia/

www.saarc-sec.org/

www.aseansec.org/

www.apecsec.org.sg/

6

Southeast Asian Security Dynamics

G V C Naidu

In his State of Union address in early February 2006, when U.S. President George Bush emphatically referred to China and India as the emerging new competitors and that there is need for others to face the challenges these giants will pose [1] he did not mean to suggest the kind of political/ideological rivalry one could see during the cold war, but meant an essentially healthy competition in the domains of economy and technology. By all indications, China is likely to emerge as the largest economy in the next three decades and India, if it manages to maintain the current momentum, will be one of the top three world's largest economies. This is in stark contrast to what many American analysts vociferously argued how unipolar movement can last for a long time (citing Roman Empire as an example) and how it is not necessarily a destabilising phenomenon. Surely, the U.S. continues to be the sole super power and there is no other power that can challenge it's reach its economic might, and military prowess, but there is no mistaking of the fact that there are already signs of American overall superiority being undercut especially with the rise of China and India. That America has recognised this fact in a nutshell, summarises the remarkable changes that are taking at present.

This is symptomatic of tectonic shifts that are beginning to be felt all across the world and these changes are going to dictate the nature of global security and economic order in the coming years. Analysts need not lament anymore, that no new paradigm has emerged after the end of the cold war. It is a new world and in this, the great powers, particularly the Asian, are going to witness increased competition from each other but as the U.S. Secretary of

State rightly pointed in her comment in the *Washington Post,* [2] the new world would be marked not by open armed conflicts, but 'competition in peace.' What it means is, that analysts need to develop new ways and techniques to analyse the effects and consequences of these developments.

This brings us to an important question of the use of appropriate conceptual and analytical tools to examine, understand, and evaluate the emerging Asian security in general and Southeast Asia in particular. Barring Europe, perhaps no other region in the world has felt so strongly the impact of the cold war and its end as the Asia Pacific region and probably no other region has come up with such varied ideas to deal with new circumstances, as this region has done even as it began to confront certain significant developments. Briefly speaking, with the end of the cold war, ended the super power-dominated bipolar regional order. However, a much-anticipated multipolar region as a viable alternative for regional stability, failed to emerge. Consequently, the U.S.-led unipolar movement continued to be the predominant feature of regional security.

Yet, regional great powers, which neither had much say nor role during the entire cold war period, but virtually and unabashedly remained as appendages of one or the other super power in the cold war balance of power, and started steadily asserting themselves. The initial signs of a four-cornered regional multipolarity which had centred around the U.S., China, Japan, and India, are beginning to appear. There are obviously power asymmetries in this, with U.S. continuing to be a global power China rapidly emerging as a strong regional power. Japan, on the other hand, better known for its economic might than military power, is still largely dependent on the U.S. for its security, though it is trying hard to carve out some strategic autonomy, by gradually breaking down some of the self-imposed shackles. India is another rising power that is entrenching itself as a power and player in the regional security matrix. All these three regional powers are yet to exhibit signs of independent actors. China still needs Russia for strategic partnership and for its defence modernisation and cannot stand up to American pressures; India, notwithstanding its pretensions of pursuing an independent foreign policy, is cozying up to Washington, partially due to 'commonly shared concerns' in East Asia; and despite some bold decisions, Japan is still heavily tied to the U.S. for its security needs. In this context, some major trends in dealing with the security issue in East Asia, warrant our attention.

Multilateralism

As part of new ideas, multilateralism came into picture for the first time in the region. When encouraged by the European experience (CSCE/OSCE), attempts were made to replicate multilateralism in East Asia to deal with security issues, the result was the creation of the ASEAN Regional Forum (ARF) in the early 1990s. Though Japan was the original proponent of the idea, Australia and Canada strongly pitched for it. Interestingly, neither ASEAN nor the U.S. nor China was interested in supporting the security multilateralism for a variety of reasons. ASEAN felt that a new regional framework, encompassing the entire Asia Pacific, would certainly undermine its overall political significance, especially at a time when ASEAN was striving hard to find a suitable role after the cold war ended. Because of open conflicts amidst claims and counter-claims in the South China Sea over the Spratly and Paracel Islands during the late 1980s and early 1990s, China did not want to get involved in a multilateral forum where it might be cornered.

On the other hand, the U.S. was totally reluctant to throw its lot behind an entirely new initiative by giving up its time-tested strategy of the forward deployment and bilateral alliances especially when India, on the other hand, hardly figured in any of the deliberations, let alone becoming a factor. There were many other issues as well such as, the usefulness of multilateralism as a viable mechanism in complex region such as the Asia Pacific, questions over the extent of institutionalisation, creation of a mechanism to enforce decisions, leadership, etc., that began to cast doubts on the viability of multilateralism. However, some of these issues were addressed once the ASEAN, mantle fell on, though many questions remained unanswered.

Once the U.S. (soon followed by China), expressed willingness to try out the experiment, ASEAN came out with a Concept Paper in 1995 with an ambitious three-staged blueprint for the ARF- confidence building measures (CBMs), preventive diplomacy, and conflict resolution. [3] While China ensured that none of the contentious issues concerning territorial/border disputes that it is involved became part of the ARF agenda, especially the South China Sea and Taiwan, the U.S. wanted the ARF to 'supplement' but not 'supplant' its existing strategy, based on the alliance system. ASEAN wanted multilateralism under its leadership as the mainstay of addressing regional security problems, rather than worry about many of the above intrinsically complex issues and the challenges they would pose. Ironically, though Japan had been the biggest supporter of multilateralism, almost parallel to the formation of the ARF, it was taking measures to further strengthen its bilateral alliance with the U.S. Thus, there were fundamental contradictions in positions right from the beginning, along with divergent expectations.

Notwithstanding its grandiose plans, the ARF's progress since its inception in 1993, has nothing to write home about. The record of CBMs has been scanty and far from being satisfactory and serious differences have arisen over moving to the next stage of preventive diplomacy. Moreover, certain recent developments have further undermined the ARF, prominently, the weakening of ASEAN consequent on the 1997-98 financial crisis, the rise of new power centres such as China and India, the American reluctance to fully commitment itself to multilateralism, and the renewed efforts at creating a separate forum for Northeast Asia. The ARF was also found to be wanting when crises actually arose. Both in the case of the East Timor and more recently the North Korean nuclear imbroglio, the ARF had absolutely no role to play. If a Northeast Asian security forum (or dialogue) came into being, it will further take winds out of the ARF's sail, for many of those issues with potential to undermine regional security, are located in that region- the Taiwan problem, the North Korean nuclear issues and problems of Korean unification, the future of American troop presence, and the growing row between Japan and China.

As if to underscore their waning interest, most of the foreign ministers of great powers, failed to show up in Vientiane in July 2005, for the annual ASEAN meetings. It was U.S. Secretary of State Condoleezza Rice who first announced her inability, which was soon followed by the Japanese Foreign Minister Nobutaka Machimua, and a little later the Indian minister Natwar Singh, leaving only the Chinese foreign minister to make his presence, which, also turned out to be a half-hearted one as he found it more expedient and useful to meet his friends in Myanmar than attend, what is increasingly perceived to be ineffectual, the ASEAN Regional Forum (ARF) meetings.

Economic Dynamics

In spite of a variety of security problems, the economic bonds are growing very rapidly with each other in the Asia Pacific. This is happening regardless of any institutional mechanism or conscious or concerted efforts but entirely driven by market conditions. Trade, for instance, is growing faster within the region rather than without. The share of intra-East Asian trade out of total trade volume increased to nearly 56 percent, compared to 33 percent a decade or so ago, with China's dramatic emergence as a major trading nation. China has already emerged as the largest trading partner of both Japan, which has crossed US$ 200 by 2004, [4] and South Korea, two of America's closest allies and for more than five decades the largest trading partners. In the case of ASEAN-China too, the bilateral trade has gone up to nearly 100 billion by 2004 from less a few billion in 1990, and India-China trade is expected to exceed more than 18 billion by 2006 from virtually an insignificant position just a few years back. Similar trend is also seen in the case of investments within the region, in particular with regard to Japanese, Korean, Taiwanese and

Singaporean direct investments. They are headed to Asia more than to other regions. This overall trend is like to pick up momentum if India too manages to maintain the current growth rates in trade and economy.

With a view to further strengthen the fast growing economic bonds across the Asia Pacific region, new intra-regional linkages are being forged, and a number of new mechanisms and political initiatives are being taken, both at the sub-regional level and at the larger regional level. ASEAN's agreement to create a free trade area in Southeast Asia is an example. At the regional level, on ASEAN's initiative, a new consultative forum with annual summit meetings as its hallmark, has been created and aimed at regional economic coordination so that the 1997 type of financial crises could be prevented. It initially comprised ASEAN and the three Northeast Asian economic giants- Japan, China and South Korea, called ASEAN Plus Three but was extended to India in 2002 called ASEAN Plus India. This process which is expected to become the basis for an Asian Union idea, aimed at further integration, but faced serious problems to create an East Asian community if the December 2005 inaugural East Asia Summit (EAS) is any indication.

Changing economic relations are also beginning to influence the nature of political relationships too. China is gaining its influence in the region because of its growing economic clout and that may be happening at the cost of Japan (and the U.S.) leading to the inference that Tokyo is getting marginalized in regional political equation. It is true, that both Japan and the U.S. are much too important to be ignored because of the vast investitive capital they possess and their control over advanced technologies. That however, may change in the coming years. China has already made a beginning by investing over a billion US dollars in Southeast Asia and is committing itself to vast resources in the energy and commodity sectors. This trend is likely to intensify in the coming years. Given its size and rapid growth, China most likely will emerge as the regional economic locomotive and correspondingly, its overall political influence will also increase, commensurate with its economic might. It is obvious how acutely conscious ASEAN has become in the recent past to Chinese sensitivities and concerns. It is against the above backdrop of fundamental transformation in the regional geostrategic and economic landscape that the Southeast Asian security is evaluated below.

Southeast Asian Security

It is imperative to keep in view both global and regional geopolitical and geo-economics shifts to locate Southeast Asia, its security, its role, and its importance. Unquestionably, that the strategic focus is moving away from Europe to East Asia even as the region itself undergoes remarkable changes. Within the Asia Pacific, much of the attention is moving largely to Northeast Asia and to a less extent to India in terms of both geopolitics and geo-economics. Southeast Asia continues to be an important region because of its strategic location straddling some of the most important sea lines of communication and the vast natural resources that it is endowed with. However, the region's strategic salience is undoubtedly on the wane for a number of reasons. Despite relative tranquillity and considerable economic progress in the recent past, there are numerous issues that seem to undermine the overall significance of the region.

Comprising mostly small and medium-sized countries and possessing extreme complexity in terms of ethnic diversity, history of wars, insurgencies and instability, long spells of external interventions, vast disparities in economic development, and an absence of a single common attribute by way of religion, language, culture or history, except that they all belong to a broad geographic entity called Southeast Asia coined by the colonial powers, there does not seem to be a tangible glue to bind them together. There were compelling political reasons during the cold war that brought them together, but even together, they faced many constraints. Despite these limitations, the region has witnessed a steady growth of regionalism and multilateralism centring around the Association of Southeast Asian Nations

(ASEAN). [5] ASEAN has been at the centre stage of Southeast Asia's international politics ever since the Cambodian problem began in 1979. In the aftermath of the cold war, ASEAN tried to bolster its standing and weight by incorporating the rest of the countries under its fold though, to what extent it has enhanced ASEAN's weight and strategic importance is a debatable question, still. At a time when ASEAN was beginning to consolidate itself by a variety of means of engagement with the great powers, the financial crisis dealt a severe blow to its aspirations. It has not been the same ever since and Southeast Asia appears to be unlikely to emerge as an autonomous power centre in view of certain recent developments such as the rise of new power centres, terrorism, Northeast Asian security issues becoming more critical, and fundamental changes in regional order and balance.

A major aspect of this region's security historically, has been in terms of the role of and relations with great powers and the nature of inter-great power relations vis-à-vis Southeast Asia, which is undergoing major shifts. Any assessment of Southeast Asian security thus, has to take into account the changing dynamic of the region's relations with great powers and the existence of a vast number of regional traditional non-traditional security concerns. Both the U.S. and Japan, for instance, find it more useful to befriend India to countervail a rising China than take recourse to multilateralism.

Southeast Asia is also beset with both traditional and non-traditional security concerns. Apart from the unsettled issue of Spratly and Paracel Islands in the South China Sea, a vast number of unresolved border/territorial and maritime boundary problems persist. Furthermore, despite nearly four decades of ASEAN solidarity, mutual suspicions and apprehensions among many of the ASEAN countries have not withered away. At the same time it should be mentioned that the chances of a conflict breaking out among the ASEAN countries or with any outside power are unlikely, periodic tensions on certain issues, notwithstanding. It is apparent that any sign of a conflict would further undercut

Southeast Asia's strategic importance and bargaining power. Moreover, the threat to regional security, if any, is more likely to emanate from within, due to domestic reasons such as armed movements, inter-ethnic tensions, religious fundamentalism, etc., rather than from without.

Additionally, two issues, *inter alia*, need to be mentioned that can affect Southeast Asian security. One is terrorism and the other is a number of maritime-related security concerns. The uncovering of well-knit terrorist networks, especially that of Jamaah Islamiyah (JI), and certain high-profile terrorist acts such as the October 2002 attack on the Sari nightclub in Bali which killed 220 people, the suicide bombing at the Marriott Hotel in the heart of Jakarta in August 2003 that took another 12 lives, and a series of terrorist acts in other parts of Southeast Asia have brought forth the kind of dangers, that terrorism can pose. There is evidence that some of the terrorist organisations in Southeast Asia, have established links with notorious Al Qaeda and have undertaken coordinated activities. Despite considerable progress in counter-terrorism, Southeast Asia remains a major cause for concern, although not necessarily the second front for terrorism after Southwest Asia.

Maritime security is another critical element of Southeast Asia. Geographically, among the ten countries of Southeast Asia, only one, i.e., Laos is land-locked, while all others either are archipelagic nations or have long coastlines and substantial maritime interests. More importantly, barring a few exceptions, most of them have unsettled maritime boundaries or have claims for offshore assets, islands or seabed resources. Hence, sea power and maritime issues dominate the security concerns of the countries of Southeast Asia individually as well as collectively, at the regional level. A clear manifestation of this can be seen in the attempts to develop the naval forces in the region. Secondly, most of these countries are critically dependent on sea-borne trade. Some of the world's busiest and most important sea-lanes are located in this region. A related issue that has emerged as of a major concern, is the problem of piracy on high seas. The waters of Southeast Asia are the most prone, to piracy attacks than any other region in the world.

The other dimension is the strategic location of the islands of Spratly and Paracel in the South China Sea. The existence of large quantities of oil and gas reserves, may be proven right or wrong, the piracy issue may be tackled, the shipping may not get disturbed after all, but no one can deny the fact that the control of these islands offers enormous strategic importance leading to radical changes in the entire security calculus. This prospect would be very much unnerving to most other great powers which have developed considerable stakes in the region. What needs to be underscored is that the Southeast Asian countries, individually or collectively, do not possess the requisite military capabilities to address the above concerns.

ASEAN and Future of Regionalism

Since its inception, ASEAN has become the principal tool of regionalism in Southeast Asia. However, at every stage of a major event or development at the global or regional level, it had to reinvent and find ways to adjust to present itself as a viable mechanism. If anti-communism was the common objective that compelled the original five to work together, the Cambodian issue was handy for political cooperation to be forged later on. The concerns about regional peace and stability because of shifts in regional power balance, once again forced ASEAN to reinvigorate itself. Expansion of ASEAN was seen to be a way to enhance its importance, but it brought its own problems. The much talked about 'ASEAN way' of doing business that is, peaceful settlement of disputes and non-interference in each other's internal affairs among others, has largely remained relevant only to Southeast Asia. Its negative side is that it precluded ASEAN from emerging as a genuine vehicle for regionalism not just in terms of greater economic cooperation, but also in the larger political and security affairs. As a former foreign minister of Thailand boldly admitted, "ASEAN would seem unlikely to find itself called upon to play a major regional security role for the simple reason that circumstances are unlikely to arise when its ministrations would be required. And if they were, ASEAN would almost certainly have difficulty in rising to the occasion because its governments have yet to demonstrate sufficient common interest and political will to act with one mind." [6]

The 1997-98 financial crisis and the political developments that followed further, exposed the serious limitations and weaknesses of ASEAN, prompting the then Singapore's Prime Minister to point out that the events had "taken the shine out of ASEAN... (ASEAN) is seen as helpless and worse, disunited in a crisis." [7] Most of the worst affected countries have managed to tide over the crisis, nonetheless its political repercussions still reverberate in certain quarters such as Indonesia, the largest and the most influential member of ASEAN.

Similarly, the attempt to create a free trade and investment zone in Southeast Asia under the aegis of ASEAN in order to boost the region's political and economic importance does not have a smooth sail. The fact, that countries such as Singapore, Thailand, the Philippines, etc., are looking beyond the ASEAN framework to enter into bilateral free trade area agreements with a large number of nations, is a clear indication of the kind of impediments that exist. Southeast Asia as an economic entity too, has become less attractive when compared to large and fast growing economies such as China and India if the strength of the economy is rather taken in its totality than just one component such as trade. In PPP terms, the combined GDP of entire Southeast Asia is less than half of India's GDP and less than one-third of China. And the gap is growing. It is no secret that foreign direct investments (including Japanese) are going to East Europe, China, and India because of Southeast Asia's growing unattractiveness. In November 2002, Singapore's the then Deputy Prime Minister Lee Hsien Loong (now Prime Minister) observed that "Southeast Asian countries are under intense competitive pressure, as their former activities, especially labour-intensive manufacturing, migrate to China. One indicator of this massive shift is the fact that Southeast Asia used to attract twice as much foreign direct investment as Northeast Asia, but the ratio has reversed." [8]

The unravelling of ASEAN, has been much more stark since the 9/11 events and the growth of terrorism in Southeast Asia, which has been billed as the second front of global terrorism. [9] In its inimitable style, ASEAN tried to dismiss terrorism in the region as a non-issue or at best a minor problem. Subsequent events, however, have proved otherwise, especially periodic bloody bombings in Indonesia and unearthing of several militant cells all across the region. This also brings to the fore the issue of building a security community in Southeast Asia, which has failed to materialise because of basic differences.

India and Southeast Asia

Until recently, India had not been a factor in regional economic or political calculus but it has been rapidly changing. Today, no debate on the regional security in the Asia Pacific is complete without a mention of India. New Delhi's growing stature is not so much because of its participation in regional multilateralism, of which it had been wary for a long time, as because of its potential to balance China as an economic and military power and its rising strengths in mastering certain advanced technologies. Within ASEAN, there have been mixed reactions over India's involvement in regional affairs. The differences over extending an invitation to India to attend the EAS, are a sign of ambivalence. The Look East policy that India has been pursuing for over a decade and half, as it was originally envisaged, is not limited to Southeast Asia any longer. It is multi-dimensional and multi-pronged, and aims at the entire Asia Pacific region. These changes need to be recognised in order to comprehend India's policies in a proper manner.

As the former Singaporean Prime Minister Goh Chok Tong pointed out, China and India should form two wings of Southeast Asian jumbo jet. The signing of comprehensive economic cooperation agreements (CECA) with Singapore and Thailand and a framework agreement with ASEAN (to create a free trade area between India and Southeast Asia), are clear indications of India's commitment to increasingly align itself with the Asia Pacific region. To be sure, the economic dimension is not confined to Southeast Asia as talks are in an advanced stage to conclude similar agreements with Japan and South Korea and a little later with China. The same trend is also seen in India's strategic and political interaction, which had been focused on Southeast Asia until recently but now extends to the Northeast Asian region. The dilemma the Southeast Asian nations face in dealing with China, are understandable as it poses challenges as well as offers opportunities, but it would be a mistake to underrate India. Like other great powers, India too would be taking cognizance of the emerging power balance in East Asia, its relations with those powers will gain importance.

Hence, the Look East policy is unlikely to be an ASEAN-centric but would aim at the larger Asia Pacific. The big picture today is not how ASEAN would be instrumental in moulding the regional security but what the nature of relations among the great powers is going to be. If the growing rift between Japan and China and its impact on India's relations with Japan, and the U.S. the assessment of India as a strategic partner and China as a potential military challenge in the years ahead- as indicated by the February 2006 Quadrennial Defence Review Report (QDR) [10] are any indication, it is the balance of power rather than multilateralism, that is going to be the principal dimension of regional security. There is already a talk of India-U.S.-Japan trilateral strategic cooperation in Asia, though it is unlikely to manifest itself as an alliance but would be a hedge to deal with contingencies.

Conclusion

After the end of the cold war, Southeast Asia's strategic significance has been on the decline and the focus within the Asia Pacific is shifting increasingly to Northeast Asia. Though ASEAN-led regionalism, has made considerable progress, it is still facing with problems. Economically too, the region is becoming less attractive. ASEAN's major drawback is that it has failed to project Southeast Asia as an autonomous power centre. Hence, intra-great power relations largely will determine the nature of regional security order rather than ASEAN taking a lead role in shaping it. Similarly, ASEAN-led multilateralism, both economic and security, has not made much headway, in particular, the ARF.

There are both traditional and non-traditional issues that can affect Southeast Asia's security, which the region alone is not able to tackle effectively but, at the same time, is unwilling to involve external powers, thus getting its own weaknesses aggravated. Unfortunately, the Southeast Asian countries are neither successful in forging common solidarity by evolving as an economic and strategic community nor overcoming mutual suspicions that persist among several member states at the bilateral level. Moreover, Southeast Asia has been dubbed as the second front of terrorism thus further getting its credibility as a stable and economically fast growing region.

Southeast Asia's overall weight is on the decline in relative terms even as the attention within the Asia Pacific region increasingly moves towards Northeast Asia, and it is also becoming economically less attractive with the rise of China and India. ASEAN's failure to emerge as an autonomous power centre and its insistence on managing regional affairs on its own terms without realizing its limitations, may not contribute to an overall stability and prosperity of the region. Unless ASEAN comes up with new ways, it is difficult for Southeast Asia to become altogether invulnerable to external pressures. India's Look East policy will continue to be a major aspect of India's foreign policy and it is being expanded to cover the entire Asia Pacific region. The nature of this policy would largely depend on the kind of relations it would develop with great powers such as the U.S., Japan, and China.

Notes

1. http://www.whitehouse.gov/news/releases/2006/01/20060131-10.html

2. Condoleezza Rice, "The Promise of Democratic Peace: Why Promoting Freedom Is the Only Realistic Path to Security," *Washington Post*, December 11, 2005.

3. Under Chinese pressure, the conflict resolution was changed into "elaboration of approaches to conflicts."

4. Shen Caibin, "As China expands, Japan must look outward," *The Asahi Shimbun*, July 19, 2005, http://www.asahi.com/english/Herald-asahi/TKY200507190130.html

5. Notwithstanding regional sensitivity, there is no denying of the fact that ASEAN was a cold war creation with a strong external impetus.

6. Surin Pitsuwan, *Future Directions for ASEAN*, Trends in Southeast Asia No. 38, (Singapore, Institute of Southeast Asian Nations, September 2001), http://www.iseas.edu.sg/102001.pdf.

7. Roger Mitton, "Now, ASEAN Becomes Ten", *Asia Week*, April 30, 1999, p. 23.

8. China Online, November 14, 2002.

9. David M. Jones and Mike L. Smith, "The Changing Security Agenda in Southeast Asia: Globalization, New Terror, and the Delusions of Regionalism," *Studies in Conflict & Terrorism*, No. 24 (2001), pp. 271–288.

10. http://www.globalsecurity.org/military/library/policy/dod/qdr-2006-report.pdf

7

Emerging India in Asia–Pacific: Implications on Southeast Asia

C. Ravindranatha Reddy

Asia is emerging as the most dynamic region of the world in twenty-first century. [1] In the region, East Asian community which encompasses ASEAN, China, Japan, South Korea, is gradually developing as the centre of gravity of global economy. The increasing integration of ASEAN countries with Japan, Korea and China and with Australia and New Zealand`, can easily promote India's trade and investment initiatives in East Asia and Southwest Pacific. [2] India has not only acquired a deep "geographical foot print" in Asia-Pacific, but also stands out distinctly as an integral part of the region. [3] India floated the idea of broad Asian Economic Community (AEC) and called for the creation of Pan-Asian Free Trade Area (FTA). [4] Asia's growing weight in international relations, empowered by China and India and their respective economic strength, could generate mutually reinforcing growth across the continent especially, in the region of Southeast Asia. [5] The underlying transformation of Asia has already moulded the dynamics of India's foreign policy.

Emerging India

India is a major power with an enormous potential. India with physical, cultural and economic dimensions, has remained a medium sized continent. [6] It is the seventh largest country in the world in terms of total land area and with a population of over one billion, it is the world's second most populous country. [7] India has already established itself as the world's largest democracy. India is the cradle of great religions, Hinduism and Buddhism, and one of the second largest Muslim countries in the world. The impact of the influence of India's ancient civilisation may be felt in various parts of the world.

India has been playing an increasingly important role since her independence. [8] She has brought remarkable distinction and substantial contribution to the cause of United Nations, the Afro-Asian conference, the Non-Aligned Movement, North-South Dialogue and South-South Cooperation and many other international fora. As a founding father of several of these bodies, India not only helped shape them, but also defended and protected their principles. India, with the distinction of possessing the fourth largest standing army in the world, has been known as one of the nuclear powers outside the 'Nuclear Power Club' and aloof from it. This will guarantee not only Indian security, but also international stability. [9]

The Indian economy has been growing rapidly, displaying wholesome signs. India is the fourth largest economy in 2000, in terms of Purchasing Power Parity (PPP), the eighth largest industrial economy, the world's largest pool of scientists and engineers after the United States, and a large middle class (300 million). [10] Indian economy has grown at an annual average of 7-8 per cent, placing India amongst the world's better performing economies in terms of GDP growth rate. [11] The stock market is booming, reaching more than 10,000 points. Foreign exchange reserves had crossed over US$100 billion mark. The interest rates are low. The results of the corporate sector, continued to show profits.

The Indian economy has a number of strengths poised enough to grow rapidly on a sustained basis. It is established that Indian economy could grow to the third largest in the world by 2050, after the United States and China. [12] Henry Kissinger predicted to the effect, that in the twenty first century, the international system will be dominated by six major powers: the United States, Europe, Japan, Russia and probably India. [13] Similarly Samuel Huntington foresaw that, during the coming decades, "India could move into a rapid economic development and emerge as a major contender for influence in world affairs". [14]

India's image has been qualitatively upgraded with regard to software and IT enabled services. India is today recognised, not only as one of the important emerging economies, but also as a leader in the field of science and technology, human resource development and provision of services. Politically also, there is stability of government in India. Social transformation of India has been remarkably impressive. Indian culture has gone global. Overseas Indians are moving up in their chosen careers and their contribution to the success and prosperity in the countries they live, is immensely substantial.

India has been in search of a major power status. An important running theme of Indian foreign policy since independence, has been the attainment of a major power status. One could discern variations of emphasis and change of means to attain that goal, from Jawaharlal Nehru, to Vajpayee. [15] The outgoing NDA government headed by Vajpayee, stressed plans to turn India into an economic super power and the new UPA government of Manmohan has been targeting an annual economic growth of 7-8 per cent. [16] In spite of change of government in April 2005, Indian transition to a more important role of an active participant in the international economy, is unlikely to be reversed.

India which demonstrates a growing economic strength, plays an increasingly significant role in the international economy. It is also likely to play a major role in the over all world in view of a close kinship between India's growing economic strength and its status in the offing, as a prospective super power. India's current demographic and economic size has already placed it fairly high in terms of international power rankings. The growing economy of India will add weight to its foreign policy. India is strategically located between the major energy producer of Middle East and the dynamic economies of East Asia. Several analysts believe that India, along with China, will be a central shaper of any future balance of power in Asia. In the emerging new world order, India has a significant place and a pivotal role to play on the world stage. [17]

Emerging India in Asia-Pacific

It is a universally accepted surmise, that 21st century is going to be the century of the Asia–Pacific. Its stability or instability will have far-reaching consequences for the global order as whole. It is in this region that the impact of the presence of almost all major global players – the USA, Russia, China, Japan, ASEAN and India, is felt. It is an international area, accommodating convergence of diverse kinds of economic dimensions, natural resources and the presence of massive, competent technical trained human resources. [18]

Nehru had long ago, visualized that the Pacific is likely to take place of the Atlantic as a future nerve centre of the world. [19] Though not directly a Pacific state, India will inevitably exercise a significantly salutary influence there. In his famous Singapore lecture, Vajpayee has remarked that the Indian economy has been rapidly getting integrated into the global mainstream [20] and that India's linkages with the major economies of the Asia-Pacific have been gaining enough of a momentum to reinforce development, peace, security and stability in the region. He added that the fact of India belonging to the Asia-Pacific community, is a geographical one as well as a political reality. It does not require anything like a formal membership of any regional organisation, for its recognition and sustenance.

India recognised the importance of ASEAN as a desirable pathway of reaching the pacific front nations. ASEAN also recognised that the Indian economy and political sagacity are a vital importance to the region. India's Look East policy has been accommodating a multi-pronged approach, encompassing political, strategic and economic aspects. India has successfully established the institutional linkages with ASEAN and got its bilateral relations with the member states strengthened. [21] India has been an enthusiastic participant and a staunch supporter of multi-lateralism in Asia-Pacific and has become a significant part of the larger Asia-Pacific landscape.

By virtue of the geographical situation as well as the civilisational contacts in culture, religion, language and trade, the growing business and the investment in contemporary time and the presence of large Indian diaspora, denote India's deep contacts in Asia-Pacific which stands clearly an integral part of the region. Having realised ASEAN's strategic importance in the Asia-Pacific region, India has continued its cordiality with the Southeast Asian countries in the 21st century. It also tried to use the ASEAN platform, as a spring board for its further successful integration with the Asia-Pacific region. [22]

India's participation in the ASEAN Regional Forum (ARF) demonstrates New Delhi's increasing engagement in the Asia-Pacific region both in the politico-security and economic spheres to sustain regional peace and stability. A place for India in the emerging politico-economic architecture of Asia-Pacific, becomes a logical corollary. India appears a natural candidate and a legitimate claimant for APEC and ASEM. [23] The inclusion of India in the East Asian Summit (EAS) in December, 2005 shows the significance accorded to India, by the Asia-Pacific countries in the region. While welcoming this opportunity with great deal of warmth, India displayed poise and a determination to throw in its lot, with Asia-pacific region. [24]

Implications of Emerging India on Southeast Asia

The rise of India in Asia-Pacific carries certain important implications for Southeast Asia. The end of seemed to augur Cold War well for India's shift to the role of an outward oriental model and for its growing economic and strategic importance in the world, which have all led to an enlargement of the scope for engagement, besides boosting India's relative importance to Southeast Asia. The Look east policy launched by India in the 1990s, was a vigorous response to the extended neighbourhood in the East, in the post cold war situation.

Under this policy, India has achieved notable success in securing an institutional integration with the ASEAN region. This includes not only the membership of ASEAN ARF, but also the holding of the annual ASEAN plus Summit, since 2002. The progress that India has achieved in cultivating multifaceted relationships with ASEAN and its member states, is remarkable. Though India's Look East Policy encompasses the entire Asia-Pacific, the primary focus undoubtedly has been on Southeast Asia. However, the policy has played a vital role in enabling India, to emerge as one of the major powers.

In the first phase of its Look East Policy, India's relations were ASEAN-cantered and focussed primarily on trade and the investment linkages. The growth in India's trade was the fastest, with Southeast Asia, compared to any other region, during 1990s. India has put across concrete plans to increase the economic interaction and integration through institutional arrangements. Thus the economic dimension has acquired a significant place in India's relations with these countries and the trade scenario between India and Southeast Asia derived strength from the emerging complementarities between their economies.

By the turn of the century, began the second phase of the Look East policy. The new phase of the policy is characterised by an extended definition of the East that embodied a range from Australia to East Asia, with ASEAN at its core. India's trade with East Asia and ASEAN was growing, making a handsome profit out of the deal. In the years to come, the investment flows would figure prominently in the exchanges between India and ASEAN and East Asia. The level of current contacts, reflected the fulfilment of India's Look East Policy.

The new phase of policy focussed on developing wider and more intense economic contacts than usual. The emphasis is on trade, by mobilising investments from Southeast Asia region. Creating a Free Trade Arrangement (FTA) with ASEAN as a whole, as well as with selected individual countries, is an important aspect of the strategy of economic integration. India has set a target of trade turn over of 30 billion dollars with ASEAN by 2007, and a Free Trade Area by early years of the next decade. There is a growing realisation in Southeast Asia, that India's expanding economy is more than double that of all

Southeast Asian countries put together in PPP terms and it is one of the largest emerging markets for products and services in the world. [26]

An interesting dimension of India's Look East policy, is the new found interest in regional multilateralism. India came up with a number of new multilateral initiatives, involving Southeast Asian countries. Prominent among these were the BIMSTEC in 1997, and MGC in 2000. India aims at physical connectivity with Southeast Asia through Myanmar and Thailand. India's participation in the sub-regional organizations of BIMSTEC and MGC, ensured development and stability of its turbulent and strategically resistive region of the north-east. [27] There are tremendous opportunities for cooperation in the areas of transport, energy, telecommunications, tourism, environment, Human Resource Development trade and investment. [28]

India also expands and gets contacts in the field of defence and security cooperation reinforced. The Southeast Asian countries are engaged in a massive defence modernisation and also form an alternative market for Indian products and services. India can play a very significant role in peace-keeping anti-piracy, anti-terrorism and search and rescue operation against the transport of illegal arms, drugs, fissile material through Indian ocean. The growth of mutual trust and confidence between the two sides was quite explicit in the enhanced strategic interaction between them which manifested itself in the holding of joint naval exercises. [29] ASEAN's perception of New Delhi as an emerging power, and China as a source of security threat, had convinced ASEAN of the need for a paradigm shift in India-ASEAN linkage. [30]

India's partnership with ASEAN helped to improve its diplomatic position, international political credibility and strategic interests. India integrated its security with the countries of Southeast Asia and beyond. India's membership of the ASEAN Regional Forum ARF, offers to discuss issues of peace and security in a wider region of Asia-Pacific. It also gives an opportunity to explain and defend its own policies and action.

[31] India's summit status on par a with China, Japan and South Korea is a boon in the sense, that it had offered a rare opportunity to meet the leaders of ASEAN, East Asia and western countries on the sidelines of their meetings, to exchange their views on important bilateral, regional and global issues.

India enjoys traditional cultural bonds with Southeast Asia. Culture becomes a powerful instrument in India's Look East Policy. The MGC and BIMSTEC have highlighted the importance of culture, in promoting the regional cooperation. The cultural aspect facilitated better trade and commerce and promoted tourism which is a major economic activity and India's biggest foreign exchange earner. An important dimension of the cultural diplomacy is, strengthening the bonds between Indian diaspora in Southeast Asia and India. The Indian diaspora has been an important factor in India's maintenance of the relations with Southeast Asian countries. [32]

East Asian Community

East Asia is calling for the reconstruction and an innovation of cooperation mechanism. The forming and strengthening of ASEAN 10+3 and 10+1 cooperation indicates East Asian regional economic group, inclusive of all East Asian countries. This trend has a long term and deep influences on the international situation and many aspects of the global economy. India is the market on which ASEAN and East Asian powers viz., China, Japan and South Korea should focus. The rate of growth between India and ASEAN as well as India and East Asia, has been impressive. [33] It is to be noted that South Korea is today, the second largest investor in India.

To foster prosperity, peace and security in the region, India, China and Japan should spearhead strenuous efforts in both economic and political areas. The significant development underway, is the rise of China and India recording high economic growth rates simultaneously. Its implications will continue to engage the attention of Southeast Asia, the Asia-Pacific region and beyond. [34] It is a misconception that India and China are competitors as the two countries are partners involved in a healthy competition. India continued its efforts to engage China in greater economic interaction. The relations between India and China are moving in a fruitful direction. The implementation of ASEAN proposal of an East Asian Summit, has been influenced by an intervention from China and India. To their credit, neither India nor China has rocked the ASEAN boat or hurt each other. [35]

As India has been invited to attend the inaugural East Asia Summit in Malaysia in December 2005, India can legitimately claim that its Look East Policy is bearing fruits and hence, its being considered a serious player, in the Asia-Pacific region. [36] On its part, India is comfortable with the idea of ASEAN driving the East Asian Summit process forward. New Delhi favoured an annual meeting of the countries invited for the East Asian Summit which includes ASEAN nations, India, China, Japan, South Korea, Australia and New Zealand.

India's participation at the first East Asian Summit is an achievement of India's foreign policy. India's participation in the summit which issued the 'Kuala Lumpur Declaration', is an encouraging sign of its integration with the region. A fortified integration of the Indian economy with Asia-Pacific region, would benefit not only India, but also the Asia-Pacific economies. The inclusion of India in the EAS, also shows the importance accorded to India, by the Asia–pacific countries in the region. The summit host and Premier of Malaysia, Abdullah Badawi claimed, "The East Asia Summit was a great and unqualified success. There was high degree of acceptance that we are community with a common interest in peace, stability and prosperity." [37]

Towards Asian Economic Community

The vast geographical stretch of Asia is indicative of its importance in global affairs. Asia occupies a little more than one-third of the landmass of the world's territorial spread and is populated by more than half of the world's largest energy resources, which ensures a formidable clout in the global affairs. Contemporary Asia is changing and in many a way, it is quite different from what it appeared to be, in the last century. Asia is incomparably far more developed than what it was, at any stage of its development. [38] Blackwill, the former American Ambassador to India argued, "Asia's century is now under way - Asia is prised to become the strategic centre of gravity in international politics". [39]

Compared with Europe and North America, Asian economic integration and collectivisation are much slower. But driven by globalisation and regional collectivisation, Asia has made some progress. Gradually, Asian countries realised that they do have certain similarities, and may have, some differences too. The best way to remove poverty and promote prosperity in Asia is, to take recourse to a full exploration and exploitation of Asian gigantic natural and human resources potentiality. There is an urgent need for Asian countries, to carry out an internal cooperation to consolidate and to deepen the economic relations. This will lead to the improvement of economic interest and political status of the Asian countries.

Asian Economic Community could be built in a gradual manner, to begin with ASEAN, India and East Asian community. Asia has attracted the considerable attention of the world, on account of its rapid economic growth over the past decades. China and India are very convincing examples of this trend. More significantly, the Asian Economic Community is in the making. There is broad realization in Asia that the formation of the community, would ensure enormous advantages and benefits, because of closer integration. [40]

India as an Asian country and the developments in Asia, have their own impact directly on India's security and strategic interests. Full Asian cooperation is necessary for future global order. Asia is holding the key to collective global prosperity and security. At the heart of Asia, lies India and in view of its proven strength in the science and technology, human resources and economic development, it is logical for India to stretch the scope of its diplomacy towards the formation of Asian Economic Community. [41]

The East Asian Summit could be eventually expanded to cover other Asian countries in an Asian Economic Community. Economic integration in East Asia, would enable the region, to resume its rapid growth and help it to emerge as a centre of gravity in the world economy. Integration of Indian economy with East Asia is a win-win for Asia. With a US$ 700 billion economy, growing at 7-8 per cent per annum, a sizeable large middle class and strong macro fundamentals, India is able to add its own dynamism to the East Asian integration. The East Asian Summit in December 2005 in Malaysia, provides an opportunity for Asia to take an initial first step in the long journey towards broader regional economic integration of Asia. [42]

Conclusion

India's route to great power status on world stage, will depend on its ability to alter the dynamics of its own neighbourhood. Therefore, India will certainly intensify its efforts to carry forward Look East Policy. India's regional initiatives were presented in terms of mutual economic benefit, restoration of historical links and forging of the strategic relations. The results have been impressive and have given rise to hopes for a significant increase of influence in the East. The growing India-ASEAN partnership has also looked beyond their mutual engagement. ASEAN is currently engaging for the success of East Asian Economic Community which includes India also. There is need to consolidate these attempts into economic grouping, that could provide a framework in due course, to an Asian Economic Community.

Notes

1. R.R. Sharma, *India and Emerging Asia*, (New Delhi, 2005).
2. *India-ASEAN Partnership in an Era of Globalisation: Reflections by Eminent Persons*, (RIS, New Delhi, 2002).
3. Sudhir Devare, *India and Southeast Asia: Towards Security Convergence*, (Singapore, 2006).
4. See http://pmindia.nic.in/visits/content.asp?id =88.

5. Srinivasan and Others, *Reintegrating India with World Economy*, (Washington, 2003). p.2.

6. For details see N.S. Sisodia and G.V.C. Naidu, *Challenging Security Dynamic in Eastern Asia*, (New Delhi, 2005).

7. For details see Sandu Gordon, *India's Rise to Power: In the Twentieth century and Beyond*, (London, 1995).

8. *Ibid.*

9. *India-ASEAN Partnership in an Era of Globalisation*, (RIS, New Delhi, 2002) p.118.

10. Baldev Raj Nayar and T.V. Paul, *India in the World Order*, (Cambridge, 2002), p.9.

11. *The Hindu*, 2 January, 2006.

12. Dominic Wilson and others, *Goldman Sachs Dreaming with BRICs: The Path to 2050*, (New York, 2003) cited in Mark P Thirlwell, *India: The Next Economic Giant*, (Canberra, 2004), p.3.

13. Henry Kissinger, *Diplomacy*, (New York, 1994). pp. 23-24.

14. Samuel P. Huntington, *The Clash of Civilisations and Remarking World Order*, (New York, 1996), p.121.

15. C. Raj Mohan, *Crossing the Rubicon*, (New Delhi, 2005).

16. Mark P. Thirlwell, *India: The Next Economic Giant*, p.4.

17. S. Bhatt and V.S. Mani, *India on the Threshold of the 21st Century: Shape of things to come*, (New Delhi, 1991), p.360.

18. Prakash Nanda, *Rediscovery Asia: Evolution of India Look East Policy*, (New Delhi, 2003) p.466.

19. Jawaharlal Nehru, *Discovery of India* (Calcutta, 1945).

20. Cited in Mark P. Thirlwell, n.16.

21. For details see K.S. Nathan, *India and ASEAN: The Growing Partnership for the 21st Century*, (Kuala Lumpur, 2000).

22. Rahul Sen, Mukul G. Asher, and S. Ramakishan Raja, (eds.), *ASEAN-India Economic Relations: Current Status and Future Prospects*, (RIS, New Delhi, 2004).

23. Sudhir Devare, n.3, p.212.

24. Nageshk Kumar, Rahul Sen and Mukhul, Asher, *India-ASEAN Relations: Meeting the Challenges of Globalisation*, (New Delhi, 2005).

25. For details see, Frederic Grave and Amitabh Matto (ed.), *India and ASEAN: The Politics of India Look East Policy*, (New Delhi, 2001).

26. Mark P. Thirlwell, n.16, p.103; 106.

27. See Vajpayee address to the second Northeast Business Summit in New Delhi, 20 January, 2003, http://pub.nic.in/release/release asp?relid+754.

28. *India–ASEAN Partnership in the Age of Globalization*, n.2, p.XXXI.

29. G.V.C. Naidu, Wither the Look East Policy: India and Southeast Asia", *Strategic Analys*is, Vol. 28, No.2, April-June, 2004, pp.331-46.

30. Tridib Chakraborti, "Disparate Priorities: Explaining the Penumbra of India's Look East Policy" in *India and ASEAN*, (New Delhi, 2002), p. 53.

31. Lakshmana Chetty, "India and ASEAN Regional Forum" in *India and Southeast Asia: Problems and Prospects*, (Tirupati, 1999).

32. Sudhir Devare, n.3, pp.211-212.

33. Mukul G. Asher and Rahul Sen, *India – East Asia Integration: A Win-Win for Asia*, (RIS, New Delhi, 2005).

34. Yang Bojiang, "East Asia's Economic Integration. Realities and Prospects" *Contemporary International Relations*, 2003, p. 2.

35. Mukul Asher, n.33.

36. Nauda Mallik "Look East Policy set to get a boost" http://specials.rediff.com/menery /2005/see 0aseau.htm.

37. Quoted in Andy Mukherjee, "What is in name? East Asia has yet to decide", *International Herald Tribute*, December 13, 2005.

38. R.R. Sharma, *India and Emerging Asia*, (New Delhi, 2005) p.13.

39. Robert Blackwell, Lecture delivered at the *IDSA 5th Conference on Asian Security*, New Delhi, January 27, 2003.

40. "Emerging New Asia" *New Asia Monitor*, Vol.1, No.1, March, 2004, p.1.

41. Sudhir Devare, n. 3, p.157.

42. Nagesh Kumar, *Towards Broader Asian Community: Agenda for the East Asia Summit*, (RIS, New Delhi, 2005).

8

Reflections on Nation-building in Southeast Asia

V. Suryanarayan

The Pakistani political leader Abdul Wali Khan (Son of Khan Abdul Ghafar Khan) was asked few years ago by a journalist: "Are you a Pakistani, a Muslim or a Pathan?" Wali Khan replied that he combined all the three characteristics. The journalist persisted and asked what his primary identity was. Wali Khan responded: "I am a Pakistani for thirty years, a Muslim for 1,400 years and a Pathan for 5,000 years". The multiple identities of South and Southeast Asians, an intrinsic feature of the socio-political profile of the two regions, have made the task of nation building an exciting and fascinating exercise. But before analyzing the problems of nation building, few preliminary observations are in order.

Political Scientists unfortunately use the terms nation and state as synonymous and this semantic confusion has done incalculable harm in understanding the politics of developing countries. Louis Halle, for example, maintained that a "prime fact about the world is that it is largely composed of nation states". The statement is not true. The world consists of states, not nation states. A survey of the world's 132 states in 1971 found that only 12 (9 per cent) could justifiably be called as a nation in the sense of the boundaries of the "territorial juridical entity being co-terminous with the distribution of a particular national group". The comment made by Massimo d' Azeglu, with special reference to Italy after unification, holds true of most of the states which came into existence after the Second World War: "We have made Italy, now we must make Italians".

The rise of ethno-nationalism and intensification of ethnic conflicts in different parts of the world) raises an interesting theoretical question, which many Marxian Social Scientists have so far not only ignored, but also considered as taboo. They subscribed to the view that the process of industrialization and modernization would dissolve ethnic identities and create new identities based on class considerations. However, recent developments belie this claim. The political assertion of various nationalities in the Soviet Union, the revolutionary changes that have taken place in Eastern Europe and Central Europe, the demands of the Blacks in the United States, the Irish conflict in UK, the developments in Fiji, the problems of the Chinese minorities in Southeast Asian countries - all these are not only illustrations of the pervasiveness of ethnicity, but also underline the possibilities of more conflicts in the new millennium. An important point, however, should be kept in mind. Whether conflict or harmony governs inter-ethnic relations hinges to a large extent, upon the provision in the political system for tolerance of each other's beliefs and value systems. In those countries where the dominant theme is "ethnicisation of politics and politicization of ethnic communities", the chances of escalation of ethnic conflicts are in plenty. As Sumantra Bose has highlighted, "The topsy-turvy world where nation has meant state, nationalism has meant loyalty to the state, and nation state has most often meant a state that contained a multiplicity of at least potential nations, has obscured the vital issue - the emergence, growth and apparent mass appeal of nationalisms that define themselves in sharp opposition to the juridical state".

In his absorbing book, *Revenge and Reconciliation: Understanding South Asian History,* Rajmohan Gandhi underlines two features of identity politics in South Asia, which are equally applicable to Southeast Asia. First, "articulating the unreasonableness of the other". The "other" could be a neighbouring state, a government, a secessionist movement, an opposition party or a coalition partner. Second, and a more saddening spectacle, "political mobilization around a religious, linguistic or ethnic group or around a class or caste - in short identity politics - has generally seemed more promising than a political effort focusing on the needs or grievances of the citizens as a whole".

I would like to submit three propositions, which can be considered as the yardstick for the success of nation building in multi-ethnic societies in South and Southeast Asian countries. First, the political system should provide sufficient space for minorities so that they can preserve, promote and foster their distinct identities, while continuing as a part of a united country. Second, a federal system with entrenched provisions for sharing power between the centre and the states, can lead to a softening of the secessionist demands and pave the way for eventual integration. Third, we must distinguish between citizenship and nationality. Citizenship implies political loyalty to the state and every citizen, irrespective of his ethnic origin, should subscribe to this fundamental axiom. Second, nationality implies cultural moorings. You can be a Chinese, follow the Chinese culture and yet can be a citizen of Malaysia. In other words, the political system must provide sufficient space for multiple identities to co-exist harmoniously. The statement of Rupert Emerson assumes great significance here: "The simplest statement that can be made about a nation is that it is a body of people who feel that they are a nation; and it may be that when all the fine-spun analysis is concluded, this will be the ultimate statement as well".

The past weighs heavily on the present and it is necessary to highlight certain historical realities for a proper appreciation of the complex problems of nation building in Southeast Asia. The inter-state boundaries in Southeast Asia are imperialist creations and they have tended to follow a colonially inspired pattern of demarcation arrived at for reasons of administrative convenience. States have been formed in a region, the main characteristic of which, is social and cultural diversity. Instead of uniting people who belong to the same ethnic group, speak the same language and follow the same religion, these boundaries have tended to divide them. And in the post independence era, when the nation building experiment started, in many cases based on the language and religion of the majority community, the minorities were unwilling to reconcile themselves to the political dominance from the culturally alien centres. Regional minority dissidence and demands for separate states have been most marked in Southern Thailand, in Southern Philippines and parts of Indonesia. Complicating the situation, had been the extra-regional and regional support to these movements.

As is well known, the United States was deeply involved in the regional uprising that took place in Indonesia in the 1950's. The US policy has turned full circle, Washington is providing support to the Indonesian President to tackle the problems posed by the Achenese rebels. The relations between Malaysia and Thailand deteriorated on the question of activities of the Muslim separatists in Southern Thailand that abuts on the northeastern parts of Malaysia, which are predominantly Malay. Similarly, the separatist movement in Southern Philippines, which dates from October 1972, was sustained by external support, from the neighbouring state of Sabah in East Malaysia and later, in financial terms, from Libya and other members of the Organisation of Islamic States. The independence of East Timor is a classic illustration of a combination of factors, the high handedness of the Indonesian military and gross violation of human rights, the alienation of East Timorese from the rest of the archipelago and more important, the external support from countries like Australia, who were waiting for an opportunity to fish in the troubled waters. What I want to highlight is the fact that the demand for separate political identity (despite external support) has an autonomy and momentum of its own; and, what is more, these cannot be tackled merely at the level of law and order and military reprisals. The ruling elite must undertake soul searching to find out what went wrong with nation building experiments.

An overview of the political developments in Southeast Asia clearly illustrates, that the cartographic changes have been taking place rapidly, which again have affected the concept of nation building. Take the Malay peninsula for an example. Before the Second World War, there was no political entity called Malaya. The states and settlements of the Malay peninsula, including Singapore, formed three distinct political groups, namely 1) The Straits Settlements, which included the settlements of Singapore, Penang and Malacca; 2) The Federated Malay States, comprising the states of Negri Sembilan, Pahang, Perak and Selangor and 3) The five Malay states of Johore, Kelantan, Kedah, Perlis and Trengganu, not included in the Federation, but known as the Unfederated Malay States. After the Second World War, the British undertook far reaching constitutional changes. In order to provide unity and enable the immigrant communities to develop loyalty to Malaya, the unitary state of Malayan Union was created. Singapore was separated and was made into a Crown Colony. A common citizenship was introduced and the liberal provisions entitled the Malays, the Chinese and the Indians to become citizens.

However, due to opposition from the Malays, the Malayan Union proposals were abandoned and the Federation of Malaya was established in 1948. In 1963, in order to accomplish the decolonisation of British possessions in Southeast Asia and also, at the same time, retain their strategic and economic interests, the British colonies of Singapore, North Borneo and Sarawak were united with Federation of Malaya and the Federation of Malaysia came into existence thus. Malaysia did not last long, and later a bitter and acrimonious experiment lasting less than two[s] years, Singapore seceded from Malaysia and became an independent Republic in August 1965.

How did these changes affect the concept of nation building? Take Singapore for an example. From 1954 to 1963, Lee Kuan Yew and other political leaders of Singapore emphatically maintained that Singapore was not a nation and cannot be a nation and that it should seek its independence only through merger with the Federation of Malaya. In fact, the first essay on Singapore's independence, was in the context of Malaysia. Even before the ink turned dry on the Malaysia Agreement, a bitter war of words between Singapore and Kuala Lumpur started and the situation reached a point of no return by early 1965 and on August 9, 1965, Singapore, not without reason, had to separate from Malaysia. Lee Kuan Yew and other leaders made a sudden *volte face;* they began to assert that Singapore can be a nation, it could be a nation and started their own unique experiment in social engineering and nation building. A Chinese island in a Malay sea; a city of immigrants, a state without a hinterland and no natural resources but only for its location and the ingenuity of its hard working population, Singapore has emerged, over years, as the most prosperous state in Southeast Asia. And in a region plagued with xenophobia, it remains an oasis of stability and tolerance.

The main objective of the British administrators was to provide political stability to the country, encourage large scale immigration of the Chinese and the Indians and accomplish the economic exploitation of Malaya. Education, which is recognized as an instrument of integration, was not all neglected, and the British adopted a policy of laissez *faire* in this crucial area of development. As Martin Rudner has pointed out: "The conception of education in British Malaya had been narrowly confining, both socially and scholastically. Indeed to the end of the colonial period, education was segregated into separate and disjointed linguistic ethnic streams; English, Chinese and Tamil, with impoverishment of resources their common lot". No attempts were made to standardize the syllabi and to give it a Malayan orientation. On the contrary, the educational systems only widened existing schisms among various communities. As far as the Tamil boys and girls in the plantations were concerned, the attempt to transplant Tamil Nadu into Malaya resulted in a deprived education. The schools performed the custodial and not the instructional function. What is more, they only allowed the Tamil children to tap and weed out, to build roads, to live on the rails, to clear cars and to clear the malarious jungle.

Parallel systems of education that existed in Malaya were divisive in nature. Totally lacking in integration, there was a marked disparity in the quality and content of education offered by them. English medium schools looked to Britain for inspiration, the Chinese schools towards China and Indian schools towards India. The divisive character of the school system in Malaya has been rightly described as follows: " Thus it was that a local child in an English school would recite Wordsworth's lines on the daffodils, never having seen them, sail up the Thames in imagination, accompany Bonnie Prince Charlie through Scottish burns and braes, and pay for imaginary purchases in pounds, shillings and pence. His opposite number in the Chinese-medium school, on the other hand, referred to the Middle Kingdom, as "My country". He was taught to repeat the will of Sun Yat Sen, founder of the Chinese Republic, and he learnt to sing the Chinese national hymn. His cultural heritage came from China; his aspirations and loyalties remained, not with the land of his birth, but with the land of his fathers". As a result of the British neglect, a national system of education was introduced only after the independence of Malaya in August 1957.

The immigrant peoples in Malaya - Chinese, Indians and Indonesians - had always been subject to pulls and pressures from their motherlands. In the beginning, it was economic and a large proportion of their savings was remitted to China, India and Indonesia. With the growth of nationalism in China, India and Indonesia, political pulls also started exerting in subtle ways. Just as Mahatma Gandhi's baptism into politics took place in South Africa in defence of Indian community, the initial activities of the revolutionary movement in China were related to the Chinese communities abroad. Dr. Sun Yat Sen himself was a migrant from Honolulu and had his higher education in Hong Kong. From its inception, the Kuomintang began to enlist the support of the Chinese communities abroad. The Nationalist

Government, after the Revolution in 1911, started a Ministry of Overseas Chinese; Consulates were opened in Malaya, East Indies and the Philippines.

What is more, the new Government initiated a new principle of citizenship. The doctrine of "Once a Chinese, always a Chinese" came into force. It meant that citizenship went by ethnic origin and not by place of birth. It had dangerous implications and it was viewed with great suspicion both by the colonial governments and by Southeast Asian nationalists. The Chinese in Southeast Asia, gave financial support to the Nanking Government during the Sino-Japanese War. Branches of Kuomintang and the Chinese Communist Party were opened in Southeast Asian countries. It must also b mentioned that communism came to Malaya and Singapore from China and it was from the local Chinese that it drew its support. Very few Malays and Indians joined the Malayan Communist Party. In Malay perception, the MCP was Malayan only in name, but was Chinese in theory and practice. It was the inability of the Communist Party to build up a multi-racial following that led to its eventual downfall. The powerful ideological support the Chinese Communist Party (CCP) extended to the MCP during its armed struggle for power, created further misgivings among the Malayan nationalists. They viewed the Chinese minority as a "potential fifth column" of China.

Compared to the Chinese, the political consciousness among the Indians and the Malays was less. Most Indians were plantation workers and had no interest in politics. But, with the growth of the nationalist movement in India educated Indians began to take a lively interest in Indian political developments. This received a further impetus as a result of the visits of important Indian leaders like Jawaharlal Nehru, AK Gopalan and EV Ramaswamy Naicker. During the Second World War, the Indians rallied round the Indian National Army and joined the *Azad Hind Fauj* in great numbers. The *Thondar Padai* sensitized the Indians and imparted to them the legitimately proud feeling that they were in the vanguard of Indian independence. In the same way, number of educated Malays began to evince interest in the political developments in Indonesia. They began to advocate that after the end of the colonial rule, Indonesia and Malaya should join together to form a great *Indonesia Raya.*

The existence of a plural society prevented the growth of anti-British feelings in a big way. Unlike India, Malaya was politically a backwater. But beneath the surface, powerful forces were at work. Thus, long before the concept of Malaya and Malaya alone arose, the three largest countries of Asia - China, India and Indonesia - were pulling the three communities apart in different directions.

An overview of the nationalist movements in Southeast Asia would reveal that while the primary objective of the nationalists were to get independence from colonial domination, the nationalist movements were also directed against the immigrant communities who were working hand in glove with the imperialists. In Myanmar, the Burmese nationalists not only agitated against the British, but also were conscious of the economic exploitation of the Indian Chettiars. In Indonesia, from the days of the *Sarekat Islam,* the Indonesian nationalists were sensitive to the presence and economic domination of the Chinese who were working as the compradore classes of the Dutch.

In Malaya, the political awakening of the Malays following the introduction of the Malayan Union proposals and the unity that they forged under the United Malays National Organisation (UMNO) had far reaching repercussions on the political evolution of Malaya. Not only did it compel the British to withdraw the Malayan Union proposals, but also did it clearly reveal that the Malays would never surrender their pre-eminent position in the political life of Malaya. While in later years, the Malay leaders did co-operate with the Malayan Indian Congress and the Malayan Chinese Association in the larger interests of Malaya as a whole, the dynamic leadership of Malayan nationalism has always remained in the hands of the Malays. The inter-communal alliance and later the Barisan Nasional was not an alliance of equal partners, but was one in which, the supremacy of the Malays was clearly established.

The independence of the Federation of Malaya in 1957 did not lead to any revolutionary break with the past. With the Malays and the non-Malays divided roughly in equal numbers, the economic predominance of the Chinese would be offset by the political dominance of the Malays. The nation building experiment in the Federation of Malaya was based on the premise that the kernel would be provided by the Malays, while the outer covering would be provided by the Chinese and the Indians. The retention of the Malay Sultanate, the provision that Malay would be the national language and official language after ten years and the special rights and privileges accorded to the Malays as the Bhumiputras symbolized the Malay kernel. The provision of citizenship to the Chinese and the Indians and the assurance that they there would be no restrictions on their business activities were illustrations of the concessions made to the non-Malays. However, after the communal riots in May 1969, the political system was radically altered and Malay supremacy was further entrenched in Malaysia.

The Malayan nationalists were also sensitive to the fact that the best way to accomplish inter-communal co-operation and maintain the unity of the country, was to adopt the consociational system of democracy. According to Arend Lijphart, its "first and most important element is a grand coalition of the political leaders of all significant segments of the plural society". Unlike the majoritarian democracy, which as in the case of Sri Lanka, got degenerated in the dictatorship of the majority community, the consociational democracy accords to all communal groups a stake as well as meaningful role in the political system.

During 1963-65, when Singapore was a part of Malaysia, the question of nation building assumed controversial proportions. The leaders of the Alliance Government and the leaders of Singapore realized the delicate nature of the ethnic balance in Malaysia and the dangerous consequences that would follow if ethnic harmony was disturbed. There was a general reluctance on the part of the Alliance leaders to discuss communal issues in the open because they considered them to be potentially divisive. Therefore, the decisions on vital issues were taken behind the scenes by the leaders of the Malays, the Chinese and the Indians on the basis of co-operation and compromise. The leaders of Singapore said that they followed a diametrically opposite course. They believed in free, unfettered and open discussion of the communal problems, so that the dangers of communalism might be realized by the common people. They also wanted the development of political parties on the basis of non-communalism to be encouraged. As Prof. Milne has pointed out: "The resulting paradox was that the Alliance was a Party with a communal structure, which believed that too frequent open discussions of the problems of communalism is itself "communal"; the PAP was a Party, with a non-communal structure, which nevertheless believed that communal problems should be subjected to perpetual scrutiny".

Indonesia, the largest and the most populous country in Southeast Asia, encapsulates all the problems of nation building. Indonesia also holds the key to the stability of the region. The long spell of Suharto rule and the apparent political stability and high economic growth convinced many observers that Indonesia was the sheer anchor of the region's stability and progress. Since the removal of Suharto from power in 1998, the country has been beset with many problems affecting its unity, cohesion and development. Will Indonesia be balkanized into several independent islands? Will Indonesia become the Yugoslavia of Southeast Asia? Implications of hazardous large-scale violence and the consequent disintegration tend to form wild conjecture only.

Despite the apparent stability, the Suharto regime carried seeds of its own destruction. The administration was highly centralized and the provinces lacked political and economic autonomy. Under the system of divi fungsi (dual functions), the armed forces dominated the country. Armed struggles began in

Acheh, East Timor and Irian Jaya. Corruption was endemic and the compradore Chinese tycoons and the members of the Suharto family enriched themselves at the cost of the vast majority of the poor people. The regional and economic crisis of 1997-98 opened the Pandora's box. Large-scale violence against the Chinese community ensued, culminating in the downfall of Suharto. The interim administration led by Habibie, paved the way for parliamentary elections and eventual restoration of democratic rule.

Indonesia is the largest Islamic country in the world, with 87 per cent of the population following the Islamic faith. But Islam in Indonesia is not a monolith; the overwhelming majority of the people in Java practice animist traditions and are referred to as *abangans* or nominal Muslims. And, what is more, Indonesia is not an Islamic State. The pendulum swings between two extremes - the secular nationalists advocate the continuance of the secular character of the State, while the orthodox Muslim leaders want Indonesia to be a theocratic state. The Indonesian ideology - *Pancasila* - implies that the State considers all religions as equal, a principle that was dear to the heart of Sukarno. During the early years of his rule, Suharto also adhered to the same principle, but gradually his attitude towards Islam began to change. In order to neutralize the growing dangers of discontent, expressed through orthodox Islamic forces, President allowed a "Religious Court of Law" and a "National Education Law" to come into force. In December 1990, he permitted the formation of the Association of Indonesian Muslim Scholars (ICMI). It is interesting to note that the two popular Muslim organizations, the Nadahtul Ulema and the Muhammadiyah, dissociated themselves from the ICMI. They were conscious of the dangers of Islamic fundamentalism. They wee advocates of greater democratization of the polity and political tolerance. They were afraid that the supporters of the Islamic State would use the ballot box to come to power and then attempt to make Indonesia a theocracy.

Southeast Asian and international perception of Indonesia underwent a change following the bombing of the nightclub in Bali and the Marriot Hotel. An increasing pressure was exerted on Jakarta to crack down on the terrorists. Though Indonesia has enacted an anti-terrorist law and has arrested number of suspects in connection with the bombings, it has not yet banned the Jemmah Islamiyah, the reason given being that there is no evidence of the existence of such an organization in the country. According to the international community, Indonesia continues to be the weakest link in regional co-operation against international terrorism.

Bambang Harymurti, the well known Indonesian journalist and the editor of the *Tempo*, has summed up the challenges facing Indonesia as follows: "If Indonesia is to grow into a more mature and modern nation, it must successfully come to grips with four key issues - the politics of Islam, the political role of the military, ethnic Chinese domination and tensions between the center and the periphery. The international community should do all it can to help Indonesia overcome these challenges ...If Indonesia succeeds in meeting these challenges, it will become world's third largest democracy and the largest democracy in the Muslim world, making it an important beacon of hope in the Islamic community. If it fails to do so, there is the danger that the country could disintegrate into a mosaic of thousands of small, scattered, and mutually hostile units, with disastrous consequences for Southeast Asia and the world".

9

Religion, *Consciousness* and *Mental Images* in Southeast Asian Society

K. Syamalamma and P. Krishna Mohan Reddy

The study of religion, in the context of Southeast Asia, especially in the modern context, has been gaining prominence, since 1990s. Although there are several studies on the ancient and medieval religion in Southeast Asia, most of them deal with the influence of Buddhism, Hinduism or Islam on the art, architecture etc. However, the concept of how the religion shaped the society or influenced the collective consciousness of people through ages in Southeast Asia is yet to receive anything like a serious study.

The study of religion in general, is influenced by the anthropologists, sociologists and historians so much so, that the study of religion from the perspective of religion itself, (and/or from the perspective of scholars in religion) seems to have become blurred, as other disciplines threaten to dominate it. The approach of Marxist historians has always been to search for a materialistic base in the religion. The sociologists and anthropologists understood religion as an essential tool for the society, to maintain order and to control the groups and divisions in the society. For them, society created religion. Anthropologists often try to understand religion as a 'world view', 'belief systems' etc., especially, of the tribal groups. The general trend has always been, to study religion as part of society or economy. The result, naturally has been to view religion from the angle of society, economy etc. Scholars in religion, in the context of understanding an integration of the diaspora in the host countries, have criticized the Sociologists and Anthropologists for ignoring the study of the role of religion, let alone, studying religion from its own angle. [1] In the present paper, we propose to view society, social norms and behaviour, from the angle of religion based on the hypothesis, that religion is the primary force that frames the society as a whole. In this sense, contrary to the belief of earlier scholars, their disciplines and approaches, we propose to view society, behavior, etc., as components of religion by adopting almost a Reverse Approach.

To understand the connotation of the word 'religion', we need a comprehensive definition.

Albanese defines religion, dividing it into ordinary religion and extraordinary religion. [2] According to her, ordinary religion 'is the trunk of the tree of culture'. In the most general sense, ordinary religion is 'the source of distinguishable cultural forms and the background out of which the norms arise that guide us in our every day lives,' and in a more specific sense, it can reveal itself in many customs and folk ways that form only part of a culture such as habits of diet, expected ways of greeting people, wedding etiquette concerning clothes, manners, and obligations etc. [3] Contrary to the belief cherished by the leftist historians, the sociologists and anthropologists in general, Albanese deduces that religion tends to mould the society. By contrast, extraordinary religion is outside the ordinary circle of society and involves an encounter with some form of otherness, whether natural or supernatural.

It is specific and particular, easily recognizable as religion, and possible to separate from the rest of the culture. [4] For example, the practices of meditation or any practices aiming at salvation, can be called extraordinary Hinduism and the rest, such as the daily home worship, temple going, festivals, fastings, belief in the planetary influence, superstitions and all other things connected with life which is lived on this earth, as ordinary Hinduism. Even the minutest details of the daily life of a Hindu such as waking up from bed, the particular gods and goddesses any individual should pray after he wakes up, brushing his teeth for which the particular plants' branches he could use, the quantity of water to use and the way of using water while cleaning his mouth or face, the directions in attending the calls of nature, including the places and facing a fixed direction, the manner of taking bath and the number of times etc, are all dictated by the Hindu religious texts. [5] Therefore, it is necessary to study even the minutest details of the daily life of the Hindus to understand Hinduism to a considerable extent.

By following this definition, we face no ambiguity in understanding the role and the effect of religion on the society, as it not only becomes the part of everyday life of the individual person and the society as a whole, but also dictates it. An individual acquires his religion as a hereditary characteristic from his parents and family like his physical characters, food habits, manners, customs and behaviour. So, in a way, religion is, in his blood. Society too, in a similar way, inherits its characters from religion and is shaped by it. To put it more clearly, like human brain, which controls every aspect of a person, religion acts as the 'brain' of a particular society. The brain controls all the actions of a human being, both physical and mental. The ability to walk, talk or fight or to sleep, worship or meditate is controlled by the brain. Likewise, the 'consciousness' developed by the 'brain' of the society viz., religion, controls not only the physical behaviour of the society but also its arts as much as its administration, law, punishment etc. In the ancient and medieval periods, all over the world, religion formulated all these features.

In the medieval Europe, Middle East or in India, the punishments for crimes such as robbery and rape were similar and the 21st century man feels that they were barbarous. But, during the medieval period, they were normal for the contemporary men as their 'mental images' of crime and punishment were shaped by the contemporary 'consciousness'. In the ancient and medieval period all over the world, whether it is Hinduism, Christianity or Islam, every aspect of life such as administration, law, punishment, birth, marriage, food habits, dress etc. were formulated and regulated by religion. The 'brain' of the society was virtually the religion. By the time the literary sources are available (though we are not sure about the pre historic period); we can see all over the world the 'consciousness' or the 'mental images' of a given society being operated by its religion or religions. It is a mistake to name this 'consciousness' as 'tradition' which is but another name for religion.

Very recently, a research that is being conducted on the study of 'mind maps' in relation to the use of language, symbols etc. in human beings has begun bringing forth interesting results. Our brain functions may be divided into two categories, the left one handles reason and logic, while the right one deals with emotion and creativity. 'Mind maps' make use of key words and images. The visual nature of mind maps makes them easy to remember. A mind map is a graphic technique for representing ideas, using words, images, symbols and colour. It reflects the pattern of thinking in the human mind. Anyone with a logical mind, can easily draw them, and use them with some ease. [6] It is understood, that certain parts of the brain are responsible for understanding, action and reaction of an individual with reference to grammar-verbs, nouns etc. in the language part. 'We don't think about all the things that are going on behind the curtain when we are doing something as simple as talking on the phone or reading the paper.' To map the brain regions connected to word processing, the Harvard group used magnetic resonance imaging technology that reacts to increases in the flow of oxygenated blood. [7]

Some symbols of religion like the temple, church or mosque, have been implanted in the brains several centuries ago. Even today, any person, on seeing these symbols, recognizes and gets influenced by them since there has been a perpetuation of these occupying a permanent place in the brains of the respective individuals. Like these symbols, there are mental images of physical, legal, administrative and spiritual symbols that should have been formulated by the 'consciousness', in the past. The reaction of a Muslim who is offered pork or for that matter a Hindu, who is offered beef, can be better imagined than described. It is obviously their respective religions which insist on certain animals being omitted from their food menu. This feature of the human brain is evidently the result of its previous development of 'consciousness' and 'mental images'.

By constant interaction between the communities in a given society, the 'individual consciousness' develops into a 'collective consciousness' in their own community as also the 'consciousness' of that particular 'society' develops into 'collective consciousness' of their 'country'. The leaders in the community-religious leaders and intellectuals play a dominant and significant role in shaping and formulating this 'consciousness' in the society. The length of the 'consciousness' depends on the nature of religion practiced by that society from ancient times, and that of the influences from other religions both in ancient and modern period, and in the 20th and 21st centuries; effect of modernity, secularism etc. If a given society is multi-religious, then its 'consciousness' is shaped by the dominant religion/religions in the past and present. The influence of a religion on an individual or a society (when practiced for centuries) can be a continuing force on some aspects, even when the individual or the society changed to some other religion. The marriage practices of south Indian Christians such as the wearing of a *mangala sutra* and *mettelu* or the caste system among the Christians and Muslims in India, can be cited as examples. These are evidently, the remnants of the Hinduism practiced by their forefathers.

Generally, while describing a society, terms such as culture, values, system of values, behaviour, norms, action etc. are used, which are in many instances, vague and do not give us an idea of how a society operates. Takdir Alisjahbana uses these terms in a vague manner. According to him, what we call culture is the totality of the manifestations of the life of a society which exists in any given period and is based on a certain system of values. Its system of values may have very varied characteristics. It may be clear, ordered and stable, with each value within the system hierarchically subordinated to a supreme value, but it may also be fragmented and indistinct, with tension and conflict apparent between the various values within it. Such characteristics do not depend on the type of culture alone, but on the stage of its development.

In its incipient days, when a culture is still healthy and vigorous, its system of values is usually clear and ordered. But if the culture has grown old enough to become feeble, its values become disparate and turn out to be contradictions. A society of this kind, is bound to lose has ,lost its sense of direction, as its ideals forfeit their sense of certainty. It is from the system of values that the members of a society obtain guidance and an orientation for their everyday existence and for the enduring pattern of their lives. The entire society with all its rules like custom, convention, statutory law etc. and all its institutions such as government, education, family, religion etc. is itself a concrete expression of that system of values and its purpose is to provide the means whereby both its members and the society itself, may realize the values of its culture in all their totality. [8]

In this definition, we see the classical sociological or anthropological approach towards religion and society. Religion is supposed to be part of government, education, family etc. Again, there is no clue as to how a 'system of values' develops in a society or whether that system has been different from the religion that the society has been practicing for several centuries. In truth, it is the other way round. The system of values is derived from the religion or religions the society had practiced and is still practicing. Alisjahbana, while describing the development of the Indonesian culture, says that '...although the cultural patterns in the Indonesian archipelago vary very widely owing to the varying historical influences, we can still see in Indonesian culture as a whole, three cultural 'layers', which can easily be distinguished. [9] They are Indigenous Indonesian Culture, Indian Culture and the Islamic Culture. [10] Evidently, Alisjahbana directly referred to the native religion in terms of Hinduism and Islam when he classified the Indonesian Culture into three layers. If we apply our concept of 'consciousness' or 'mental images', we can clearly see that the earlier 'Indonesian consciousness' was altered by Hinduism considerably, and later also, by Islam. As a result, a wonderful blend of indigenous, Hindu and Islamic 'consciousnesses' or 'mental images' was achieved by Indonesia and a distinct 'Indonesian consciousness' developed. This composite consciousness' can be seen all over Southeast Asia.

In the present paper, an attempt is made to apply the concept of 'mental images' or 'mental maps' or the 'consciousness' of the individual as well as the society in Southeast Asia, shaped by or altered by different religions, especially Hinduism. In other words, any given society operates by the 'mental images' or the 'consciousness' shaped by the religion/religions it practiced. Religion offers guidance and makes the individual and the society, follow strict discipline as dictated by it. The basic element of religion, especially of Hinduism, is ethics or morals. Unlike law, ethics seldom change, in a given society as ethics are shaped by religion. Religion also plays a role in offering solace to the day to day problems and struggles of men and women in society. But, the true meaning of religion is 'consciousness of God'. This 'consciousness' leads an individual and a society towards understanding God and salvation as also it shapes the total behavior and thinking of an individual as well as the society.

Before the advent of Islam in the Middle East, the 'consciousness' of the society was in a different form. There was a vogue for an idol worship and the concept of God was different. The ethics, morals and the 'consciousness' or the 'mental image' of the society were different. This was radically changed by the succeeding Islam. The definition and concept of God, worship, prayer, law, punishment, ethics, morals etc were totally shaped by Islam. The 'mental image' or the 'consciousness' of the Middle Eastern society was shaped by Islam since then. By and large, this consciousness seems to be continuing in the Middle East even today. The Islam influenced punishment of 'tooth for tooth and nail for nail', is still practiced in the Middle Eastern Islamic countries, as just the rules of Shariat including the dress code for women are followed. The rights on abortion, gay and lesbian marriages, gay bishops, even in the 21st century U.S.A. and Europe, are dictated by the ethics formulated by Christianity.

Therefore, the 'consciousness' of the 'medieval Christian society', one way or the other, is still in operation in the 'modern' U.S.A and Europe despite the progress in technology, secularism etc.

By contrast, though Islam became the dominant religion in Southeast Asia, the 'consciousness' or the 'mental images' it formed there in the Southeast Asian society, is drastically different from that of the Middle East. The reason, evidently, is that, no religion during the pre-Islamic era in the Middle East, could develop a long lasting 'consciousness' or withstand the 'consciousness' to the 'mental image' shaped by Islam. In the case of Southeast Asia, for example, in Indonesia, Islam was introduced in the 15th century A.D. But the 'consciousness' formed by Hinduism and Buddhism practiced for several centuries influenced heavily the latter 'consciousness 'of Indonesia partly shaped by Islam.

Here, Islam was not able to erase the earlier 'mental image' formed by Hinduism and Buddhism. We can call this Southeast Asian 'consciousness' as a 'composite consciousness' shaped by Hinduism, Buddhism, Islam and to a lesser extent by Christianity. This feature is unique when we compare this, with European countries where the 'consciousness' was predominantly formed and shaped by Christianity or the Middle Eastern 'consciousness' which was fundamentally formed and shaped by Islam. The history of the spread of Islam in the medieval and modern periods in Southeast Asia and how it emerged as a tolerant and accommodative variety, is too well known to be discussed in detail. [11]

The following observations make it clear, as to how the Indonesian 'consciousness' took its shape in the post Islamic period, until as late as the 19th century. By studying these examples from some nations, we can understand how religion acts as the 'mind' of the society. Islamic teachers in Indonesia usually did not attack the Hindu system directly but preferred generally to redefine the traditional religious practices and symbols under the covering canopy of the endless recitations of the Islamic confession of faith in Allah and the Prophet. 'Arab fairies took over for older spirits, and the heroes of the Hindu epics took on Sassinid Persian names'. [12] In both Malacca and Java, a Sufi pantheistic sect gained wide acceptance for a time under a presupposition not very different from Brahmanism. Malay spirit mediums or Shamans, found the same stimulation for their magical capacities under the Islamic regimen of austerity, fastings, and abstinence which the older Hindu rituals had previously provided.

The older culture retained its social vitality (our 'consciousness' or 'mental images'), including the adat law in Java. It absorbed the elements of Islam just as it had absorbed the Hindu and Buddhist accretions. Javanese standards survived the Islamic impact in the higher status of women, in village cohesion and wizardry, in music and puppet shadow plays, in the magical control of evil spirits and the calculation of lucky days, and even in the veneration of ancestral saints, including their embodiment in Hindu and Buddhist statuary. 'The Islamic confession of faith became for many a new kind of incantation.' [13] As late as early 19th century, the Muslim faith in Java was not firm; most of the Javanese paid little attention to prayer and fasting regulations, ignored the prohibition of the intoxicants and opium, and participated openly in the usury. They generally refused to eat pork, but many also observed the Hindu taboo on beef.

As the indigenous culture exhibited less vitality, the general practice in Malaya, which was Islamized more thoroughly than Java, was to add an Islamic confession to a familiar Hindu ritual. Allah's aid was invoked under a great variety of names; love charms from the Hindu Vedas were legitimized by appending a confession of faith in Allah. The Arab texts, properly written in perfumed ink at the right astrological moment, afforded protection from evil spirits. The Malay words for religion, fasting, teachers, heaven, and hell were all drawn from Sanskrit roots. The symbols of royal power and enthronement rites, including the twelve steps of purification, followed Brahman standards in Muslim Malaya as in Theravada Buddhist countries. Indra's thunderbolt symbol continued to appear on the armlets worn by the sultans. The capitals in Pahang were still called Indrapura and Brahman and the heralds functioned at their courts. Mount Meru astrological and numerological considerations influenced the organization of the palace area and the choice of the royal regalia. Hindu practices in cremation and in payment of bride dowries, also continued in Muslim Malacca after 1511 A.D. [14] The small city-kingdom of Acheh is an exception as it vigorously tried to follow Islam, in a purer form.

The cultural transformation accomplished by the advent of Islam in Indonesia, was not homogenous or revolutionary in its effects. Along with the pre-Hindu practices, much of the Hinduized Indonesian culture survived.

The ancient and medieval Southeast Asia, especially Indonesia, developed Hindu and Buddhist 'consciousness'. Besides economic and political factors, the religious symbolism like the royal ceremonies, temple rituals, mantras, secret symbolism of/in the Hindu temples etc. played a vital role in creating a long lasting 'consciousness' or shaping the 'mental image' of Southeast Asia. The Balinese believe that they are the descendants of the Aryans who came from Jambudvipa to liberate the island from the brutal tyranny of the demon king Mayadanava and these Aryans were considered as divine beings or as incarnation of the gods.

This belief is the result of the 'consciousness' shaped by Hinduism and Buddhism practiced by the people for many centuries. The study of Hinduism and Buddhism has a special significance since Hinduism and Buddhism are still living religions in Bali and some parts of Lombak. Not only during the ancient and medieval times, even now modern Balinese authors writing on religions, philosophy, ethics, worship, meditation and yoga couch their works in the Hinduistic vein, quoting scriptures and verses in Sanskrit. Therefore, Hinduism and Buddhism are matters of living faith not only in terms of mythology, tradition and history but also in terms of forming and shaping the 'consciousness' or the 'mental image' of the Indonesian society. There was no doubt a mix of native religious and ritual practices and those which came from India. In the temples of Bali, we can see the influence of pre-Hindu megalithic culture. In the Balinese temples, unlike in India, a stone seat is erected for Surya, into which the godhead is supposed to descend in an invisible form, when the priest invokes him. In ancient Indonesia and Polynesia, the sanctuary was always an open space, usually surrounded by a wall and often paved with great stones where all religious ceremonies took place.

Here, the great nature gods, such as the god of the sun, of the mountains, and of the sea etc., were invoked as well as the souls of the ancestors, whereupon they descended upon the megaliths which were erected for them. Some times, these were simply upright stones, some times, stone tables, consisting of a flat stone on top of some smaller stones, some times stone seats, consisting of a prostrate (female) stone and at the back as a support an erect (male) stone. These megaliths are destined for Surya the God of Gunung Agung etc. and are the forerunners of the shrines which are found at the last temple court of the Balinese temples. Ancestral worship also played a prominent role among the ancient Indonesians. Their souls are believed to descend on to the stone seats of the megaliths. Since the chiefs and the oldest men of the village were supposed to represent the ancestors, they had the right to sit down on these stone seats and at ceremonies and meetings. [15]

The Hindu caste system and the Indian religions can be studied even today in Bali and Lombok, where these have persisted with some novel features. Significantly, though Balinese introduced some new elements into Balinese Hinduism, some old feature which were lost in India were retained in Balinese Hinduism. The various kinds of *mudras* which went from India, have now become somewhat dull and meaningless movement of fingers in India, but they have still retained their vitality and primary importance in the rituals of the Balinese priests. [16] Even a casual look at some of the nationalist movements in Southeast Asia denotes a strong influence of religion in them.

Indonesia

The first organization with mass appeal dealing with broad political and economic issues, was the Sarekat Islam (Islamic organization), founded in 1912. Its focus of activity was economic and anti Chinese. The membership of the Sarekat was principally drawn from the *santri* and the lower *priyayi* classes. Educationally, the members were above the general level of Indonesians, mostly with an exposure to the west and from mostly middle class families. Because of the flexible nature of Islam in Indonesia and more specifically because of the influence of modernist Islamic doctrine, religion could play a significant role as a vehicle for Indonesian nationalism, the people's social and political aspirations. The most radical of the socialist groups with in the Sarekat fold, was the Indies Social Democratic Association (ISDA), founded in 1914 by the future leader of the Dutch Communist party, Henrick Sneevliet. Its Indonesian leaders included Semaun and Tan Malaka, who insisted on the Sarekat coming out openly as a political organization with a radical and revolutionary programme to overthrow the Dutch rule and the establishment of a socialist state. In 1920, they broke away to form the Partai Kommunis Indonesia (PKI), or Communist Party of Indonesia. The PKI detested Sarekat's emphasis on religion and preference for evolutionary rather than revolutionary means of attaining independence. In 1921, the Sarekat Islam prohibited its members from joining any other political organization and expelled the communists from the Sarekat.

One of the important factors for the failure is, PKI's secession from the Sarekat Islam, and the moderate central leadership of the Sarekat being closer to the bulk of religious minded Indonesians than the atheistic communists could ever hope to be. [17]

The development and consolidation of this system of 'consciousness' or 'thinking' of the Indonesian society spanned many centuries of the pervasive influence of Hinduism and Buddhism. For example, the theory of the divine origin of kingship, as in India (the Manusamhita says: *mahati devata hyesa nararupena tistati*), influenced also by the ancestral worship in

India and in the Indonesian society led to the deification of kings, rather in excess in Indonesia. The king came to be called *saksat trivikrama*, in the copper plate charter of Kancana. [18] This belief mustered strength and persisted with the passage of time so much so, that even today in Southeast Asia, the persons of the ruling class and caste or noble origin, are highly venerated, evidently as a result of the earlier 'consciousness' formed by the religion, though the concept of divine origin no more plays a role in the present India, or Southeast Asia.

Malaysia

At the time of the Portuguese arrival in Southeast Asia, Malacca was the most prosperous port of the region [19]. The Portuguese held Malacca for 130 years, often precariously because of the hostility of the Muslim rulers of nearby Johore, Acheh, and Java. A major weakness of the Portuguese policy was, linking religion with trade and politics. The uncouth, unruly and uncultured Portuguese of the time could not have impressed the Southeast Asians as being the torchbearers of European civilization. Even a great missionary, Saint Francis Xavier, was so disgusted with their debaucherous way of life that he shook the dust of Malacca from his feet vowing that he would never return to the cesspool of vices again. And their use of force in proselityzation, only created animosity in the minds of the Southeast Asians, who had historically been receptive to peaceful penetration of the religious influences. Consequently, the conversion to Christianity was very marginal. Instead, by trying to force Christianity on the people of the region, the Portuguese inadvertently glamorized Islam, as a weapon against the Portuguese oppression.

The rapid spread of Islam in the insular Southeast Asia in the sixteenth century, could be reckoned among Portugal's indirect and, indeed, unintended cultural contributions to the region. The new converts to Islam preferred to trade with their religious brethren and worked to prevent the trade from falling into Portuguese hands. [20] The method of propagating religion by the

Portuguese, was rapidly different from that of the amicable way of Indians, be it Hinduism, Buddhism or Islam. The Portuguese could not understand the general, receptive and accommodative nature of the Southeast Asians who successfully assimilated animism, Hinduism, Buddhism and Islam, when propagated peacefully and friendly.

Philippines

The Spaniards registered their great success in the field of religion in Philippines. [21] Unlike the other areas of Southeast Asia where Hinduism, Buddhism, and Islam struck firm roots, the northern and central Philippines, lacked a potent sacerdotal hierarchy.

By thc timc the Spanish arrived, Islam was already well established in Mindanao and Sulu archipelago. Elsewhere, a belief in animistic spirits and the supreme being called Bathala predominated. Such beliefs continued even after the people in the central and northern Philippines were converted to Christianity. Thus, many Christian converts wore necklaces of charms (anting anting) marking a compromise between Christianity and animistic folk beliefs. Many Filipinos still practice their traditional ancient rites, and continue to believe in the spirits like anitos and nunos. The church had to compromise on all these practices to attract the indigenous people to Christianity. The traditional Filipino social organization was hardly affected. The Philippinos identified themselves with the particular barangay (boat-load) that supposedly brought their ancestors from the Indonesian islands.

Myanmar

The British administration destroyed the old system. The most important single factor disruptive of Burmese society had been the British neglect of the Buddhist *sangha* (association). Traditionally, the monks had played a crucial educational and cultural role helping social cohesion. The opening of government and missionary schools competed directly with the Buddhist schools. The cultural inroads made by the west, were opposed by the Buddhist monasteries, which became centers of resentful opposition to the West. The Myanmar nationalist movement began with the establishment of the Young Men's Buddhist Association (YMBA) in 1906. Originally patterned after the Young Men's Christian Association (YMCA), the YMBA established schools conforming to the governmental curriculum requirements and also started interpreting lessons in Buddhist scriptures to counter the Christian missionary schools, which had been offering Bible lessons. The YMBA schools soon became centers of the community's social life and national awareness. They restored to religious organizations as a politically safe way to promote nationalistic sentiments. Buddhism provided common platform for those who deeply resented the colonial government's neglect of and injury into their faith. Numerous political parties of later times, were led by the former YMBA volunteers.

When the Japanese drove the British out of Myanmar, most of the Burmese, who had been fascinated by the Japanese slogan "Asia for the Asiatics" expected immediate independence. The warmth the Burmese held for the Japanese, soon dissipated because of the callous disregard shown by the Japanese military towards the Burmese susceptibilities. Atrocious acts such as face slapping of the village notables, forced labour, mandatory and unanswered requisitions for cattle and rice, and strangely enough fellow the *abuse of the fellow Buddhists, pagodas as latrines and the burning of the Buddhist scriptures* earned an undying Burmese hatred for the Japanese. [22] Not surprisingly, the insults meted out to religion, resulted in a war with the Japanese.

Vietnam

Vietnamese nationalism was nurtured in the cradle of the country's history of resistance to Chinese domination. The direct Chinese rule from 111 B.C. to A.D 939 and again from 1407 to 1428, was punctuated by numerous uprisings and final ouster of the northern invaders. However, the hatred of Chinese rule didn't preclude a willing absorption of some of the traits of the culture of China, the Chinese civil and moral law, the Confucian glorification of bureaucracy, the civil service examination system, and finally, the institution of an emperor, whose primary duties included establishing harmony between earth and heaven. More importantly, it should be noted, that the sinicization of Vietnam affected mainly the upper classes of society, while the villagers were left for themselves. The peasants clung to the Vietnamese habits of chewing betel nut and worshipping hosts of village genies, spirits of their ancestors, and mountains and rivers. They rejoiced in the ceremonies and festivals that predated the advent of the Chinese culture. In that sense, The Chinese domination has never posed much threat to the traditional modes of Vietnamese rural social behaviour as the French administration did, particularly, toward the end of the nineteenth century.

The French administration in Vietnam, destroyed the peasants' traditional civilization, which had persisted with the nominal external interference for two thousand years.

The activities of the major religions also tend to require the presence of physical structures where collective religious activities can be undertaken. In this manner, whenever a sentiment of believers of a given religion has become sufficiently large, pressure will develop to set up buildings to accommodate the religious activities that have to be undertaken collectively by members of the religious community. Each house of religion, be it a church, mosque, or temple, has its own requirements. Consequently, the house of religion of any given religion, tends to be distinctly different from that of other religions.

'Religious orientation is necessarily based on beliefs which are ordinarily not acceptable to purely rational thinking. They are rooted in sentiments and emotions which provide basic meaning in the life of the individual concerned. The teaching of a given religion, therefore, gives meaning to human existence as well as to the universe and its constituent elements. It also contains basic values that the believers are expected to adhere to, in their activities particularly, in their social relations.' [23] Therefore, religious cause seems to be a very significant cause even in the modern history of Southeast Asia

Terrorism: If we apply the concept of 'consciousness', 'composite consciousness' or the 'mental image' in the study of terrorism, we can see the clear difference in its formulation in the case of Southeast Asia. First and foremost, we have to be cautious in dividing extremism or terrorism into different categories, viz., terrorism for independence or regional autonomy based on a regional territory, based on language, based on ethnicity. The terrorism influenced or shaped by ideology like Marxism or Maoism should not be clubbed with the 'religious terrorism' as religion is also some times vaguely (which is incorrect) referred to as ideology. Political ideology like Marxism should not be compared with a religious ideology like militant Islam. The peaceful, tolerant and accommodative fabric of the Southeast Asian society formed by the earlier 'composite consciousness,' has been slowly deteriorating since 1990s, because of the Jihadi Terrorism. Evidently, these terrorist activities are influenced and shaped by the fundamentalist forces operating from the Middle East, Pakistan, and Afganistan etc.

As such, Jihadi terrorism was virtually unknown in Southeast Asia until recently, since the earlier 'consciousness' of Southeast Asia was shaped by Hinduism, Buddhism, Christianity and Islam which is utterly different from the 'Middle Eastern consciousness' shaped exclusively by Islam. Though the earlier consciousness continued to operate in Southeast Asia, the 'Islamic consciousness' seems to be threatening to erase the earlier 'composite consciousness', now discernible in some groups. We have to wait and see whether this phenomenon is temporary or long lasting. However, we can see one significant difference in Southeast Asia, in the history of Jihadi terrorism. Though radical Islam started in Egypt, Middle East, Pakistan etc. in the 1970s, and has been continuing till today, the militant kind of Islam was altogether absent in Southeast Asia until recently. As Jasjit Singh puts it 'If terrorism has acquired the personality, form and characteristics of a war, and is no longer a random phenomenon or merely targeted acts of violence like assassination of individuals, then it should be true that it is made in the *minds* of men, and then acted upon real life....'. [24]

He uses the term 'Intellectual foundations of terrorism' exactly in the same way as the present authors are using phrases like 'consciousness' or 'mental images'. 'All significant changes in human history, benign or destructive, have their roots in belief systems and ideas that shape actions of people.' [25] As discussed earlier, the 'belief system' is another name for religion. This observation strengthens our thesis that it is the 'consciousness' of the society or the groups in the society, that decides the direction of the society.

It is very important to note here, that the 'intellectuals' and 'leaders' in the militant type of Islam, are implanting the 'mental images' of Jihad in the Muslim youth. Though Islam mostly influenced extremist activities in Southeast Asia such as in Malaysia, Cambodia, Myanmar, they are regional in nature and are in pursuit of autonomy of their respective regions in their countries. Thanks to the 'composite consciousness', there has not been any terrorist activity, motivated by religion on a large scale, so far. Even when there were regional, religious problems or aspirations, Southeast Asians never gave a clear mandate to Islamic parties. For example, in Indonesia, where almost 90 per cent of the population is Muslim, in the 1955 election, six Islamic parties got 43 per cent of votes and the figure dropped to 38 per cent in the 1999 elections.

From the 1940s to 1960s, every Islamic party in Indonesia supported a constitutional amendment to oblige Muslims to uphold Islamic law or Sharia known as the Jakarta Charter. But in the 1999 election, the first free election following the Suharto regime, the Islamic championing of the Jakarta charter got only 4 per cent of the vote. In 2002, Indonesia's two largest Islamic organizations, Nahdlatul Ulama and Muhammadiyah, with a combined membership of 60 million, flatly rejected the Jakarta Charter. [26] If we go back to the period of independence, we must note that, even with a 90 per cent population of Muslims, they adopted a secular law and not an Islamic law evidently by the 'composite consciousness' they had inherited. This feature can be noticed all over Southeast Asia.

By contrast, because of the 'Islamic consciousness', the Middle eastern countries adopted Islamic law. If we observe the results of Malaysian general election in 2004, the National Front coalition got 90 per cent of the seats in the national parliament, a 77 per cent of rise from 1999 and also succeeded in getting control of 11 out of the 12 state governments at stake, and its share of the vote jumped from 57 per cent to 64 per cent, 'clearly signaling *rejection* of a fundamentalist Muslim party that wants to impose an *Islamic state* in the country.' [27] These election results of the Muslim majority countries, do not seem to suggest that these countries are getting more fundamentalist. 'In fact, these results don't surprise those who know that Muslims in Southeast Asia prefer a moderate path.' [28]

Though Islam is a political factor throughout this region, Islamic parties espousing Islamic fundamentalism, do not govern political life in the region and therefore the existence of the radical Islamic political groups in Southeast Asia, does not necessarily mean that the region is destined to live through Islamic-inspired violence that has occasionally racked the Middle East and South Asia. [29] However, there is a growing danger of these struggles being sucked into an Islamic jihad of international dimensions. What is often ignored or not discussed openly even by the academicians, is the opportunity for terrorism in Islam itself. A Canadian writer, Irshad Manji ridiculed many concepts of Islam leading to fundamentalism. [30] As Kumar Ramakrishna points out 'What can not be over-emphasised is that it is actually incorrect to hold that the Islamists are guilty of *twisting* Islamic scripture to jihad, against the West.

There is in fact, sufficient backing in the Quran and other sources, for a *fully legitimate defensive* jihad against any enemy judged by the prominent Islamic scholars as committing aggression against Islam. So at the level of justification for waging jihad, Islamic clerics need not distort scriptures. They merely need to persuade young Muslim men that the ummah is under attack and that legally speaking all Muslims are supposed to take up arms to defend the wider Muslim community.' [31] The radical ideologues, will precisely exploit any mistake or badly conceived action of the US or its allies, in order to sustain the Grand Narrative of Muslims under attack by the so called *Jewish-Crusader axis*. [32] 'The power of this message over thousands of young alienated Muslims,' especially when articulated by religious figures, should not be underestimated. [33]

In fact, progressive Muslim scholars ought to even 'fight fire with fire' at the grand strategic level, in the wider contest for the future trajectory of Islam with in Southeast Asia and even worldwide. In this respect, Indonesia, for all the bad press it gets for being a so-called haven for militant Islam, also happens to be a tremendous source of very erudite, learned Islamic scholars as Azyumardi Azra, Bahtiar Effendy, Narcholish Madjid Abdurrahman Wahid who are quite capable of engaging with their Middle Eastern counterparts on the finer points of Islamic law. They are especially well placed to mount well-reasoned critics of the cosmic Jewish-Crusader Axis versus Islam story line integral to Islamism of the Al Qaeda and JI kind.

Moreover, such scholars have sought to do away with the binary "us-verses-them" dichotomized world view favoured by the Islamists and have generally celebrated the value of religious pluralism. Abdurrahman Wahid, for instance, has called for a cosmopolitan Islam that is fully capable of functioning in a pluralistic religious and cultural context. [34] Indonesian scholars are extremely well placed, moreover, to lead more extensive discussions of topics such as various understandings of jihad; ways to reconcile the obligations of dual citizenship in both a national state and a transnational Islamic community or ummah; and the challenges and rewards of practising one's faith within a modern, secular, multi-religious society. [35]

Particularly important, is an elaborate discussion on the various interpretations of the *dar al islam* or realm of Islam. An open and extensive debate within the Muslim community in Southeast Asia, will also foster greater critical thinking that might well be an antidote to Islamist recruitment. [36] The growing influence of the TV channels, internet etc. in the world today, can be easily exploited by the extremist intellectuals, to plant images of hatred in the brains of the youth. Particularly vulnerable, are the ones aged between 14 and 20 years. If the present trend continues unchecked, in the coming two or three decades, Southeast Asia might not be as beautiful, hospitable and peaceful, as it is now.

To check and control the menace of terrorism, we should have a two pronged approach; must use the same means and methods that are used by the terrorists .As already explained, the intellectuals and leaders create and transplant 'mental images' of suffering and humility as well as the heroic deeds of the terrorists and suicide bombers who (are made to) believe that they would reach the abode of Allah .The governments, NGOs who are fighting terrorism should take the help of the moderates and secular intellectuals from their 'own' religion to create and to transplant the tolerant, secular and accommodative images in the vulnerable sections. They can use the electronic media and the internet, for this purpose, because of visual images and texts have a powerful and long lasting effect on the minds of the people, especially the teens and the youth.

The present authors wish to emphasize, that the terrorism influenced by religion, has to be tackled in a different way from the terrorism, caused by ideological, regional, ethnic, linguistic reasons since religion creates the 'consciousness' of the societies and states, which sometimes leads to terrorism of the international dimensions crossing boundaries of language, ethnicity, region, nation etc., The significant difference in the case of Southeast Asia, is its peaceful, accommodative and secular society formed by the centuries old 'composite consciousness'. Despite the impact of '9/11'or the Bali bombings of 2002 or the London Bombings, this consciousness is still continuing. When we compare this situation with that of the Middle East, we have to note that in Turkey, Iran, Iraq, Kuwait, or Saudi Arabia, as in the past, even now Islamic parties are gaining popularity and winning elections. The 2006 elections, just concluded in Palestine, gave a resounding victory to Hamas.

In Southeast Asia, so far no political party with a militant ideology was supported by the people. Even the non-violent Islamic parties like the Islamic Party of Malaysia (PAS), received a setback. The party's deputy president, Nashruddin Mat Isa said, that they wanted to change the image of the party and increase their appeal to non-Muslim, non-Malay Chinese and Indian minorities. 'We still want an *Islamic state*. But we want to discuss it in the context of *universal values* and *rights*, good governance, and justice issues.' [37] Thus, there is a fundamental difference in approach even when the aim is to achieve an Islamic state. The militant 'Islamic consciousness' is not born in Southeast Asia nor is it likely to be born. This is being exported from the Middle East, especially Saudi Arabia, and Pakistan. Another recent example of publishing a cartoon, depicting the Prophet Muhammad in a Danish newspaper, resulted in a spontaneous reaction from Saudi Arabia which recalled its ambassador to Copenhagen. An Iraqi militant group called for attacks against Danish and Norwegian targets. There were demonstrations in Karachi. [38]

When the newspapers in Germany and France reprinted the same caricatures, the protest seemed to take an 'Asiatic' turn, if not a global turn. Libya closed its embassy. The French daily *France Soir* defended that it has the right to caricature God; it published a cartoon of Buddhist, Jewish, Muslim and Christian gods floating on a cloud. [39] On February 4th, Afghanistan's Prime minister and Indonesian Foreign ministry, condemned the cartoons while the Iranian foreign ministry summoned the Austrian Ambassador, as representing the E.U., to protest against the publication. [40] There were demonstrations in Indonesia. On the same day, in the 'Hard Talk' in the B.B.C, the representative from the Danish daily *Jyllands-Posten* defended the publication, while the representative from the Danish Muslims, could not fully defend the reactions from the Muslim countries. By February 5th, demonstrators in London carried banners 'Kill the one who insults the Prophet' and demanded punishment by 'Islamic law' so that they can be 'executed'.

Iranian President ordered the cancellation of economic contracts with the countries, where the caricature is published. Pakistan's parliament passed a resolution condemning the cartoons as blasphemous and derogatory as protestors chanted 'death to France' and 'death to Denmark'. Interestingly, with the largest Muslim population in the world, in Indonesia, in Jakarta, about 300 persons invaded the lobby of the Danish embassy shouting 'Allahu akbar'(God is great). [41] On February 6th, the demonstrations in Kabul became violent, when 2000 protestors clashed with the police and four persons were killed. Iran's largest selling newspaper *Hamshahri*, announced an international cartoon contest on the Holocaust. In Malaysia, a newspaper ran one of the drawings, to accompany an article about the lack of impact of the controversy inside the country. [42]

The pattern in this controversy, indicates, that even today, in Southeast Asia, there is no perceptible 'militant consciousness' pervading the whole region, and still the 'composite consciousness' is in operation. The funding for the propaganda of the militant 'global' jihadi variety and the training for the same, is happening in the Middle East and Pakistan. Therefore, to counter this 'militant consciousness', efforts should also be made in *these centres* .Moderate scholars and intellectuals of Islam from these centres, should try to build a 'consciousness' of tolerant and moderate variety of Islam, in these centres. Also, more number of Islamic schools with a moderate outlook, should be established in Southeast Asia and youth and students should be encouraged to study in these schools rather than going to Saudi Arabia or Pakistan. More attention should be paid by the academicians, scholars and governments in trying to understand the functioning of a society in the light of 'religion' as it's the 'mind' and the 'consciousness' that it formulates.

The theme of 'mental maps' was introduced to us by our friend Dr. Marc W.D. Tyrrell, M.A., Ph.D., Research Associate, Research Resource Division for Refugees, Carleton University,

Ottawa, Canada. The discussions and arguments with Marc both in person and through internet, since September 2005, gave us an opportunity to develop the hypothesis for the present paper. We are grateful to him for his support and encouragement.

Notes

1. See editorial in H. Coward, J.R. Hinnells and R.B. Williams, (eds.), *The South Asian Diaspora in Britain, Canada, and the United States*, (Albany, 2000).

2. Catherine L. Albanese, *America Religions and Religion*, (Belmont, 1999), p.6.

3. *Ibid.*

4. *Ibid.*

5. Srira Chandra Vidyaranya, *The Daily Practices of the Hindus Containing the Morning and Midday Duties*, (Allahabad, 1918) (Reprinted 1979, pp.1-6.

6. *The Hindu*, January 23, 2006.

7. *Ibid,*, January 18, 2006.

8. S. Takdir Alisjahbana, *Indonesia in The Modern World*, (New Delhi, 1961), pp.1-2. Sociologist Durkheim used the term 'collective consciousness' as the basis for social solidarity and in the context of how the division of labour and the development of autonomous individuality affect the social solidarity .His concept differs from ours in the sense that our definition transgresses the division of labour in society. Our definition of religion, following Albanese, encompasses the total behaviour of the society, not restricted only to sacred things as defined by Durkheim. Our definition and concept also are different from Durkheim's 'sacred' and 'profane' or secular ones since the 'secular' nature of society is also, in our view, shaped by religion. Durkheim's approach to 'tackle religion sociologically' is substantially different from our approach of 'tackling society religiously'. For details, see Emile Durkheim, *The Division of Labour in Society* (W.D. Halls, Trans). London, 1893/1894, pp.38-39 and Emile Durkheim, *The Elementary Forms of Religious Life*, (Joseph Ward Swain, Trans. New York, 1912), pp.62-69.

9. S. Takdir Alisjahbana, n.8, p.9.

10. *Ibid*, pp.9-16.

11. An elaborate discussion can be found in Ahmad Ibrahim, Sharon Siddique and Yasmin Hussain, (eds.), *Readings on Islam in Southeast Asia*, (Singapore, 1985).

12. John F. Cady, *Southeast Asia Its Historical Development*, (New York, 1964), pp.170-171.

13. *Ibid*, p.170.

14. *Ibid*, pp.170-177.

15. Himansu Bhuşan Sarkar, *Some Contributions of India to the Ancient Civilizations of Malaysia and Indonesia*, (1970), pp.163-171.

16. *Ibid*, p.163.

17. D.R. SarDesai, *Southeast Asia: Past & Present*, (New Delhi, 1997), pp. 168-170.

18. See *Ibid*, p.133.

19. D.R. SarDesai, n.17, pp.64-66.

20. *Ibid*.p.66.

21. *Ibid*, pp.71-72

22. *Ibid*.

23. *Ibid*, pp.176-180.

24. Jasjit Singh, 'Strategic context of terrorism', in Wilson John and Swati Parashar (eds.), *Terrorism in Southeast Asia Implications for South Asia*, (Delhi, 2005), p.14.

25. *Ibid*.

26. Surat Horachaikul, 'Thailand' in Wilson John and Swati Parashar (eds), *Terrorism in Southeast Asia Implications for South Asia*, (Delhi, 2005), pp.216-236.

27. *Ibid*.

28. *Ibid*.

29. *Ibid*, p.220.

30. Irshad Manji, *The Trouble with Islam Today-A Wake-Up Call for Honesty and Change*, (New Delhi, 2005). Also see review of the book by Rasheeda Bhagat, *The Hindu*, February 5, 2006.

31. Kumar Ramakrishna, 'Singapore' in Wilson John and Swati Parashar eds. *Terrorism in Southeast Asia Implications for South Asia*, (Delhi, 2005), p.167.

32. *Ibid*.

33. *Ibid*.

34. John L. Espito and John O Voll, (eds.), *Makers of Contemporary Islam*, (New York, 2001), p.208, Cited in Kumar Ramakrishna, n.31, p.64.

35. *Ibid*, p.176.

36. *Ibid*.

37. *The Hindu*, January 21, 2006.

38. *Ibid*, February 1, 2006.

39. *Ibid*, February 3, 2006.
40. *Ibid*, February 4, 2006.
41. *Ibid*, February 5, 2006.
42. *Ibid*, February 7, 2006.

10

India's Southeast Asia Policy in the 21st Century: Perambulating the Horizon

Tridib Chakraborti

India's policy of new regionalism towards the Southeast Asian countries, and later on towards East Asia, arose, in response to the prevailing international environment at the end of the Cold War. In order to cope with this new.international ambience, New Delhi announced its New Economic Policy in July 1991 under the leadership of P.V. Narasimha Rao and this was guided more by an economic imperative etc., and judiciousness than by the political rhetoric. This paradigm shift in India's overall economic reforms and market liberalization policy naturally attracted many countries of Southeast Asia to develop better economic linkages with the former. The ASEAN members also realized the growing importance of the role of economic diplomacy in relations between nations and were also convinced of the seriousness of India in her liberalization policy. This new economic dynamics and re–orientation of foreign policy, promoted India to the role of a 'Sectoral dialogue' partner of ASEAN in January 1992 on trade, investment, tourism and science and technology. New Delhi's status in ASEAN was further elevated to a 'full dialogue' partner in 1995, as well as a member of the ASEAN Regional Forum (ARF) in 1996, and a Summit level partner (on a par with Japan, China and South Korea) in 2002.

So far, India has participated in four India–ASEAN Summit meetings, the first in 2002 at Phnom Penh, the second in 2003 at Bali, the third in 2004 at Vientiane and the fourth in 2005 at Kuala Lumpur. However, the most major achievement of India within the orbit of 'Look East' policy, has been its participation at the First East Asian Summit, held in December 2005, at Kuala

Lumpur, Malaysia. This unprecedented event, in the words of Manmohan Singh, the Indian Prime Minister, was a 'historic meeting,' which had marked an auspicious beginning of its ultimate integration with the East Asian region and can be viewed as a first stepping–stone for success for India to play a major role in global affairs in the twenty first century. This paper seeks to analyse India's Southeast Asia policy in the 21st century against the background of its past posture towards this region.

India's Southeast Asia Policy in the Cold War Years

With the end of the Second World War, the emergence of Cold War ushered in, an era of alliances and counter–alliances. India, in the perplexing new global environment, indicated clearly that it did not wish to be drawn into any alliance. This initiative of India, later came to be known as non–alignment that emanated out of strategic compulsions and socio–economic and political requirements of the country at that point of time. New Delhi's response to the bipolar world, therefore, stood differently from the experiences of the South East Asian countries, most of which, were getting entangled with the Cold War military alliances. Obviously, India's foreign policy strategy towards the Southeast Asian countries during the Cold War years, had always been determined by their super power relations and political turbulence within that region.

For all its cultural and religious links with Southeast Asia from the beginning of the Christian era, and the utmost sympathy and support of the Indian intelligentsia extended to the anti–colonial movements in the British, French and Dutch colonial possessions in Southeast Asia, the independent India's interest in the region began to wane soon after the heady days of the Afro–Asian Conference held at Bandung, Indonesia in April 1955. Although, our foreign policy decision–makers did recognize the strategic location of Southeast Asia – an area between the Pacific and the Indian Ocean controlling major trade routes and sea lanes used by foreign naval forces this region usually received the lower priority in the formulation of India's foreign policy strategy, for several reasons. [1]

Instead, West Asia began to receive much more attention than the Southeast Asian countries. [2] India forged her links with the countries of the Southeast Asian region, in terms of its non–aligned ethos based on the enunciation of certain principles namely anti–colonialism, anti–racialism, non–alignment etc. Therefore, India's foreign policy in the 1950s and 1960s towards the Southeast Asian countries, took the form of a "Diplomacy by Proclamation". During these years, India, in the capacity of the Chairman of the International Control Commission (ICC) for the three Indochina states (Vietnam, Cambodia and Laos), was mainly concerned with liberating Indochina from all external influences in order to ensure that the independence and neutrality of these countries were guaranteed by the Great Powers, especially, by the United States and China and to make this area, conducive to peace and non–alignment. However, this mission of India did not fully succeed. The only discernibly partial success of this policy, seems to be the enduring friendship that India could establish with Vietnam, which firmly resisted the US imperialism and military expedition.

The Indo-Soviet Treaty of Peace, Friendship and Cooperation (1971), which concluded on account of the global, political and strategic compulsions, had a telling effect upon the form and substance of relations which India had cultivated with the Southeast Asian countries, during the 1950s and early 1960s. In the changed scenario, the Indochina states – but not the ASEAN countries – started receiving more attention of the Indian foreign policy makers. This particular orientation of Indian foreign policy towards Southeast Asia, continued more or less, till the fall of former Soviet Union, in early 1990s. India's recognition of Heng Samrin government in July 1980, brought India and Indochina States closer, but alienated her from the ASEAN countries. [3]

This was in consonance with New Delhi's non–aligned image. Besides India's intimacy with Indochina states (mainly Vietnam) since 1975, their identical views and mutual support on many international and regional issues, made them intimate with each other. Though a developing country with its limited capacity and own resource constraints, India contributed a substantial credit assistance to Vietnam, to restructure its moribund economy. The rebuilding of Vietnam was in fact, considered by New Delhi, as a moral responsibility of the entire international community. This consistent political and economic support extended to Vietnam in 1970s and 1980s, clearly exhibited the priority that Vietnam received in Indian foreign policy. Therefore, India's interaction with ASEAN in the Cold War years, can be described as a tale of missed opportunities. In other words, India and ASEAN remained estranged during the Cold War years and their ties, in addition to being tenuous, lacked real essence. In New Delhi's calculations, cordial ties with ASEAN, did not produce any immediate and palpable gains, be it political, economic and strategic.

Shift in India's Economic Policy: The First Beacon of New Regionalism towards Southeast Asia

The years between 1989 and 1991, formed a watershed in the history of the 20th century witnessing a series of swift and bewildering events–like the reunification of Germany, the collapse of the Communist Parties in Eastern Europe and the Soviet Union and the eventual disintegration of the latter, the end of the Cold War and the impact of the Gulf war on the functioning of the United Nations Security Council and the Cold War giving a way to a new multi–polar world and new global order, characterised by positional shifts among all the actors. The ideological struggle between capitalism and communism vanished in no time and paved the way for globalization.

The world, previously polarized by an ideological struggle, rapidly got blended together as economic blocs. ASEAN, hitherto a bulwark against communism in Southeast Asia, rearranged itself within a short span of time to include Vietnam, Cambodia and Laos. Thus, in the post Cold War era, two main and often opposing trends emerged. The first was a willingness of the international community, particularly the US, to play a mediating role in settling conflicts from Northern Ireland to East Timor. In consort with this trend, was the break up of larger countries into smaller nations of Eastern Europe and the Commonwealth of Independent States of the former USSR.

Concurrently, neighbouring states realized the benefits of economic interdependence and blended into trading blocs. Among the most notable groupings were NAFTA, European Union and ASEAN. Thus, the sudden fall of the former Soviet Union, largely impelled New Delhi to make a frantic search for new trade doorways and links throughout the world, which led to a drastic paradigm shift in India's overall foreign policy outlook. India's shift in foreign policy priority towards ASEAN was expressed in bold relief when the Ministry of External Affairs, in its Annual Report: 1992–93, clearly stated that "India [has] decided to give a special policy thrust to its relations with the ASEAN," [4] and "desired improved relations with individual countries in the ASEAN region and with ASEAN as a collective entity." [5]

The evolving structural similarities between the economies of the ASEAN countries and India, and India's growing and affluent middle class of about 150 to 250 million out of a total of 900 million people, naturally attracted many Southeast Asian countries to develop a favourable economic and strategic partnership with India to initiate various measures for promoting better ties with New Delhi.

The ASEAN countries in the post–Cold War globalized phase, having vividly realized the growing importance of the role of economic diplomacy in the relations between nations, were also convinced of the seriousness of India in her liberalization policy. ASEAN's positive response was vindicated by India's elevation from 'Sectoral-dialogue' to 'Full dialogue' and finally a 'Summit partner' of ASEAN within a short span of time. Thus, ASEAN's growing ties with India brought to an end decades of ASEAN's relative ignorance of an economically emerging, politically matured and strategically vital and dynamic India. This close interaction also gave India an opportunity, to develop an "Asianist" discourse.

India's Southeast Asia Policy: Unmasking of Look East Diplomacy

The priority to the idea of New Regionalism given by India in its foreign policy agenda towards the Southeast Asian countries in the 21st century was officially unveiled by Indian Prime Minister P.V. Narasimha Rao through his 'Singapore Lecture' on September 1994. In this speech, Narasimha Rao clearly spelt out the basic outlines of India's Look East model and tried to convince his interlocutors that India was "worth their time and money" and that "investment in India is an investment in the future–a future not only for the investor, but for a population of one billion which will remain a force for stability for the world", and insisted on the fact that "in return, countries of the Asia–Pacific will find in India a reliable partner, a vast market; the process of whose development will simultaneously involve the renaissance of a great and noble civilization which we all share in some measure..." [6]

The Ministry of External Affairs (MEA), rudimentally used the term 'Look East' in its Annual Report of 1995–96 and officially accepted this policy as part of its major foreign policy agenda, although its genesis lay in the announcement of India's New Economic Policy in 1991 that took shape in the context of changing global order. While projecting the importance of this policy, the Report stated: "As a part of India's 'Look East' policy, efforts to strengthen the already existing good relations between India and the countries of Asia–Pacific and Southeast Asia continued during the year." [7] And pointed out "to the intrinsic and emerging complementaries between the dynamic and fast consolidating economies of ASEAN and the large economy of India." [8]

I.K. Gujral, the first Minister for External Affairs, to attend an ASEAN conference (July 1996, in Indonesia), expressed New Delhi's approval of the new relationship in the following emphatic terms:

"We see the full dialogue partnership with ASEAN as the manifestation of our 'Look East' destiny. This is because we are geographically inseparable, culturally conjoined and now more than ever before, economically and strategically interdependent and complementary .... What the 'Look East' policy really means is that an outward looking India is gathering all forces of dynamism – domestic and regional – and is directly focussing on establishing synergies with a fast consolidating and progressive neighbourhood to its east in the mother continent of Asia... [India] would work with ASEAN as a full dialogue partner to give real meaning and content to the prophecy and promise of the 'Asian Century' that is about to drawn upon US." [9]

On September 4, 2003, the External Affairs Minister of India, Yashwant Sinha, at the Plenary Session of the Second India–ASEAN Business Summit, held at New Delhi, officially declared:

"India's Look East Policy has now entered its Phase–II. Phase–I was focussed primarily on the ASEAN countries and on trade and investment linkages. Phase–II is characterised by an expanded definition of 'East' extending from Australia to China and East Asia with ASEAN as its core. Phase–II marks a shift in focus from exclusively economic issues to economic and security issues including joint efforts to protect sea lanes, coordination on counter terrorism etc. On the economic sphere, Phase–II is also characterised by arrangements for FTAs and established of institutional economic linkages between the countries of the region and India." [10]

Therefore, the announcement of 'Look East' Phase–II policy, naturally raised doubt as to why New Delhi proclaimed the Phase–II, without announcing the period of Phase I of 'Look East' policy earlier. Does this mean that the Phase I 'Look East' policy of India had failed to generate the impetus which the foreign policy makers have expected initially? The fact is, that India's 'Look East' policy in Phase I was confined to offering confidence–building measures to the countries of Southeast Asia. Hence, New Delhi, in its initial years, concentrated more on developing ties with the economically developed members of ASEAN (i.e. Singapore, Malaysia, Thailand, Indonesia and the

Philippines) rather than with members who were economically weak, politically vulnerable, religiously indifferent and belatedly incorporated into the ASEAN orbit (i.e. Brunei, Vietnam, Cambodia, Laos and Myanmar). Further, New Delhi's sluggish pace of reforms to liberalize its economy, lack of stable governments in New Delhi, and the 1997 financial crisis faced by ASEAN members, considerably hindered the pace and momentum of India's Southeast Asia policy, during the 'Look East' Phase I.

Sub-Regional Hubs Initiatives: The Bridge between India and Southeast Asia

In terms of geo–politics, the contiguous sea spaces of the Bay of Bengal – South China Sea could be regarded as hubs of geo–economic and geo–strategic advantages and opportunities for New Delhi to look far into the East. The safety and security of sea lanes of communications in the straits of Malacca, are best exemplified in joint naval exercises in the required support of the cooperative maritime security. This new environment, clearly provided the operational aegis for India aiming at political partnerships, physical connectivity through road and rail links, and free trade arrangements. Having realized the need for the development of the regional cooperation with its immediate neighbourhood, India has actively supported the creation of the bilateral and sub–regional groupings, which would complement New Delhi's larger goal of enhancing ASEAN–India ties, as well as to promoting the cooperation between the economically dynamic regions.

India, which has been a member of the Bangkok Agreement ever since its inception in 1975 (when India signed a regional preferential tariff arrangement with a number of Asian countries), had taken new initiatives at the intra–regional level by signing a Draft Framework Agreement for an FTA with ASEAN. The two agreements–FTA with Thailand (in October 2003) and Comprehensive Economic Cooperation Agreement (CECA) with Singapore–will act as a bridge between India and China, besides offering the Indian investors, an access to the large Chinese market, in its 'Look East' Phase II process.

India has also begun to realise that the economic integration of India's Northeast region (NER) with Southeast Asia, will foster regional political integration. New Delhi's initiatives of the transnational and sub–regional fora between NER and Southeast Asian states, allowed the artificial political barriers between the South and Southeast Asia, to recede. In 1997, India and Thailand proposed a new organization called BIMSTEC – Bangladesh, India, Myanmar, Sri Lanka, Thailand Economic Cooperation – as a vehicle to promote the trade and economic cooperation between countries around Bay of Bengal with initial focus on fisheries, tourism, energy, technology, trade and investment, transport and communication. This BIMSTEC sub–regional organization also effectively represented an inter–regional cooperation forum, bringing together the five SAARC countries and two ASEAN members (Myanmar and Thailand). In linking five South Asian countries with two Southeast Asian nations, it shattered the old notions of a South Asia as separated from its eastern neighbours. [11]

In February 2004, Bhutan and Nepal joined the grouping, and the organization retained its acronym of BIMSTEC which henceforth stands for the Bay of Bengal Initiative for Multi–Sectoral Technological and Economic Cooperation. Its members agreed that each country would take a lead role in planning and implementing programmes in the six areas targeted for cooperation. Through this initiative, India could reach out to the Southeast Asian region and beyond to the Asia Pacific community and play a constructive role in South and Southeast Asia. India's pro–active involvement in the Southeast Asian region, also testifies to India's security interests linked with the latter. To quote one strategic analyst:

"With an eye on China's growing influence in Southeast Asia, India has created an intriguing model of regional cooperation that plays on the historical, religious and cultural ties between India and Southeast Asia. More important, BIMSTEC conveniently lays out an ambitious agenda that will serve to advance India's security agenda in the region." [12]

Like BIMSTEC, the Mekong–Ganga Cooperation (MGC) scheme enabled India to get itself associated with five of its eastern neighbours–Myanmar, Thailand, Cambodia, Laos and Vietnam. The initiative, which was fructified on November 10, 2000, aims at the broadening and the intensifying of the joint efforts at economic cooperation between India and ASEAN and the development of the overland transport links between India and the countries of Mekong basin that would facilitate cross border movement of goods and services and thereby ASEAN-India FTA. [13] Therefore, two important cooperative frameworks at the sub–regional level, BIMSTEC and MGC, are also credited with the creation of a geographical connectivity, to promote the economic partnerships between India and the countries of Southeast Asia in the 21st century.

India's Southeast Asia Policy Gains Momentum

India's re-look, re-activated and re-accelerated new regionalism outlook towards Southeast Asia, reached its height when the first ASEAN–India Summit took place on November 5, 2002, in Phnom Penh. A Joint Statement, issued at the end of the Summit, clearly highlighted both the principles and the future road map of ASEAN–India cooperation. [14] It was agreed by India and ASEAN in this summit, that an ASEAN–India Annual meeting will be held regularly. While highlighting this Summit as a major achievement of India's 'Look East' policy, the Ministry of External Affairs in its Annual Report: 2002–03, described this Phnom Penh Summit, as "a significant development in our relations with ASEAN countries, as India joined the ranks of a handful of countries with which ASEAN has summit dialogues, namely, China, Japan, and South Korea. This up–gradation is a natural culmination of ten years of progressive engagement with ASEAN.... It is also a vindication of India's 'Look East' policy which seeks to build on our historical and cultural ties with the region to create a mutually beneficial strategic and economic relationship." [15]

India's growing proximity with the Southeast Asian countries, gathered more dynamism. Prime Minister Atal Behari Vajpayee who had attended the Second India–ASEAN Summit held in Bali, in October 2003, sent a strong message about New Delhi's seriousness and commitment in forging closer links with the region. [16] In this Bali Summit, three broad accords were signed on comprehensive economic cooperation, combating terrorism, and facilitating India's accession to the Treaty of Amity and Cooperation (TAC) with Southeast Asia. [17] Taken together, these steps promise a considerable improvement in the economic political and security cooperation between India and its Southeast Asian neighbours – extending from Myanmar to the Philippines.

India's Southeast Asia policy in 'Look East' Phase II, got strengthened further, when India and the ASEAN members signed a historic partnership pact entitled "India–ASEAN Partnership for Peace, Progress and Shared Prosperity" at the Third India–ASEAN Summit, held on 30th November, 2004, in Vientiane, Laos, attended by the Prime Minister Manmohan Singh. The pact outlines a multi–pronged action plan for boosting trade, investment, tourism, culture, sports and people to people contacts. In a significant move to strengthen economic ties, India and ASEAN members have decided to set up a RITA, to facilitate the flow of Foreign Direct Investment (FDI) in the region and to enhance regional monetary and financial cooperation besides promoting an Asian market.

The pact covers a long–term plan committed to creating a free–trade area by 2011, with five ASEAN members (Brunei, Indonesia, Malaysia, Thailand and Singapore) and by 2016, with the rest of the members. The Agreement, comprising a 4-page partnership accord and a 9-page action plan, addressed the "common challenges of economic, food, human and energy security," besides laying special emphasis on the infrastructure and transport development and the cooperation in gas–related projects. [18] Besides the road map, containing the areas of cooperation between India and Southeast Asian countries, the Third India-ASEAN Summit envisaged a cooperation in multilateral forums like WTO. This sort of cooperation, according to the Ministry of External Affairs of India, "forms the inner core of countries in ASEAN's political relationship with the rest of the world." [19]

Another landmark event of the Vientiane Summit was, that on 30 November, in Vientiane, the Indian Prime Minister and ASEAN leaders flagged off the India–ASEAN car rally. [20] In the words of the Secretary–General of ASEAN, the car rally "is not merely a social encounter between ASEAN and India, but a trial–blazing beginning." [21]

At the fourth ASEAN–India Summit, held in Malaysia on December 13, 2005 and chaired by Malaysian Prime Minister Abdullah Ahmad Badawi, the ASEAN members expressed their deep satisfaction with the overall growth of ASEAN–India dialogue relations since the upgrading of these relations to the Summit level in 2002 and also thanked India for its contribution of $5 million to the ASEAN–India Cooperation Fund and $5 million towards ASEAN Development Fund. They also discussed the issue of exploring every avenue for enhancing and strengthening their partnership further in the face of the growing challenges of globalization, terrorism, rising oil prices and the threat severely posed by avian influenza and other emerging diseases. In this meeting, the Indian Prime Minister put forward the six point proposals before the ASEAN community, pertaining to various sectors:

- Establishing Centres for English Language Training in Cambodia, Laos, Myanmar and Vietnam. The objective would be to equip students, civil servants, professionals and businessmen with adequate skills relating to English language and communication abilities;
- Proposed that a tele–medicine and tele–education network would be set up for Cambodia, Laos, Myanmar and Vietnam, and these countries would be linked with India through a satellite–based network;

- A special training course to be organized for diplomats from ASEAN countries through the Foreign Service Institute;
- Proposed an India–ASEAN Technology Summit in 2006, through the Department of Science and Technology and Confederation of Indian Industry (CII);
- Proposed that Education Consultants India Ltd. would organize education fairs and a road show in ASEAN countries in 2006. Both public and private Universities and educational institutions, would be associated with the initiative;
- It was proposed, that an India–ASEAN IT Ministerial and Industry Forum be organized in 2006 through the Department of Information and Technology. [22]

Besides these proposals, the Indian Prime Minister Manmohan Singh said, that New Delhi was ready to adopt a "flexible and pragmatic" approach to the proposed Free Trade Area (FTA) agreement with ASEAN, and made a forceful plea for a Pan–Asian FTA and for establishing an Asian Economic Community, on the lines of the European Union and NAFTA.

India's Role in the ASEAN Divide Problem

The Initiative for ASEAN Integration (IAI) has been a regional framework that aimed at narrowing the gap in development, within ASEAN and at enhancing regional integration. This issue had serious implications for ASEAN that had faced the development gap problem after achieving the ASEAN 10 by admitting the CLMV (Cambodia, Laos, Myanmar and Vietnam) countries in the late 1990s. At the Fourth Informal Summit in November 2000, at Singapore, the Singapore Prime Minister Cooh Chok Tong proposed the IAI, that aimed to narrow the development divide between ASEAN's old and new members, by way of promoting equitable economic development, and help alleviate poverty in the new member-states. In February 2001, ASEAN Secretariat and representatives of CLMV, agreed to set up the Task Force on the IAI. At the thirty fourth ASEAN Ministerial Meeting (AMM) in July 2001 in Hanoi, the Foreign Ministers recognized the need to address the development gap by issuing the Hanoi Declaration on Narrowing Development Gap for an effective ASEAN Integration. The declaration contained basic guidelines for measures in four areas: infrastructure, human resource development, information and communication technology, and regional economic integration. In November 2002, ASEAN leaders approved the IAI work plan for Narrowing the Development Gap within ASEAN. The initial number of projects in the Work Plan was 48, and the number increased more than 100 by May 2005.

Besides the ASEAN–6 contribution to the IAI Work Plan, the nine Dialogue Partners have also supported IAI Work Plan projects by providing funding assistance to the less fortunate members of ASEAN. The top five donors are the Republic of Korea, Japan, Australia, European Union and UNIDO (Norway). India being a responsible 'Dialogue Partner' of ASEAN, had actively played a very constructive role on the IAI programme by undertaking Railway Training Programme, India-Singapore Joint Training Programme, and an Entrepreneurial Development Project. [23] This active focus of New Delhi on the IAI, have been looked upon by ASEAN countries as a sign of India's commitment to ASEAN and its processes.

India's Southeast Asia Policy: The Economic Sequel

India's Southeast Asia policy in the post–Cold War years, started with a lot of impetus, but it was not a unilinear projection. One can classify this policy into three separate phases. The first phase marked a prodigious earnestness and a flutter of activity and exchanges. The second one exhibited by mid–1990s, when there was considerable cooling down of the earlier ardor on the both sides, got further depressed by the 1997–98 financial crisis. The third and the latest phase displayed the revival of interest and currently there has been a upward mobility in the India–Southeast Asia economic and political ties.

India and ASEAN as regional trade partners, offer a huge and attractive interconnected, geographically contiguous market of more than 1.5 billion people. There is also a compelling rationale for strengthening the business relationship between India and the ASEAN in view of their emerging complementary economies. Both India and ASEAN have attained higher growth rates in their exports than the global average in the last two decades. India's exports to ASEAN countries in recent past, have too registered much higher growth rate in comparison with the other important destinations, although imports from other regions, have achieved faster growth than ASEAN's imports into India.

The deepening of the ties between India and the ASEAN over the years, have resulted in an upward trend in their trade ties which is due, in large part, to a sharp increase in India's exports to the ASEAN member states. In 1980, ASEAN accounted for 3.6 per cent of India's exports to the world which by 1992 increased, nearly 6 per cent. In terms of value, India's export to ASEAN countries, had more than quadrupled in 1992. Subsequently, the trade turnover declined quite sharply in 1997 and 1998, as a result of the 'East Asian Financial Crisis', mostly due to sharp fall in New Delhi's exports. Since 1999, there has been a recovery and the trade flow once again started its normal long–terms trend. Though the Balance of Trade, save in 1993–94, has always titled in favour of the Southeast Asian countries (Table 10.1), India's trade with ASEAN increased very rapidly. In the last five years, for instance, India's exports to ASEAN have increased by over 280 per cent while its imports from ASEAN countries have also increased by around 220 per cent. India's trade of US $ 16552.81 million with the Southeast Asia countries, in 2003–04, was 4 times more than that, in 1992–93. If the total merchandise trade of about $ 17 billion in 2005 is of any indication, the exports target of $ 30 billion to the region by 2007, looks very realistic. Compared to other regional groupings in the world, ASEAN is the fifth most important market for India's exports and the fourth, in terms of imports. In 2004, for example, ASEAN accounted for 9.34 per cent of India's global trade of $ 142 billion which remained much below the potential. While Malaysia and Singapore have been India's most prominent trading partners,

India's trade, in value terms, with Laos, has been the least among the Southeast Asian countries, (as per 2003–04 trade statistics).

Table 10.1: India's Trade with Southeast Asia (Value in US $ Million)

Year (April–March)	Exports	Imports	Total Trade	Balance of Trade
1990–91	748.00	1474.00	2222.00	–726.00
1991–92	1022.30	1274.60	2296.90	–252.30
1992–93	1508.25	2230.24	3738.49	–721.99
1993–94	1981.71	1950.00	3931.71	+31.71
1994–95	2326.27	3059.50	5385.76	–733.23
1995–96	3177.77	3881.88	7059.65	–704.11
1996–97	3353.46	4492.58	7846.04	–1139.12
1997–98	2987.21	5177.91	8165.12	–2190.70
1998–99	2090.35	5865.13	7955.48	–3774.78
1999–00	2721.05	6281.73	9002.78	–3560.68
2000–01	3362.20	5210.49	8572.69	–1846.31
2001–02	3945.86	5767.12	9712.98	–1821.26
2002–03	5219.16	6565.61	11784.77	–1346.45
2003–04	6494.35	10058.46	16552.81	–3564.11
2004–05 (April–August)	3232.98	4603.25	7836.23	–1370.27

Source: Compiled by the author from various tables and pages based on Ministry of Commerce Annual Reports, Government of India, New Delhi, April–March 1990–91 to April–August 2004.

India's economic liberalization also attracted ASEAN's investment in crucial infrastructure sectors, such as telecommunications, heavy industry, fuels, hotel and tourism services, chemicals, fertilizers, textiles, paper and pulp and food processing. Malaysia, Thailand and Singapore have become the major source of FDI into India. From a negligible amount in 1991, ASEAN's cumulative approved FDI has, so far reached more than

US $ 5 billion. However, compared to other dialogue partners of ASEAN, the investment flows, like the volume of trade between India and ASEAN, remained very low. Between 1993 and 2003, India accounts for 0.2 per cent of FDI in the ASEAN region while the inflow of FDI from ASEAN represents, 3.4 per cent of the total FDI flows into India.

India's Southeast Asian Policy: Strategic Gains

India's Southeast policy in the post–Cold War years, has benefited her considerably on the defence and strategic front in this region. The resolution of the decade long Cambodian crisis and the sea change in ASEAN's outlook towards Vietnam, as a potential ally rather than an enemy, generated a fervent hope, that the winds of peace would at last blow over the entire Southeast Asian region. This favourable situation in the region and the scepticism of some countries regarding China, gave India an opportunity to enter the region. In fact, many Southeast Asian nations began to look upon New Delhi as a power for a kind of 'balancing role.' These convergence of interests of India and Southeast Asia created a new strategic interaction in the post–Cold War years. In its report "ASEAN Regional Forum's Annual Security Outlook," (2001), the Government of India argued that its security concerns in the post–Cold War years, extend beyond the conventional geographical definition of South Asia. New Delhi made it clear that "given its size, geographical location and trade links, security environment ranges from the Persian Gulf to the Straits of Malacca across the Indian Ocean including the Central Asian region in the North–West, China in the North–east and Southeast Asia." [24] But, China, which always regarded the Asia–Pacific region as vital to its security, became averse to any Indian attempt to intrude into this region.

India has a vital interest in seeing that the Straits of Malacca remain in friendly hands. Similarly, the sea lanes to further east, are growing in significance for its energy security, as New Delhi is looking for oil and gas supplies from Myanmar, Vietnam and Indonesia. Further, the idea of upgrading the security structure of the Andaman and Nicobar islands and the surrounding areas by way of establishing a 'Far Eastern Maritime Command' at Port Blair, clearly exhibited New Delhi's seriousness about its maritime policy in the post–Cold War years. This importance has grown further due to growing Chinese presence in the waters close to India, in the form of radar facility on Myanmar's Coco islands capable of providing Beijing necessary information regarding India's missile test programme in Orissa.

Besides this, the Naval Operations Directorate's announcement in April 2000 about New Delhi's plan of unilateral naval exercises in the South China Sea, clearly signals its move to expand operations from the north of the Arabian Sea through the South China Sea and to establish an expeditionary–capable force that will not only threaten China's areas of operation but also alter the balance of naval power in the Asia–Pacific region. Thus, New Delhi's plans stem from several important reasons like counter–piracy, protection of trade routes. As against such a background, India's Southeast Asia's 'naval diplomacy', embodying new naval doctrine, has been high on the agenda of Indian foreign security policy. This resulted in a number of confidence building measures (CBMs) being undertaken by India and greater appreciation of Indian maritime capabilities by the Southeast Asian countries. New Delhi's joint naval exercises, regularly held with Singapore, Malaysia, Indonesia, Vietnam and other countries of Southeast Asia, clearly manifested the formation of a more systematic and strategic 'Look East' policy.

Furthermore, in the post–Cold War years, militarily, there has been a change from security dialogue and joint naval exercises to a role stressing joint training and sales of defence equipment. This change comes at an appropriate time, since many Southeast Asian countries have increased their military budgets and enhanced their security strategy in the face of increasing Chinese military might. This naturally forged defence ties between India and many countries of Southeast Asia (like Vietnam, Thailand, Malaysia, Singapore and Indonesia) in areas such as exchange of defence personnel, transfer of relevant technologies and repair, maintenance and upgradation of defence information and equipment.

Besides naval exercises and defence ties, Indian navy's role in the Tsunami disaster in late December 2004, has no doubt, demonstrated the extended neighbourhood policy of New Delhi and strengthened its strategic ties with the countries of Southeast Asia. The Tsunami environmental disaster offered a window of opportunity to restrengthen New Delhi's regional relations within the cooperative conceptual framework of human security. The Tsunami environmental problem also seemed to have forced the foreign policy makers of India to wake up fully to the strategic importance of the water ways around it.

India's Southeast Asia Policy: From Look East to Move East

One of the path breaking achievements that India has made during Manmohan Singh's visit to Kuala Lumpur in December 2005, is its participation at the first East Asian Summit (EAS). [25] The EAS represents a logical next step forward from the ASEAN + 3 process. Yet the EAS is more than a near and next extension of the ASEAN plus. One significant difference is the effort to include other states. The criteria that have been laid down for new members include, an acceptance of the Treaty of Amity and Cooperation (TAC), a central agreement on inter–state relations among ASEAN states and others in relation to ASEAN. Based on such criteria, the EAS has been expanded beyond the ASEAN + 3 states and the new entrants are India, Australia and New Zealand. Surprisingly enough, the United States has been excluded altogether from this East Asia Summit. [26] The formation of the EAS can be termed as the first step for establishing an East Asian Community on the lines of the European Economic Community, a landmark decision to create a forum for dialogue on broad, strategic, political and economic issues of common interest, with the aim of promoting peace, stability and economic prosperity in East Asia.

Prime Minister Manmohan Singh, who described EAS as a "historic meeting" said, that it was important for India to be in a group that had the "potential to play a major role in global affairs. Its composition, its evolving agenda and format give it the potential to play a major role in global affairs. India's presence in this group from its very outset is an opportunity we value." [27] Thus India's presence and participation, first in a Summit with the ASEAN and then in the First East Asian Summit, are no doubt a good beginning to the country's ultimate integration with that region. In fact, rapid integration with East Asia as part of India's 'Look East' Phase II policy, has made the region India's biggest trade partner, ahead of the EU and the US.

India has been evolving an FTA with ASEAN, and is presently studying Free Trade Area's (FTAs) with Japan, China and South Korea and trying to integrate as a part of the growing web of FTAs in the region. In the East Asian Summit, economy and trade formed the core issues and a historic decision was taken to work towards the world's largest free trade area, covering some developed and developing economies. In the Kuala Lumpur declaration, the 16 members have committed themselves in promoting "development, financial stability, energy security, economic integration and growth", besides narrowing the development gap through technology transfer.

For New Delhi, the EAS can be seen as the penultimate step in its integration with the East, and a stepping–stone to joining the Asia Pacific Economic Cooperation (APEC) forum based on solid state of emerging ties with the countries of Southeast Asia. In other words, in the context of emerging regionalism idea in Asia, different countries are signing multiple agreements and are vying with each other to emerge as hubs. With its excellent trading and transport links and emerging preferential trading arrangements with South, Southeast, and West Asian countries, India could emerge as a hub between East on the one hand, and South, West and Central Asian countries on the other, where Southeast Asia could act as a bridge between these countries. [28]

Once India's Southeast Asia policy in the 21st century against the background of its past posture through the Cold War and post–Cold War years is analyzed it becomes amply clear that

India's interaction with the countries of Southeast Asia before the fall of Soviet Union, was built on an idealistic connection of Asian brotherhood based on shared experiences of colonialism and cultural ties. New Delhi's interaction with the then ASEAN members in the cold war period, can be described as a narrative of over–sighted opportunities, since India had declined to get confederated with ASEAN, despite positive gestures from the latter. India's priority towards Southeast Asia in the Cold War years, mainly in the 1970's and 1980's (unlike 1950s' and 1960s'), was towards the Indochina states, rather than the ASEAN members. The dynamic of the Southeast Asian region is at present determined as much by trade, investment and production, as by history and cultural leanings. It was only through the formulation of the 'Look East' policy in the early 1990s', that the Southeast Asian region has received its uniform importance in India's policy planning. This in turn, has led to a better appreciation of the benefits of integrating foreign and economic policies. Such an approach has naturally made the economically vibrant ASEAN countries, more attractive towards India, and has led to the new phase of "rediscovery and renaissance" in India's pragmatic outlook towards the countries of Southeast Asia.

India's comprehensive new Southeast Asia policy has grown over more than one and half decades. The intensification of the economic ties with the Southeast Asian countries, have quietly led New Delhi into a Second Phase of its 'Look East' policy. Its Phase–I policy was characterised by trade and investment linkages. Phase–II is marked by creation of arrangements for free trade area and for establishing institutional economic linkages between the countries of the region and India. The Phase–II initiative of New Delhi has an ample geographic scope because, from the initial focus on Southeast Asia, it presently includes East Asia and the South Pacific. It is clearly marked by an expanded definition of the 'East', stretching from Australia to China and East Asia with the ASEAN as its path. The recent East Asian Summit, held in Kuala Lumpur on December 14, 2005, has been a major achievement of her 'Look East' policy, which can serve as forward posts for New Delhi's trade and investment initiatives towards Northeast Asia and Southwest Pacific. India, having realized ASEAN's strategic importance in the Asia–Pacific region, has continued its cordiality with the Southeast Asian countries in the 21st century.

It also tried to use the ASEAN platform as a springboard for its further integration with the Asia–Pacific region, NAFTA and other successful world trade groupings. Comprehending the potential for gains of the Asian Economic Community (AEC), India has actively searched for cementing its ties with the ASEAN plus three nations by way of involvement in cooperative frameworks both at the sub–regional and bilateral levels. New Delhi's participation in the East Asian Summit, could open up a fresh dimension to the efforts at regionalism in Asia, which were hitherto being confined to the countries of Southeast Asia. The recent defence agreement between India and China, signed on May 30, 2006, which aims to develop a 'strategic and cooperative partnership for peace and prosperity", is a clear signal of a sustained dialogue between these two countries, in the context of a changing global environment.

Furthermore, it can be argued that India's participation in the East Asian Summit, might make the grouping more balanced and less susceptible to domination by any particular big country in the region. Therefore, it can be said that India's policy of new regionalism towards the countries of Southeast Asia, has ushered in a dense network of collaborative relations with the countries of ASEAN and East Asia. It seems that finally, India's Southeast Asia policy in the post–Cold War years, has sensitized the Indian foreign policy makers to the need of embracing a concept of regional integration. In the context of the changing global order, New Delhi is looking at present towards the Asia–Pacific region with an anticipation and a hope. However, this outlook and the attendant initiatives, need to be sustained steadily over a long period with the focus on the core objectives. On the whole, India's Southeast Asia policy in the 21st century, has evolved a definite destiny of its own and is poised for further improvements in the coming days.

Notes

1. India began to turn away from the Southeast Asian affairs, mainly for the following reasons:

- New Delhi's pre–occupation with Pakistan;
- With Southeast Asia, specially Indochina, emerging as a major arena of contention between the two Super Powers in the 1960s, the non–aligned India's ability to influence the events in the strategic region, was extremely limited; and
- Military defeat at the hands of China in 1962 circumscribed New Delhi's ability to act outside the borders although some countries of Southeast Asia wanted India to counter Chinese influence and leadership in the region.

2. Concentration of Indian capabilities–economic, technological, diplomatic–in the West Asian region became directly related to the dramatic increase of oil the prices that begin in 1973. Besides India's dire need for assured sources of oil supply at concessional prices, it was interested in carving out a niche for itself in the booming economics of the oil–rich Gulf region. The availability of a large pool of technologically skilled manpower in India, the considerable sophistication of its industrial and manufacturing base, and its capacity to export relatively cheap semi–skilled and unskilled labour, combined, to provide India with a respectable share of the booming market available in the oil producing countries of West Asia.

3. For details see Tridib Chakraborti, *India and Kampuchea: A Phase in their Relations – 1978–81*, (Minerva Associates, Calcutta, 1985).

4. *Annual Report: 1992–93*, Ministry of External Affairs, Government of India, New Delhi, 1993, p.27.

5. *Ibid.*, p.6.

6. *P.V. Narasimha Rao Selected Speeches: 1994–95*, July 1994 – June 1995, Vol.IV, Publication Division, Ministry of Information and Broadcasting, Government of India, (New Delhi, 1995).

7. *Annual Report: 1995–96*, Ministry of External Affairs, Government of India, (New Delhi, 1996), p.17.

8. *Ibid*, p.viii.

9. *The Times of India,* 25 July, 1996.

10. See www.meaindia.nic.in/.

11. C. Raja Mohan, "A foreign policy for the East," *The Hindu*, 24 July, 2004.

12. For details see http://www.atimes.com/atimes/South Asia/FB11Df06.html.

13. A major vision of this programme, is to establish a Delhi–Hanoi road and railway link in the near future, and also to develop transportation networks including the East–West Corridor project and the Trans–Asian highway. Further, the linkages between India and these countries of Indo–China region over land, might give New Delhi, an opportunity to speed up economic development of its North–East region.

14. The Summit also outlined several areas of cooperation, namely trade and investment, human resources development, science and technology including information technology and people–to–people interaction. The leaders further agreed to consolidate the close economic relations by promoting trade and investment, facilitating market access, improving the flow of technology and enhancing the flow of and access to trade and investment–related information and decided to work towards AFTA–India linkages.

15. *Annual Report: 2002–03*, Ministry of External Affairs, Government of India, (New Delhi, 2003), p.24.

16. The Indian Prime Minister's offer included a unilateral "open skies" policy to specified Southeast Asian airlines, which will be allowed free, to operate daily flights to the four Metros in India and unlimited flights to eighteen tourist destinations in India and also New Delhi's decision to extend special and differential treatment to ASEAN countries, depending on their levels of development, to improve their market access to India.

17. *Annual Report: January 2003 – March 2004*, Ministry of External Affairs, Government of India, (New Delhi, 2004), p.38.

18. As part of cooperation in infrastructure, the plan called for expediting the completion of India–Myanmar–Thailand trilateral highway and its extension to Laos and Cambodia, apart from strengthening air connectivity, and agreed for investment promotion and double taxation avoidance. It also aims at improving financial stability, regional monetary and financial cooperation and further development of the capital markets of the region.

19. See pib.nic.in/release/release.asp?relid=6154

20. This rally, which had lasted for a period of 20 days and travelled across 11 countries, covering nearly 8,000 kms, was an important step in New Delhi's ambitious plan to link its NER with Southeast Asia. This car rally thus, opened up the frontier and land locked the areas of India and ASEAN, linking the peoples at the common borders. The major objectives of this car rally were:

- To demonstrate the proximity of India with the Southeast Asian countries;
- To develop public awareness of India–ASEAN relations;
- To promote connectivity, especially road–transport;
- To enhance trade, investment, tourism and mass links between India and the ASEAN members.

21. For details of speech, see www.aseansec.org/16594.htm.

22. See, http://pmindia.nic.in/visits/content.asp?id=88.

23. India has successfully completed the "Railway Training Programmes for 48 trainers from CLMV countries in India." In addition, India is presently implementing a project namely, "India–Singapore Joint Training Programme for CLMV in English language Training". New Delhi is also involved in an Entrepreneurial Development project in each of the CLMV countries. The objective of this project for India is to provide technical and advisory services to CLMV for the establishment of Entrepreneurial Development Institute in each of these countries, as part of efforts to train entrepreneurs and to prepare small enterprises for those who face the challenge of globalization. So far, New Delhi has already established Entrepreneurship Development Centres in Cambodia, Laos and Vietnam, and in Myanmar, it will be set up soon. See, www.aseansec.org/ pdf/IAIdoc16904.pdf.

24. *The Dawn*, 18 June 2001.

25. The road to this first EAS, has been paved by events in recent years, especially the ASEAN plus formula. This process has brought together, several leaders from the 10 ASEAN members with their counterparts from the northeast Asian States of China, Japan and South Korea. Indeed, the ASEAN + 3 process has grown beyond summitry to provide a framework for initial Asian Cooperation on diverse transnational issues such as finance flows (with the Chiang Mai initiative) and public health.

26. The understanding among the members is not to allow any non–regional powers to get into this group. For the US, the EAS represents a diplomatic challenge. Although the US is a leading trading partner for all EAS participants and has security relationships with

significant players including Japan, the US would not participate in the Summit, as long as it is unwilling to accede to the TAC, which requires an agreement not to introduce nuclear weapons in the area. See http://yaleglobal.yale.edu/display.article?id=7484

27. See, www.literateworld.com/india_lead1.htm.
28. See, www.bilaterals.org/article.php3?id_article=2952.

11

India in 21st Century Asia-Pacific: Some Aspects of Strategic and Economic Issues

S. Gopal

For the past few decades, the economies of a number of countries in the region, referred to as Asia pacific have been dynamic. In the post world war II period, the rapid economic growth of Japan and the Newly Industrialised Countries (NICs) has thrust Asia pacific into the world stage of international trade, technological innovation and foreign investment. The gravitational shift of the economic growth from Atlantic to Asia Pacific since 1970s, has inspired many to call the current century as the "Pacific Century. The economies of China, Japan, India, – a late comer, Indonesia and South Korea particularly dominate the region.

China, taking purchasing power parity as a measure, dominates with a consistent robust growth. Both China and India are set to drive the economic growth in the region. In terms of Purchasing Power Parity (PPP) China's per capita Gross Domestic Product is already about $5,700, or more than four times, the more often cited 2004 level of $1,230. In both the measures, China's GDP is roughly double that of India's. According to one report (*Mapping the Global Future* National Intelligence 2020 Project Report), by 2020, China's Gross National Product (GNP) will exceed that of individual Western economic powers except the United States. India's GNP will have overtaken or be on the threshold of overtaking the European economies. In fact, China revised its economic data on December 20, when $280 billion were discovered in hidden economic output in China, for 2004. China's gross domestic product in 2004 was nearly $2 trillion, not $1.65 trillion as previously reported. With its GDP up at 17 per cent, China was the sixth-largest economy in the world, last year. With an expected big growth in 2005, its economy may already be ranking fourth, trailing only that of the United States, Japan and Germany.

An indication of strong economic growth is the increased energy consumption and that has been the case in Asia Pacific. In October 2003, Goldman Sachs released a report which predicted that within 40 years, the economies of India and China, if added to those of Brazil and Russia (the "BRICs") would be larger than that of the United States, Germany, Japan, Britain, France and Italy combined. China would overtake the United States as the world's largest economy and India would be third, outpacing all other industrialized nations, and thus dominating the world.

Before discussing India's Place in the Asia Pacific, it would be pertinent to examine the relations of the intra Asia Pacific countries as well as their relations with some outside countries like the U.S. and Russia.

China

China's advantages in leaving India far behind, being in search of a major power status, are its ability to push through its economic reforms with a single party autocratic rule, an ability to undercut prices in the international market through an administered price scheme, and economic investments by expatriating Chinese in neighbouring countries (estimated to be 60/70 million in Southeast Asia) with large Chinese population. China had started its reform process a decade earlier in 1978 – when it was poorer than India – and the Chinese communist regime paid more attention to human development like health care and education for the poor than successive Indian Governments had done. For example, in public health expenditure, China spent 2 per cent of GDP while, India spent 0.6 per cent (1990-1998). As a result, infant mortality rate in China was 31 for 1000 births and it was 70 in India; life expectancy at birth in China 68 (males) and 72 (females), in India 62 (males) and 64 (females). Similarly, the literacy rate (per cent of population) in China was much higher than India (in China, males 9 per cent and females 25 per cent whereas in India, males 33 per cent and females 57 per cent) (1998). China is expected to grow by more than 9 per cent this year, and its export-led growth is generating a huge trade surplus of more than $100bn - with China's total foreign currency reserves now totalling more than $700bn.

The OECD has forecast the growth of 9 per cent for the whole year for China. In fact, the Chinese govt. is so concerned that it is attempting to slow the pace of economy by putting interest rates up, revaluing the Yuan, and restricting credit levels. It is also trying to limit investment in industries such as steel, cement and aluminium, but high-tech industries are still investing heavily. China grew by an average of 8.5 per cent between 1990 and 2003 while India grew at 4 per cent. China has grown to be 70 per cent richer than India (*Economist*, March 2005).

Sensitive to the concerns of the countries of the region about what it calls as "peaceful rise " China has also been inclined to accept multilateralism and collaborate with the South East Asian countries , essentially to make American led bilateral alliances irrelevant. It has also shown other indications of cooperative behaviour. It continues to engage in ASEAN Regional Forum (ARF) security dialogues and cosponsored (with Philippines) a major confidence building workshop convened in Beijing in 1996. While asserting its right to use force to regain Taiwan, if it moves towards independence, China had put most other territorial disputes on hold, including Spratly islands (without of course giving up its claims of sovereignty over the islands) and control over five Diaoyutai/Senkaku islands 22 kms. north of Taiwan. It has accepted existing boundaries as a basis of settlement in recent talks with Russia, India and other central Asian states. It has agreed with the South East Asian states that UN Convention on Law of the Seas (UNCLOS) should be the governing criterion for resolving the territorial dispute and has agreed to discuss the issue multilaterally.

It is however worried over recent trend in Japan's strategic assertiveness including shifting of its military deployments from

North to west facing the Korean peninsula and China. In fact, there is a view among many scholars that China retains a stake in US military presence in the region to contain a Japanese remilitarization. In a symposium organized by the Chinese communist party central committee and Central military commission in November-December 1993 many Chinese strategic scholars, however expressed the view that the US is the most important threat to China's national security. 60 per cent of them however felt that Japan would be the most serious security threat by 2020. It would thus appear that while China is determined to end American strategic involvement in Taiwan straits and reduce US strategic influence in Asia Pacific, it would not want a total removal of American Presence, at least in the near future, in view of its concern about Japan.

Though many Chinese view the United States as a major threat to their nation's security and domestic stability, the reality of the United States being a global leader in economics, education, culture, technology, and science, is important for China . A close relationship with the United States is the *sine qua non* for China if its modernization efforts are to succeed. The United States needs China's help on issues such as counterterrorism, nonproliferation, the reconstruction of Iraq, and the maintenance of stability in the Middle East. More and more, Washington has also started to seek China's cooperation in fields such as trade and finance, despite increased friction over currency exchange rates, intellectual property rights, and the textile trade.

With respect to India, China has always followed a policy of containment of India, although some constructive engagement is seen in China's policy after the 1980s. Neutrality in Kashmir issue has been a notable change in this regard though this could change as the situation and relationship with India warrants. Chinese worry is over Indian influence in Tibet and the consequent interference. China has deployed tactical weapons in Tibet designed to deter India from interference in Tibet in case of a revolt. It has deployed land based intermediate range missiles against Indian cities. As part of its containment efforts, It continues to favor and support Pakistani efforts to match Indian military capabilities. It has even helped Pakistan in the latter's quest for nuclear and missile capabilities. It is also a matter of interest that China has been resisting India's attempts to expand ASEAN to form a larger Asian Community. It resists India's suggestion that the present ASEAN+3 (inclusive of China, South Korea and Japan) and ASEAN+1 (inclusive of India) should be merged into a single ASEAN+4. The current status would confine India to South Asia and not become a key player in the expanded East Asian community.

The Chinese are adopting a conflict avoidance strategy to give themselves time to modernize China's economy, strengthen its political system and develop its military capabilities to a standard which will meet its global ambitions. Right now, china's capabilities, despite being the only major power with a land route to South East Asia, are unable to match US or Collective ASEAN control over key maritime choke points and archipelagic waters. Currently, U.S. is determined to contain China. Even in the case of Taiwan, China is trying to find a political way of unifying Taiwan with the mainland. Top opposition politicians from Taiwan, Lien Chan and James Soong were feted in historic visits to Beijing, It is trying to use its contacts with the opposition parties to gain an unprecedented predominance in Taiwan's domestic politics. It has also offered perks to farmers in the south, traditionally an independence stronghold. China's tourism minister visited Taipei. All these indicate a certain anxiety on the part of China to solve the issue politically and avoid, if possible, armed confrontation on the issue, particularly with the U.S. Many Taiwanese seem to believe that the military threat has dramatically been abated.

Japan

Historically, Japan's hunger for the resources of Southeast Asia and its concern with American interference led it to attack Pearl Harbor. It is an irony that it was the United States that helped Japan to resume its economic push into Southeast Asia and to create, in effect, the sphere of economic dominance it had been seeking. The Japanese dominance grew in the later decades in a model some Japanese economists called the "flying geese," with Japan in the lead and its lesser partners moving forward in its economic slipstream.

Japan believes that it should be a more influential power in the region. It follows many sided strategy combining a policy of strong bilateral alliance with the U.S. while participating in multilateral organizations like Asia Pacific Economic Cooperation (APEC) and ARF to deal with the changes taking place in the strategic scene in the region , most important being the rise of China. Japan has however made it clear that trade issues need to be kept separate from US Japan defence relations when it petitioned the WTO against US retaliatory trade measures.

There has been recent fears that the deteriorating Sino-Japanese relations could lead to destabilizing conflict in the region. However, the positive feature is, that the vibrant Sino-Japanese commercial relationship has remained unharmed despite the political hostility and is perhaps an insurance against such destabilizing conflict. Strengthening cultural and economic exchanges between China and Japan in the 1990s did not mitigate mutual suspicion and antipathy. Public opinion polls in Japan show a decline in pacifist sentiment and a majority preference for a more robust national security policy. Both Japan and China have staked their rights to the natural gas deposits in the East China Sea and have not been able to resolve the dispute. Tensions escalated following exploratory operations by China in May 2004 when Japan responded by allowing private Japanese companies to explore the disputed areas in May 2005.

It is interesting to note that in December 2004, Japan's National Defense Program Guidelines identified North Korea and China as threats. Foreign Minister Taro Aso told the press on December 22, 2005 that neighbouring China, a nuclear weapon state with one billion people, is becoming a "considerable threat" because of its rising but opaque military spending which is posting a double digit growth and nuclear weapons. There is also a growing feeling in Japan that it needs to amend its constitution to give more teeth to its defence forces.

Koizumi the current PM who has returned with a large majority is essentially pro American and is determined to make Japan a major partner in Ballistic Missile Defence (BMD) development with the United States. He has changed the command and decision-making structure of the Japanese Defense Forces to allow fast, decisive and flexible decision-making to launch anti-ballistic missile interceptors against possible attacks. He has pushed through major purchases of BMD systems and co-production agreements with the United States. These deals gave America's high-tech industries the urgently needed infusions of capital.

On the other hand, there is considerable concern, not only in china but also in South East Asia about Japan's ability to move to be a strong military power, if it chooses to. Its equipments are superb, second only to the U.S. It has enough wealth to support a large standing army. It has the industrial capacity to equip itself with advanced weapons and could turn nuclear within months, if not weeks, if it decides to do so.

Australia

During the past two decades, Australia had projected itself as part of the region. It is a major advocate of regional interdependence and provided intellectual leadership in multilateral security politics both within South East Asia and Asia Pacific. Its active interest in East Timor is an indication of its changed priorities. It spearheaded the International emergency force in East Timor. Australia, like Japan, is committed to 1. a continuing US presence to realize and sustain regional security and 2.strengthening multilateral security as a key component of Asia Pacific regional security framework.

If Australia becomes more and more an Asia Pacific middle power, any bilateral relationship it develops with an Asian power would not override the cultural affinity and mutual bonds in Australia – American relationship.

Southeast Asia

Southeast Asia has about 500 million people with a combined gross domestic product of $737 billion and a total trade of $720 billion. The states in the region are able to perceive the advantage of regional security commitments under which they will be able to engage China and minimize the "China Threat" The former Prime Minister of Singapore, Lee Kuan Yew recommended free trade and economic competition as guarantees of peace, quoting the post war examples of Japan and Germany. Activities like involvement in regional arrangements and active participation in defense talks and information exchanges, could impose restraint on its possible maverick behaviour, in future.

Some of the Southeast Asian countries including Vietnam, have seen the strategic importance of their locations which is traversed by some of the world's most important sea lanes of communication and trade routes. They therefore, are determined to get their naval and air power strengthened, in order to control these routes and defend their offshore territorial claims and long coast lines. China's naval expansion has been a major cause for these maritime states, to get their naval and air capability upgraded.

Inter relations between Southeast Asian Countries have not been without some strains. Naval activities of Myanmar off the Isthmus of Kra, are increasingly viewed with concern by Thailand In 1998/99, and there has been an incidence of naval skirmishes between Thai and Myanmar naval vessels in disputes concerning fishing waters along the Isthmus.

South China sea and contiguous areas of contention are South east Asia's flash points. For South East Asian countries like Indonesia, keeping a balance between domestic stability and preserving domestic sovereignty and dealing with external security threats, essentially from a rising China, are major preoccupations. Indonesia had nearly half of ASEAN's land space and straddles most of the sea lanes between Indian and Pacific Ocean. It also encourages over the horizon, the strategic presence of the U.S. as a check against Chinese expansionism. It maintains its influence in the regional economic institutions. It had entered into the "Agreement on Maintaining Security (AMS) with Australia in December 1985, the first formal security commitment. By entering into security accord with one of the important allies of the U.S., Indonesia gravitated more closely towards the U.S. security networks. Unfortunately, the AMS came to nothing and was abrogated after strains, in relations over East Timor. The need to maintain a stable relationship with Indonesia has thus become an important and immediate problem for Australia.

Malaysia which has moved from counterinsurgency to external contingencies, follows a policy of building and maintaining a small but relatively effective military, to deal with limited external military threat. Singapore is a highly vulnerable state from security point of view depending solely on trade for its well being and believes that the U.S. is the only strategic ally who matters most as an acceptable balancer to Chinese power. Lately, Singapore has also been contemplating, seeing India as being capable of performing an important role to play, in the region.

Philippines remains highly suspicious of and hostile to, China after the Chinese constructions of airstrips and installations in Mischief Reef, only 300 kms from Philippines and within Philippines' 200 Nm EEZ, an action referred to by Filipino defense secretary as "a dagger at our underbelly." Without the wherewithal to enhance its strategic capability, Philippines have to depend on substantial US military assistance and cover.

Given the security problems of the individual ASEAN states, ASEAN cannot work only for cosmic unanimity but has to focus more on security challenges of individual ASEAN states. The ARF remains a cooperative security arrangement rather than collective defense mechanism Till it progressed beyond a debating society, the individual ASEAN states would look up to the U.S. presence for their security. The other balancer, who could be welcomed, is India as many south East Asian states see power balancing in a multi polar strategic setting as the best way to avoid regional dominance.

U.S.

The critical American interests in the Asia Pacific region are: (1) to prevent major Asia Pacific wars which can lead to strikes against US territory or forces and (2) to prevent China from achieving regional hegemony at US expense. This would call for a policy of avoiding total withdrawal from the region and controlling critical sea lanes there and facilitating Asia pacific regional prosperity as economic relations are viewed by the US policy makers as a crucial aspect of national security policy.

U.S. relations with Southeast Asia are not without its problems. Malaysians, Singaporeans, the Chinese and other regional elites oppose American efforts to devalue their policies of thrift, family loyalty and primacy of community interests. They resist American efforts to impose their brand of democracy and believe in strong Govts. to safeguard economic growth and social cohesion for its citizens.

However, both Clinton and Bush administrations have underscored the importance of alliances in Asia pacific as important components of US security politics in the region. Asia pacific region continues to be important for US global strategy. For example, the U.S resumed (stopped in 1991 after the bloody Indonesian crackdown on East Timor Independence movement) extending assistance to Indonesia for specific military programs and units that will help modernize the Indonesian military. This is intended to boost Indonesia's anti-terrorism efforts, maritime security and disaster relief.

Russia

Russia under Putin, seems to have realized the importance of this region and has started paying a lot of attention. Energy Minister Viktor Khristenko said in November 2005 that by 2020, 30 percent of the country's oil exports would go to Asia, compared with the current 3 percent. Asia also buys more than 90 percent of Russia's $5 billion annual arms exports. For these reasons alone, Russia is pushing for permanent membership in this bloc. Putin, attending the ASEAN meeting recently and then attending the first East Asia Summit as Malaysia's guest, promised to increase the oil deliveries to Asia, from the present 3 percent of Russia's total exports to 30 per cent by 2020. In a joint statement, leaders of the 10-nation group pledged to build a "comprehensive partnership" and provide boost to trade and security cooperation with Russia. A new Siberian pipeline should be operational by 2008, with early deliveries going mainly to China.

Russia is also transferring advanced military technology to Asia, particularly China and India which could give the Asian countries enough of home grown defense industries in five or ten years so that, the U.S. suppliers would have much diminished influence over their behaviour.

India Factor

India, with its sub continental size, and large population ($1/6^{th}$ of humanity) and potential economic and military strength, has all the qualification of being a major power. It has also consistently defended its autonomy in foreign policy. It has the fourth largest army, the fourth largest economy (in terms of purchasing power parity (PPP), the eighth largest industrial economy, and the world's largest pool of scientists and engineers after the U.S. and a middle class (300m) double that of Japan and growing. It has been a major contributor to the U.N. peace keeping operations. Despite all this, it still remains only a potential power with influence largely confined to South Asia

One of the reasons for this is, that India had remained less integrated in the international system, particularly, on issues that affect its security and economy , partly due to external reason like the U.S. keeping India isolated , specially in the technology area after the Indian nuclear test in 1974 and partly due to its own economic and strategic policies. If it can maintain the current growth of 5 per cent to 7 per cent, it can become the third largest power behind the US and China in another couple of decades. On the economic side, the isolation was self imposed with an insular economy with productivity of the Indian work force being lower than that of the countries comparable to it. India is also called by many, as the soft state where enacted policies are not enforced.

Other constraining factors on its search for great power status include, its inability to remove social and economic maladies like grinding poverty, regional and gender based inequalities and most of all, rural urban disparities. It has been argued that a country with high levels of social and economic deprivation, is unlikely to be internationally respected, let alone attaining a major power status.

On the economic domain, India completely neglected the export led growth for a long time, even as East and South East Asian countries were changing in this regard and some of them like the Newly Industrialised countries (NICs) of Taiwan, South Korea and Hong Kong were becoming economic tigers. Poor taxation revenues, endemic and widespread corruption throughout the country, were other maladies. Mass education was given a go by putting emphasis on higher education. Last but not least, has been the total neglect of developing infrastructure. In order to close the gap with the developed world and to catch up with China, India will have to pursue policies that endorse the support application of new technologies, good governance, universal education, and market reforms. India has already been investing in research in the next group of high technologies involving the convergence of nano-, bio-, information and materials technology and is thus well placed to become a leader in a number of key fields along with China.

Military Factor

India's ability for power projection beyond the South Asian region, is also constrained by active defense on two fronts - with a determined adversary like Pakistan in the west and a major power like China, with a border dispute, in the east. Military defeat at the hands of China forcing India into arms dependency with the Soviet Union, deflated the image of India in the developing and non aligned world of which Asia Pacific, is a large part. The continuing conflict with Pakistan has also prevented India's march to greatness. On the other hand, China actively pursued a polity of containment of India, to prevent the rise of a peer in this region. A major portion of China's arms sales goes to countries that border India. China, in addition to bolstering Pakistan by supplying arms, nuclear and missile technology, bolstered up the military junta of Myanmar with arms and other aid and in turn obtained observation facilities in Coco islands to monitor India's missile testing. The collapse of the Soviet Union by the beginning of the 1990s and the end of the Cold War, has also altered the scenario in South Asian strategic scene. Soviet union was no longer available as a political , economic and security anchor for India . India had to adjust its foreign policy to work out new political equation with major powers, especially the U.S. which, of course, had no more reason to see India as a Soviet surrogate

There are however, hopeful signs that India could still move towards a major regional, if not a global power.

The International Monetary Fund has revised India's 2005 growth forecast by half a percentage point to 7.1 per cent, and said that an opening of Indian economy with a young population and rapid growth rates could become a key engine of world growth over the next decade. According to it "If India continues to embrace globalization and reform, Indian imports could increasingly operate as a driver of global growth as it is one of a handful of economies forecast to have a growing working-age population over the next 10 years“. India's exports, although coming from a relatively low level, were forecast to more than double by 2010 while imports will nearly triple. The IMF said that the imports were growing at about 33 per cent but sounded a note of caution that such a boost to world demand will present major challenges to the global economy as well as obvious opportunities. It is also a matter of interest to note that according to World Bank, India emerged as the top recipient of remittances from expatriates abroad to the tune of 21.7 Billion dollars in 2004, overtaking China at 21.3 billion dollars. India China two way trade was expected to reach 19 billion dollars, making China, India's second largest trading partner. India is also now no 2 destination for FDI behind China and above the U.S .as per the FDI confidence index prepared by consulting firm AT Kearney.

Regrettably, India still only accounts for 2.5 per cent of global trade compared to more than 10 per cent for China. Over the past two years, India accounted for just under a fifth of Asian growth and 10 per cent of world growth, compared with 53 per cent and 28 per cent respectively, for China. India's growth prospects are related to progress toward continued economic reforms presently stymied by partisan politics. Its financial system with one of the highest fiscal deficit needs strengthening. The second stage of reforms is yet to be actively pursued. One positive aspect is the declining rate in population which was 1.95 per cent from 1991 to 2001.There has been some decline in total no. of illiterates as well as in the gap between male and female illiteracy. One small example of India's foibles is indicated by the comparison of the performance of the American A/C manufacturer "Carrier". They set up shop both in China and India in 1987. By 1995, they had five times revenue in China, compared to that in India.

India has also a much larger proportion of its population in desperate poverty. Communal tensions (communal riots in Gujarat in 2002 is a negative publicity internationally), growth of regional and caste-based political parties, are seen as evidence of a worsening trend.

India's relations with Asia pacific

Historically, India's link, with Asia Pacific, specially what is now called South East Asia, has been civilisational for centuries with close connections in the fields of culture, commerce, art, architecture etc. This link went into hibernation with colonial conquests of both India and the South East Asian countries. In the post colonial period, the cold war kept the region apart from India due to India's ideology of command economy not being sync with that of these countries .There was also the cold war divide of the countries in the region for being in the western camp while India was perceived as a Soviet supporter. India's controlled economy with the "Hindu" rate of growth and the military defeat at the hands of China in 1962, hardly impressed these countries about India's position as a major economic and military power in the region. In the first few decades after independence, India also chose to follow a policy of benign neglect of this region, more concerned with West Asia . However, the geographical reality is that India is in the immediate neighbourhood of these countries and the vital waterway from West Asia to South East Asia is also straddled by India in the Indian Ocean. It is thus in the interest of India as well as these countries to have a closer economic and strategic relationship..

Another important fact is, that these countries have placed utmost importance in technical development in anticipation of future competition. Japan is superior even to the U.S. in 25 of the 34 critical areas of high technology. Some of the important technological changes required are centered in micro electronics, information technology, biotechnology and new materials technology.

A welcome development is, the invitation to India to attend the first East Asia summit at Kuala Lumpur on December 14 2005. The summit decided to set up an EAS forum for a dialogue on broad strategic, political and economic issues of common interest and concern to promote peace, stability and economic prosperity in East Asia. The leaders of the countries who attended, committed themselves to promoting development, financial stability, energy security, economic integration and growth besides narrowing the development gap through technology transfer. India' participation in the summit which issued the "Kuala Lumpur declaration, is an encouraging sign of integration of India with the region. Aware of India's economic clout and the opportunity it presents, ASEAN is keen on expediting India ASEAN free trade area, which is to come into force next year. This would also be the first step to India towards joining the Asia Pacific Economic Cooperation (APEC) forum. India has also agreed to participate in the regional maritime security. The ASEAN would be the driving force for the Forum. The most interesting aspect is that the U.S. was not invited to this summit while Putin of Russia addressed the gathering as a guest of Malaysia. He said he was keen on obtaining full membership when the second East Asia Summit is held in Manila, in the next year. Russia agreed to renounce the use of force in the region and has signed an economic cooperation agreement.. The United States declined to join because of reluctance to sign a pledge renouncing the use of force and interference in the internal affairs of the region.

With its recent economic growth and increased prowess in science and technology, particularly space, Information and biotechnology (projected earnings from IT in 2008 is 87 billion dollars), India could well become a bridging power in the new century between South and South East Asia. Greater integration of the Indian economy with the Asia-Pacific region, would benefit not only India but also the Asia-Pacific economies. India can draw useful lessons from the success stories of the East and Southeast Asian countries, particularly Japan, South Korea and Taiwan. The reasons for the success are:

- High investment ratios
- Small Public sector
- Export orientation
- Labour market competition and
- Govt. intervention, when needed, in economic matters.

Strategic Importance of India for the Region

Apart from Japan which has constitutional Impediments to militarise itself, India is the only regional power that can provide a balance against possible growth of China's militarism in the region. It is interesting to mention here that the U.S. seems to acknowledge this fact and has initiated moves favouring India. India's hard power is also increasing with its indigenous missile capability increasing in the form of Agni I and II and projected Agni III. As home to 1 billion people, India has to be integral to any regional process pertaining to the Asia Pacific.

The Look East Policy seems to be taken more seriously by the present Govt. of India with Prime Minister Dr. Manmohan Singh calling for a dynamic, open and inclusive PAN Asian Free Trade Area (FTA) when addressing the business advisory council of the ASEAN in Kuala Lumpur. He saw India ASEAN free trade agreement as a first step in the process. He called on the ASEAN and the East Asian Nations, to focus on India as a market. The East Asian Summit (EAS) in which India has been included after some initial reluctance from China, and the Shanghai cooperation organization, seem to be moves towards a new security architecture with countries within the region itself taking responsibility of their security. The inclusion of India in the EAS also shows the importance attached to India by the Asia Pacific Countries in that region.

To conclude, India has all the advantages of playing its role in Asia Pacific in this century. But it has to get out of its mindset beset by caste and communal polity. I end this by quoting part of Finance Minister Chidambaram's 2004 budget speech

"If we bring thought and passion to our governance and walk the path of honour and courage, we can make the future happen. And this century will be India's century."

12

Russia's Renewed Interest in Southeast Asia

R.G. Gidadhubli

In analyzing the issues of external relations of the South East Asian and Pacific countries, it is necessary to examine their relations with Russia which has a direct access to the Pacific Ocean through its eastern part. Moreover, Russia has been actively pursuing its policy initiatives with these countries. In fact, after the break-up of the Soviet Union, there had been dramatic changes in Russia's policy towards these countries. During the Soviet era, Marxist-Leninist ideology was the prime consideration in the framework of the foreign policy. Based on this policy, the communist countries including North Korea, Vietnam, which were part of the 'Socialist Block,' were closer to the Soviet Union politically and economically than Thailand, Malaysia, South Korea etc.

The relations of the former USSR with China were altogether on a different level and scale and were determined by issues concerning international communist movement and the leadership of the communist world. After the Soviet break-up, socialist ideology became irrelevant to Russia's foreign policy as the ideology was replaced by National interest in the foreign policy consideration of Russia. Guided by this principle, Russia began to cherish the partnership with the West as its primary objective and this was visualized in its Foreign Policy Concept of 1993. An important element of this policy Concept was that, holding national interest of the country in the high esteem, the Russian leadership under Boris Yeltsin, did not abruptly declare the agreements entered into by Mikhail Gorbachev in political and economic spheres as annulled.

Thus, in the initial phase, under the presidency of Boris Yeltsin Russia was trying to develop normal relations with the USA with a view to establishing sympathetic rapport prior to establishing any strategic partnership determined by the context, and possible alliance in the future. The then foreign minister of Russia, Andrei Kozyrev, played a pivotal role in formulating this policy. It is significant to note that at that time, Russia badly needed the western aid and technology to overcome its crisis, and to tide over the difficulties. Hence Russian leadership began to cherish the notion that close political and economic relations with the western countries were indispensable. This view might have gathered strength when the USA had offered $1.6 billion to Russia, consequent on the meeting between the Russian president Boris Yeltsin and the US president Bill Clinton in April 1993.

However, at the same time, Russia was not able to get reconciled to the idea of the sole super power status of the USA in the aftermath of the disintegration of the USSR. Moreover, there was a group of political leaders in Russia which was not at all in favour of Moscow's excessive preoccupation with the idea of the west as a 'development model and business partner. Thus, according to Sergei Goncharov, the then head of the Sino-Soviet section at the Institute of Far East in the Russian Academy of Sciences, warned Kremlin not to neglect other regions including the Eastern countries since they were of paramount importance for Russia. Thus, in the early 1990's, there were conflicting views prevailing in Russia on all issues, including the country's foreign policy. There was another group known as Eurasianists that was formed in this period, which had a distinct school of thought to its credit.

This group contended that Russia should assume the role of a bridge connecting Europe and Asia. It appears that this group wanted to assert that the strategic location of Russia, the vast territory of which lies both in Europe and Asia, could be exploited for the economic and political development of the country. On the issue of Russia's role at the international level, a somewhat similar view was expressed by some academics from the Center for International Studies at the Moscow State Institute for International Relations. According to them, Russia's main foreign policy objective should be to prepare the ground for raising the status of the country from periphery to the core of the World economy by concentrating on developing the country's economic power. While there were debates and discussions in Russia on these issues, in the initial period after the Soviet break-up, Russia did move away from the 'Third world' countries. There was a prevailing view among a small section of policy makers that the developing countries could not contribute to the economic development of Russia. This could have been partly based on the contention that some developing countries, mainly those that were in the former communist block as well as those which were considered to have had strong communist/socialist orientation, having received liberal economic aid and assistance from the erstwhile USSR, could not repay the debt for their own reasons.

In the second phase, which covered the period 1994-1998, a realization dawned on Russia that the national interest of the country could be served by developing closer relations with the countries in the East. Apart from the possible impact of the debate on the country's foreign policy as noted above, there were many other factors that might have contributed to this shift in foreign policy. For instance, Russian policy makers were worried about the continued expansionist policy of NATO towards the east, as the former East European countries and the Baltic countries, are bound to enfeeble Russia's role at the international level. In fact, there was a view put across by some sections in Russia that after the Soviet break up, the Warsaw Pact, the communist military alliance, was dissolved and the perceived threat to the west ceased to exist, and on this analogy, they told themselves in a mood of complacency, that NATO would also cease to exist.

However, the fact of NATO getting expanded and thus mustering strength, was contrary to the expectations of certain political groups in Russia. Moreover, Russia was not able to get the expected status as a partner with the developed countries, particularly the USA. The amount of economic assistance from the west was also far below Russia's expectations for overcoming the economic crisis. Hence Russia seems to have considered that a policy emphasizing an alternative line such as focusing on 'multi-polarity' in world affairs to counter the US influence, would be to its advantage. In evolving this alternative approach, Russia's policy makers including Yevgenii Primakov, played an important role. Thus, several Asian countries including India, china, South East Asian countries started gaining more importance in Russia's foreign policy and economic relations with these countries. This revised foreign policy of Russia benefited the country and thus on 17th- November 18, 1998, Yevgenii Primakov attended the Asia Pacific Co-operation Summit at Kuala Lumpur during which Russia was admitted as a full-fledged member. Russia's entry into the APEC was thus, a recognition that was needed to enhance its international status. According to some experts, this membership had more of strategic significance for Russia than of economic consideration.

Russia's Foreign Policy under Vladimir Putin

Under President Vladimir Putin, Russia's foreign policy seems to be really pragmatic and assertive. This is evident from the fact that while co-operating with the west particularly after 9/11 episode, Russia has disagreed with the West on various issues such as NATO expansion, war on Iraq, ABM Treaty, Caspian energy issue etc. However, Putin has managed to see that the disagreements did not lead to confrontation with the West. On the other hand, Russia has developed closer relations with Germany and France during the last few years. Thus, Russia has developed a multi-sectored foreign policy. Considering the realistic assessment of the situation in the world, Russia had announced a new Foreign Policy Concept in July 2000, which had replaced rhetoric with realism. In this new foreign policy, it is stated:

'.... a distinguishing feature of Russia's foreign policy is that it is a balanced one. This has been predetermined by the geopolitical position of Russia as one of the largest Eurasian powers, requiring an optimal combination of efforts of all sectors'. (Foreign Policy Concept of the Russian Federation 10th July 2000). Thus it is evident that Russia wants to reemerge as a major power in the world. As opined by some experts, Russia has national interests everywhere. An important observation has been made by Putin with regard to Asian countries when he stated '...it is essential to intensify participation in the basic integration process of the Pacific region and consistently expand friendly relations with the leading states including our neighbors, perhaps giving them priority'.

Russia's strategic course has aimed at an integration into the world economy, as Putin has given high priority to the integration into the world economy in his foreign policy. This is evident from the concept paper in which it is stated '... under conditions of accelerating globalization which is causing so many discussions, our country is still to find its place in the world'.

Under Putin's leadership, Russia has increased its political and economic relations with the South East Asian and Pacific countries. With a view to becoming a full-fledged member of the ASEAN, Russian leaders undertook necessary measures. For instance, Russia signed a non-aggression pact with the ASEAN, in fulfillment of a requirement to be considered for membership. Similarly, Russia became a dialogue partner with the ASEAN countries. However, Russia's economic ties were relatively tenuous and feeble. For instance, in 2002, Russia's trade with the ASEAN was only 0.4 per cent of the region's global trade. Hence, to strengthen trade and economic relations, Putin attended the Summit meeting of the ASEAN in 2003 during which, several co-operation agreements were signed to increase trade and to combat terrorism. All these measures indicate the seriousness on the part of Russia to increase political and economic relations with these countries.

Russia-Southeast Asia: Arms Exports

During the last few years, Russia's Military Industrial Complex (MIC) has shown considerable renewed interest in promoting defense exports to the South East Asian countries. This new development is in sharp contrast to the situation that prevailed in the early 1990's when military programs were either suspended or scaled back. Prior to that, during the Soviet era, the former communist block countries did receive defense equipments at a cheaper rate and on barter basis. As a result of the policy initiatives of Mikhail Gorbachev, arms supply and military-technical co-operation with these countries were curtailed. Subsequently, with the end of the cold war and under the prevailing conditions in post-Soviet Russia, defense exports to Vietnam, North Korea substantially declined. In fact, in the first half of the 1990's, Russia's defense expenditure declined drastically. For instance, between 1992-1997, defense expenditure went down by about 50 percent from $ 80 billion in 1992 to about $ 30 billion in 1997. This had a major impact on the defense production and exports of Russia. [1]

However, since 1998, an increase in defense expenditure and arms production in Russia and arms exports from the country has been witnessed. This rising trend in defense expenditure is evident from the fact that national defense budget shot up from Ruble 95 billion in 2002 to Ruble 344 billion in 2003, that is more than three and half times in one year. This was the largest growth sector of Russia in 2003. By then the Russian leaders had readily realized the economic benefits from the exports of arms. As the Russian economy was facing various constraints of growth, the defense sector and energy sector emerged as the main sources of export earnings for the country. Realizing this situation, at the Security Council meeting of the Russian Federation held in February 2003, Vldimir Putin approved of the new military technical policy for the rearmament plan. This new policy emphasized Research and Development of new generation weapons systems. [2]

Evidently, the recent qualitative shift in Russia's exports of arms to the South East Asian countries was a result of change in the assessment of the Russia's MIC. For instance, according to Vladimir Artyakov, Russia's arms expert Director General of

Russia's state arms export organization ROSOBORONEXPORT, arms export market in the South Asia region was estimated at $ 20 billion, during the present decade. This assessment was made when Artyakov attended the Asian Aerospace 2002 Exhibition in Singapore. This visit coincided with the Russian search for market for exporting its defense equipments as remarked by the editor of Asia Pacific Jane's Defense weekly. According to defense experts, by the end of 1990's, the fact of Russia's defense industry desperately requiring to rebuild itself and to focus on export, was considered as part of this policy. This is also evident from the fact that the then prime minister of Russia Mikhail Kasyanov, during his visit to Vietnam in March 2002, was trying to promote strategic partnership with Vietnam which also included the issue of co-operation in nuclear energy as also sale of arms to the Soviet military equipments.

Moreover, under the new dispensation, some of the South East Asian countries, which were denied new technology and defense equipments, were able to get them from Russia. From the reports available, it may be stated, that Russia has been able to export a large quantity of defense equipments to many countries of the South Asian countries. In 2002, Russia's 'Lomo Corp' delivered 50 portable SA-18 surface-to-air missiles to Vietnam under $64 million contract. Maynamar took delivery of dozens of Russian MiG-29 fighter jets and was negotiating to build its first nuclear reactor with the help of Russia. Similarly, the Malaysian air force was also planning to purchase a squadron of general-purpose fighter planes from Russia. Moreover, Russia's Sukhoi Corp was offering S-30K fighter to Malaysia. From these accounts, it is clear that Russia was driven to evince interest in Southeast Asia not only by commercial consideration but also by way of seeking new direction for promoting its strategic interest and regaining its status in the world affairs after the disintegration of the Soviet Union.

From the foregoing details, it is obvious that Russia has effected an enhancement of its military co-operation with the Southeast Asian countries. The increased military sales necessitate service centers in the Asian region. In view of the fact that India had been importing defense equipments for army, navy and air force on a very large scale and for over the last four decades from the former Soviet Union and post-Soviet Russia and that both the countries have entered into agreements for joint production of some of Russia's defense products, India should consider the possibility of building a service centre which can cater to the needs of Russia's equipments sold in the Asian region. This will further add to the promotion of strategic co-operation between India and Russia. The needs of some Southeast Asian countries can be catered to, by such a service centre.

Russia-China Relations and their Implication for Southeast Asian Countries

Russia-China relations have considerable relevance for the Asia-Pacific and South East Asian countries. In particular, close defense relations between these two countries during the last few years, have raised academic debates and view-points. It appears that as China has emerged as a global power, some of its policies and actions have created conflicting situations. For instance, in the late 1980's, China initiated oil-exploration work in off shore areas where its sovereignty was disputed by Vietnam. Similarly, there were reports that in January 1995, China evicted Filipino fishermen from that part of Spartly archipelago which was within the Exclusive Economic Zone of the Philippines and was 1,000 kilometers away from the Chinese Island of Haiman.

Some defense experts from Australia have contended that Russian arms would increase China's capacity to project power and use force, which would affect the interests of the countries in the region, particularly countries such as Australia, Philippines, Indonesia, Vietnam etc. In this regard, it is important to note that in December 1995, Indonesia signed a defense agreement with Australia and augmented the security on some of its oil deposits, which are also claimed by China.

In the opinion of some academics, large quantity of defense purchases by China from Russia, could exacerbate arms competition among the Asian countries including ASEAN countries. It is pointed out in this regard, that there was a relative lack of transparency with respect to long term objectives of China in buying new and hi-tech defense equipments during the last decade. China has acquired latest military equipments such as attack aircrafts, in-fight refueling technology, modern surface combatants, submarines, surface-to-air missiles which involve strike capability with offensive connotations. In the opinion of some western defense experts like William Tow, increased military co-operation between Russia and China could lead to a new strategic coalition, which could isolate Japan and neutralize American power in the region. [3]

On some of these issues there are different kinds of assessment. Some scholars consider that Russia-China relations are not as threatening as they have been made out to be. It is felt that China might not be able to project its power and capability to the South East Asian and Pacific region. As observed by Rajan Menon in 1997, China lacked sea-based air support and that its ariel refueling technology is not advanced. [4]

It is worthwhile to examine the views of some Chinese and Russian specialists. According to some Chinese experts, China has undertaken major defense modernization program since late 1980's and that the military build up of China was modest as compared to some other Asia Pacific countries. It is also pointed out that China did not spend more than Japan, South Korea or Taiwan on defense and that it did not possess more sophisticated weapons than what these countries had procured in the 1980's and 1990's. In the opinion of some Chinese scholars, China was not filling the military 'power vacuum' in the region and that no such vacuum had been left by the USA and Russia.

Russian scholars are also trying to justify the position of their own country. It is stated that if Russia had not supplied defense equipments, China could have procured them from other sources any way. Yuri Savenkov has observed in 1998 that China might not become a military super power even in the next 20 years, much against what was claimed by some experts.

In conclusion, it may be stated, that during the Soviet era, the communist ideology was the primary consideration of the USSR in its policy towards the South East Asian countries. In the immediate aftermath of the Soviet disintegration, Russian leadership was looking more to the west than to the east. Hence, Russia's interest towards the South East Asian countries had declined. This situation, however, changed and a more balanced approach in foreign policy was adopted. Under the leadership of Russia's president Vladimir Putin, a more dynamic policy has been adopted by Russia with the South East Asian countries, which is evident from the interest of the country to become a member of the APEC and the ASEAN. The export of arms to several countries of this region since the last few years, has made a qualitative difference in the relationship between Russia and the ASEAN. It has also strengthened Russia's strategic interest in the region. At the same time, Russia's sale of sophisticated defense equipments to China has generated concern among many South East Asian countries.

Notes

1. *Sipri Yearbook 2000*, p 260.
2. *Russia's Military Balance 2003-2004,* p 267.
3. William Tow, "Changing US force levels and regional security," *Contemporary Security Policy.* Vol. 15, No. 2 August 1994, p 20.
4. Rajan Menon, "The Strategic Convergence between Russia and China," *Survival*, 39 (2), Summer 1997.

13

India and China Rapprochement: Cautious Moves

K. Raja Reddy

The two Asian giants, India and China, have been making efforts to come closer to each other. These two big nations, in terms of their size and population, have been trying to shed their animosities inflicted by a border war in 1962 in favour of an unprecedented economic integration through trade and investments. India's acceptance of Tibet as an integral part of China and in turn China's recognition of Sikkim's merger with India and an opening of Nathu La trade route by increasing the volume of border trade between India and China are some of the decisive steps taken to improve the relations between the two countries. Some of the vivid issues such as border disputes, nuclear concerns and China's special relationship with Pakistan against India are being addressed cautiously by both the sides as they carry security implications for both the countries.

A Historical Turning Point

The frozen relations between India and China acquired some movement with the appointment of ambassadors by either side in 1976 but the progress in the relations, has been rather tardy. However, India rediscovered China during Rajiv Gandhi's tenure as Prime Minster. Rajiv Gandhi's visit to China in December 1988 was a turning point because it was during this visit that a 'road map' was prepared to improve the relations between the two countries. After the meeting, having been impressed by the statesmanship of the paramount leader of China Deng Xiao Ping, almost double his age, Rajiv Gandhi was inspired to reciprocate the Chinese urge to resolve all the problems with all its neighbours, including India. It was during this visit, that a Joint Working Group (JWG) was established for future negotiations on the boundary problem and to discuss ways and means of maintaining peace and tranquility along the Line of Actual Control.

Another important milestone in the relations between India and China has been the visit of the Prime Minister P.V. Narasimha Rao in 1993. His visit was significant because both India and China formalized the high level visits and their proceedings between 1988 and 1993. Since the maintenance of peace along the disputed border assumed importance as both the parties agreed to maintain peace and tranquility along the Line of Actual Control (LAC), this agreement was formally signed during Rao's visit to China. An important feature of Rao's visit was the enormous thrust given to increase the volume of trade between India and China. It was also a manifestation of India's penchant to attach importance to the countries in the East. The economic reforms initiated at the beginning of 1990's, catapulted India's image in the eyes of the Chinese getting enriched through their economic reforms, which were already more than a decade old. By 1995-96 the bilateral trade rose to US$ 5 billion from 675 million in 1993.

Jiang Zemin's visit to India in 1996, was a further demonstration of China's urge for the maintenance of cordial relations with India, keeping their past animosities on the back burner. The Chinese President signed a land mark agreement which covered military confidence building measures along the border and honoured the earlier accords with regard the Line of Actual Control.

The next high level visit by a Chinese dignitary after Jiang Zemin, was the five day visit of the Chinese Prime Minister Zhu Rongji in January 2002. He was responsible for many economic initiatives taken to boost China's trade and investments. During his visit he made a deep impression in the business community in India that China was a potential and suitable country for Indian investors and traders. He compared the prices of manufactured products between India and China and invited businessmen to invest in China by explaining that goods in China are five to six times cheaper than in India. He also gave an outline of the immense scope for business in the sectors such as IT, Services and Engineering.

Indian Prime Minister Atal Bihari Vajpayee visited China on June 20, 2003. The visit assumed greater significance because it not only boosted the trade relations between the two countries but also made them express their willingness at the diplomatic level to get the border problem solved, by special envoys appointed exclusively to look into the matter. The trade and investment scenario greatly changed with the visit of Zhu Rongji. The two sides agreed to fix the target for bilateral trade at US$ 10 billion by 2005. It is surprising that ever since 1993, the volume of bilateral trade has been surpassing the targets fixed by the two countries. Soon, China became the principal trading partner to India, next only to the United States and European Union. The two sides for the first time, also agreed to recognize the sovereign authority of China over Tibet and India's authority over Sikkim. In spite of security implications, the two sides demonstrated that the political and security matters are intertwined with economic development.

The booming trade activity between India and China encouraged Chinese leadership to pay much more attention on the bilateral relations. Prime Minister Wen Jiabao return visit to India in April 2005 helped both the nations to declare that the establishment of the strategic cooperative partnership is for peace and prosperity. According to the Chinese Ambassador to India Sun Yuxi, Wen's visit "opened a new chapter for the comprehensive development of our relations". The increasing economic cooperation between India and China evidently inspired the description of the economic integration as "Chindia" scenario with China leading in the economic growth, followed by India. It is appropriate to quote here, an apt and appealing expression of the sentiment by the ambassador San Yuxi at a FICCI Symposium held in New Delhi in October 2005. He said: "today, I am very pleased to see that, with continuous development of the China – India relations, the word Chindia emerges as the times require. When we use only one word to denote our two countries, I think the relationship between China and India is much closer than brotherhood." This cryptic expression is appropriate so far as the economic relations between the two countries, are concerned. In recent years, India closely collaborated with China in bidding oil prices bearing in mind the energy needs of the two countries. After an initial competition for oil resources, both the countries realized that by collaborating, they save precious foreign exchange considerably. Both India and China entered into an energy partnership and cooperation with each other in their bid for oil in Russia, Central Asia and expressed their preparedness to work together in America and Europe.

Cautious Moves

Not withstanding the economic and trade boom between India and China, both allowed their individual apprehensions about each other, to operate on the political and security matters willingly or otherwise. Prolonged animosity and lingering mutual suspicion, seem to exert an influence on both the sides in matters of building bridges between the two nations. The traditional friendship between China and Pakistan, targeting India, got altered after 9/11 incident in the United States. India's troubles and tribulations due to cross border terrorism received much attention as the United States was all sympathy for India. Both India and the United States came closer than before. The strategic partnership between these two nations effected a change in the political scenario in Asia. China, having begun to aim at the domestic economic growth, did not want to get itself disturbed by the changing political equations in South Asia. Therefore, the visiting Chinese Premier in 2002 made it clear to both India and Pakistan, to resolve their differences bilaterally, including Kashmir issue. However, it is very hard to transform the Indian national psyche against the humiliation of not only the Chinese inflicting a defeat on India in 1962, but also the indirect promoting of cross border terrorism by supporting Pakistan.

The border problem between India and China has not been solved so far. The Joint Working Group (CWG) and the appointed special envoys representing both the countries, held discussions several times but the dispute along the border, remains unsolved. The continuing non-resolved border problem gave rise to several apprehensions in India. India is alert about nuclear arsenal of China which has been producing various types of ballistic missiles. Besides, China has already taken up modernization of People's Liberation Army (PLA) in the wake of information Technology. The apprehensions in the minds of Chinese have been enhanced by the recently concluded defence pact between India and the Untied States. The pact entitled "The New Framework for the US-India Defence Relationships" and signed in June 2005, helps India to acquire wide variety of defence equipment and even sensitive military technologies. The nuclear agreement between India and China is also causing uneasiness to China.

In spite of these apprehensions, Chinese Prime Minister Wen Jiabao paid a highly successful visit to India in April 2005. Both the prime ministers of the two countries decided to celebrate 2006 as "China-India Friendship year". Accordingly on January 6, 2005, the Chinese Embassy in New Delhi hosted a reception of the celebrations to mark a beginning of "China-India Friendship Year." Messages of the respective Presidents and Premiers of the two countries were read on this occasion. This event was closely followed by the visit of the foreign secretary of India Shyam Saran to China who had held discussions with the Chinese State Councillor Tung Jiaxuan. Both of them reiterated in their joint communiqué that "China and India should go a step further to explore the framework for the solution to the border issue." But both the sides know that unless border problem is solved, it is hard to establish full normalization of relations between the two counties. Until then, India and China would tread cautiously.

Conclusion

The year 2006 is declared as "China-India Friendship Year" by both the countries as an all round boost to the relations between them. India and China got their relations enhanced almost from the scratch to a recognizably visible level. From a state of frozenness, the relations grew tremendously, especially in the realm of economic partnership. However, the impact of the unresolved border problem creating uneasiness between the two countries is bound to be felt in other fields, including trade and investment. As a result of the apprehensions, both India and China have become cautious in taking initiatives.

14

India's Role in Peace, Progress and Prosperity in Asia

G. Jayachandra Reddy

We are of Asia and the peoples of Asia are nearer closer to us than others. India is so situated that she is the pivot of western, southern and Southeast Asia.

Jawaharlal Nehru

The rise of India and China has begun transforming Asia, and the rise of Asia has been changing the world. It is widely held that the twenty first century belongs to Asia. Given the fact, that Asia is one of the least integrated regions, a section of the international community entertains certain apprehensions about the Asian nations treading the path of peace and ensuring and maintaining peace, stability, balance of power, economic growth and security, which are the prime requisites of making this century, a century of Asia. There is also a saying: "Rising powers can`destabilize their neighbourhoods and destabilize world order." [1] If India is poised enough to play an altogether new and a major role in the 21st century world order, then it must be able to evolve for itself a distinct notion quite convincing to the world also, as to what kind of role can India assume in the new millennium – a role, totally different from the one, presumably perceived in the present-day geopolitics.

With the economic boom in Asia, there comes a great diversity and also a shift in the priority-paradigm for co-existence in the region. An active collaboration in many areas is essential to guarantee peace, security and development. Despite their new found status, the rising powers should be cautious enough to keep insolence and jingoism at bay, lest they should prove to be dangerous, by resulting in sharp and internecine conflicts. Moreover, history has shown that an unbroken development cannot be taken for granted, as many set-backs in the past have been witnessed. [2]

In this paper, an attempt has been made to examine the new dynamics of geopolitics in the Asian continent, in particular. Asia has been known for its longest history and for its typical responses to the world-events. As it is very difficult to deal with all the issues of Asia, this paper seeks to focus on the assessment of sub-regions of Asia Pacific in respect of peace, unity and regional cooperation. An attempt also is made to study the potentials of the conflicts in the region that, constantly threaten, to undermine the immense potentialities of the region.

Many countries of Asia were brought under the colonial rule of the Europeans for a long period. Right now, almost all the countries have achieved independence. However, a casual glance at the nature and the behaviour of these countries is bound to expose the behavioural legacies of the past. Hence, it is said that *countries were decolonized but not their attitudes.* Crises are ubiquitous in the world but what distinguishes Asia vis-à-vis the global scenario, is the fact that Asia has been in the grip of a pattern of conflicts which are, all said and done, amenable for an easy analysis.

First, the nuclear issue comes to the fore to deserve own consideration. Out of eight nuclear powers of the world, five of them, i.e. Russia, China, India, Pakistan and Israel are located in Asia. Surprisingly enough, the present and the former world leaders of the US and Great Britain respectively, have been representing the most potential and dynamic regions of the world, along with France as another nuclear power. Whereas, the newly independent states of Asia are emerging as "*nuclear region*", competing not only in matters of the acquisition of nuclear capability but also in regard to their strategic use. What makes the situation still worse is, that these powers tend to target their neighbours but it is the nuclear belligerence, that seems to thrive in the continent.

Secondly, in the same proportion as that of the nuclear proliferation, there has arisen the proliferation of the regional organizations in the Asia pacific, contributing little to their objectives like cooperation, economic affairs and confidence building. Although these organizations were initiated in the same spirits as that of EU and other European monoliths, they turned out to serve as senseless venues for accusations and counter accusations and wide-spread distrust in the member countries. Peace and stability have been reduced to mere slogans meant for the satisfaction of certain political order and purpose exclusively. Hence, they do not give out an impression that they had any vision of, and commitment to, the economic and political stability in the region. Therefore, it is easy to conclude as to where these organizations are leading the member-countries. [3]

However, ASEAN, out of all the regional organizations of Asia, may be singled out for praise for its spirit of and commitment to broad-based unity, confidence building, stability and peace. This kind of an achievement requires, no investment but some amount of mutual trust and respect and, on top of all, an appreciation of respective compulsions irrespective of economic status, strategic importance, and future ambitions and expectations. ASEAN may be one of the smallest, in terms of quantity but it is one of the richest regional organizations, in terms of quality and spirit of cooperation among its members. Based on the strength of unity and spirit, ASEAN attracts many larger states and stronger economies to come under the ASEAN umbrella. For instance, Japan, China and India, besides EU, have been paying due attention to this region along with EU. Although the US has been a little lukewarm on the issue of its partnership, the US Secretary of State has increasingly been making the impact of his/her presence, felt in the ASEAN foreign ministers' meet consistently, for the last 20 years.

This year, however, Condoleezza Rice allowed herself to be represented by her deputy, last ASEAN should find its stature diminished. Commenting on this, Michael Vatikiotis, a strategic analyst, has rightly observed that it might be, that Washington's priorities lie elsewhere, or that the Southeast Asia's strategic significance has been giving the impression of being on the wane since the end of the Cold War. Considering the fact that Rice has been a vitriolic critic of Myanmar's military regime, [4] it may also be true, that ASEAN has made things awkward for Rice by an inability to pressure the military junta in Myanmar to restore democracy. It shows that the member countries are committed to remain united in supporting one another, in spite of strong reactions and adverse consequences. This kind of unanimity has been the modus operandi of every regional organization of Asia to achieve unity, so that the intensity of the US interference is reduced. This can be taken to be an indicator of peace and stability in the region.

For its own part, the US has been not at all concerned about the type of regime in a country, as long as the regime listens to the US voice. The issue of the type of government that rules a state, can be dismissed as an internal matter in a facile manner by the US, if the government is prepared to play a US stooge. If a state is under military rule, and should, therefore, be deprived of certain privileges, US can pretty well turn a blind eye, and keep on patting the back so long as the state in question serves US interests. Pakistan's case is a glaring example of the US brinkmanship. At one point of time, the military dictatorship of Pakistan was given the most favoured nation status by the US.

It goes without saying that South Pacific Forum (SPF) has been playing a significant role in maintaining peace and co-operation in the region, in spite of the fact that all the countries of this region are insular though they are spread over a large geographical area. Except Australia and New Zealand, the other countries have been tiny in terms of economic resources, though this region has been deemed strategically significant. The nations of this region have undoubtedly maintained socio-economic and political stability. However, the environmental disasters, due to nuclear tests in some of the island countries and the dumping of nuclear wastes by the developed nations, have been the bane of the region.

Interestingly enough, South Pacific and Southeast Asia, are the only two sub-regions of Asia Pacific which have been favourable to India in extending an economic cooperation. Of course, India has effected a paradigm shift in its relations with the countries of those neighbouring regions, following the launch of Look East policy. The ongoing Look East policy has been yielding good results in these regions especially after its entry into the second phase.

Central Asia is going to emerge as one of the potential regions of interest for the entire world because of its huge oil reserves. At the same time, the growing involvement of the US and Russia in a struggle for rival claims for power is noticeable in this region. Central Asia/Transcaucasian Region, will presumably be a new battlefield for great power rivalry. The region serves as a link between Europe and Asia, and can turn into another area of instability and local conflicts. [5] The geopolitical structure of the post-Soviet States may have greater influence over the entire Asia and world, at large. Eventualities are likely to erupt in the form of border conflicts. In addition, the US is very much interested in playing a major role to contain the Russian hegemony. As noted by many scholars and political strategists, the new development is labeled as the "new great game" in the 21st century. In all seriousness, Moscow has repeatedly stated its determination to enhance the role of the "Collective Security Treaty Organization" (CSTO). [6] Although the stakes involved, remain the same, -- i.e., power, influence, security, wealth -- the new playing field is further complicated by an array of problems such as intra-regional multinational conglomerates, and a shortfall in commercial expertise and legal infrastructures. [7]

The Middle East has incessantly been afflicted by age-long insecurity syndrome. This region can be treated differently from other regions of Asia because of chronicles of conflicts. Many conflicts nevertheless internal have been responsible for inviting the outside intervention in this region. Ultimately, it is quite obvious that the political instability, resulting from the immense economic potentialities of the oil-wealth, leads to disunity and unrest in the region. In addition, this region attracts many big players of the world, and Iran's nuclear issue has been hitting the headlines in the front page of world geopolitics. The US role in the region is going to be the key role and the fact of the dependence of the emerging economies of the world like those of India and China has been to the hilt for their oil imports, creates a complex situation in the Middle East. Peace and political stability of this region demand political liberalization and democratization. In this context, many observers view the greater Middle East and the Islamic world as an anomaly, because, an authoritarian rule continues to dominate, albeit in varying degrees. The spread of democracy which had remained subterranean was set in motion the internal reforms that contributed to greater openness and the multiparty competition in the Middle East during the 1990s. Ultimately, the drive toward more substantive reform was cut short, as the incumbent leaders did not want to face the risk of their positions getting endangered by their embarking on genuine democratization processes. [8]

East Asia has been endowed with good economies, particularly Japan and China. But these countries have been playing two different kinds of roles; Japan and China are known for their pro US and anti US policies respectively. Based on the political ideology and the issue of nuclear technology, North Korea has been at the centre of East Asian geopolitics. Though this region has attained top rank in terms of its economic and technological potentialities, the uncertainty of cooperation among the countries, leads to an underestimation. During her Asia tour in March 2005, Rice repeatedly stressed, that Washington would back Japan in the region and support the Japanese desire for a permanent UN Security Council veto status. In Tokyo, she called on Japan and other countries in the region, to get united to demand that China "eventually embrace democracy." She openly opposed the recent effort of the European Union to lift the 1989 arms embargo on China as well, and warned of a new Chinese threat against Taiwan. [9] Apart from China and Japan, there are other countries playing a major role in the world economy and also notable for strategic importance. The entire region from Korea to Taiwan is part of one strategic complex which threatens to go awry to the detriment of the growth of the world economy and finance flows. In response to the new Japan-USA front against China on Taiwan, China reacted with coolness, and even tried to mediate a Korean solution. In response to the US-Japan "Taiwan Card" game, China is apparently playing at the moment, its "Korea Card" game. [10]

The subcontinent can not at all be dismissed. It is a region with a massive population, long-range nuclear weapons and uneven but rising economic growth. At the same time, India is increasingly wary of China's intervention in this region. There has been an opinion developed that Sion-India relations are on the verge of making a "new beginning." For instance, on the issues like Afghanistan's membership and China's induction into SAARC as observer, India has been cornered by Nepal, Bangladesh and Pakistan. At the 13th SAARC summit, held in Dhaka in November 2005, India's physical presence was overshadowed by China's invisible presence but growing influence. [11] China's involvement in this region may give greater opportunities to intensify the existing tensions, especially in India and Pakistan relations. So, India ought to go ahead with specific strategies to contain China and to maintain good relations with the member countries of SAARC.

One thing, however, would seem evident: the manifold economic and financial ties among the Asian countries are no guarantee for either support or solidarity amongst them. Perhaps quite the contrary is the case: as long as these economic linkages are not sustained by some kind of political commonality or solidarity, the individual countries will remain vulnerable. Economic interdependence has thus, a political price: either that of increased vulnerability or of delegating some national authority to a common international institution. [12]

At the present juncture of economic crises and political reform, it can be argued that the regional security cooperation would seem to be of secondary importance. In some regions, this may be so, in others rather less. Thus, if Asia, wants to be an area of stability, safe for foreign investment and capable of managing crises or even conflicts by itself, it will have to pay greater attention to this dimension of stability and predictability. As long as it does not, the "Asian Century" will have to wait for a while. [13]

A brief account of the sub-regions of Asia-Pacific is that of an order based on the requirement of peace. Accordingly, Middle East and South Pacific occupy the first and last places respectively, followed by South, Central and East Asia in the second, third and fourth places. In view of the nature of politics and conflicts, the resultant economic order supports the search for new means and measures for protecting the big continent. A few of the leading countries of this region are engrossed in promoting their own interests and priorities, but there is an immediate need to float the idea "Cooperation for Peace". The "Partnership for Peace" programme is useful and also historically and conceptually unique. It promotes cooperation and possibly concertation. [14]

Conclusion

Asia is endowed with a wide range of resource base, and also keeps pace with the sustainable economic growth rate and many experts refer to this as the image of the 21st century of Asians. But the reality is totally different. We can conclusively say that many sub-regions of Asia have been witnessing internal conflicts, dissensions series of wars and apprehensions. In this geopolitical scenario, what is in short supply is an enduring peace and sustainable economic growth – these two realities are deeply enshrined in workable unity. In fact, these dimensions of geopolitical realities, if realized at least in routine affairs of the countries, can solve the destabilizing problems and can be directed towards future, to play an important role in the world politics.

At present the geopolitics are driven by muscle power and aggressiveness. In view of the transition of geopolitics into geo-economics, mankind looks for peace rather than war, sustainable economic growth rather than brinkmanship, and a safe world without radicalism. Moreover, Asia is seemingly an epicenter of the world crises. At this juncture, any country initiating the policy of peace and stability certainly touches the hearts of people in general. US rule the roost now, after the termination of the Cold War. Russia can be considered a sleeping lion. China now fires the shots and tries to ride roughshod in economy and politics in its own terms. In the new millennium, there are new probabilities for the rising countries in the world arena, to spell out new prospects for world peace and stability and contribute positively by working out their own roles, in geopolitics. Such a nation can emerge as a real leader of the region/world. For instance, winning a war does not mean achieving target. Wars leave behind fallouts that keep fermenting from generation to generation. None pays any attention to the conqueror in the war who is very soon forgotten.

Literature on geopolitics spells out that 21st century is the century for the Asians. One wonders as to how it is achievable without unity and integrity. It requires a lot of commitment and basic faith in peace, non-violence, and brotherhood. If we excavate the history of the world, we learn that India took lead many times on many occasions with distinction, and therefore, India has to play a proactive role in establishing peace and stability in the Asia Pacific region. This leads to the assumption of the ongoing Look East policy as extended to other sub-regions of this region. This is to be strongly promoted and supported by researchers, in the form of Area Studies Programme. There is also a dire need to go for a research commission to coordinate the research works of different Centres of Area Studies Programme of the country. If needed, such a commission may design the required strategies and initiatives for the Indian government on a time-frame basis.

Notes

1. Surakiart Sathirathai, "Managing the Rise of Asia," *FEER*, July 2005, p.14.
2. Andre Gunder Frank, (2004), Reorient World History, Social Theory, and the 19th Century.

3. Towards the 21st Century: Trends in Past-Cold War International Security Policy, Paper prepared for the 3rd International Security Furum, Switzerland, 1998.

4. Michael Vatikiotis, (2005), No Rice for ASEAN this year, International Herald Tribune.

5. Towards the 21st Century: Trends in Past-Cold War International Security Policy, Paper prepared for the 3rd International Security Forum, Switzerland, 1998.

6. Federico Bordonaro, (2006), Why Russia must be strong, http://www.atimes.com/atimes/Central_Asia/HB24Ag02.html

7. Rosemarie Forsythe, (1996), The Politics of Oil in the Caucasus and Central Asia, Adelphi Paper, No.300, p.6.

8. Marina Ottaway and Thomas Carothers, (2004), Think Again: Middle East Democracy, Foreign Policy, No. 145, also see, Chris Zambelis, (2005), The Strategic Implications of Political Liberalization and Democratization in the Middle East, Parameters, Autumn, pp. 87-102.

9. William Engdahl, (2005), Japan and China Tensions and Washington's Asia Geopolitics.

10. *Ibid*

11. Mohan Malik, (2006), Delhi and Beijing tread warily, http://www.atimes.com/atimes/South_Asia/HB14Df02.html

12. Towards the 21st Century: Trends in Past-Cold War International Security Policy, Paper prepared for the 3rd International Security Forum, Switzerland, 1998.

13. *Ibid.*

14. *Ibid.*

15

East Asia Summit: First Impressions

A. Lakshmana Chetty

On the occasion of ASEAN's inception, many a political observer within and outside the region, sneered and scoffed at ASEAN, as they felt that it only represented a region, marred by mutual suspicions, war and intra-regional conflicts. The impressive performance of ASEAN defied all the cynics who had wrongly predicted that it would eventually fall apart. [1] ASEAN not only fulfilled its founders' vision of an association encompassing all the ten countries of Southeast Asia but also established "effective forums for consultation and dialogue" where they interacted with outside powers concerned about the political and security issues of the region. What is more, ASEAN leap frogged to unveil a new regional architecture, East Asia Summit (EAS), which is viewed as the harbinger of a pan-Asian forum. Though constrained by the lack of a thorough grasp of the mainsprings of the EAS initiative, India, driven by its penchant for associating itself with too many regional groupings in the period following the opening of its market, had made a determined bid to become a founding father of this forum. This paper, while describing various events that led to the emergence of EAS, aims at analysing its political and strategic dimensions and seeks to offer certain insights into India's perception of and attitude towards EAS.

Genesis of the Proposition

Disenchanted with the unfruitful Uruguay Round of GATT negotiations and deeply concerned about the threats to the external economic relations of East Asia by the growing trend of protectionism manifested in the emergence of regional trade groupings such as European Community and NAFTA, Malaysian Prime Minister Mahathir Mohamad promulgated in 1990, the idea of setting up of the East Asian Economic Group (EAEG) with ASEAN members, the three Indochina countries, Myanmar, China, Hong Kong, Taiwan, South Korea and Japan to discuss, debate and jointly resolve economic issues of common concern and to take a united stand at international economic forums such as GATT. The exclusion of the United States from the proposed economic regime, not only impeded the support of Japan and South Korea but also incurred the wrath of the US and its allies such as Canada, Australia and New Zealand. In order to win a wider acceptance for the new entity proposed by him, Mahathir changed the focus by rechristening it as East Asian Economic Caucus (EAEC) in October 1991.

However, the US, which did not want the APEC to be diluted, remained obdurate, while some of the ASEAN countries like Indonesia adopted rather lukewarm attitude to the Malaysian move. [2] There were also other factors which prevented the Malaysian proposal from taking a concrete shape in the early 1990s, China and India being yet to emerge as great powers capable of moulding the destinies of Asia. The trade among Asian countries, paled into insignificance, in comparison with that between Asia and the rest of the world. With APEC covering the entire Asia-Pacific, EAEC had no worthwhile appeal to make. With the expectations of "multipolarity" remaining high, following the end of the Cold War, Mahathir's move to limit the power and influence of the US in Asia through the proposed forum of EAEC, was felt redundant.

Pushing through the Concept

However, it was left to the successor of Mahathir, Prime Minister Abdullah Badawi to realize that the time was ripe to pick up threads from his predecessor and to push through Mahathir's pet project. The demand for an institutional mechanism was great more than at any time before, for meeting the challenges in three vital sectors – economic, energy and security. This was more so at a time when Asia was emerging as the 'centre of gravity of global economy' against all odds and hazards like tensions between China and Japan, the rising level of extremist threats in the Philippines and Indonesia, and the increasing dependence of Asia's economies on the US. The region's prospects had brightened, thanks to India's robust economic growth and rising global significance, China's phenomenal-economic growth and ASEAN's emergence as a geopolitically vital and economically vibrant region. Singapore's Senior Minister and former Premier Goh Chok Tong has pointed out that the renaissance of Asia was led by China and India. [3] Asia continued to lag behind America and Europe in multilateral trading arrangements despite the growing supportive environment as well as a spurt which occurred in the bilateral Preferential Trading Areas (PTAs) in Asia by way of catching up with the rest of the world. Intra-Asian trade has begun to gallop. China has been in the process of snatching the U.S. position as a major trading partner in Asia. China has replaced the US, as a major trading partner of South Korea. India's trade with the developing Asian countries had already shot up from 11.8 per cent to 24 per cent, during 1990-2000. [4]

India and China, the two Asian giants, have been in quest of energy security. As the Petroleum Minister Mani Shankar Aiyar has pointed out, to both India and China "the most crucial sector of economy which will determine their future prospects of growth and the possibilities of eradicating poverty will be the energy sector." [5] Members of ASEAN have turned to Russia, to get their dependence on West Asian Oil minimized. South Korea hoped to secure "stable deliveries of oil and gas from Eastern Siberia and Sakhalin." [6] India and China have been investing huge sums in oil exploration in Africa, Central Asia and Russia. India has invested a record US$·2.7 billion in the Sakhalin-I oil and gas project, in order to meet 20 per cent of its energy requirements. [7] A sad part of the story is, that China and Japan are sharply divided over the route of a planned oil pipeline from the rich East Siberian fields. [8] Since Asia is emerging as the fastest growing energy market there is need to build an "Asian oil and gas community" which is likely to lead to a "closer alliance between Asian nations", [9] besides the meeting the challenges in the energy sector.

It is said that Asia, which is the most dynamic and a rapidly changing and modernizing region, is seriously challenged by a wide array of security issues, including the scourge of international terrorism, particularly, after 9/11, gun running, narcotics trafficking and deployment of foreign forces to mention a few. Setting out with a conviction that these challenges could be effectively addressed, by coordinated and collective action, and certainly not by "compartmentalised approaches," ASEAN and BIMSTEC have already initiated counter-measures. Mention may be made of "ASEAN-India Joint Declaration for Cooperation to Combat International Terrorism," adopted on October 8, 2003. [10]

Malaysia's initiative for a broader economic integration was given a major boost when Japanese Prime Minister Junichiro Koizumi dilated in a speech in Singapore in 2002 on the concept of a Community in East Asia involving ASEAN+3 and Australia and New Zealand. [11] Two years later, the ASEAN Summit in Vientiane, Laos, decided to hold the first ever East Asia Summit in Malaysia, in December 2005. [12]

Membership Wrangle

The participants of the three hour EAS meeting held in Kuala Lumpur on December 14, 2005, included ASEAN+3 (plus three being China, Japan and South Korea) besides India, Australia and New Zealand. This meant that minus EU, Canada and the US, most of the non-ASEAN members of ARF, were accommodated in the EAS.

To begin with, India did not figure in the list of participants of the proposed East Asian outfit. Former Malaysian Prime Minister and the promoter of the idea of East Asian grouping Mahathir Mohammad insisted on excluding the 'peripheral' nations like India. [13] He was opposed to making the geographical definition of East Asia elastic. [14] Mahathir's successor, Prime Minister

Badawi, held fast to his mentor's view which was shared by China. No doubt, India has a great attraction for ASEAN nations by virtue of its fast growing economy marked by a GDP of US $ 700 billion and an annual growth rate of seven to eight per cent. [15] But ASEAN countries, particularly, Singapore, Thailand and Malaysia, have been unhappy with India which, having entered into a slew of pacts, agreements and FTAs failed in matters of their implementation which was glaringly obvious in the poor follow up of the Indo-Thai FTA and CECA with Singapore. This was attributed to the hurdles in the process of liberalization – due to considerable opposition from the Indian industry which suffered from the lack of competitive efficiency – the dogmatic political parties and the nonchalant bureaucracy. While committing that India would bring down its tariffs to ASEAN evels, dismantle unwarranted barriers and expand capital flows, the Indian Prime Minister Manmohan Singh, in the course of his address to the ASEAN Business Advisory Council on December 12, 2005, described as follows:

"We must walk this road together, so that enterprises in our countries find it a beneficial process, not a hurtful one. There may be losers, and there will certainly be gainers, but on the whole, we will obtain a win-win outcome." [16]

India had to face an embarrassing situation, when ASEAN countries launched a scathing attack on India, for including not only strategically important items like oil and gas, but also trifles like lavatory seats, dolls, and chewing gum in the 1414 "negative items list" in the proposed FTA with ASEAN. [17] Malaysia expressed doubts about India's preparedness to participate in an Asian Free Trade Community, citing New Delhi's belated and slow approach, towards economic reforms. [18]

Despite New Delhi's poor show in the economic front, ASEAN countries like Singapore and Indonesia had supported India's participation in the EAS so as to neutralize the fast growing Chinese influence. An Asian analyst remarked that "India must be aware that it has not been invited to EAS because of its rising economic potential alone but more as a balancing force to offset the China factor." [19] The Chinese officials admitted unofficially, that Beijing's preference was for a smaller Asian grouping which would facilitate rapid advances in the economic sphere and thus help China to influence in a significant way. [20] An Indonesian diplomat Wiryono Sastrohandoyo, asserted that it was the fear of this increasing influence of China that prompted the ASEAN nations like Singapore and Indonesia to create the EAS in the first place and coopt India, Australia, New Zealand and even Russia (which was invited as an observer) into the EAS. He added:

"We see the central problem as China. China is growing so fast and people are not sure of its intentions. It needs a balancer. That could be India, Australia, New Zealand–at least economically." [21]

This glaring China syndrome prompted the Chinese Prime Minister Wen Jiabao to dispel these concerns. Addressing the East Asia Summit on December 12, 2005 Wen said: "China will continue to seek peace and development through cooperation and will strive to achieve development that will bring about peace, openness, cooperation and harmony as well as benefit to itself and other counties." [22]

Analysis of Kuala Lumpur Declaration

The first ever East Asia Summit brought together all the economic power houses in East, Southeast and South Asia, besides Australia and New Zealand whose heads of government alone (without the presence of advisors and senior officials), met in a "retreat" format, and got engaged in an exchange of views that focused on burning issues of the day including international terrorism, maritime security, prevention of infectious diseases. The 16 heads of government issued the "Kuala Lumpur Declaration" establishing the East Asia Summit as a forum for "dialogue on broad strategic, political and economic issues of common interest." The leaders agreed to focus on key areas such as – cooperation in political and security issues – financial stability, energy security, economic integration and growth, eradicating poverty and narrowing down the development gap in East Asia, deeper cultural understanding and people-to-people contact. The Summit fondly hoped that the efforts of the EAS "to promote community building in this region will be consistent with and reinforce the realization of the ASEAN Community, and will form an integral part of the evolving regional architecture." EAS also called for cooperation in environmental protection, prevention of infectious diseases and natural disaster management.

Outlining the 'plan of action' of the EAS, the Chairman of the EAS said: "We recognized the increasing inter-linkages and growing inter-dependence among our countries and agreed to deepen integration and cooperation in order to promote the creation of a harmonious and prosperous community of nations." [23]

Future Membership

The Kuala Lumpur Declaration stated that the East Asia Summit will bc an "opcn forum". It augurcd wcll from Indian perspective because, keeping the grouping open and inclusive would facilitate the formation of an Asian Economic Community, which New Delhi has been contemplating for quite some time. It also comforted the American allies who advocated the American participation in the EAS. Singapore favoured the idea of Washington's future involvement. [24] Japan went a step further to lobby hard with personal letters to all leaders of the ten ASEAN nations and to South Korea and India for its view that while India, Australia and New Zealand should be included as members, the US should be offered an observer status in the EAS. Tokyo also called for keeping the EAS open.

Interestingly enough, the Deputy Foreign Minister Hitoshi Tanaka had been charged with the organization of this lobbying campaign to counter China's plans to dominate the EAS by restricting the membership only to ASEAN + 3. With the U.S. precluded, China was so confident of its pre-eminent role in the EAS that, on the ever of the holding of the EAS, Beijing proposed to host the second Summit. [25] As the International Herald Tribune has pointed out, the US was "absent from an Asian association for the first time in the post war era." [26] The US had strong claims to be a member of EAS. The Foreign Minister of Singapore, George Yeo, while underlining the stabilizing role of the US, argued that the US should continue to play a key role in the region, citing the enormous relief efforts by the American military including the deployment of 16,000 military personnel, 26 large ships, 58 helicopters and 43 fixed wing aircraft, besides the recovery effort during the December 2004 tsunami disaster that ravaged around a dozen countries located along the Indian Ocean coast leaving at least 288,000 people, dead. [27] In fact, the EAS, though originally conceived as an East Asian forum to the core, was subsequently redefined so as to accommodate extra regional powers for their economic and political importance, the US got its own case spoiled.

The ASEAN diplomats maintained, "the US was not frozen out – it just didn't bother to ask to join." [28] The exclusion of the US did not point to Washington's forfeiting the diplomatic influence in favour of China. The outgoing Deputy Secretary of State Richard Armitage lamented, that China has done well in its "charm offensive" to win over Asia, while the US had lost ground in Asia, due to its obsession with the ideas of fighting in war on terror and perceiving Asia as the second front for terror activities. By frowning on multilateral initiatives such as the ARF, and regarding them as merely a talk shop, Washington had unwittingly defaulted the leadership to Beijing. [29] Further, the US declined to join by refusing to sign a pledge renouncing the use of force and interference in the internal affairs of the region. Sharing the sentiments of Armitage, Jusuf Wanandi, Director of the Jakarta-based Centre for Strategic and International Studies, said: "I know about the mess in the Middle East, but don't be distracted. There's a bigger region that you have to pay attention to for the long term. This is definitely, whether you like it or not, the most important region in the future." In sharp contrast to the US, the Federation of Russia was represented at the EAS by its

President Vladimir Putin as an invited observer but not as a member. Russia which, besides satisfying the criteria for membership by agreeing to renounce the use of force in the region, [30] successfully lobbied for full membership at the second EAS, scheduled to be held in Manila next year.

Issue of Stewardship of EAS

The one issue on which the inaugural EAS sharpened focus was, as to who would "lead" the forum – would it be ASEAN, "ASEAN+3 or all the members of the forum. This was particularly so, in the light of criticism of ASEAN's continuing leadership of the ARF. The ASEAN, some of whose members were labelled as "Asian tigers" was firm that the steering role should be reserved for itself. The Chairman's statement of ASEAN Summit held ahead of EAS proclaimed, that ASEAN would remain the "driving force" of EAS. [31] ASEAN was uncompromising on this subject as it did not want to get embroiled in the power politics among the big Asian powers as well as among countries such as Australia and New Zealand which were noted for their "blunt style of diplomacy" in contrast to Southeast Asia's more stolid approach.

Occupation of the driver's seat would also facilitate for ASEAN, the balancing of the key powers in the region. [32] Further, the fact that ASEAN remained the core of the EAS, reinforced the Southeast Asian grouping's title to the leadership role of the EAS. [33] Malaysia, the chief advocate of the EAS, asserted that ASEAN nations were the ideal choice for leading the EAS process and making the EAS "a meaningful" and the result-oriented forum. [34] With ASEAN – and not the heavy weights such as China, Japan and India – in the drivers' seat, the interests of the smaller nations of ASEAN in EAS would be best served. Michael Vatikiotis, a top notch strategic analyst, quipped: "To establish for itself a steering role in a nascent East Asian Community is perhaps the best way to avoid being totally squeezed." [35]

The rift between China and Japan also favoured ASEAN's leadership role. An Indonesian economist of no mean repute observed:

"That the Asian economic integration movement has thus far been ASEAN-driven, however, is simply because ASEAN is the least objectionable player to take the lead. The rivalry between China and Japan has made it impossible for either of these two powers to formally lead the process." [36]

Long before the EAS was held, Japan had advocated a system of Co-chairmanship (with the Chair rotating between an ASEAN and a non-ASEAN country). [37] Curtain on the issue was dropped following the unveiling of the Kuala Lumpur Declaration on East Asia Summit, which read in part stated: "The East Asia Summit will be hosted and Chaired by an ASEAN member country that assumes ASEAN Chairmanship and held back-to-back with the annual ASEAN Summit...."

India's Attitude to EAS

India which took long to join the ASEAN process because of its preoccupation with the inward looking policy was impatient to join EAS for more than one reason. First and foremost, it would facilitate the legitimization of India's claims for the status of a major power. Speaking to the media on his way to Kuala Lumpur to attend summit meetings, Prime Minister Manmohan Singh told the media: "The fact that India was invited to the (EAS) meet speaks volumes about the region's acceptance of India as a regional power." [38] India's association with EAS would also impart "a major impetus" to India's 'Look East' policy. Premier Manmohan Singh noted: "It (participation in EAS) is in a way, fulfilment of our commitment to the 'Look East' policy." [39] Already Look East policy had paid good dividends. In 2004, the trade between India and ASEAN stood at US $ 18 billion, a year on growth of almost 25 per cent. [40] India's trade with South Korea and China has been growing at a "handsome rate". As the Indian Premier claimed "South Korea is one of the most bullish investors in India." EAS would not only offer India an opportunity to hold a summit level dialogue with ASEAN, the Plus Three and Australia and New Zealand, but also strengthen India's claims to join APEC, a forum, larger than the EAS. [41] India's deep interest in EAS was also influenced by geopolitical considerations. New Delhi, which has been keen on carving a niche for itself in Asia, was determined not to "miss the first train" of the Asian integration. An entry into EAS, would send across message that India's foreign policy focus was not confined to South Asia only. Bringing out EAS' strategic significance to India, a Southeast Asian analyst remarked:

"Saddled with a troubled neighbourhood (terrorism, Kashmir, a royal coup d'etat in Nepal, growing Islamic militancy in Bangladesh, among other problems), India wants to avoid at all costs becoming a 'second-class member' of Asia. So India is seeking to be incorporated into the EAS' inner circle at whatever price." [42]

The chilly atmosphere in Sino-Japanese relations offered an excellent opportunity to India to play a benign major role in the regional affairs. But, as the strategic analysts have pointed out, India is constrained by its "clumsy diplomacy and continuing tardiness in opening up its economy." [43] This was admitted by the Indian Premier Manmohan Singh himself when he told a press conference in Kuala Lumpur on December 12, 2005:

"All is not rosy with India. Since 1991, India has taken a break from old practices and a great deal has been done, but the process is not over and there are miles to go." [44]

In the international circles particularly in ASEAN, it is widely held that India could "balance" China. In fact, it was this perception of the ASEAN grouping that played a major role in ensuring invitation to India to join the East Asian grouping. [45] But Indian leadership was prompt to express its disapproval of the misreading of the India's positive disposition towards China. Premier Manmohan told the media on his way to Kuala Lumpur on December 11, 2005: "India and China are not in competition. We are partners. Our relations with China are evolving in a healthy direction." [46] It may not be out of context to mention here, a piece of advice offered to India by the former Prime Minister of Singapore Lee Kuan, while delivering the 37th Jawaharlal Nehru Memorial Lecture in the presence of Premier Manmohan Singh and Congress Party President Sonia Gandhi:

"Whether Asia will take its place in the world as Jawaharlal Nehru wanted depends on how both India and China work together as they rise and actively set out to avoid ending up in opposing camps." [47]

India's abiding interest in EAS and its commitment to make this century the century of Asia found an expression in Indian Premier's lavish praise of ASEAN for its determination and commitment to see the job of holding the EAS through. India not only hailed ASEAN's steering role, but also made a fine gesture by stating that "a safe and experienced driver" would take the forum to its destination. [48] Premier Singh also made explicit, India's deep concern for Asian peace and prosperity. Addressing the EAS Summit, Manmohan Singh quoted Jawaharlal Nehru, saying: "Today time is moving fast in Asia and the old continent is waking up." The Prime Minister said: "Future is our present, and Asia is India's destiny." [49]

ASEAN returned the gesture by openly declaring that India's role in the growth and development of the region was in no way inferior to that of China, Japan and South Korea. The statement of the Chairman of the EAS thus read:

..., we believed that the East Asia Summit together with the ASEAN + 3 and ASEAN+1 (ASEAN+India) processes could play a significant role in the community building in the region.

Evaluation of EAS

Ever since the convening of EAS became certain, arguments in favour of and against the East Asian grouping came to be advanced.

The pessimists argued that the diversity and vastness of the region would serve as disincentives in shaping the EAS into a cohesive regional outfit. Further, the prospects of the EAS as a new security mechanism would depend on the chemistry of relationship of big powers like India, China and Japan which could make or mar the career of the grouping. One analyst pointed out that smaller powers like the ASEAN nations do matter but more in terms of facilitating dialogue than in shaping the agendas. He added that the EAS may turn out to be just another talkfest, but its one saving grace was its potential to promote greater institutional collaborations. [50] Critics pointed out, that whatever ASEAN might do to remain in the East Asian driver's seat, it was inevitable that big power influence would come to play. "China, Japan and India increasingly cast large foot prints across the region and eventually across the world," said an observer. [51] One critic affirmed: "ASEAN's leadership of Asian integration is a case of the tail wagging the dog. That is another reason why the East Asia community, for all the hype, may never materialize." [52]

Optimists, on the other hand, hailed the EAS as the dawn of a new era. The summit host and Premier of Malaysia, Abdullah Badawi claimed:

"The East Asia Summit was a great and unqualified success. Let me repeat it, the summit was a great success. There was a high degree of acceptance that we are one community with a common interest in peace, stability and prosperity." [53]

Similar sentiments were expressed by Malaysia's political scientist Murugesu Pathmanaban:

"The very fact that all the invited leaders attended and that they discussed and agreed to some things is itself a success. It is the first step to major things in future given time." [54]

While dismissing the criticism that the EAS was "another talk shop" a senior diplomat from Thailand noted: "The new grouping will have a major say in shaping Asia's engagement with itself and rest of the world." [55]

Several proponents asserted that ASEAN was ideally suited to take driver's seat in the EAS. ASEAN, founded as far back as in 1967 and endowed with sound leadership, has been universally acclaimed as one of the most viable and vibrant regional groupings which was admitted by no less a person than the UN

Secretary-General Kofi Annan when he declared "Today, ASEAN is not only a well-functioning, indispensable reality in the region, it is a real force to be reckoned with, far beyond the region." [56]

ASEAN's steering role in EAS was defended by citing the driver's seat ASEAN has been occupying in all its interactions with the non-ASEAN members of ASEAN forums such as ARF and ASEAN+3+1 and in the meetings with its dialogue partners.

Going by the past experience of ASEAN, optimists ruled out the possibility of the grouping's prospects being undermined by the members of varying stages of development and diverse interests. Malaysia's leading English daily, *The New Straits Times*, observed:

"While ASEAN members have developed a comfort level among themselves over years, it will take some time for EAS members to do the same. The differences between some Northeast Asian nations and the different views of countries like Australia, from those of ASEAN, will require time for a rapport and a comfort level to develop. But that has not stopped ASEAN from engaging others with different views." [57]

One Southeast Asian analyst emphasised that ASEAN was eminently suited to the role of steering the EAS by citing the diplomatic dexterity ASEAN had displayed in bringing round the non-ASEAN members of EAS: "While ASEAN was able to persuade China to accept a more inclusive membership (of EAS), India could not stop China from influencing the recent summit of the South Asian Association for Regional Cooperation nations over the membership of Afghanistan." Pointing out ASEAN's commendable role "in forging an international peace agreement on Cambodia more than a decade ago", he further said: "Neither India nor China can yet notch up achievements like this on the global stage. Doesn't this make Southeast Asia a regional player, quite apart from its collective market place of 550 million people." [58]

A Summit of no mean dimensions of this kind, being the first of its kind need not be dismissed as a mere fortuitous event that carries not much of significance but is to be viewed as a rare event that augurs well for the countries involved as well as for the neighbouring ones and that it inaugurates a series of the kind.

Since the Summit would provide a convenient rostrum for a debate, one may entertain a hope that, out of the opinions' clash there would emanate a fruitful mutual understanding that forms a firm basis for developmental activities.

Any attempt to view this event with suspicion would only betray our pessimistic opinion only.

Notes

1. ASEAN, *ASEAN at 30*, ASEAN Secretariat, Jakarta, 1982, p. 51.
2. See Daljit Singh," A Political Overview of Southeast Asia," *Southeast Asian Affairs 1992*, (Singapore, 1992), p.6; Shefuddin Hashim, "Malaysia 1991: Consolidation, Challenges and New Directions," *Ibid*, p.198.
3. *Hindu*, January 16, 2006.
4. Siddharth Varadarajan, "Asian Interest and the myth of 'balance', " *Ibid*, December 13, 2005.
5. *Ibid*, January 12, 2006.
6. Vladimir Redyuhin, "Russia sees energy as key to unlock Asian doors", *Ibid*, December 19, 2005.
7. *Ibid.*
8. *Ibid.*
9. *Ibid*
10. For text of the Joint Declaration, see http://www.aseansec.org/15276.htm.
11. Makoto Taniguchi, "An East Asian Community could be established sooner than it is thought," *Asia-Pacific Perspectives*, (Tokyo), August 2005, p.38.
12. For text of Chairman's Statement of the 10th ASEAN Summit, Vientiane, November 29, 2004, see http://www.aseansec.org/16631.htm.
13. Jehangir S. Pocha, "A Continent Divided", *Business world*, (New Delhi), January 2, 2006, p.40.
14. Henry Leong, "East Asian Summit-just another talkfest?", http://www.onlineopinion.com.all/view.asp?article=3956.
15. *The Hindu*, December 12, 2005.
16. *Ibid*, December 13, 2005.
17. Pocha, n. 13, p.41.

18. *Ibid.*

19. C.S. Kuppuswamy, "India's Look-East Policy: More aggressive, Better Divideds".

20. *Ibid.*

21. *Ibid.*

22. For text of the speech of Chinese Premier Wen Jiabao, to the East Asia Summit at Kuala Lumpur, see *News from China* (Embassy of Peoples Republic of China, New Delhi), February 2006, pp.6-8.

23. For text of Chairman's Statement of the First East Asia Summit, Kuala Lumpur, December 14, 2005.

24. Henry Leong, "East Asia Summit just another talkfest?, http://www.onlineopion.com n. .

25. Martin Walker, "Battles around new Asia Summit," *Washington Times*, April 2, 2005.

26. Seth Mydans, "Leaders meet to discuss 'the Asian century'", *International Herald Tribune,* December 15, 2005.

27. Leong, n. 14.

28. Pocha n. 13 p.41.

29. Leong, n.14.

30. Mydans. n.25.

31. For Chairman's statement of the 11th ASEAN Summit see http://www.aseansec.org/18039.htm.

32. Amit Baruah, "A real forum for the future?" *The Hindu*, December 16, 2005.

33. Editorial, "A New Regional Architecture," *Ibid*, December 15, 2005.

34. Baruah, n.31.

35. Michael Vatikiotis, "EAS offers bullish view of Asian regionalism, *New Strait Times*, December 19, 2005.

36. Hadi Soesastro, "East Asia: Many clubs, Little Progress, *Far Eastern Economic Review*, January/February 2006, p.51.

37. Eric Teo Chau Cheow, "East Asia Summit's birthing pains." *The Strait Times*, February 22, 2005.

38. Nandita Mallik, "We do not need to 'Look West': Dr Singh," http://specials.rediff.com/money/2005/dec/11asean1.htm.

39. *Ibid.*

40. Nandita Mallik, "Look East' policy set to get a boost," http://specials.rediff.com/money/21005/see/10asean.htm.

41. Mallik, n.36.

42. Cheow, n.36.

43. Pocha, n. 13, p.41

44. Nandita Mallik, "All is not rosy with India: Manmohan Singh," http://in.rediff.com/money/2005/dec/12asean2.htm

45. P.S. Suryanarayana, An ambiguous entity", *Frontline*, January 13, 2006, p.53.

46. Mallik, n.36.

47. V.M. Gokuldas, "Letter from India no longer content to play second fiddle," *New Straits Times*, December 12, 2005.

48. Amit Baruah, "East Asia Summit, a forum for dialogue on strategic issues," *The Hindu*, December 15, 2005.

49. Nandita Mallik, "East Asia Summit ends with high optimism." http://www.rediff.ocm/money/2005/dec/14asean2.htm.

50. Leong, n.14.

51. Baradan Kuppuswamy, "East Asia Summit, Another Talk shop?," http://www.ipsnews.net/news.asp?idnews=31433.

52. Andy Mukherjee, "What's in a name? East Asia has yet to decide," *International Herald Tribune*, December 13, 2005.

53. *Ibid.*

54. *Ibid.*

55. *Ibid.*

56. Hardev Kaur, "ASEAN is still firmly in the driver's seat," *New Straits Times*, December 9, 2005.

57. *Ibid.*

58. Michael Vatikiotis, "EAS offers bullish view of Asian regionalism," *Ibid*, December 19, 2005.

16

India's Look East Policy: Posture and Reality

Man Mohini Kaul

India's Foreign Policy towards Southeast Asia not only reflects the change that has taken place in India's perception of the region, but also reflects the transformation of international relations in the contemporary world of globalisation. The process of globalisation has given a new dimension to the meaning of security, which now includes non-military threats that states and the international society face due to the complex pattern of interdependence. There are shared economic and security interests in the profound transformation that has taken place in the contemporary world after the end of the Cold War. In India, the end of the Cold War, brought about some soul searching, which resulted in Prime Minister Narsimha Rao initiating the economic reforms as soon as he came to power in 1991, and announcing the "Look East Policy" in 1992. Closed economy and set attitudes of Indian policy makers had not done much for Indian image either globally or regionally. [1]

New Approach

By the end of 1980's, it was clear that India was being marginalised from every other regional or sub regional forum regardless of its being ASEAN or APEC. Taking for granted, that India's involvement in Southeast Asia had begun immediately after its independence in 1947, it had taken decades for it to mature into constructive partnership. On the one hand, there was a peaceful country like India, with no hegemonic leaning in Southeast Asian region, and on the other hand, there was China gaining a strong foothold in the region, irrespective of its dubious past record. With one masterly stroke, Narsimha Rao's "Look East Policy," wiped away the earlier constricted thinking and approach that had been a handicap in ASEAN's acceptance of India as a country of consequence in the region. The new strategy to promote India's links with the ASEAN , had immediate positive fallout with the ASEAN responding immediately by making India a sectoral dialogue partner of the ASEAN in January 1992 and a full dialogue partner in December 1995. In July 1996, India was made a member of the ASEAN Regional Forum (ARF). India's elevation to a Summit partner of ASEAN during the Phnom Penh summit of November 2002, is an acknowledgement of India's emergence as a key player in the Asia Pacific region and with most other countries catching what Singapore Minister for Trade and Industry called the India, "fever". [2]

With the change in the international environment the new thinking was, that commonality of interests must take precedence over differences due to diversity. Thus in today's world, where interdependence is pushing nations together, there is a dire need for getting engaged constructively, with the neighbouring region. The key factors underlying India's growing ties with Southeast Asia, can be categorized as follows:

- India's desire to be an influential regional power
- Geopolitical significance of Southeast Asia, to India's security
- India's cognizance of the importance of ASEAN.
- China's rising role in Southeast Asia.

Some of the principal considerations behind a growing position, are a sense of geography, a sense of history, a need for economic growth, and a concern for security. To find its place in Asia, India realized that it is only through regional cooperation in the economic and social fields that it could achieve security not only for itself but also for the region as a whole. The primary concern of India, as that of other Asian countries is, poverty reduction, which can be done in cooperation with the neighbouring countries and by ensuring that the region remains free of tension and strife.

For some time now, Indian analysts, academicians, and former diplomats, have been calling for a new approach towards regional cooperation with Southeast Asia. It is obvious, that an effort has been initiated by the Foreign Office, to have a well-defined Indian policy towards Southeast Asia that keeps pace with China's strategy for cooperation with the ASEAN. At the fourth India-ASEAN Summit in Kuala Lumpur in December 2005, the Prime Minister of Malaysia acknowledged in his statement: "Although India has only assumed Dialogue Partner status with ASEAN, India has emerged as one of ASEAN'S most active partners in enhancing cooperation with ASEAN. This is demonstrated by the fact that "our Dialogue (had) been upgraded to the Summit level since 2002". [3] Prime Minister Manmohan Singh in his speech in Kuala Lumpur on January 24, 2006, described India's Look East Policy. He stated: "Some of you might recall that in 1992, our Government launched India's "Look East Policy". This was not merely an external economic policy; it was also a strategic shift in India's vision of the world and India's place in the evolving global economy.

Most of all it was about reaching out to our civilizational neighbours in South East Asia and East Asia. I have always viewed India's destiny as being inter-linked with that of Asia and more so South East Asia. I reiterate India's commitment to work with ASEAN and East Asian countries to make the 21st century truly an Asian century." [4] Essentially, it is the recent accelerated pace of Indian economy and the capacity of its business to go global that has led to a closer partnership through the separate dialogue process. According to a view: "India's unilateral liberalization, and deregulation, and a shift in its economic paradigm towards integration with the world economy-consistent manner have contributed to creating a favourable environment for the emergence of New Asia which is not tied to the cold war thinking and institutions." [5]

Regionalism

Of the many challenges facing the policy makers, a search for energy security is an important factor shaping the foreign policy of all major powers including India and China. In order to ensure its national interest, India is engaging not only with Southeast Asia but also with China as well. Indian political elite is giving credence to those variables that are essential for the promotion of bilateral and multilateral cooperation. India's rise as a leading global player, is a recognised fact, which received further momentum when President Bush, during his visit to India in March 2006, acknowledged "India's economic rise". [6] India's "new regionalism" towards Southeast Asia is a response to the "new framework" of Asian century, which according to many, is based on the economic trends of China and India. Michael Yahuda, analysing the new geopolitics, writes: "...the re-emergence of India as an economic political and strategic power with influence that extends beyond South Asia, to which it had been confined for most of the Cold War, has brought it increasingly into the Asia-Pacific region as a major power, rather than one confined to its periphery". [7]

India's diligent pursuit of closer trade relations with the ASEAN countries and the strengthening of security ties with this contiguous region, are clearly visible from its growing cooperation in all fields, from comprehensive economic cooperation to combating terrorism and ensuring maritime security in the region. It is obvious that the ASEAN countries want India to play more active role in the region, so that it can balance China. In India's relations with Southeast Asia, the China factor looms large and comparisons between the two are inevitable. The United States, with which India's relations have improved dramatically, sees India playing a stabilising role in the region. Although, the United States has massive trade relations with China, the long-term intentions of China are a risk factor. The Pentagon Report for 2005, cautioned about China's defence spending, which amounted to $90 bn. It also reported that there were up to 730 missiles in China, while in 2004 there were only

500. According to the report, China's military build-up put regional balances at risk. [8]

President Kalam's visit to Myanmar in March 2006, soon after President Bush's visit to India, must have come as a surprise to many in the United States, especially after Bush had stated in New Delhi, on March 3, 2006: "India's leadership is needed in a world that is hungry for freedom. Men and women from North Korea to Burma to Syria to Zimbabwe to Cuba yearn for their liberty. In Iran, a proud people is held hostage by a small clerical elite that denies basic liberties, sponsors terrorism, and pursues nuclear weapons. Our nations must not pretend that the people of these countries prefer their own enslavement. We must stand with reformers, dissidents, and civil society organizations, and hasten the day when the people of these nations can determine their own future and choose their own leaders. These people may not gain their liberty overnight, but history is on their side." [9] The reason behind Indian President's visit, can be understood better in the context of India's strategic and economic needs. [10] The Indian political elite is guided by the requirement to secure a safe neighbourhood through economic cooperation and strengthening of political relations. India would not like to get caught in the "balance of power" game in Southeast Asia or elsewhere.

Despite its commitment to democracy, it does not want to lose sight of its economic and security interests, by allowing the US perceptions to affect its efforts at engaging Myanmar. Nor does it want to compromise its image as an independent country, with an independent foreign policy, irrespective of its special relations with the US. Sharing 1600 kms. long border with Myanmar, India does not want to push Myanmar further into China's arms by openly espousing the cause of democracy. There are serious strategic implications for India, in China's gaining access to vital ports in Myanmar. [11] A former secretary in MEA, Mr Sudhir Devare writes "The latter's [India's] neglect of its major eastern neighbour would not only aggravate Myanmar's isolation but would further postpone the addressing of serious issues of development and security of India's northeast which has a close connection with ethnically similar regions of Myanmar. Equally importantly, India cannot but pay attention to the strategic dimension of China's growing relationship with the Myanmar regime, especially in the military field." [12]

In its pursuit of finding effective ways of enhancing its relations with Myanmar, India has taken various bilateral and multilateral initiatives like the BIMSTEC, which was founded in 1997. Initially, the membership was limited to the littoral states of, Bangladesh, India, Myanmar, Sri Lanka and Thailand, but later in 2004, Bhutan and Nepal joined as members. In July 2004, the grouping was renamed as Bay of Bengal Initiative for Multi-Sectoral Technical Cooperation (BIMST-EC). The wider membership was hailed by the regional news papers, as indispensable for bridging the gap between SAARC and ASEAN. The objectives of BIMST-EC were enshrined in the Summit Declaration of June 6, 1997, which stated: "Desiring to establish a firm foundation for common action to promote sub-regional cooperation in the areas of trade, investment, technological exchange and other interrelated areas in a spirit of equality and partnership and thereby contribute towards peace, progress and prosperity in their common region; Conscious that in an increasingly interdependent world, the cherished ideals of peace, freedom, and economic well-being are best attained by fostering greater understanding, good neighbourliness and meaningful cooperation among countries of the same sub-region already bound together by ties of history and culture." [13]

Further contacts with Myanmar, were initiated through yet another sub regional grouping called the Mekong Ganga Cooperation (MGC). Formed on November 10, 2000 in Vientiane, MGC includes Myanmar, Thailand, Cambodia, Vietnam and India as members. Closer economic cooperation with Mekong countries, is the rationale of this grouping with an emphasis on building infrastructure for better connectivity, and is expected in the long run to lead to the formation of Bay of Bengal Community by 2020. [14]

Bilateral engagement with the junta has also helped in joint military operations against insurgency in India's North-eastern region, as well as against drug trafficking and illegal immigrants. Andrew Selth points out that there is a school of thought that believes: "China has not been as successful in winning Burma's confidence as sometimes reported." [15] With the new relationship evolving between India and Myanmar, positive results are already showing – there is an agreement now to have a gas pipeline from India through Bangladesh to Myanmar known as the "Eastern Corridor Pipeline". [16] The relationship has equally been positive for Myanmar, with India promising various economic and trade incentives. During the visit of General Than Shwe to India in October 2004, the two countries agreed to set up Tamarathi hydroelectric project in Myanmar. A "Memorandum of Understanding on Cooperation in the field of Non-Traditional Security Issues" was also signed. [17] To strategise, the furthering of trade and economic relations with Myanmar, the Confederation of Indian Industry (CII) established a task force for this purpose. BIMSTEC is expected to help the economic cooperation and regional integration, yet mutual suspicion and political instability in some of the nations can hinder its progress.

During President Kalam's visit, India signed an MOU with Myanmar on the supply of gas. There were talks of finding an alternative route for the gas pipeline, in case Bangladesh continues with its delaying tactics. The strained relations between India and Bangladesh, seemed to have pushed Myanmar, to grant contract to a Chinese firm Petro, which was a setback to Indian overtures. According to media reports, the Indian Joint Secretary from Ministry of Petroleum, who was in Myanmar to forge a gas agreement with Myanmar, had to cut short his visit when Myanmar authorities informed him of the deal with China. Ostensibly, they had been irked by the delay in finalising the gas pipeline project. [18]

Despite the focus of BIMST-EC & MGC on the development of infrastructure, the sub regional groupings are still in the initial stage and there is much that needs to do before positive results can be seen. Till now only one project, i.e. Tamu-Kalemyo road network has been accomplished though it needs to be stressed, that the initiating of a new proposal each time an Indian Minister visits the region, is neither pragmatic nor strategically correct. It is far better to stick to a few meaningful projects. Here China's example can be emulated. Already ten road networks, linking Yunnan province of China with the Mekong basin countries, have either been developed or are at a stage of implementation under the Greater Mekong Sub-Region (GMS) Economic Cooperation Program. The success of these projects is attributed by some influential Indians, to the financial assistance given to GMS by the Asian Development Bank. [19]

The China Factor

Thus, compared to China's diplomatic forays, India has 'miles to go'. Prime Minister Manmohan Singh acknowledged this, when he stated: "China is ahead of us in planning for its energy security-India can no longer be complacent." [20] In a recent comment, the managing director of the world's second largest beer company expressed, what many have felt when doing business with India. He said, "Despite India's reputation as the world's biggest democracy where business is booming, we have found it a difficult place to do business compared with China". [21] According to some analysts, there is a perceptible strategy of China's to contain India. Therefore, it is engaging India's small neighbours with this aim in mind. [22] However, There is no second opinion about China's growing economy, that is now regarded as the fourth largest economy after the US, Japan and Germany. In Southeast Asia, it is an economic giant and has initiated the establishment of Free Trade Area with tariff cuts begun in 2005, and to be completed by 2010. [23] The two-way trade is expected to surpass $ 100 billion in the year 2006. [24]

In spite of China's "workable and cooperative relations with its neighbours," [25] the South China Sea dispute and the Taiwan issue are regarded as potential flashpoints. Besides, the increase in China's defence spending since 1990 by more than 10 per cent annually, could be a destabilising factor in East Asia, especially keeping in view of its strained relations with Japan. [26] As part of the core group of East Asia Summit, it is difficult to predict as to which way the China- Japan relations would go eventually. There are those who go a step further in doubting the benefits accruing to ASEAN from the much hyped ACFTA. Perhaps the reason behind such doubts are due to what Mark Beeson observes: "Yet somehow paradoxically, even after the Cold War, when China is actively seeking to integrate itself into an increasingly global capitalist economy, the 'China threat' has not entirely diminished: concerns about China's long term hegemonic ambitions in the region have, to some extent, given way to immediate concern about its potential as an economic rival to a Southeast Asian region still coming to terms with the aftermath of economic crisis." [27]

In order to counter these fears, China is trying to play by the rules, especially through the ASEAN plus Three processes. It has signed the Treaty of Amity and Cooperation and the Declaration on the Conduct of Parties in the South China Sea. Chinese Prime Minister Wen Jiabao, also assuaged the regional apprehensions, when he stated in a speech during the 8th ASEAN Summit that, "China will continue to seek peace and development through cooperation and will strive to achieve development that will bring about peace, openness, cooperation and harmony as well as benefit to itself and other countries". [28] As part of Confidence Building Measure (CBM), China established Kunming initiative on August 17, 1999, in Kunming, the capital of Yunnan Province of China. The member countries China, India, Myanmar and Bangladesh agreed through this initiative to cooperate towards "equality and mutual benefit, sustainable development, comparative advantages, adoption of international standards, and infrastructure development in order to enhance connectivity and facilitate widest possible economic cooperation." [29]

Simultaneously, Track II exercise was initiated to further promote regional economic cooperation among Bangladesh, China, India and Myanmar and is known as BCIM Forum. So far six BCIM Forum conferences have been held including the one held in Kunming in August 1999. According to a background paper, the BCIM Forum, "represents the combined endeavour by the four countries to increase connectivity, culture, trade and tourism ties and people to people contact among them, in the border regions in particular". [30]

Though there is a talk of Asian integration, the ground reality is different. One, the strategic scenario is becoming extremely complicated and is difficult to predict. Two, the internal challenges in some of the countries of South and Southeast Asia have serious security implications, as these could jeopardise prospccts for peace and stability in the region. Three, if at one level there are CBMs being under taken, at another level there are regional jealousies and suspicions. There is China wooing South Asian nations with as much vigour as India is doing so, in Southeast Asia and East Asia. If India sees China intruding in South Asia the feeling is mutual. China never wanted India to be part of East Asian Summit, while India was not keen to see China included as an observer in SAARC. [31] However, in spite of these competing interests the trade between India and China is increasing at an incredible level and there is an admiration in India for China's economic success. China is now India's second largest trading partner after the US. Indian and Chinese business community, is jubilant at the enhanced economic and trade relations between the two countries with bilateral trade, expected to go up to twenty billion by 2008, and with such strengthening of economic integration, it is expected to have a positive fallout on the political relations as well.

Economic Integration

India is focusing on a strategy for closer economic ties through bilateral Free Trade Agreements (FTA's). To facilitate the process of economic integration, a number of multilateral forums have been established, like the India-ASEAN Business Summit, which is held regularly by the Federation of Indian Chambers of Commerce and Industry (FICCI), CII, and the

Government of India. Such initiatives have positively impacted on the bilateral trade. The McKinsey Report of the Second India – ASEAN Business Summit of September 2003 stated: "If India and ASEAN are able to implement policy changes in line with other trade blocs to remove trade and investment barriers, the business between India and the ASEAN countries could increase significantly as experienced by other trading blocs like the North American Free Trade Agreement (NAFTA). [32] India – ASEAN bilateral trade is targeted to grow from US $ 13.25 billion in 2003-2004, to US$ 24-30 billion in 2007. [33] To encourage investment and trade links, an ASEAN-India Economic Linkages Task Force (AIELTF) was set up, which drafted a Comprehensive Economic Cooperation Agreement (CECA) that was signed between ASEAN and India at the Bali Summit in October 2003. [34] India also signed the Joint Declaration for Cooperation to Combat International Terrorism. [35]

To promote the integration process further, India- ASEAN partnership was institutionalised through the India-ASEAN multilateral dialogue at the highest level and expanding areas of cooperation, which was given a concrete shape at the Vientiane Summit of November 30, 2004, when India and ASEAN signed the declaration titled "ASEAN- India Partnership for Peace, Progress and Shared Prosperity." [36] They agreed to; Work through both conventional and innovative trade and economic arrangements, and full implementation of the ASEAN-India free trade area by 2011 for ASEAN-5 and India, 2016 for the Philippines and India and by 2011 by India and 2016 by the 4 new ASEAN Members Countries, including the early implementation of the Early Harvest Programme, to achieve freer movement of goods, services, investment, and cooperation in other economic areas. [37]

At the bilateral level, India has improved its trade relations, and is trying to keep pace with changing pace of economic cooperation in the region. It is Singapore's fastest growing partner, overtaking China. A Comprehensive Economic Cooperation Agreement (CECA) with Singapore was signed on

June 29, 2005. This agreement, which came into effect on August 1, 2005, will facilitate trade including FTA. With Thailand, India's relations have grown after the Cold War ended. With expanding economic and political relations with Thailand, India, signed a framework for FTA in October 2003. With Indonesia, there is a healthy understanding of each other's security concerns and both have agreed to establish a "strategic partnership" based on shared values and commitment to democracy and aimed at broad based development of relations in the political, security, economic, commercial, cultural, and in science and technology fields. [38] With Malaysia, inspite of sometimes strained political relations, the bilateral trade has grown to US$ 4.5 billion with Malaysia being India's second largest trading partner in the ASEAN.

Prime Minister Badawi's address to Malaysia – India Business Forum, on December 20, 2004, in New Delhi reflects Malaysia's desire to play a major role in India's rising economic potential He observed, "I cannot emphasise enough the role that Malaysia can play as a gateway to ASEAN, which has emerged as a dynamic and competitive region with a combined G.D.P. of 686 billion U.S. dollars in 2003, with a population of more than 540 million, with high literacy rates, and an expanding industrial sector and abundant natural resources. With the various economic integration measures in place, ASEAN offers Indian businessmen and women ample trade and investment opportunities". [39]

Critics feel that in view of India's deepening relations with Southeast Asia, it is generally accepted that India will have to remove barriers that impede the free flow of goods, services and investment for 'deep integration'. India is lagging behind China, in implementing FTA's with the ASEAN, and that even though India's participation in the economic and political affairs of the region is growing; it is still on the margin. [40] In a special report the *Financial Times* wrote: "Trade just represents 29 per cent of Indian GDP, compared with about 57 per cent of China's Although India has made some progress in eliminating trade barriers since it joined the World Trade Organisation in 1995, import tariffs remain high. India is still a min- now in world trade, with its goods exports accounting for just 0.8 per cent of the global total, compare with 6.4 per cent for China's." [41]

The Confederation of Indian Industry (CII) has suggested that India must focus on the commodity groups that are of maximum importance to ASEAN so that Indian exports to the region may reach the targeted level of USD 30 billion by 2007. The most important constraint in the multilateral cooperation is the bureaucratic hurdle and lack of political initiative. The delay in the implementation of projects has often had a negative impact on the investors from the ASEAN countries. It has to be recognised that recent initiatives have had positive fallouts on the trade figures and are reflective of the more open and less discriminatory regime coming into force. In 2003-2004, India-ASEAN trade was "about US$13.25 billion, over 5 times the 1939-94 trade figures of US$2.s billion." [42]

Moreover, the presence of the "new Indian Diaspora", which consists of highly skilled people, has enhanced India's image in Southeast Asia. The Government of India is taking great interest in the Indian Diaspora, which is evident from the setting of Ministry of Overseas Indian Affairs to forge closer links with people of Indian origin. Increased growth in trade and investment between India and ASEAN has had a positive effect with a surge of skilled workers, professionals and business people to almost all the countries of ASEAN. There is a great demand for these Indian professionals, who command respect.

Security Perceptions

Although, regional integration is regarded crucial for economic growth, security cooperation is equally essential. There are many asymmetrical threats to India's security, such as smuggling of illicit arms into India's Northeast from Myanmar and Thailand (which has become a market for illegal weapons), and maritime piracy and terrorism. The safety of the sea-lanes and their choke points like Malacca straits are crucial to "India's economic well being". [43] Joint military exercises with the countries of the region are a witness to the growing security cooperation with the countries of Southeast Asia. This multilateral cooperation is based on common threat perceptions especially after 9/11. [44] Terrorism is a trans-national problem requiring active coordinated cooperation. Such cooperation is now the basic component of India's foreign and defence policy in the region. The second occurrence of bombing in Bali on October 1, 2005, was a reminder that Jemmah Islamiyah in Indonesia is active and is working for Al Qaeda. Jemmah Islamiyah is also alleged to have masterminded the earlier bomb blasts at Bali. A politically weak and economically poor Indonesia has seen the rise of Islamic fundamentalism especially in the aftermath of the 1997 Financial Crisis. The activities of Islamic fundamentalist groups have at times threatened the secular and accommodative character of Indonesian Islam. The October bombing in Bali once again raises the question of Al-Qaeda penetration of Islamic organisations in Southeast Asia. [45]

Since, it is not possible to fight these "asymmetrical wars" alone, India is seen as a natural partner by some of the ASEAN states, for maintaining stability and peace in the region. Its navy has the capability to respond immediately to threats in its neighbouring seas. It is held by security analysts, that with the proliferation of non-traditional and trans-national security threats, there is a need for a multi dimensional and cooperative approach. Many of these cooperative efforts especially those related to intelligence sharing and enhanced military contacts, will help in assuaging anxieties about India's emerging dominant role. At the Vientiane Summit of 30 November 2004, it was agreed that "India and ASEAN would cooperate in combating the menace of international terrorism and other transnational crimes such as trafficking in drugs, arms smuggling, human trafficking particularly in women and children, cyber crimes, international economic crimes, environmental crimes, sea piracy and money laundering, through effective institutional linkages and programmes of cooperation giving priority to information exchange and capacity building". [46]

Yet there are apprehensions regarding the naval competition among various regional powers in the waters of ASEAN countries. *Jane's Defence Weekly* reported, "that influential Indonesian academics recently called for Thailand and Indonesia to work more closely to establish a maritime bloc to balance the maritime power of countries like China and India. Other Southeast Asian countries might also be sympathetic to such an arrangement." [47] However, there is a need for cooperative measures for maintaining security, whether it is Bay of Bengal, or the Indian Ocean or Malacca Straits. Also, in the face of natural calamities like tsunami, cooperation and coordinated approach is needed to bring relief to the affected people.

Conclusion

In order to emerge as a global power, India has to give up being the proverbial tortoise of "slow and steady wins the race". In this century, only those that are "fast and steady", seem to be getting ahead in the race. The reality is, that it is a competitive world, where action counts more than maintaining a posture in order to benefit from the rapidly growing regional integration in East Asia and Southeast Asia. Today, in the new geopolitics of the region, India is an important player. Competition between India and China especially for overseas markets and energy supplies, will continue. Regional jealousies and competing interests were apparent with China's reluctance to include India in the East Asia Summit .According to Mohan Malik, a China expert: "Beijing fears that India's participation would shift the balance of power and make the EAC less susceptible to domination by China." [48]

In the ASEAN too, there are differences of opinion and perceptions between mainland and maritime Southeast Asia. [49] Also, there is lack of homogeneity, particularly with the inclusion of Cambodia, Laos Myanmar and Vietnam (CLMV), which some analysts refer to, as a two-tier organization. [50] Within the original ASEAN core group, the Philippines still carries the Cold War perceptions in its attitude towards India. President Kalam's visit to the Philippines in February 2006, is perhaps a welcome step towards a country that has remained on the fringe for too long. It was after fifteen years, that an Indian President had visited the Philippines. With Malaysia, in spite of India's growing trade links, its stand on ASEAN forging a "strategic partnership" with India, is not yet clear. [51] Myanmar of course continues to remain an enigma notwithstanding the policy of constructive engagement of ASEAN and India towards it. According to a report in *The Economist*: "Even the Junta's supposed friends in the Association of Southeast Asian Nations (ASEAN) have been cold shouldered of late." [52] With the former, Indo-Chinese states, India's relationship remains as warm as ever, and the need for increased connectivity has been initiated through GMC.

As part of Look East Policy, India is building linkages with the South Pacific Island states. They have not been a focal point of India's foreign policy until now. In the changing global environment, India could play a significant and constructive role in the economic development of the South Pacific Island countries. The growing convergence with Australia on issues concerning security and trade only reinforces this. In an address at the second India ASEAN Summit in September 2003, the then Foreign Minister Yashwant Sinha stated that India's Look East Policy which had focused primarily on ASEAN countries earlier in Phase 1, had expanded in Phase II, following the "definition of East extending from Australia to China and East Asia with ASEAN as its core". [53] He also clarified, that the focus had shifted "from exclusively economic issues to economic and security issues including joint efforts to protect sea lanes, coordination on counter terrorism etc." [54]

India's interaction with the South Pacific has grown with its dialogue status in the Pacific Islands Forum (PIF) in 2002. In spite of their small size, these countries are rich in seabed resources. The bigger countries such as the Solomon Islands and Papua New Guinea (PNG) natural resources, with PNG possess the coveted natural gas in abundance. The ASEAN and the PIF are involved in economic cooperation and close links through dialogue process is being maintained. PNG has been given an observer status in

ASEAN and is a member of the ARF. Australia and New Zealand have been interacting with Southeast Asia for a long time as the security and stability of the region directly affects their own. In relation to Australia, India is again lagging behind China in the diplomatic game. China has built close links with Australia and on April 3, 2006, Australia signed a uranium deal with China, which is a signatory to NPT. Australia has about 40 per cent of world's uranium deposits and has so far refused to supply uranium for India's nuclear energy sector, as the latter is not a signatory to NPT. It is however, expected that President Bush's nuclear deal with India will certainly soften the Australian stance in the future.

After the India – ASEAN Summit became a reality in November 2002; a new lease of life seems to have been injected into India's Look East Policy. The reality was that even though India's dialogue status had led to a significant deepening of its relationship with the ASEAN states, they still considered India in the same bracket as Australia and New Zealand rather than China. Moreover, India's policy initiatives had lost momentum in the face of the challenges to the Southeast Asian region during the 1997 financial crisis and its drastic impact on internal dynamics of the ASEAN countries. India's nuclear tests in May 1998 also had a negative impact on its image as a benign power in some of the ASEAN nations. Moreover, India's posture alone was not enough to deepen the relationship into a cooperative and constructive partnership. Many of India's initiatives seemed to have remained unaccomplished, sluggish, slow and not in tune with its capacity to forge significant links. India must not allow its new activism towards Southeast Asia and South Pacific, to dwindle into old ways. The multilateral and bilateral diplomacy has to move forward to keep pace with the new regional initiatives towards closer engagement. At the same time, there are new security paradigms that are evolving, and this needs a well thought out strategic approach.

Notes

1. This paper builds on the work of the author in the previously published papers " ASEAN- India Relations During the Cold War" in

Fredric Grare and Amitabh Mattoo (ed.), *India and ASEAN; The politics of India's Look East Policy,*(New Delhi: Manohar Publishers,2001), pp.41-66. and "Indian Perspectives on Security Dimensions of India and Southeast Asia", in V.R. Raghavan and Karl Fischer (ed.), *Security Dimensions of India and Southeast Asia*, (New Delhi: Tata McGraw-Hill, 2005), pp.3-21.

2. app.fta.gov.sg/data/fta/file/Ministerspercent520CECAAdress.pdf
3. http://aseansummit.bernama.com/speech.php?id=398
4. http://www.newasiaforum.org/speech_pm.htm
5. Mukul Asher and Rahul Sen, "India; An integral Part of New Asia", January 2005 (Version 2) - unpublished.
6. http://usembassy.state.gov/posts/in1/wwwhspconmarapr06.html
7. Michael Yahuda, *The International Politics of the Asia –Pacific* 2nd ed (London: Rutledge, 2003), p.341.
8. http:/www.sinodefence.com/news/2005/news05-07-20.asp
9. http://usembassy.state.gov/posts/in1/wwwhspconmarapr06.html
10. See C.S. Kuppuswamy, "Myanmar: Visit of the Indian President", *http://www.saag.org per cent5Cpapers 18 per cent5 Cpaper1732.html*
11. Christina Fink, *Living Silence: Burma under Military Rule*, (London: Zed Books, 2001), pp. 222-223.
12. Sudhir Davare, *India and Southeast Asia: Towards Security Convergence*, (Capital Publishing Company, New Delhi) p.188.
13. http://mofa.gov.bd/bimstec/dec_estalis.html.
14. http://www.hinduonnet.com/2000/11/28/stories/05282523.htm.
15. Andrew Selth, Burma: "*A Strategic Perspective*", (Asia Foundation Working Paper May 13, 2001) p.30.
16. http://www.atimes.com\Southeast_Asia\F J I 9AeO I. html.
17. The Economist Intelligence Unit, *Country Report: India*, (London: EIU, 2004), p.17.
18. http://www.expressindia.com/fullstory.php?newsid=61157.
19. 19.See *ADB Review*, August 2005,pp.16-17.
20. *The Times of India,* New Delhi, January 23, 2005.
21. *Financial Times*, 26 January 26, 2006.
22. Mohan Malik, "*China's Strategy of Containing India*", http//www.pinr.com/report.phb?ac+ view_printable&report_id=434&language_id=1.

23. Kevin G. Cai, "The ASEAN- China Free Trade Agreement and East Asian Regional Grouping", *Contemporary Southeast Asia,* vol.25, no.3, 2003, pp.387-404.

24. www.ipnews.net/news.asp?idnews=32473.

25. Michael Yahuda, *The International Politics of the Asia Pacific*, (2004: RoutledgeCurzon, London) p.283.

26. http://www.nni.nikkei.co.jp/FR/FEAT/china2/

27. Mark Beeson," Southeast Asia and -the Major Powers: The United States, Japan, and China", in Mark Beeson (ed.), *Contemporary Southeast Asia: Regional Dynamics, National Differences* (Palgrave Macmillan, Hampshire, 2004) p.209.

28. http://www.us-asean.org?/ASEAN/business_Investment_Summit_03/chinese_pm_speech.asp.

29. http://www.hinduonnet.com/fline/fl 1707/17070980.htm

30. Background Paper of the Sixth BICM Forum, New Delhi, 30-31 March 2006.

31. Mohan Malik, "*China's Strategy of Containing India*", n.20. 7language

32. Second India-ASEAN Business Summit, *Boosting Trade and Investment between India and the ASEAN Countries,* (New Delhi: MckKinsey, 2003), pp.18-19

33. Animesh Roul, "ASEAN: Towards Asian Arc of Prosperity?" http://www.ased.org/artman/publish/ article_668.shtml

34. See for full text in Sudhir Devare, n.12, pp.116-28.

35. *Ibid.*, pp.229-31

36. CS. Kuppuswamy, "India's Look East Policy More Aggressive, Better Dividends", *http://www.saag.org/ per cent5Cpapers17 per cent5Cpaper1663.html*

37. http://www.aseansec.org/16839.htm

38. C.S. Kuppuswamy, n.36.

39. www.ficci.com/media-room/speeches-presentations/2004/dec/dec20-yk.htm

40. Michael Yahuda, n.25, p 214.

41. *Financial Times,* January 26, 2006.

42. www.ciionline.org/common/92/default.asp?page=ASEAN per cent20Countries.htm

43. http://www.defenceindia.com/defenceindia/indian_navy.html

44. Jonathan T. Chow, "ASEAN Counter Terrorism Cooperation since 9/11", *Asian Survey,* vol. xlv, no.2, March/April 2005,p.303

45. Man Mohini Kaul and Vibhanshu Shekhar, "Extremism in Indonesia", *The Hindu*, 2 November 2002.

46. For full text see Sudhir Devare,n.12,p.229-31

47. *Jane's Defence Weekly*, vol.42, 11May 2005, p.25.

48. Mohan Malik, "The East Asia Summit: More Discord than Accord", *http://yaleglobal.yale.edu/ display.article?id=6645*

49. *Janes Defence Weekly*, n.47, p.25.

50. Ralf Emmers, "The Indochinese Enlargement of ASEAN: Security Expectations and Outcomes," *Australian Journal of International Affairs*, vol.59, no.1, pp.71-88, March 2005.

51. Faizal Yahya, "Challenges of Globalisation: Malaysia and India Engagement", *Contemporary Southeast Asia*, vo.l27, no.3, 2005, pp.472-98.

52. *The Economist*, 14-20 January2006.

53. http://www.ficci.com/media-room/speeches-presentation/2003/sep/sep4-asean-yashv

54. *Ibid.*

17

India and Asia-Pacific Economic Integration: A New Hope

T. Nirmala Devi

India's increasing engagement with the economic affairs of the Asia-Pacific countries in recent years, is a step towards its deeper economic integration with the region in the 21st century. Despite its historical and cultural affiliations with the region, India chose to remain an outsider in the Southeast and East Asian political and economic matters, until the last decade. The country could not get any membership in the major regional groupings and remained contented with its dialogue partner status in the Association of South East Asian Nations (ASEAN). Its role as a major player in the South Asian Association for Regional Cooperation (SAARC), has often been viewed with suspicion and mistrust by other members in the region.

However, its membership in the Bay of Bengal Initiative for Multi-Sectoral and Technical Cooperation (BIMSTEC), serves as a bridge between South Asia and South-east Asia, which enables its intensive economic interaction with Southeast Asia. The changing global scenario, the increasing role of Asia in the progress of the world, India's continued 'look east policy' from the early 1990s, and its attempts to translate this into an early launch of a pan-Asian regional cooperation, coupled with its recent impressive economic performance, are the factors contributing to its participation in the recently held East Asia Summit. The reduction of tensions between India and China in the region and the emphasis on the security environment, are also responsible for India being recognized as a partner in the development process of the Asia-Pacific region.

Thus, India's participation in the ASEAN Summit, which was ensued by the East Asia Summit, comprising 16 countries - stretching from India to Australia and New Zealand - is considered as an auspicious augury. This is likely to culminate in an ultimate integration in the region through trade and economic cooperation. Evidence suggests, that it is imperative for India to be increasingly engaged with the South-east and East Asian countries in future along with its ongoing interaction and evolving partnership with the industrial countries, particularly with the U.S and the E.U members. The political ideology of India in the past was such that it threatened to some extent, to impede the trade and economic relations with some of the Asian countries, which had the bearing of American imperialism. Even now, countries like Australia, Japan, Philippines, South Korea and Thailand continue to be the American military allies.

If Singapore, despite its multinational links with the U.S., seeks an economic engagement with India in the region, it is mainly because of its compatibility with India, rather than with China (Sunanda K. Datta-Ray 2005). In the backdrop of changing global context and the current political developments, India cannot afford to miss the opportunity of engaging itself with the economic powerhouses. Viewing against this background, the present paper makes an attempt to examine the possibility of widening the scope of avenues to successful India's economic interactions of India with the Asia-Pacific region, in the new millennium. It argues for an in-depth economic engagement of India with the countries in this region in the light of the prospects of Asian Economic Integration and also in the wake of the bleak prospects of the developing countries at the multilateral trading system, WTO.

Socio-Economic Scenario

The Asia-Pacific region not only includes three industrial countries, but also combines the fastest growing economy of China, along with other better performing economies and thus, provides a huge global market. The select Asia and Pacific countries, display diverse characteristics in the dimensions of population, economy and their performance, as detailed in Table 17.1. India's fast growth in population in the 1980s and the early 1990s, came closer to that of China's size. But the considerable reduction in India's growth rate of population in recent years, is not enough to affect its population stabilization. The country is in the phase of demographic shift, as the share of working age population is bound to increase, in the coming years. In the selected group of Asian countries, Japan has the least growth rate of population owing to its high density. Malaysia and Philippines have two per cent growth rate of population, which may be attributed to the encouragement of the 'sons of the soil' in the former country and the influence of religion in the latter one. It is surprising to note that Singapore, a country with high density, has nearly two per cent growth rate, notwithstanding the significant decline from the preceding decade. India's per capita income in absolute terms, was the lowest among the countries under consideration, mostly as a result of a huge variation between its absolute and purchasing power parity (PPP) terms of per capita. The growth of GDP per capita, became significant in China, Singapore, India and Thailand in the region in 2003-04, despite the steep decline in Thailand from the decade 1985-95.

The social infrastructure is the focal point of the economic development of the country and hence the necessity of the review on social performance. In contrast with most of the developing countries, India has been suffering from high incidence of poverty as a considerable section of its population is deprived of the basic needs. Table 17.2 shows the highest incidence of poverty in India, in terms of one dollar a day. Along with the three industrial countries, viz., Japan, Australia and New Zealand; Singapore, South Korea, Malaysia and Thailand also registered the lowest incidence of poverty. However, it becomes surprising to note that Thailand has registered nearly one-third of poverty, if it is measured in terms of national poverty line. Basing on the same line, Philippines recorded the highest ratio of poverty during the period 1990-2002. India's low social status is explained by an

Table 17.1: Key Indicators of Select Asia and Pacific Countries

Region/ Country	Total Population (millions)		Annual population growth rate (per cent)		Gross national income per capita ($)				Gross domestic product per capita growth (per cent)	
					Absolute		PPP			
	1990	2004	1990-2000	2000-04	1995	2004	1995	2004	1985-95	2003-04
India	849.5	1079.7	1.8	1.5	340	620	1,400	3,100	3.2	5.4
ASEAN-5:										
Indonesia	178.2	217.6	1.7	1.3	980	1,140	3,800	3,460	6.0	3.7
Malaysia	17.9	25.2	2.5	2.0	3,890	4,650	9,020	9,630	5.7	5.2
Philippines	61.5	83.0	2.2	2.0	1,050	1,170	2,850	4,890	1.5	4.3
Singapore	3.0	4.3	2.8	1.9	26,730	24,220	22,770	26,590	6.2	6.3
Thailand	55.8	62.4	0.9	0.7	2,740	2,540	7,540	8,020	8.4	5.4
China	1133.7	1296.5	1.1	0.7	620	1,290	2,920	5,530	8.3	8.8
Korea, Rep. of	42.8	48.1	1.0	0.6	9,700	13,980	11,450	20,400	7.7	4.1
Japan	123.5	127.8	0.3	0.2	39,640	37,180	22,110	30,040	2.9	2.5
Australia	17.1	20.1	1.2	1.2	18,720	26,900	18,940	29,200	1.4	1.8
New Zealand	3.4	4.1	1.1	1.3	14,340	20,310	16,360	22,130	0.8	3.1

Source: World Bank (1992, 1997 & 2006), *World Development Report*, New York: Oxford University Press.

Table 17.2: Social Indicators of Select Asia and Pacific Countries

Region/ Country	Population below income poverty line (per cent)		Popn. with sustainable access to improved sanitation (per cent)		Popn. with sustainable access to improved water source (per cent)		Popn.undernourished (per cent of total)		Life expectancy at birth (years)		Adult literacy rate (per cent ages 15 and above)	
	$ 1 a day	National poverty line										
	1990-2003	1990-2002	1990	2002	1990	2002	1990-92	2000-02	1990	2003	1990	2003
India	34.7	28.6	12	30	68	86	25	21	59.1	63.3	49.3	61.0
ASEAN-5:												
Indonesia	7.5	27.1	46	52	71	78	9	6	61.5	66.8	79.5	87.9
Malaysia	< 2	15.5	96	--	--	95	3	2	70.1	73.2	80.7	88.7
Philippines	14.6	36.8	54	73	87	85	26	22	64.2	70.4	91.7	92.6
Singapore	--	--	--	--	--	--	--	--	74.0	78.7	88.8	92.5
Thailand	< 2	32.5	80	99	81	85	28	20	66.1	70.0	92.4	92.6
China	16.6	4.6	23	44	70	77	16	11	70.1	71.6	78.3	90.9
Korea, Rep. of	< 2	--	--	--	--	92	2	2	70.1	77.0	--	--
Japan	--	--	100	100	100	100	--	--	78.6	82.0	100	100
Australia	--	--	100	100	100	100	--	--	76.5	80.3	100	100
New Zealand	--	--	--	--	97	--	--	--	75.2	79.1	100	100

Source: UNDP (1993 & 2005), *Human Development Report*, New York: Oxford University Press.

inadequate and impoverished provision of the basic amenities like sanitation, proper hygiene and potable water and also by the highest number of undernourished people in 2000-02. Its poor play is further revealed by its three-fifths of adult literacy rate and a slightly above that of life expectancy at birth in the year 2003 and all these are reflected in its low Human Development Index value among the selected group of countries. The social spending on education has increased in all these countries in 2003. For instance, the public expenditure on education in terms of the percentage of GDP was 8.1 in Malaysia, 5.2 in Thailand, 4.2 in South Korea, and 4.1 in India, but these facts and figures did not contribute to anything like a significant improvement in the literacy and enrolment ratios, in India. The public expenditure on health in terms of GDP was however, not at all significant in these countries, with the singular exception of three industrial countries, which had allocated a sizeable share, both on health and education (UNDP 2005).

The main economic activity of Asia-Pacific region, is seen from Table 17.3. In the chosen group, India's GDP size was ranked only next to Japan and China in 2004 and its GDP growth rate was second to China during 2000-04. In fact, a significant decline in GDP growth rate was witnessed in Singapore, followed by South Korea, Malaysia and China owing to the impact of the financial crisis in 1997. Australia too registered a fall in the growth rate, while Japan experienced stagnation. Among the group of countries, the agricultural productivity was impressive in the three industrial countries, besides the substantial productivity gains in Singapore. In the rest of the countries, India's low agriculture productivity, is quite noticeable. In the sectoral value addition as a per cent of GDP in these countries, services sector by and large dominated the economy in a majority of the countries and the shift towards services from 1990 to 2004, was mostly at the cost of agriculture. The exception to this trend, is China and Malaysia in which, industry was the high priority sector. In this group of countries, Thailand showed a departure from the general

Table 17.3: Economic Activity in Select Asia and Pacific Countries

Region/ Country	Gross domestic product ($ billions)		Gross domestic product		Agricultural productivity (agrl. value added per agrl. Worker		Sectoral Distribution of GDP (per cent)					
			Avg.ann per cent growth		2000 dollars		Agriculture value added		Industry value added		Services value added	
	1990	2004	1990-2000	2000-04	1989-91	2001-03	1990	2004	1990	2004	1990	2004
India	254.5	691.9	6.0	6.2	341	397	31	22	29	26	40	52
ASEAN-5:												
Indonesia	109.3	257.6	4.2	4.6	477	556	22	17	40	46	38	38
Malaysia	42.4	117.8	7.0	4.3	3,694	4,571	--	10	--	48	--	42
Philippines	43.9	86.4	3.2	4.2	910	1,016	22	14	35	32	43	54
Singapore	34.6	106.8	7.8	2.8	25,523	32,980	0	0	37	35	63	65
Thailand	80.2	163.5	4.2	5.3	493	588	12	10	39	44	48	46
China	364.9	1,649.3	10.3	8.7	242	357	27	15	42	51	31	35
Korea, Rep. of	236.4	679.7	5.7	4.7	5,312	9,888	9	3	45	35	46	62
Japan	2,942.9	4,623.4	1.3	1.3	19,163	25,339	3	1	42	30	56	68
Australia	296.3	631.3	4.1	3.3	20,601	26,957	4	3	31	26	64	71
New Zealand	42.8	99.7	3.0	3.9	19,930	26,526	9	--	27	--	65	--

Source: World Bank (1992, 2002 & 2006), *World Development Report*, New York: Oxford University Press.

trend – a contraction of services along with agriculture, in favour of industry.

If the strength of these sectors can be judged by their productivity in terms of employment potential, India's above one-fifth share of agriculture in GDP, absorbs more than three-fifths of workforce (60.5 per cent), while ASEAN region with a lower share of agriculture, creates employment to 46.5 per cent of workforce, owing to its high farm productivity. India employs only 22.7 per cent of workforce in services sector, which has a share of above 50 per cent in GDP, whereas ASEAN creates more than two-fifths (41.5 per cent) of employment in this sector. China's share of agriculture in GDP is 15 per cent, but it registers an impressive share (50 per cent) of employment. Likewise, China's share of above one-third of services in GDP, contributes to the employment for about 28 per cent. China outshines both India and ASEAN, in the performance of industry, as it is able to generate half of its income from this sector. However, the presence of modern production technology is responsible for limiting the industrial sector of China to absorb only 22 per cent of workforce (Mohan Guruswamy 2005).

Trade Competitiveness

Trade was not the central feature of the Indian economy till the initiation of economic reforms, as it had not contributed significantly to the growth process. Insufficient exposure to international trade was thus the main characteristic of the economy in the pre-reform period. If the proportion of the trade to GDP indicates the openness of the economy, it can be said, that the trade has never become an integral part of the Indian economy, unlike that of ASEAN. In the post-reform period, India had registered a significant improvement in its proportion of trade to GDP – from 17 per cent in 1990 to 32 per cent in 2002, indicating a rise of exports from 7.5 per cent to 15.3 per cent and imports from 9.7 per cent to 16.5 per cent (IMF 2005)

As seen from the structure of the trade of Asia-Pacific countries in Table 17.4, the overall share of exports in GDP was

Table 17.4: Structure of Trade in Select Asia and Pacific Countries

Region/ Country	Imports of goods and services (per cent of GDP)		Exports of goods and services (per cent of GDP)		Primary exports (per cent of merchandise exports)		Manufactured exports (per cent of merchandise exports)		High technology exports (per cent of manufactured exports)		Current account balance (as per cent of GDP)	
	1990	2003	1990	2003	1990	2003	1990	2003	1990	2003	1990	2003
India	9	16	7	14	28	22	71	77	2	5	-2.3	1.1
ASEAN-5:												
Indonesia	24	26	25	31	65	48	35	52	1	14	-2.6	3.0
Malaysia	72	93	75	114	46	22	54	77	38	58	-2.0	12.9
Philippines	33	51	28	48	31	10	38	90	--	74	-6.1	1.8
Singapore	--	--	--	--	27	12	72	85	40	59	8.5	30.5
Thailand	42	59	34	66	36	22	63	75	21	30	-8.5	5.6
China	14	32	18	34	27	9	72	91	--	27	3.1	3.1
Korea, Rep. of	29	36	28	38	6	7	94	93	18	32	-8.0	2.0
Japan	9	10	10	12	3	3	96	93	24	24	1.5	3.2
Australia	17	22	17	20	73	61	24	30	8	14	-5.2	-6.0
New Zealand	17	31	27	32	75	67	23	29	4	10	-3.4	-4.2

Source: UNDP (2005), *Human Development Report*, New York: Oxford University Press.
IMF (2001 & 2005), *International Financial Statistics Yearbook*, Washington D.C.

not significant in Japan and India in the selected group of countries. This share ranged from about one-third in New Zealand, Indonesia and China to more than a cent in Malaysia. In most of the countries, the share of exports exceeded that of imports thus, registering a favourable trade balance.

The developing countries in general, experience chronic problems in their balance of payments. But most of these countries including India, which had experienced a deficit in their current account in 1990, have successfully managed to get the negative balance in 2003 erased. Among the selected countries, Singapore registered a significant size of current account balance in terms of its GDP in the year 2003, while Australia and New Zealand experienced a current account imbalance, as against the general trend. In the export composition, the share of primary products declined and the share of manufactured exports increased in general, with the exception of the two advanced countries, New Zealand and Australia. In the rest of the countries, Indonesia and Malaysia which had registered a well above three-fifths and two-fifths of primary products in 1990 respectively, shifted their production pattern to manufactured exports. The hike in manufactured exports from 1990 to 2003 was particularly striking in Philippines, followed by Malaysia and China. The share of high technology exports in the manufactured exports, was nearly three-fourths in Philippines, and about three-fifths in Singapore and Malaysia and a below one-third in South Korea and Thailand, and the lowest share of five per cent in India.

India's Trade with Asia-Pacific Countries

The evaluation of India's trade with major trade blocs in the world, explains to a major extent, the rationale behind India's trade relations with the Asia-Pacific region. Table 17.5 presents India's trade with the trade blocs in the world, in the three selected years 1995-96, 2001-02 and 2004-05. Despite the moderate decline in recent years, a well above half of India's exports, was directed to the Organization for Economic Cooperation and Development (OECD) bloc, comprising the industrial countries in the world. India's imports sourced from this bloc, declined from a well above half in 1995-96, to a well below two-fifths in 2004-05. However, the European Union (E.U) and the North American Free Trade Agreement (NAFTA) - the majority of these two regional groupings which constitute the OECD bloc - are still the major export destinations of India.

Table 17.5: India's Trade with Trade Blocs (per cent share in total)

Blocs	Exports			Imports		
	1995-96	2000-01	2004-05	1995-96	2000-01	2004-05
SAARC	5.41	4.21	5.43	0.70	0.87	0.84
ASEAN	8.51	6.52	10.09	7.32	8.12	8.23
OECD	57.71	54.65	46.08	55.30	41.70	38.39
EU	27.39	23.98	21.76	28.09	21.00	16.86
NAFTA	18.50	22.90	18.21	11.74	6.58	6.64
OPEC	9.68	10.90	16.06	20.83	5.37	9.15
CIS	3.57	2.35	1.32	3.31	1.36	1.73

Source: CMIE: (2001 & 2005), *Foreign Trade & Balance of Payments*, Mumbai.

In the three selected years, the country enjoyed an appreciable trade surplus with the NAFTA region (of which the U.S is the major partner), despite considerable decline in the year 2004-05. India also had a favourable trade balance with the E.U., except in the year 1995-96. The country's exports to the Organization of Petroleum Exporting Countries (OPEC), registered a significant hike from 2000-01 to 2004-05 and recorded a trade surplus, notwithstanding the rise in imports, during the same period. With ASEAN grouping, India's exports also registered a considerable growth during the above period, resulting in a favourable trade balance for the country. It is surprising to note that India, a major partner of SAARC has had a low share of trade especially, in matters of imports, with the region. India's share of exports ranged from four to five per cent with this bloc, whereas the share of imports was less than one per cent, reflecting the foregoing of the benefits of geographical proximity. The impact of South Asian Preferential Trading Arrangement (SAPTA) and its ongoing transition into South Asian Free Trade Area (SAFTA) is thus limited, on this grouping. India's trade with the Commonwealth of Independent States (CIS), was also lower.

India's trade with selected Asia-Pacific countries in the years 1990-91, 1995-96, 2000-01 and 2004-05, is provided in Table 17.6. India's export trade has undergone a sea change in its major partners in this region, during the past one and half decades. Japan, which was once the major export destination of India, had gradually lost its prominence in the late 1990s.

India's export trade with Japan contains gems and jewellery, marine products, iron ore, cotton yarn fabrics and cotton ready-made garments. Japan's share in India's imports had also declined gradually, like its share in exports. India's imports from Japan consist of non-electrical machinery, electronic goods, transport equipment, primitive and semi-finished iron and steel, professional and optical goods. China, which initially had a minimal share in India's total exports, absorbed a major share in the year 2004-05. Iron ore, primitive and semi-finished iron and steel, plastic linoleum products, processed minerals and inorganic, organic and agro-chemicals, are the major exports to China. Surprisingly enough, China was the major import source of India too, in the year 2004-05, and this reflects an elevation of its status as the major single market, in Asia. Electronic goods, coal, coke briquettes, organic chemicals, non-electrical machinery, are the main imports from China. Singapore has been the steady market for India's exports, since the last decade. India of late, has been experiencing a trade surplus with Singapore by accelerating its exports. Gems and jewellery, machinery and instruments, transport equipment, electronic goods and dyes and intermediates, are the major Indian exports to Singapore, while electronic goods, organic chemicals, transport equipment, printed books, newspapers etc and non-electrical machinery, are the prime imports.

Table 17.6: India's Trade with Select Asia and Pacific Countries (per cent share in total)

Countries	Exports				Imports			
	1990-91	1995-96	2000-01	2004-05	1990-91	1995-96	2000-01	2004-05
World	100.0	100.0	100.0	100.0	100.0	100.0	100.0	100.0
Indonesia	0.60	2.08	0.89	1.63	0.34	1.26	1.81	2.34
Malaysia	0.82	1.24	1.36	1.26	2.31	2.46	2.30	2.07
Philippines	0.15	0.45	0.46	0.50	0.02	0.06	0.13	0.17
Singapore	2.09	2.84	1.95	4.79	3.31	3.04	2.87	2.41
Thailand	1.36	1.49	1.20	1.08	0.27	0.46	0.63	0.78
China	0.10	1.05	1.88	5.79	0.13	2.21	2.99	6.30
Korea, Rep. of	1.01	1.41	1.01	1.21	1.50	2.25	1.78	2.98
Japan	9.30	6.97	4.04	2.50	7.52	6.73	3.67	2.81
Australia	0.99	1.18	0.91	0.87	3.40	2.79	2.12	3.33
New Zealand	0.12	0.19	--	--	0.28	0.17	0.16	0.10

Source: As in Table 17.5.

The other major export destinations for India's exports, are Thailand for gems and jewellery, non-ferrous metals, iron, oil meals and drugs and pharmaceuticals; Indonesia for dyes, intermediates, primitive and semi-finished iron and steel, oil meals, machinery and instruments and inorganic and organic chemicals; South Korea for cotton yarn, oil meals, other ores and minerals, iron ore and primitive and semi-finished iron and steel; and Malaysia for meat preparations, electronic goods, machinery and instruments, man-made yarn fabrics, dyes and intermediates etc. The other important import sources for India in the region are, Australia for gold, coal, coke briquettes, metal ferrous ores, raw wool and non-ferrous metals; and Malaysia for electronic goods, vegetable oils, wood and wood products, organic chemicals and non-ferrous metals etc.

The role of Foreign Direct Investment (FDI) in facilitating economic development, has gained momentum in the present global economy. Statistics show that the FDI flows in India, are much lower than in China and the five major countries of the ASEAN. So far, the FDI into India is mostly from the multinational corporations of the advanced countries and accordingly, India is acting as a manufacturing hub for them. With regard to the inward FDI stock as percentage of GDP, India's over five per cent share in 2003, is not comparable with the significant shares of South-east and East Asian countries. Besides the substantial share of 161 per cent of the inward FDI stock in GDP in Singapore in the above year, Malaysia registered an appreciable share of 57 per cent; China, 36 per cent; Indonesia, 28 per cent; and Thailand, 26 per cent. South Korea had the lowest share of eight per cent in these selected countries with the exception of India. The share of outward FDI stock in GDP was also substantial in Singapore (nearly 100 per cent) and to some extent in Malaysia (nearly 29 per cent) in 2003, whereas it was less than one per cent in the case of India (UNCTAD 2004). The share of net FDI inflows in GDP has not shown considerable improvement and in fact, declined from 1990 to 2003 in a majority of these countries. The share of Singapore dropped from

15.1 per cent to 12.5 per cent and that of Malaysia from 5.3 per cent to 2.4 per cent in the above years. The exceptions to this trend are China, where its share of net FDI inflows in GDP increased from one per cent in 1990 to 3.8 per cent in 2003 and India, in which the minimal share of 0.1 per cent had increased to 0.7 per cent (UNDP 2005).

Conclusion

In the backdrop of Asia-Pacific region's vast experience and expertise in overcoming the hurdles and in attaining rapid growth, India's engagement with these countries in a number of economic and political spheres, is imperative in the coming years. The development challenges, particularly, on the human development count, compelled India to emulate the social transformation process of East Asia and thereby follow a rapid path of economic growth. Evidence suggests that India had already learnt some lessons from the neighbouring region in formulating the trade and investment policies. However, the simplification procedure of trade facilitation in the country is yet to be done to a major extent, in order to acquire the desired export earnings and to reduce the unauthorized and illegal trade.

If India's proven edge in the IT sector, is supplemented with the acceleration of growth rate along with its required accessories, naturally, the entire Asia-Pacific region, would engage with our country in their economic processes. India's signing of FTA with the individual East Asian countries, reveals its legitimate ambition of future integration with the region as well as its sincere attempt at it. This is supported by India's increased trade (nearly two-fifths) with this region. Bilateral investment flows between India and some countries of Asia can be promoted through organized institutional campaign. Statistics show that some specific Asian countries, particularly Japan, South Korea, China and Singapore, have made significant investment in India's portfolio investments. If the strength of the software prowess of India together with its capacity-building mechanisms and its vibrant entrepreneurial class, are combined with the manufacturing potential of the East

Asian region, the economies of the region will get benefited. No doubt, there are some clashing economic interests among the Asian countries, but the unification process has already been in the making and taking shape. India's increased competitiveness can be exploited by the region, for better results; and for India too, the region holds future promise and bright prospects. With the earlier regional cooperation attempts, viz., Bangkok Agreement and Asian Clearing Union and the recent BIMSTEC etc, India is already linked economically with the South-east and East Asian countries.

The participation in the latest East Asia Summit elevated India's position considerably and also added to the responsibility of setting right its home by enhancing the capacity of the market via industrial restructuring and by making trade a broad-based one. Thus, India has a lot to do in order to utilize the synergies of the vast Asia-Pacific region properly. The East Asia Summit may be subjected to an overnight transformation into East Asian Community on the lines of the erstwhile European Economic Community (EEC), and this, appears to be an ultimate goal of most of the Asia-Pacific countries, which are striving to meet the challenges of their economic, political and security concerns. The vision of Asian economic integration is bound to get translated into a reality, provided the participants of East Asia Summit scrupulously follow certain rules of the game and exploit the existing complementarities and meticulously use the strengths, readily available in the region to the purpose.

18

Problems of Indian Diaspora in Fiji

Amit Singh

"Indians abroad always should give primary consideration to the interest of the people of those countries; they should never allow themselves to be placed in a position of exploiting the people of those countries; in fact, we have gone thus far and said, if you cannot be, and if you are not, friendly to the people of that country, come back to India and do not spoil the fair name of India".

Jawaharlal Nehru, 1957

The notion of 'Diaspora', used first in the classical world, had acquired renewed importance in the late twentieth century. While the term, was historically applied on in principle to Jews and less commonly to Greeks, Armenians, Chinese, Africans and Indians, today, on their own or as claimed by others, at least thirty ethnic groups declare that they constitute a 'Diaspora'. [1]

Etymologically speaking, 'Diaspora' is an ancient word which is derived from the Greek term *diasperien* to mean dia-, "across" and *sperien,* "to sow or scatter seeds". Thus, semantically speaking, 'Diaspora' refers to the displaced communities of people who have been dislocated from their native homeland, through the movements of migration, immigration, or exile. Accordingly, Diaspora suggests a dislocation from the nation state or the geographical location of origin and relocation in one or more nation states, territories or countries. [2]

Contemporary Diaspora are minority ethnic groups of migrant origins, residing and acting in the host countries but maintaining strong, sentimental and material links with the countries of their origin i.e. their respective homelands. The Diaspora are almost ethnically distinct, often differing from the population of their host country in their race, religion, culture, and to a great extent, in their language. In the past, the host society did not encourage the migrants to get assimilated with the native population, or to change their national identity or to mix socially with the locals. [3] Being a minority in their host countries, the Diaspora assiduously preserve their ethnicity, religious identity and solidarity. It is this solidarity based upon a kind of an identity of ethnic exclusiveness, that gives the Diaspora a cutting edge in matters of the maintenance of its relations with the people of the host country. [4]

It may be considered erroneous to say that Diaspora had its origin only in the recent past. The new immigrations are being recognized as an international force. The increased globalization has created an environment, which enables the Diaspora to look beyond the rigid national boundaries for an effective realization of their interests. Prior to the 19th century, it was difficult to maintain linkages with the homeland due to lack of communication constrained by distance and cost. Also, there were no large-scale international migrations to threaten the host culture. The migrant communities largely had no alternative but to form their own identity which is distinct socially and culturally from what they had left behind. In the modern period (post 19th century) migration and its characteristics were quite different. In fact, Diaspora phenomenon became more pronounced only after the European expansion and the colonization of the African and Asian continents. [5]

The Indian Diaspora has emerged as one of the leading and largest Diaspora of the world. Indian Diaspora has a global presence. There are more than 20 million people of Indian origin (PIO) and some six million non-resident Indians (NRIs) spread in 136 countries. [6] Majority of them are located in Africa, the Caribbean and the Oceania. There are regional variations in their adaptations. But in many ways, they exhibit common identity, which is not regional but global. Their adaptability has never eclipsed their identity, which springs from a deep faith in their civilization and spiritual heritage and is demonstrated through their abiding prized faith in the prized Indian value system. It is expressed in their aspirations and inspiration that they derive from their country of origin. For settlement, they may relish the idea of their children prospering and growing in their adopted countries, but globally, they want the children to adhere to the Indian family value system. The global identity of Indian Diaspora is distinct, because of these preferential practices and aspirations. [7]

Over years, Indians have been migrating by different waves, in different capacities. In ancient times, they went under three different capacities- (i) as indenture workers in sugar colonies of the Caribbean, Oceania and Africa, (ii) under Kangani/maistry system to Malaya and Ceylon (iii) and as free or passenger Indians primarily to East Africa. The free Indians went in small numbers to many other places as well. In the third phase, during the 20th century, Indians immigrated as skilled and semi-skilled workers to the Middle East, Europe, North America and Oceania. [8]

Journey of Indian Diaspora in Fiji

The Republic of Fiji situated in South West Pacific Ocean, comprises over 300 Islands of which approximately, 100 are inhabited. It is characterized by racial diversity. Fiji was colonised by the British in 1874. [9] Britain needed a labour force for its plantations in Fiji and preferred to import labour force, especially from India. The Indian population numbering about 61,000 were originally brought to Fiji as indentured labour from 1879, to work on the Sugarcane Plantations. About 75 per cent of these Indians had been recruited from what are now UP and Bihar, and the remaining 25 per cent from Andhra Pradesh and Tamil Nadu. [10] From India, as indenture labour, there were 85.3 per cent Hindus, 14.6 per cent Muslims and 0.1 per cent Christians. [11] The Hindus were from a variety of castes; Brahmins and other high castes comprising 16 per cent of those who came to Fiji through Calcutta, the Agricultural castes, 31.3 per cent artisans, 6.7 per cent, low castes 31.12 per cent. An analysis of ages reveals that

68.7 per cent of those who had left from Calcutta, were between twenty and thirty years old and 17.9 per cent, between ten and twenty; those between thirty and forty, comprised 4.9 per cent, those over forty, 0.2 per cent. [12] It was because of this labour based migration, that the Indian community came into existence in Fiji and still continues to be in significant numbers.

With the abolition of indenture system in Fiji, the Indo-Fijian leased land from ethnic Fijians, and became a sugarcane cultivator. That is why, the economic prosperity ensued for Indo-Fijians, and attracted Gujarati traders into the wholesale and retail business in Fiji. From 1921 to 1936 the Indo- Fijians increased rapidly in number, from 60634 to 85002, as in the early 1920 and 30s. Their numbers swelled by fresh immigrants from the trading sector who had set up small shops once, but today own some of the largest retail sectors in the country. [13] Many of them had moved from the plantations to occupy themselves in trade and commerce, which became almost an Indian monopoly. In the main streets of the growing towns, Gujarati names were prominently displayed on the shops. Some of the Indians started driving the latest models of the British and Japanese cars, even as the Fijians languished for subsistence in agriculture, despite owning 83 per cent of the land area of Fiji. The all-too obvious prosperity and higher standards of living of the Indians led to growing resentment by the indigenous people, who felt outclassed in what they regarded as their own country. [14]

The hard work of Indian migrants laid the foundation of the sugar industry. This is one of the major earners of the country's foreign exchange and provides a substantial part of the government revenues. The Indians operate much of the transport system of the country; they are also artisans and shopkeepers and form the bulk of the urban populations. Fiji may well give the impression that it is an India in miniature or rather a 'little India of the south-west pacific'.

In the beginning, the condition of the Indians in Fiji was not much better than that of the slaves. The proportion of women to men was totally skewed during that period. A settled family life was impossible in the barracks, provided to them by the planters. The different castes and even the more distinctive religious differences between Hindus and Muslims had become dim as they had to live together, being compelled to forget the divisions that had separated them in India. Christian missionaries from Britain and elsewhere, who had succeeded in converting most of the Fijians to one or the other of the various Christian sects, had little effect on the Indian settlers who remained loyal to what they recalled as their ancient religions and traditional customs. [15] Once it became certain that Indians were to stay there permanently, they started working hard and progressed in every sphere of life and there population increased. The British, in accordance with their policy of 'Divide and Rule,' enacted the 1966 Constitution, as they did not intend to share the power with Indians. The British maintained and inspired the belief, that the Indians who had multiplied and outnumbered all the others in population, held a predominant share of economic power and if they were to be given equal political rights, they would take over the country which legitimately belongs to the Fijian. [16]

Status of the Indo-Fijian, after the Independence of Fiji

Fiji became independent on October 10, 1970, and the Constitution, which they adopted, was very much on the lines of the old British Constitution. The Constitution of the newly independent Fiji was adopted in April 1970, which provided Fiji with a parliamentary form of democracy based on the Westminster model. It provided a bicameral legislature with one of the most complex legislative systems of the world. As the Melanesians in Fiji were in numerical minority, the Constitution was stretched out of the way from Westminster democracy to safeguard the interests of the indigenous populations. [17] By and large, the Fijian Constitution is a repetition of the British Constitution.

The political system worked out by the British, was based on a communal instead of a common electoral role. The Fijians had been advocating a communal roll throughout the colonial period.

They wanted their interests to be protected and the political power, ensured to them. Therefore, a unique voting system had been evolved by which Fiji voter had four votes to cast in the elections.

According to the New Constitution (1970s) of Fiji, the Lower House which was called the House of Representatives, had 52 members. Among these, 12 Fijians, 12 Indians and 3 general members, were to be elected on the basis of the communal voters roll. Besides that, 10 more Fijians, 10 Indians and 8 general members, had to be elected on national roll. The members of the general category represented minority communities. Each voter had a total of four votes, one in the communal electorate and three (one for each social grouping) in the national electorate. The Upper House was called the Senate which had 22 members 8 nominated by the Council of Chiefs, 7 by the Prime Minister, 6 as the opposition leader's nominees and 1, to be the nominee of Council of the Rotuman. [18] The special representation given to the Council of Chiefs in the Senate, was of most crucial significance in establishing the supremacy of Fijian interests. The Constitution gave the veto power to any three nominees of the 'Council of Chiefs', an effective veto on any legislative attempt to interfere with core Fijian interests such as land, customs and way of life. The Constitution also gave a guarantee to the indigenous Fijians, regarding the granting of the traditional rights over 80 per cent of the country's land. The elected House of Representatives had no rights over these provisions. Thus "the outwardly symmetrical parity of ethnic representation was more than outweighed by defence of Fijian interest through the composition and powers of the nominated senate". [19]

Under this condition, it was absolutely impossible to achieve a reasonable basis for any representation, based on majority rule. The NFP (National Federation Party) had always opposed the system of communal representation. In fact, the National Federation Party (support base predominantly among Indo-Fijians) insisted from the beginning, on the rights of the majority being accepted. The only proper way to identify a majority, was to establish the principle of one man, one vote. [20] But this idea was rejected by most of the Fijians on the ground that it might dilute their political identity. They also were scared of placing the numerically and economically strong Indians on an equal footing. It may be noted here that at the time of independence, Indians (51 per cent of total population) outnumbered the Fijians. [21] Thus ultimately, the NFP had to accept the system of communal roll in order to allay the Fijian fears of Indian domination. In the elections thus held in 1972, Alliance Party (support base among Indigenous Fijians) won the majority and Ratu Mara became the first Prime Minister of independent Fiji. In the words of Shanti Sadiq Ali,

"Although the 1970 constitution was not a perfect document, the Indo-Fijians co-operated with ethnic Fijians to create a society which was described as 'the way the world should be". [22]

In the General Elections of 1977, NFP got the majority of seats 26 out of 52 seats in the House of Representatives, but they could not form the government because of their internal dissensions. Once again, Ratu Mara ruled Fiji. The loyalty of Indo-Fijians has always been questioned, especially in every general election held since 1972. The 1977 election convinced the ethnic Fijian elite that the 1970 constitution did not carry enough guarantee of favouring permanent right to political power for them. [23]

In the General Elections of 1982, Ratu Mara's Alliance Party again came to power but, with a reduced majority. However, there was a great deal of discontent with the Ratu Mara government over the rising inflation and unemployment. In addition, the economic development was lopsided which favoured only the eastern part of the country. The economic measures adopted by the government to meet the crisis brought it into direct confrontation with the trade unions and because of this, the trade union movement became stronger. One of the largest trade unions, had Dr. Timoci Bavadra as its President and Mahendra Chaudhary as its National Secretary. These two leaders formed the Fijian Labour party (FLP) in July 1985. The support base of this party was urban Fijians, Indo-Fijians and those from the western part of Fiji. In 1987, the NFP and FLP formed a coalition and won the election. For the first time in the history of Fiji, the People of Indian Origin came to power under Dr. Bavadra's leadership. [24] The coalition of FLP and NFP won 28 seats in the House of Representatives, 19 of whom were won by ethnic Indians. The Governor General Ratu Sir Panaia Ganilau Dr. Bavadra and his cabinet were sworn in by Dr. Bavadra's cabinet includes seven Indo-Fijians, six Fijians and one European. It was for the first time in Fijian history, that the Indians were given an equal role in the governance of the country. [25]

1987 Coup and its Implications

The issue of land, which was already a sensitive one in Fijian politics, was made use of, as an instrument to mobilize the Fijians, against the Bavadra's government. An indigenous Fijian movement called "Taukei" (meaning our land) movement was started by ultra nationalists. The movement having got the networking of the Alliance Party spread rapidly throughout the country. Massive demonstrations were held against the new government. In fact, the government had done absolutely nothing to threaten any aspect of Fijian land, which in any case was constitutionally safeguarded in the Senate. In a sense, land became an 'anticipatory issue', meaning that it was expected by the Fijians that sooner or later the new government would begin to tamper with the Fijian land tenure and operations of the National Land Trust Board (NLTB). [26] In view of these developments and the anxiety in the minds of ethnic Fijians, Rabuka's military coup followed and toppled the government in May 1987 and subsequently, in September 1987. Rabuka brought drastic changes in Fiji; he turned Fiji into a Republic, banned all the political parties and promoted the slogan "Fiji for Fijians". Soon riots followed in Fiji, which witnessed a large-scale destruction of the Indian property due to which most of the Indians migrated from Fiji transforming the Indians from majority to a minority of population. Initially, Australia and New Zealand imposed restrictions on Fiji and it was ousted from the Commonwealth of Nations. Subsequently, Indian Government also withdrew her High Commission in Suva. [27]

The period witnessed the birth of some of the critical writings on these developments. Dr. Birj V. Lal has referred to the coup of 1987 as 'an outcome of supremacy of traditionalism'. He further adds, "Both Bavadra's class and regional origin posed the danger for traditional scheme of things in Fijian society. Dr. Bavadra belonged to the middle class and was from western part of the country". [28] In the words of another writer J. Sandy on Fiji, "The coup of 1987 overthrew a newly elected multiracial government and reinstalled the former Fijian elite led regime which espoused the traditional order and the 'Fijian way' yet also aimed to preserve its own privileged position in both Fijian society and modern economy". [29]

The new constitution adopted by Rabuka, was discriminatory. According to the new Constitution, there was to be a bi-cameral legislature with an Upper House known as 'Senate' and a Lower House, called the 'House of Representatives'. The Lower House was to have 69 popularly elected members from the communal constituencies of which 37 were allocated to Fijians, 27 to Indo-Fijians, 1 for Routman and 5, to others. In the Senate, the 'Great Council of Chiefs' was to nominate ethnic Fijians to 24 out of the total of 34 seats. The Senate played an important role in protecting the Fijian interests in Parliament especially in decisions to alter or repeal any constitutional provisions affecting the Fijians or their land, customs, traditions etc. The Senate was also empowered to appoint the President of the Republic (for a term of 5 years) and the Prime Minister from among the Fijians. [30] The late President Ratu Ganilau, commenting on the new constitution stated:

"To the Fijians the plight and fate of indigenous people in many land sounded a warning. The Fijians had to preserve their identity, their culture- and sometimes it seemed, and their very existence... It was obvious to them that the former constitution did not provide sufficient guarantees for the political rights of the

Fijian people... the new constitution rectifies in several ways". [31]

Thus, the constitution of 1990 set up a form of elective parliamentary government but even the most generous interpretation could not deny the fact that it was discriminatory and non-democratic. The 1990 constitution, drafted badly, needed an inward investment and faced a number of other problems. [32] It has been noted, that the Urban Fijians for all their constituting one third of the indigenous population, were allotted only 5 of the 37 seats in the House of Representatives. Hence, the constitution was opposed by both the NFP and the FLP and they announced that they would not participate in any elections to be held under it. Rabuka on the other hand, justified the discriminatory nature of the constitution on the grounds that it was meant to redress the political and economic inequality between the Fijians and the Indo-Fijians. [33]

President Ganilau, finally promulgated the constitution on July 25, 1990. In the legislative elections held in 1992, and again in 1994, Rabuka's Party SVT (formed by Great Chiefs and reflecting the ideas of Taukei movement) came to power with Rabuka as the Prime Minister. But during his tenure, Rabuka faced numerous problems. The negative effect of the racist constitution had resulted in a huge capital outflow, which considerably affected the economy. The economic policies followed by the new government, led to a great deal of unrest among the workers and strikes were held over wages and poor working conditions all over Fiji. Meanwhile, the racial tensions were also exacerbated during the period; several attacks on Hindu temples were reported. The issue of land, once again came to the forefront. Rabuka also aroused some controversy over corruption charges. [34]

Rabuka, trying to win over the situation, invited opposition leaders Jai Ram Reddy of the NFP and Mahendra Chaudhary of the FLP to form a Government of national unity, which the Indo-Fijians declined. And Rabuka announced the formation of a *Constitutional Review Commission*, which was expected to complete a review of the constitution by 1997. Meanwhile, the economic plight of both the urban and rural Fijians forced Rabuka to revise his earlier constitution to permit Indians to share power. Actually, due to a general economic downturn the racist card had lost its appeal. The Rabuka government therefore, had no hope of retaining power and the only way for him and his SVT Party was, to make a peace pact with the Indo-Fijian community by restoring some of their democratic rights. [35] Apart from this, the international concern regarding continued existence of Fiji's, racially biased constitution and its subsequent economic isolation, had forced Rabuka, to adopt amendments to the constitution. [36]

The new Constitution of 1997 aimed at creating a fine balance between the ethnic Fijian and Indo-Fijian. The main provision of the Constitution is that it declares Fiji to be a Sovereign Democratic Republic, which guarantees the citizens the fundamental rights, a universal adult suffrage and equality before law. It provides a Parliamentary form of government with bicameral legislature, comprising a House of Representatives with 71 elected members and a Senate with 32 appointed members; 46 seats in the Lower House are reserved on racial basis (23 for ethnic Fijians, 19 for Indians and 3 for other races and one for Ratuman Islanders) and the remaining 25 seats are open to all. The Senate is to be appointed by the President on the advice of the Council of Chiefs (14 members), Prime Minister (4 members), leaders of opposition (8 members) and Ratuman Islands Council (one member). In this constitution Indo-Fijians and the general voters are given equal status, so that the ownership of Fijian land, their rights and those of the Indo-Fijians are articulated in the specific articles of the constitution. The new constitution is hailed as a unique experiment in a complex situation. [37]

Following the adoption of the new Constitution Fiji found itself on the path of reconciliation and co-existence. This led to the re-entry of Fiji in the Commonwealth of Nations and India too re-opened its High Commission in Suva. Elections were conducted on the basis of the new Constitution in May, 1999, in which the FLP under Mahendra Chaudhary led People's Coalition (other partners being the Fijian Association and the Party of National Unity) and thus, came to power. Out of the total 71 seats in the House of Representatives, People's Coalition got 52 seats (37 went to the FLP alone). Shortly after the election results were announced, former Prime Minister Rabuka warned the Indian community as follows:

"...to the Members of the Indian Community, we the indigenous Fijians, have given so much in agreeing to review the 1990 constitution. Your vote is your democratic right but judging from the way you have bloc voted turning inward to your own communal interests, I appeal to you all to show greater responsibility to our wider common interests as a nation". [38]

Even though the FLP had enough seats to form the government on its own, Mahendra Chaudhary acted cautiously. Not only did he include his alliance partners but also did he rope Ratu Su Kamisese Mara's daughter and her Christian Democratic Alliance in his government. Another commendable step undertaken by Chaudhary was to allocate portfolios central to Fijian interests to ethnic Fijians. The Ministry of Fijian Affairs, Agriculture, Fisheries and Forests, Tourism etc. all went to ethnic Fijians, most of whom were not even members of the FLP. 12 out of 18 members of the Cabinet were ethnic Fijians. Thus, Chaudhary's Government was in no sense a sectarian government but was a genuine cultural mix. It reflected a triumph of multiracialism over racism. This Government symbolized peaceful co-existence of different communities of Fiji. However, an Indo-Fijian Prime Minister did not go well with some of the Fijian elite. After all, the suspicion of the Indians holding political power, was aggravated after Chaudhary became the Prime Minister. All kinds of rumors were spread especially, about land rights. Not surprisingly, on May 19, 2000, George Speight instigated a civilian coup and Chaudhary's government was overthrown. [39]

Civilian Coup in May 2000 and its Implications

On May 19, 2000, a group of armed men, led by businessperson George Speight, invaded the parliament building and ousted the government, taking Chaudhry and 30 other members of the governing coalition as hostages. The President Mara condemned the coup and declared a state of emergency as Speight's supporters rampaged through the streets of Suva, looting and setting fire to Indian businesses. Speight declared that he had reclaimed Fiji for indigenous people and had dissolved the constitution. Moreover, he threatened to kill the hostages if the military intervened. On 22 May, Mara formally invited Rabuka, in his role as chairperson of the Great Council of Chiefs, to seek a resolution of the crisis. In the following days, the Great Council of Chiefs convened to discuss the situation and proposed the replacement of Chaudhry's government with an interim administration, an amnesty for Speight and the rebels, and the amendment of the constitution. Speight rejected the proposals, demanding the removal of Mara also from the office. On 29 May, Mara resigned, and the Commander of the Armed Forces, Frank Bainimarama, announced the imposition of martial law and a curfew, in an attempt to restore calm to the country. [40]

Negotiations between the Military Executive Council and the Great Council of Chiefs continued throughout June 2000. Failure to reach a conclusive outcome seemed to be the result of inconsistencies in Speight's demands and an ambivalent attitude on the part of the military towards the coup. Regular patrols by the security forces curbed rioting in Suva, although the outbreak of violence in rural areas (mostly in the form of attacks on Indo-Fijians, the looting and burning of Indian-owned farms and the occupation of several tourist resorts), was reported. On 25 June, the four female hostages were released from the parliament building. The Military Executive Council announced its intention to appoint an interim government without consulting Speight and demanded the rebel leader to release the remaining hostages. Speight reiterated his threat to kill all those held if any rescue attempts were made. [41]

An interim administration of 19 indigenous Fijians led by Laisenia Qarase (the former managing director of the Merchant Bank of Fiji) was sworn in on July 4, 2000. Minutes after the ceremony a gun battle erupted outside the Parliament building in which four civilians and one rebel were injured; the rebel subsequently died. Speight announced that he did not recognize the interim authority, and most of Fiji's mainstream political parties similarly denounced it, although the Methodist Church declared its support of the body. On 12 July, nine more hostages were released, and on the following day the remaining 18, including Chaudhry were liberated. On 29 July, Speight was finally arrested, along with dozens of his supporters but nothing will happen to George Speight as he had already been appointed the President of the new Matanitu Vanua (MV- Conservative Alliance Party) party, despite facing the charge of treason for his part in the 2000 coup.

On May 9, 2001, Qarase formed the Soqosoqo Duavata ni Lewenivanua (SDL-Fiji United Party), a new contender for the indigenous Melanesian vote, thus rivaling the established Soqosoqo ni Vakavulewa Ni Tauket (SVT). Another indigenous party, the Bai Kei Viti, was launched on 28 June. In the same month, Tupeni Baba, former Deputy Prime Minister in Chaudhry's government, left the FLP and formed the New Labour United Party. The election took place between 25 August and September 1, 2001. Qarase's SDL was victorious, but failed to obtain an overall majority. The SDL secured 31 seats in the House of Representatives (increasing to 32 of the 71 seats after a by-election on 25 September). The FLP won 27 seats, the MV 6 seats and the NLUP 2 seats. International monitors were satisfied that the election had been contested fairly. Laisenia Qarase's formed the new Government but he refused to allow the FLP any representation in his new Cabinet. Qarase was accused of contravening a provision of the Constitution whereby a party, winning more than 10 per cent of the seats in the House of Representatives, was entitled to one ministerial post whereas two members of George Speight's were included in the Cabinet. [42]

Fiji's population was 819,000 in mid-2002 and Indians were now only 43.6 per cent of the total population. Their number has declined in view of the migration to other countries especially, since 1987 coup and also due to lower birth rates. From 1987, until the election of September 2001, violence against the Indian community and their property, increased and they were marginalized in every aspect. This resulted in the migration of skilled Indo-Fijians to the US, Canada, Australia and New Zealand, reducing the Indian community's share in Fiji population from 51 per cent at independence in 1970 to 43.6 per cent in 2002. [43] Currently, the Laisenia Qarase's government, is ruling Fiji as the struggle of the People of Indian Origin for equality and their rights, continues in Fiji.

Response of International Community to the Crisis in Fiji

Almost the entire world condemned the coups. Initially, Australia and New Zealand imposed restrictions on Fiji when it was ousted from the Commonwealth of Nations and India shut down their High Commission in Suva after the 1987 Coup. Australia and New Zealand were affected by the crisis in Fiji, as they were neighbours and have considerable number of investments in Fiji. Both the countries condemned the coups and at one point, it seemed that they were contemplating military intervention. However, according to a senior Australian naval officer, Australia at no stage planned an attack on Fiji, as Vietnam was still fresh in the minds of the decision makers. Now looking back through various reports, statements and scholarly works, it seems that the two countries realized that any physical intervention would be misunderstood by the South-Pacific island states. The Melanesian Spearhead Group, consisting of Papua New Guinea, the Solomon Islands, and Vanuata, condemned any suggestion that externally backed the idea of the military intervention in Fiji. Australia is extremely careful not to give the impression of being the region's policemen. [44]

Bavadra's policy of a nuclear free South Pacific, was an anathema to the US, Australia and France. It meant the exclusion of nuclear powered vessels from the South Pacific waters, as well as an end to French nuclear testing at Muroroa Atoll. The US State Department in Washington said that it was "profoundly disturbed" at the coup in Fiji. The French reaction was similarly muted. One of the various theories afloat at that time claimed, that there was an American backing of the military overthrow of an inconvenient government in the South - Pacific. [45] Within the South- Pacific, it was only Walter Lini of Vanuatu who condemned the coup, for most of the members of the South Pacific Forum sympathized with the motives of the coup. They saw it as a battle by an endangered indigenous people against a larger immigrant community. [46]

However, Fiji's, relations with the International Community, suffered a major reversal following the coup of May 2000, which was condemned by the UN, the Commonwealth, the United Kingdom, Australia, New Zealand, India, the US and several other nations in the region. In June 2000, Fiji was partially suspended from the Commonwealth, and a delegation of ministers of Foreign Affairs from the Organization visited the Islands to demand the reinstatement of the 1997 constitution. Following the democratic elections of August - September 2001, both Australia and New Zealand removed the bilateral sanctions they had imposed. The sanction imposed by the European Union (EU) remained in place until early 2002. In December 2001, the Commonwealth Ministerial Action group on the Harare Declaration (CMAG) recommended that Fiji be re-admitted to meetings of the Commonwealth. The decision by the French Government in June 1995 to resume nuclear testing in the region, was widely condemned by the Pacific Island Nations and in protest against the announcement, Fiji cancelled its annual military exercise with France. [47]

Fiji has experienced two armed ousters of democratically elected governments in an interval of 13 years (1987-2000) and both were strongly criticized by the International Communities. External powers have limitations and they cannot openly intervene in solving the Fiji crisis. They can, however, use pulls and pressures, to help Fiji solve its crisis in its own way.

Conclusion

The future of Indian Diaspora in Fiji appears to be rather bleak. It can change, if there is a change of heart towards it on the part of the indigenous Fijians. That does not, as of now, seem at all likely. Meanwhile, the cause for alarm lies in the fact that the Indo-Fijians are continuously migrating to the Pacific Rim Countries, due to the hostile atmosphere in the land of their ancestors. This cannot be good for the economic, social and political future of Fiji-where the ancestors of Indo-Fijian had worked hard, to make Fiji a prosperous place, a fact recognised by all the other island states.

India has a legitimate interest in the Fijian issue. It can play a vital role in getting the leaders of the two communities together in an atmosphere where many sensitive issues can be discussed and an acceptable resolution found, without leaving behind any room for rancour. Unfortunately, it needs to be pointed out, that the recent High Level Committee Report on the Indian Diaspora, demonstrated its lack of insight and knowledge of the Fijian problem, and the following erroneous statement is just one example of this: 'A revised constitution was adopted in 1990. It sought to introduce a more balanced distribution of legislative seats than before'. [48] In fact, and quite to the contrary, the 1990 constitution was racially biased and was most vocally opposed, by Indo-Fijians.

India needs to focus international attention on the situation in Fiji, until the country adopts a healthy and peaceful multiracial society. India has to articulate its position forcefully in multilateral meetings and bilateral interactions. It has to work in concert with the countries that wield an influence in the region, such as Australia and New Zealand. The Indian government has to maintain close co-ordination with regional powers and organizations like the Pacific Islands Forum, the Commonwealth and the European Union that have various kinds of advantage in the region. It will need to persuade them to exert pressure on the Fijian regime to develop the country as a multicultural society. Recent establishment of the Ministry of Overseas Indians, would be a positive step in improving good relations with the Indian Diaspora, including Indo-Fijians. Above all, it is high time that the Indian political elite had forged a constructive relationship with the indigenous leadership, especially considering the fact, that the crucial forthcoming General elections in Fiji, to be held in May 2006, are fast approaching.

Notes

1. The dispersion of Jews outside of Israel from the sixth century B.C., when they were exiled to Babylonia, until the present time. ii. Often *Diaspora* The body of Jews or Jewish communities outside Palestine or modern Israel. iii. *Diaspora* a. A dispersion of a people from their original homeland. b. The community formed by such a people: "the glutionous dish known throughout the [West African] Diaspora as...fufu" (Jonell Nash, Essence February 1996). iv. Diaspora A dispersion of an originally homogenous entity, such as language or culture: "the Diaspora of English into several mutually incomprehensible languages" Randolph Quirk, *The American Heritage Dictionary of the English Language*, (Boston, US, 2000).
2. Brazil, Jana Evans and Anita Mannur, (ed.), *Theorizing Diaspora*, (Oxford: Blackwell Publishing Ltd, 2003), p. 1.
3. Myron Weiner, "Labour migration as Incipient Diaspora", in Gabriel Sheffer, ed., Modern *Diaspora in International Politics*, (London: Croom Helnm, 1986), p.47.
4. Gabriel Sheffer, "A New Field of Study: Modern Diaspora in international politics", in Gabriel Sheffer (ed.), *Modern Diaspora International Politicians*, (London: Croom Helm, 1986), p.1.
5. Sadananda Saho, "Indian Diaspora at the Cross Roads: The Fiji and Malaysian Case", *Studies in Humanities and Social Science*, (SHSS, New Delhi), vol. IX, No.1, summer 2003, pp.1-2.
6. K. Mathews, 'Indian Diaspora", *World Focus*, (New Delhi), vol. 22, No.3, March 2001, p.5.
7. Ajay Dubey, (ed.), *Indian Diaspora: Global Identity*, (New Delhi: Kalinga, Publications, 2003), pp.iii-iv.
8. *Ibid.*
9. J.D. Legge, *Britain in Fiji 1858-1880*, (London: Macmillan & Co. Ltd., 1958) pp.V-VI.
10. See details in, "Report of the High Level Committee on the Indian Diaspora", Chapter-22, http://indiandiaspora.nic.in/ contents.html
11. K.L. Gillion, *Fiji's Indian Migrants. A History to the end of Indenture in 1920*, (Melbourne, 1962), pp. 209-210.

12. Ahmed Ali, "Serving Girmit in Fiji, 1879-1919", in U. Bissoondagal and S.B.C. Servenising (ed.), *Indian Labour Immigration*, (Moka, Mauritius: Mahatma Gandhi Institute Press, 1986), pp. 238-253.

13. Brij V. Lal, *Broken Waves: A History of Fiji in the 20th Century*, (Honolulu: University of Hawaii Press, 1992), pp.17-59.

14. See "Report of the High Level Committee on the Indian Diaspora", (New Delhi: Indian Council of World Affairs, December 2001) pp. 289-300.

15. Brij V. Lal, *Chalo Jahaji: On a Journey through Indenture in Fiji*, (Canberra: ANU, 2000).

16. Manmohini Kaul, "The Crisis in Fiji: An Overview", *Peace Initiatives*, vol.6, No. 1-3, January-June 2000, pp. 1-8.

17. E.K. Fisk, *The Political Economy of Independent Fiji*, (Canberra: ANU, 1970), p.18.

18. Rotumans number less than 10,000 and hail from the island of Rotuma, located several hundred kilometres north of the Fiji group but administered from Suva for more than a Century.

19. Rod Alley, "Fiji at the Cross Roads?" *Round Table*, No.342, April 1997, p.247.

20. R.K. Vasil, "Communalism and Constitution- making in Fiji", *Pacific Affairs*, (Vancouver, B.C.), vol.45, No.1, spring, 1972, p.250.

21. *Fiji, The Fareast Australia 2004* (London & New York: Europa Publications, 35th Edition, 2004), pp. 765-778.

22. Shanti Sadiq Ali, "Institutionalized Racial Discrimination" *Mainstream*, vol.30, No.10, December 2, 1991, p.15.

23. Amba Pande, "Race and Power Struggle in Fiji", *Strategic Analysis*, vol.24, No.6, September 2000, pp.1154-70.

24. Stephanie Lawson, *The Failure of Democratic Politics in Fiji*, (Oxford: Clarendon Press, 1991), pp.195-233.

25. Shubha Singh, *Fiji: A precarious Coalition*, (New Delhi: Har-Anand Publication, 2001), pp.110-120.

26. Ralph R. Premdas and Jeffrey S. Steeves, "Fiji Problems of Ethnic Discrimination and Inequality in the new constitutional order", *Round Table*, No.318, April 1991, p.164.

27. Manmohini Kaul, "Imaging the South Pacific: An Indian Construct of the Region" in N. N. Vohra (ed.), *India and Australia, History, Culture and Society*, (New Delhi: Shipra, 2003), pp.132-160.

28. Brij V. Lal, "Fiji Indians and the Politics of Exclusion", *Foreign Affairs Report*, vo.38, No.7-8, Jul-Aug 1989, pp.105-106.

29. J. Sandy, "The Coups of 1987: A Personal Analysis", *Pacific Viewpoint*, vol.30, No.2, 1989.
30. Shubha Singh, n.24, pp.134-148.
31. *The Fiji Times*, 27 July 1990.
32. Rod Alley, n.18, p.245.
33. *The Indian Express*, New Delhi, November 12, 1988.
34. Shubha Singh, n.24, pp.134-148.
35. S.P. Seth, "New Beginning in Fiji, *Economic and Political Weekly*, vol.34, No.2, June 1999,p.1413.
36. *Deccan Herald*, May 20, 1999.
37. Rajeev Dhawan, "The Fiji Crisis", *The Hindu*, July 2, 2000.
38. Deryck Scarr, "Communalism and Constitution: Fiji's General Election of May 1999", *The Journal of Pacific History*, 34(3), 1999, p. 258.
39. Amba Pande, n.22, pp.1154-70.
40. Shubha Singh, n.24, pp.149-163.
41. *Ibid.*
42. Brij V. Lal, "Fijian Constitutional Condandrum", *Round Table*, vol.372, October 2003, pp.671-85.
43. Fiji, n.20, pp. 765-778.
44. Manmohini Kaul, n.26, p.132-160.
45. Shubha Singh, n.24, pp.125.
46. *www.Fiijlive.com.*
47. *htttp//www.globalpolicy.org/security/issues/fiji.htm*
48. See, n.14, p. 299.

19

Harnessing the Potentialities of Indian Diaspora in the Southeast Asian and Pacific Region

P. Munirathnam Reddy

Introduction

By Indian Diaspora, the Government of India meant to include both Person of Indian Origin and Non- Resident Indian population. [1] People of Indian Origin (PIO) as a phrase has gained much importance in the context of globalization to denote its Overseas Indians or Expatriate Indians or Non-Resident Indians. Both People of Indian Origin and Indian Diaspora are used inter-changeably.and have become synonymous. People of Indian Origin constitute a third largest group, next only to the British and the Chinese.

Today there are nearly 25 million PIOs living in almost every corner of the world. [2] They have got themselves adapted to the shores of foreign lands. But neither the passage of time nor the distance between their ancestral lands and their new homes has been able to make the umbilical cord between Mother India and her children abroad severed. [3] But alas! India discovered the overseas Indians in 1991 when our economy went bankrupt. It was then that out of the blue, this new species of animal called the NRI, was elevated to the position of the savior of the bankrupt India. [4] Overseas Indians of some 20 million (1.7 per cent of the total population of India) at the turn of the century, contributed to about 10 per cent of India's total foreign direct investment. [5]

Historical Background of Indian Diaspora

According to Dr. Karan Singh, the Indian Diaspora is categorized as (1) pre-colonial, (2) colonial and (3) post-colonial migrations; with 1 and 2 categories termed as low-tech and the 3 as high-tech. [6] Indian emigration dates back to 2,300 years, starting with the post-Buddha era when missionaries went to Sri Lanka, Afghanistan, Southeast Asia and elsewhere. In the 7th and 8th centuries, there were Indians especially, Gujarati businessmen in East Africa very much involved in financing the Arabs in slave trade. There was no large-scale emigration until the 19th century. The European imperialist expansion during the 19th and 20th centuries created conditions becoming conducive to emigration of Indians in large numbers. With the abolition of slavery in the British, French and Dutch colonies respectively in 1834, 1846 and 1873, there was a severe shortage of labourers for working in sugarcane, tea, coffee, cocoa, rice and rubber plantations in the colonies. India and China became the obvious alternative sources of labour. Traders, entrepreneurs and white collar workers too emigrated to various colonies. Under the indentured system nearly 1.5 million persons emigrated from India. [7] Some immigrants stayed back and settled in the respective colonies and did not return home though the indentured system of labour was discontinued in 1917.

Later, in the post-World War II period, the dispersal of Indian labour and professionals became a nearly world-wide phenomenon. [8] Indians and other South Asians provided the labour that helped in the reconstruction of war-torn Europe, particularly UK and the Netherlands, and in more recent years unskilled labour from India has been the main force in the transformation of the physical landscape of much of the Middle East. Meanwhile, in countries such as the US, Canada and Australia, Indians have made their presence visibly felt in the professions. In recent times, thanks to globalization and economic liberalization, a considerable number of Indian students began emigrating to the well developed countries like USA, UK, Australia, New Zealand for pursuing higher studies/vocational courses and, on completion of their courses, most of them sought employment and settled in the respective countries.

Indian Diaspora's Contribution to India

Despite their disadvantage of numerical minority, the Indian communities living abroad, have made deep impressions on the political processes, besides making an indelible impact on culture and economy of their adopted countries. The active participation of people from India in the nationalist movement in Africa at the beginning of the 20th century is well documented. India's struggle for independence was also greatly strengthened by the substantial support of overseas Indian communities. Keeping in view the pan-Indian sentiment, Nehru observed thus: "wherever in this wide world, there goes an Indian, there goes also a bit of India with him". The Indian Diaspora maintained low profile and remained faithful to the established norms of the adopted societies. [9] The Diaspora was in any case too insecure to think beyond making the two ends meet. In occupying a category created by the Indian government in the 1970s to repatriate investment from abroad, this migrant has been lexically bestowed with a relationship to India and received benefits that would not normally be available to those living outside the nation-state, such as the right to own property within its borders, as well as the affirmation of political loyalties to what is perceived as an originary place. [10]

GOPIO: Global Organization of People of Indian Origin (GOPIO), a forum at the national and international level to voice their concerns, was formed at the first global convention of PIO held on August 28 – September 3 1989 at New York, at the initiation of National Federation of Indian American Association.

At the turn of the century as per the estimation of Dr. Thomas Abraham, president GOPIO, there were 20 million PIOs about 50 per cent of whom constitute the first generation immigrants from India. [11] Global communities of the PIOs represent a tremendous resource in intellectual, technical, scientific, professional, trade and entrepreneurial skills with high potential and keenness to contribute to the well-being and prosperity of the countries of their domicile and India. Excellent educational institutions like IITs, IIMs, IISc, Medical Colleges contributed to a large scale migration of professionals who are on the top all new technologies. Global potential, encompassing all NRIs/PIOs, was categorized by Dr. Thomas Abraham as capital, technical expertise and business expertise. Economic output of NRIs and PIOs in 2000 was estimated at $400 billion, almost the same as the total GDP of India. [12]

NR Is/PIOs have become a hot commodity to be attracted for investments. They have also been working behind the scene to create interest among multinational companies to take interest in India. The global Indians are recognized everywhere for their success and hard work and they have done a great job in building a good image for India in their respective countries.

India's Active Engagement with its Diaspora

The High level Committee on the Indian Diaspora headed by L.M. Singhvi submitted a well documented report in January 2002, dealing with the aspirations of 20 million population of the Indian Diaspora and envisaged the governmental action for tapping the resources and expertise of Indian Diaspora. To quote Bharat Gupt, "We have a situation in which borders may be defined by the older nationalism, while the social fabric is divided in into 'ethnic' categories. Every nation is, therefore, seen as multi-ethnic conglomerate. The communication technology is therefore making the cultural ethnic bonds so strong that the expatriated populations can now live in a close emotional proximity to the native land. The emotional bonds are easier to maintain in the age of Internet, TV, emails, faxes and phones than what the letters and newspapers". [13] The ICT (Information Communication Technology) today turned the entire world into a global village. The GOPIO, through the networking, could bring the Indian Diaspora of various nations onto a common platform thereby to knock at the door of their mother country to offer rich fund of knowledge, expertise, and economic resources in pursuit of making India emerge as knowledge super power and a vibrant economy. While inaugurating the convention of the first ever International Convention of GOPIO in New Delhi on January 6, 2001, the then Prime Minister Vajpayee called for "Developing a

Mutually Beneficial Relationship between India and the Indian Diaspora".

To harness the potentialities of Indian Diaspora, the GOI decided to organize a conference, Pravas Bharatiya Divas (PBD) every year in January. While inaugurating the first PBD in New Delhi on January 9-11, 2003, Vajpayee announced the decision of his government to permit 'dual citizenship' for PIOs living in certain countries.Vajpayee who presented "Pravasi Bharatiya Samman Puraskars"to the distinguished PIOs, [14] glorified the occasion and sought the richness of experience of PIOs in making India a developed nation by 2020. [15] At the 2nd PBD on January 9, 2004 once again organized in New Delhi by the NDA government, an External Affairs Ministry spokesman, explained that "the purpose of the conference was to mobilize the people of Indian origin, give them a greater sense of involvement with their country of birth and utilize their leverage in their countries". Prime Minister Vajpayee announced Pavasi Bharatiya Samman awards to 12 persons for their "outstanding contribution to the understanding of the Indian civilization and for advancing India's cause abroad". [16]

The UPA government of Dr. Manmohan Singh for the first time created a separate Ministry of Overseas Indian Affairs (MOIA) in May 2004 as to function as a 'one-stop shop' on all matters pertaining to the overseas and non-resident Indians in order to instill confidence in them. In pursuit of strengthening and deepening the relationship, there have been genuine efforts made by the Indian government to harness the potentialities of Indian diaspora.

To commemorate the 90th anniversary of the return to India of the most famous NRI Mahatma Gandhi, who alighted from the South African ship at Bombay's Apollo Bander Port on January 9, 1945, the 3rd PBD was organized by the MOIA of Government of India and the Federation of Indian Chambers of Commerce and Industry (FICCI) in Bombay from January 7 to 9, 2005. While inaugurating the 3-day conference, the Prime Minister Dr. Manmohan Singh offered dual citizenship to all those who migrated from the country after it became a Republic on January 26, 1950, provided their home countries allowed them to do so. [17]

While paying rich tributes to the 2.5 million knowledgeable and opportunity–seeking Overseas Indians , the Prime Minister extolled the idea of 'Indian-ness' [18] which would enable to develop a knowledge based sector. [19] Government of India has addressed in the recent times various issues concerning NRI investment, dual citizenship and direct cooperation and contacts among the Overseas Indians. [20] Mahendra Utchana, Secretary–General of GOPIO and former Mauritus Minister while calling for direct cooperation and contacts among the Indians of different countries, urged the Indian government to set up a PIO University in the country with overseas campuses for the benefit of the PIO students. [21]

The fourth PBD (PBD-2006) was organized in Hyderabad during January 7 to 9, 2006 against the backdrop of the confidence that India would be emerging as an economic powerhouse. The Minister for Overseas Indian Affairs, Oscar Fernandez, acknowledged that the quantum of remittances of the Indian Diaspora, which touched the 21.7 billion dollars, was higher than the quantum that any country, including China, could receive last year. [22] Prime Minister Manmohan Singh, while launching the Overseas Citizenship of India (OCI) scheme (popularly known as dual citizenship) promised voting rights to NRIs in the Gulf countries, expressed satisfaction over a memorandum of understanding duly signed by the Ministry of Overseas Indian Affairs and the American Association of Physicians of Indian Origin. He further encouraged that Indian government would welcome partnerships between overseas professional bodies and institutions such as NASSCOM, FICCI, CII, Assocham and further called for target specific outcomes. [23]

The 40,000 member-strong US India Political Action Committee (USINPAC), a US based credible PIO organization has been lobbying with the Indian caucus in the American

Congress for various decisions benefiting Indians including the rise of HI-B Visa quota to Indians. It is of much significance that the USINPC had suggested a paradigm shift in the government strategy in attracting foreign investments-- from merely looking out for big companies to small and medium enterprises that constitute 90 per cent of the industry spread over whole of US. [24] The special feature of this PBD convention was that six Chief Ministers of Andhra Pradesh, Maharastra, Gujarat, Bihar, Jammu and Kashmir and Kerala presented their state priorities and liberalized policies for NRI investments in their respective states.

To the cynical questions of Indian journalists about Pravasa Bharatiya Divas such as "What does a conference like this actually achieve?" and "how it is useful", the response of NRIs was commendable in all respects. Shashi Taroor [25] answered saying: "this was a remarkable utilitarian approach to the occasion" and also told that: "the real value of the conference lies in the conferring", it means to allow NRIs the chance to share their experiences, celebrate their commonalities, offer their ideas", and concluded that "when India allows its 'Pravasis' to feel at home, it is India that is strengthened". [26] To yet another question, "what can NRIs do to India", Prem Kumar [27] was so emphatic in his reply that " if given a chance, the NRI will become a metaphor for change" To quote him [28] further:

"For instance, some 200000 prosperous NRIs retirees in Canada and the US, a new brand of tourists, want to visit India routinely to escape the cold weather of the West. They will pour millions of dollars yearly into Indian economy, creating a ripple effect for the hospitality, health care, clothing and tourism sectors. In return, they want India to provide long-distance bus service at the major Indian air ports, more frequent air links to more cities and build some safe 3-star and 4-star motel chains. Again, a large number of foreign educated NRIs (some 25,000) such as doctors, engineers, teachers, economists, MBAs and the like, now superannuated from service and earning fabulous pensions, yearn to serve India. These NRIs, the professional elites of the affluent First world, will accept volunteer assignments in the nation's schools, laboratories and institutions of higher learning. To date, this resource remains untapped. Finally, NRIs with the dual citizenship would be well disposed to invest in the real estate field. India needs some 150 million new homes/apartments. NRIs have the money and experience of living in modern and safe apartments abroad. They would like to duplicate the experience in India".

States like Punjab, Kerala, Gujarat and Tamil Nadu needs to make special efforts as people from these regions form a major presence abroad. The states can benefit most from their ex-citizens in the field of education, who can help revive many institutions from schools to universities. [29] The greatest asset India has among the Indian Diaspora is, not their capital but the abundant reservoir of scientific, professional and intellectual talent. India can compete with China and even overtake it, provided the Indian government has appropriate policies for the NRIs/PIOs. They may be just over 2 per cent of India's population but their estimated collective income is at about $160 billion, almost one third of India's gross domestic product. [30]

Indian Diaspora in Southeast Asia & Asia-Pacific

A. Southeast Asia Region: People of Indian Origin and NRIs constituting the Indian Diaspora of colonial and post colonial or independent India (NRIs) account for more than 5 million. An age old migration of traders, Budhist monks and Hindu religious preachers, scholars of both Budhism and Hinduism and adventurers, princes was registered in Southeast Asia since the third century B.C. This emigration of specialists in religious philosophy spread Indian culture (both Buddhism and Hinduism) in Southeast Asia that catapulted Indianized Kingdoms which flourished until 15th century A.D. Indigenous people in Southeast Asia, like the Dravidians in southern India, got the Indian culture integrated with the native cultures that came to be known as Indo-Khmer in Cambodia, Indo-Cham in Vietnam, Indo-Malay in Malaysia, Indo-Pagan in Myanmar and Indo-Javanese in Indonesia. The indigenous native chiefs found the Indian culture very dear and embraced it to upgrade their status, prestige and dignity and philosophical outlook thereby to get their power consolidated and even they craved for Indians and Indian cultural ethos. [31]

Time and again, the fresh migrations of Brahmans and Buddhist scholars from Southern India (the territories of Pallavas, Cholas, Pandyas and Sathavahanas) and North India (Guptas and Palas) enriched the cultures of the Indianized kingdoms of Funan, Kambuja, Champa, Sailendra, Srivijaya, Mataram and Pagan. Gods and Goddesses of India with their respective temple models, art and architecture, dance and music, literary works of Puranic as well as ethical codes, were transplanted and flourished. The Sanskrit script imported from India became the state script of many kingdoms and it was from this Sanskrit language, that the ancient Mon, Khmer, Javanese, Cham languages developed. The two epics of India – Ramayana and Mahabharatha which occupied special position in traditional literatures of many countries of this region -- have also been serving as infinite source of scenario of theatrical plays in Southeast Asia. Wayang Kulit, Wayang Topeng, Wayang Djawa, Zat, Lakon theatres still survive and enchant the masses across the boundaries of the nations. [32]

Southeast Asia has to its credit world famous Hindu-Buddhist temples – Borobudur and Prambanan (Java), Angkor Vat and Bayon (Cambodia), Ananda and Mahabhodi (Myanmar), temples of Mison and Po Nagar (Vietnam), Watphu (Laos) Vat Chet Yat and Maha Tat (Thailand) – besides some hundreds of thousands of other temples dedicated to Siva, Vishnu, Buddha and the associated gods and goddesses. Hundreds of Sanskrit inscriptions and living arts and belief systems developed for beyond imagination, whose origins are traced to India, form a mute testimony of filial affiliation with India. [33] The accultured Brahman communities of Indian Origin are still held in esteem by royal clans and preside over the ceremonial functions of the royal courts (Cambodia and Thailand). The decline of Indianized Kingdoms paved the way for the dominance of Theravada Buddhism over Mainland Southeast Asia and the introduction of

Islam from India (Gujarat) into insular Southeast Asia (Indonesia and Malaysia) in the 14th and 15th centuries.

The Indian trade conducted by the Indian merchants, had gradually been taken over by the European colonial powers. Free emigration of Indians was encouraged by the British into their colonies and territories. The British colonies in Southeast Asia including Myanmar, Malaysia, Singapore and Brunei, received a maximum number of Indian immigrants, particularly from South India as contractual labourers in the commercial plantations and a lesser number of Indians as businessmen and white collar workers from all parts of India–Gujarat, Sindh, Punjab, Bengal, UP, Bihar and South India. The Chettiars of Tamilnadu who constituted a major community settled in these territories as business people and money lenders, owned large tracts of cultivable land. Indian migration to Indonesia, the Philippines and Thailand was voluntary and minimal.

The French territories in India, Karaikal and Pondicherry, served as important launching points for Indian migration, largely businessmen, into the French colonies of Vietnam, Cambodia and Laos. [34] Majority of Indian migrants who were hard working labour class belonging to the middle class people, could easily get integrated with the native communities and hence they could never become competitors to the indigenous middle class people. Unlike ethnic Chinese, the ethnic Indians in Southeast Asia who hardly entertained any political ambitions have been respected by the indigenous people to exclusion of any animosities and jealousies [35] Nonetheless, Malaysia and Singapore, Indians have been recognized as an important political group. [36]

The shift of Indian community from rural to urban areas, is well pronounced in Indonesia and Malaysia. After Independence, Indians continued to migrate to Thailand, Malaysia, Singapore, Brunei and Indonesia in search of employment. The Indian community is to the tune of 7,600 in Brunei, 55,000 in Indonesia, 1.67 million in Malaysia, possibly 2.9 million in Myanmar, 38,000 in Philippines, 3,07,000 in Singapore, 85,000 in Thailand and a very small number in Cambodia, Vietnam and Laos. The diverse opportunities in these booming economies—ranging from blue collar jobs in construction and hospitality industries to employment with Indian Companies, International (mainly UN) organizations, multinationals, banks, consultancy and financial institutions and recently the information technology sector – are at the base of such large scale immigration into Southeast Asia. [37]

With a good image built by the PIOs/NRIs living in these Countries, India's Look East policy (launched in 1992) augurs well for the progress of the contacts with the ASEAN, the regional Association of Southeast Asian Nations .Besides the multitude of benefits on account of India's participation in the ASEAN institutional framework, there has been an increase in the volume of Indian migration into the ASEAN countries. The scientific, naval and other potentialities of India, impressed ASEAN countries to the extent of inspiring them so much as to confer on India a 'Summit status' in 2002 to participate in ASEAN Meetings and chalk out the policies of mutual economic benefit. There is vast scope for India in Tourism Industry, to revive cultural sites of Buddhism and to create the infrastructure facilities like good roads, rail links, star hotels to attract the Indianized Southeast Asian people and other Buddhists world wide to visit India. India could also organize many more cultural events like celebration of 'Kalachakra' in Amaravathi (Andhra Pradesh) during January 2006 where in Tibetan Buddhist Head Dalailama participated and thousands and thousands of Buddhists from all over the world thronged Amaravathi and stayed for a fortnight, a substantial contribution to India's Foreign Exchange indeed !

B. Other Countries in the Asia-Pacific Region: Asia-Pacific region for the purpose of this study of the Indian Diaspora, includes Australia, Fiji, Honking (SAR), the Republic of Korea, Japan, New Zealand and Taiwan. All these countries have experienced colonial and post-colonial migration of Indian communities (PIOs and NRIs). There are only 1,000 PIOs in Japan, consisting of students, scholars, computer software engineers and yoga practitioners. Indian community in South

Korea (less than 3,000) and Taiwan (barely 2,000) is composed of mainly Sindhi business folks, diamond merchants, scientists on contract, software engineers and professionals. India's links with Hong Kong date back to150 years; and there are over 55,000 PIOs of diverse strata, ranging from wealthy businessmen to those in menial jobs. A large number of highly educated professionals are seeking employment in the banking, finance and Information technology sectors. Fiji, Australia and New Zealand have absorbed about 6.0 lakh PIOs and NRIs. One common feature of this region is that the well educated Indian community regarded as a law abiding and responsible community was found to adapt itself well to the local conditions. [38]

Fiji: Fiji, the hub of Pacific, is often regarded as Little India in Pacific. All other Pacific countries have some people of Indian origin, mostly emanating from Fiji. Fiji in Pacific has become a beacon light to the development activities and the processes of growth in the entire ocean. The Fiji Indians have not merely developed the country but "they have taken a hand in developing a new regional entity in the Pacific which they call 'the Pacific way of life' i.e. to live by consensus by discussion and never by confrontation", to quote Bhagavan Singh, [39] the former Indian Envoy to Fiji.

The deeply entrenched ethnic conflicts in the Fijian society between the indigenous Fijians and Fiji Indians have been attributed to the legacy of the British colonial policy of drafting the indentured labour from British India to work on the sugarcane fields in Fiji. The British colonial administration indentured 62837 Indians by 1916 when the indentured system was finally abolished by the British India. By 1920, when the last contracts of indenture were terminated, the Fijian colonial government allowed the Indians to settle in Fiji to meet the labour demand in the colony. The 1921 Census enrolled 60,634 Indians in Fiji. By 1986, the descendants of those third or fourth generation Fiji-born Indians constitute 48.8 per cent (3,48,704) as against 46 per cent (3,29,305) of indigenous Fijians. Along side of these predominant ethnic groups, a miniscule of 5.2 per cent (37,366)—composed of

Europeans, part-Europeans, Chinese, Tongans and other Polynesian Islanders - contributed to the emergence of Fiji society as a multiracial one, polyglot in character.

Fiji Indians got succeeded in getting Independence to Fiji in 1970. Later on, for all their long process of naturalization, the Fiji Indians had been targeted for ethnic coercion by the indigenous Fijians who began to adopt a kind of patronizing attitude, besides nurturing an overbearing contempt for the numerical increase of Fiji Indians and becoming envious of economic and political ascendancy of Indian community in Independent Fiji. Around 83 per cent of land in Fiji was held in 'Trust' by the indigenous Fijians and its ownership is still governed by the ordinances dating back to 1880. [40] Accordingly, the Fijian land can never be sold to non-Fijians. At the same time, over 90 per cent of Fiji's main export crop, sugarcane, is produced by Fiji Indians working on the land taken on a lease from the indigenous Fijian owners and from 'Trust'. About 80 per cent of the tax revenue of Fiji is generated by the Fiji Indians without whom the Fiji's economy cannot survive.

The insecurity of Fiji Indians' survival and the possession of very little land purchased from the European settlers, made them determined to seek their livelihood prospects from the sectors of education and business. [41] As their economic status improved the indigenous Fijians, betrayed their envy of this 'alien' community in their demands for Indians' forced repatriation. When independence was granted in 1970, the departing British introduced the principle of representation in the constitution in favour of native Fijians thus ensuring that the elected Indian members would not be able to form a government on their own strength. Though the Fiji Indians successfully overcame this legacy by forming a multi-racial government under the leadership of Bavadra who was a non-racist Fijian, two military coups in May and November of 1987 respectively ushered in a period of instability that continued until the rapprochement of the two major ethnic groups that resulted in the form of non-racist 1997 constitution. Though a Fiji Indian dominated government was formed in 1999 under Mahendra Choudhry, it was overthrown by George Speight, an indigenous businessman who carried a civilian coup on May 19, 2000.

Subsequent election in 2001 led to the formation of an indigenous Fijian government under Laisenia Qarase which had showed scant concern for the widely accepted 1997 constitution. With a paternalistic attitude he also introduced the Bill of "Reconciliation, Tolerance and Unity" in December 2005 in which he proposed concessions and grant of amnesty to 2000 coup perpetrators but the Fiji military took strong objections and even threatened to topple the government if it did pass the bill. In May 2006 General Elections, the Prime Minister Laisenia Qarase, promised to reintroduce the bill. The Fiji military Chief Frank Bainimarama openly campaigned against Qarase and even persuaded the elected Independent M.Ps to support Mahendra Choudhry's Fiji Labour Party. However Qarase's SDL party won the election with razor thin majority (36 out of 71seats).

Keeping in view of the possible threat of the military Chief and the limitations of his political jurisprudence, Laisenia Qarase came down to terms with his bitter rival Mahendra Choudhry, invited his (FLP) party to form the Cabinet and allotted 9 Cabinet Ministries to fulfill the 1997 Constitutional obligation. [42] As a consequence, a multi party cabinet for the first time in Fiji was formed. The racial conflicts that eventually perpetrated the 3 coups since 1985, forced a sizable highly educated Fiji Indians to settle in Australia, New.Zealand, Canada, USA, UK and other countries. As a result, Fiji Indians' population came down to 38.16 per cent (3,20,659) leading to the phenomenal increase of Indigenous Fijians to 54.3 per cent (4,56,207) and Others 7.54 per cent (63,335), as per the 2004 estimate. The rapprochement between these two major racial groups for their mutual benefit and peaceful co-existence, if achieved, would make the people of Indian origin in Fiji, not merely an asset to India but also to act as a spring board to forge economic relations with the neighbouring Pacific countries which have been endowed with vast resource potential.

Australia and New Zealand

At the turn of the Century in Australia, 1,90,000 people (PIOs and NRIs) and in New Zealand 55000, have been identified with the Indian ancestry. [43] The relaxation of the restrictive immigration policy by Australia in 1966, abolition of White Australia policy and the introduction of the policy of multiculturalism in 1972 by the Prime Minister Gough Whitlam, led to a rise in migration of Indians along side the Asian migration. Unlike the 19th century Indian migrants comprising camel handlers and agricultural workers, PIOs in the third quarter of the 20th century were increasingly composed of professionals – computer and software experts, engineers, doctors, accountants and students. The other areas that attracted PIOs included restaurant business, small and medium scale business, trading and taxi driving. There are PIO/NRI associations of Indians in almost all the major cities of Australia. New Zealand also witnessed a rise in immigration following the changes in its immigration Act of 1958. Indian immigrants are found in the domestic and retail trade as well as in the medical, hospitality, engineering and Information Technology sectors.

PIOs in Australia is a diverse group as they came from different diasporic locations not only from India but also from Malaysia, Singapore, Sri Lanka, South Africa and particularly Fiji. The term 'twice migrant', referring to the secondary migration from the countries mentioned above, has contributed to the complexities of Indian migration within the Diaspora and has now been widely applied in Australia as well. India-born migrants of Australia had grown from 15,754 in 1966 to 95,449 in 2001. [44] The early migrants, largely composed of Punjabis and Sikhs from rural areas and agriculture sector, were found to have settled in Woolgoolga (New South Wales). The most recent flows have brought Kannadigas mostly from the city of Bangalore, India's Silicon Valley – who formed the main source of labour for Australia's IT industry. There were 37,100 Fiji-born people of Indian descent in Australia in 1996, the vast majority of whom were settled in Sydney, following the two military coups in 1987 directed against Fiji-Indians. There are some 54,000 Sri Lankan-born, 20,000 Mauritius-born, 10,000 Pakistani-born and 5,000 Bangladesh-born PIOs in Australia.

All such groups in one way or another have links to those Indians who earlier migrated from India and Fiji. At the turn of the century, there were visible groups of Indians in Australia, leading to the emergence of establishments of various kind ranging from general stores and restaurants to temples, cricket teams and social clubs. Australian Universities have also attracted significant proportion of both Indian faculty and students. [45] The proliferation of temples, gurudwaras, restaurants and stores itself testifies to the spread of Indian Diaspora and its heterogeneity. I have had the pleasure of visiting two Hindu temples – Sri Muruga temple in Westmead in Sydney and Sri Venkateswara temple at Helensberg, 35 km south of Sydney, in October 2005, and it was also a pleasant surprise to find White Australians visiting these temples and paying obeisance to the presiding deities. The Hindu Association of Western Australia has a big Hindu Temple constructed (at Warton Road, Canning Vale) in Perth on a 5 acre land, the consecration ceremony (Mahakumbabishekam) of which was performed in September 2005.

Indian Cultural Association of Queensland has been conducting 'Indian Bazaar', a two-day cultural festival every year in Brisbane since 1995, showcasing the vibrant Indian culture through performances, music and food. The wider Australian community, through their enthusiastic participation, understands the exotic Indian culture. Besides the Hindu festivals like Diwali, Holi and Vinayaka Chathurthi , the newspapers (India Times and The Indian Down Under) radio programmes (of Brisvaani) and the TV programmes (Hamara TV) in Australia are fostering the Indian cultural identity as well as the spirit of social harmony among the Indian communities.

The New Zealand Indians comprise Indians emanating from India along with twice or thrice migrant PIO from Pakistan, Bangladesh and Fiji. As in Australia, the PIOs constitute businessmen, highly educated professionals and IT personnel as well as the people engaged in dairy and hotels besides, a sizable NRI students in New Zealand Universities. In the 2001, New Zealand Census recorded the following PIOs: Indians 60213, Pakistanis 1017, Bangladeshis 1143, and Fiji Indian1983. [46]

The Indian emigration to New Zealand has been traced to the late 18th Century. Some of the Indian soldiers and seamen who were working in British East India cargo ships settled in New Zealand by marrying the indigenous Maori and European women. By1916 there were 181, including 14 women. The 1951 Census recorded 2425 Indians, and the 1981 Census put the figures at 11244. The changes in Immigration policy of New Zealand along with political instability in other countries, especially in Fiji in 1980s, brought many more Indians to New Zealand. By 2001, the Indian population surged to more than 62.000 mostly settled in North Island of New Zealand.

After the Second World War, Indian women in greater numbers, migrated in pursuit of assisting their husbands and fathers in various business activities. The first settlers came mostly from Navsari and Surat regions of Gujarat and also Jalandar and Hoshiarpur in Punjab.Many Sikhs were employed as flax workers, drain-diggers and scrub cutters. They were also engaged in road building and brick-industry, while in urban areas, they worked as bottle collectors and hawkers of fruit and vegetables. As the agricultural occupations such as scrub and flax cutting got declined, more Indians moved to market gardening. Punjabi Sikhs who often had farming experience, settled mainly in Waikato district and took up dairy farming. Some moved to the towns to work in hotels and in manufacturing and processing industries. Many others, who acquired wealth, started their own fruit and vegetable stores and later caught up with super markets since 1970s.The arrival of well qualified professionals in the recent years, has provided a more vigorous profile to the Indian community in New Zealand.

Besides the Central Indian Association in Aukland founded as early as 1926, there were 9 regional Associations in the major cities predominantly composed of Gujarati Hindus to combat ignorance and hostility of Whites, to secure protection and to promote Indian values and culture. Sikhs and Muslims have established separate organizations to foster their own religious and cultural traditions. The community halls they built, were used for celebrating festivals such as Diwali, Navratri, Krishna Janmastami, and Vinayaka Chaturthi, and also for organizing religious and language classes. There are Hindu temples in Auckland and Wellington and also Sikh Gurudwaras in Auckland, Wellington, Hawkey's Bay and Hamilton. Apart from making use of the Newspapers 'Aryodaya' and 'Uday' published in Gujarati which were popular in yester years, the New Zealand Indians nowadays are catching up with community news through websites such as 'Indian Newslink' or NZ Punjabi, and the bi-monthly Hindi magazine 'Bharat-Darshan'.

The PIOs are well naturalized and well entrenched into the New Zealand politics and sports. The Fiji Indian origin --New Zealand born, Anand Satyanand, a retired Judge, was the first PIO chosen to the highest gubernatorial position as Governor General of New Zealand in April 2006 (Deccan Chronicle, April 4, 2006 :11). Some other prominent PIOs occupying high offices are: Dr. Rajen Prasad, Member Chairman of Families Commission; Mr. Swaran Singh, Judge, Manukan Court, Auckland; Mrs. Sukhi Turner (Pravasa Bharatiya Samman Awardee), Mayor of Dunedin and Ashraf Choudhray, Labour Member of Parliament.

Hockey and Cricket have always been important to the Indians in New Zealand. Inspired by the tour of All India Hockey Teams to New Zealand, sports associations were founded in 1930s in Auckland and Wellington. Notable New Zealand Indian sportsmen include Ramesh and Mohan Patel who participated in the 1976 Olympic Hockey, and cricketer Dipak Patel.

The New Zealand and Australian Indians have built a good image for India. The common linkages of Commonwealth, Parliamentary democracy, English language would definitely gain an advantage to India to forge joint ventures with New Zealand and Australia and our PIOs have a role to play.

Conclusion

The Indian Diaspora is a generic term used for people who migrated from territories which are currently within the boundaries of the Republic of India. Residing in distant lands, the members of Indian Diaspora (both PIOs and NRIs) have succeeded spectacularly in their professions and created a niche for themselves. The overwhelming majority, living abroad, belongs to the third or fourth generations; and they have become a permanent feature of the demographic profile of their countries of domicile. The Indian Diaspora today constitutes an important, and in some respects a unique force in the world culture.

Global Organization of People of Indian Origin (GOPIO) was formed in 1989 by the Indian Community in USA and it began to network the global Indian Communities in 22 countries which represent a tremendous resource in intellectual, technical, scientific, professional, trade and entrepreneurial skills with high potential and keenness to contribute to the well-being and prosperity of the countries of their domicile as well in India. When India faced the worst balance of payments crisis in the early nineties, when its foreign exchange reserves were dwindling, India turned to its NRIs the most potential group of the Indian Diaspora, and it was NRI deposits that helped it to come out of this economic crisis.

Recognizing the potentialities of Indian diaspora, India organized four Pravasi Bharatiya Divas (PBD) Conferences since 2003 to mobilize foreign investments and to utilize their expertise and resourcefulness of NRIs and offered them the dual citizenship to catapult India to become the global player. Indian diaspora has done a commendable job in building a good image for India in their respective countries of domicile. NRIs have also been working behind the scene persuading the multinational companies to take interest in India and as an effective pressure group lobbying for India in the political and governmental circles of their countries of domicile and in international bodies. When India conducted nuclear tests in 1998, the Indian Diaspora stood by India, to defend the tests.

India opened its economy to economic liberalization, privatization and globalization in 1990s. India's 'Look East Policy,' an initiative for redeeming the ties with the much neglected Southeast Asian and Pacific region, began to forge cordial relations with the countries of ASEAN, Australia and New Zealand. People of Indian Origin in Fiji accounting for nearly 43 per cent of the country's population is, a potential source on which, India could rely to forge ahead its economic relations with other Pacific countries. Australia reciprocated India's 'Look East Policy' with its 'Look West' policy to cement economic relations with its Asian neighbours.

The end of White Australia policy and introduction of 'Multiculturalism' in Australia in 1970s opened up its doors to the skilled and professional Asian migration into Australia. India is ranked a close fourth behind China as a provider of the largest number of immigrants to Australia in 2003-04 (China's immigrants 8,784 against India's 8,135). Australia, New Zealand and Singapore are now the preferred destinations for Indian students to pursue their higher studies, next to USA, UK and Canada. Most of the IT professionals, doctors, accountants, engineers, managerial professionals from India, are now settled in Australia and New Zealand. Most of the Indian merchant establishments got their way into these countries. The edge of proficiency in English language, parliamentary democracy and non-aggressive history of India and legacy of British colonial institutions in India, are at the base of Australia and New Zealand's preference to Indian immigration.

India shall find a fertile ground in Southeast Asia and Asia-Pacific region, if it could pursue the right policies, for harnessing the potentialities of Indian Diaspora in these regions. India shall become a global player, if it succeeded in winning over the hearts of ASEAN countries. Australia and New Zealand, the players in Asia-Pacific, which recognized the importance of India in ASEAN as member of ARF and its elevation to Summit status, began to take cognizance of India's efforts to become a dialogue partner with the APEC. The aim of India to become the permanent member in UN Security Council and its aspiration for the post of UN Secretary General in future, would only be realized if the full potential of GOPIO is harnessed along with India's fair play of external diplomacy. The dream of Dr. Manmohan Singh that "21st Century – an Indian Century" and 'the Vision of India' to become 'a developed nation' by 2020, would come true only through the participation of Indian Diaspora and effective utilization of their potentialities in the years to come.

Notes

1. Ministry of Information Broadcasting, Govt. of India, *21st Century an Indian Century* (Prime Minister Manmohan Singh's Inaugural Address at PBD at Mumbai, 7th January 2005), New Delhi, Feb. 2005,p.3
2. Ministry of Information Broadcasting, Govt. of India, *Developing a Mutually Beneficial Relationship between India and Indian Diaspora* (Prime Minister Atal Bihari Vajpayees's Inaugural Speech of the International Convention of the GOPIO in New Delhi on 6 January 2001), New Delhi, February 2001, p.1
3. Bhikhu Parekh, Why the Diaspora needs India, http://www.rediff.com/news/2003/jan/08spec1.htm
4. Sunil Prasad (Belgium), Can the Indian Diaspora Overtake China? http://www.gopio.net/NRI_PIO_Talk_Mumbai.html
5. Rahul Singh, *Manorama Year Book, 1994* (Kottayam, Malayala Manorama,1994)p.21
6. Indian labour emigration under the indenture system first started in 1834 to Mauritius, Uganda and Nigeria. Later, labourers emigrated to Guyana (1838), New Zealand (1840), Hong Kong (1841), Trinidad and Tobago (1845), Malay (1845), Martinique and Guadalupe (1854), Grenada, St.Lucia and St.Vincent (1856), Natal (1860), St.Kitts (1861), Japan and Surinam (1872), Jamaica (1873), Fiji (1879), Burma (1885), Canada (1904) and Thailand (1910) (Centre for the Study of Indian Diaspora, University of Hyderabad, *Brochure*, Hyderabad,2002, p.4)
7. Centre for the Study of Indian Diaspora, University of Hyderabad, *Brochure*,Hyderabad,2002,p.5
8. Bharat Gupt, Guest Article- Indian Diaspora, http://www.gopio.net/guest_article_0702.htm
9. Sandhya Shukla, *India Abroad*, New Delhi,2005, p.10

10. The estimate of PIOs are: (a) North America (most of USA and Canada) 2.8 million; (b) South America (Trinidad & Tobago, Guyana, Surinam, Jamaica, etc.) 2.0 million; (c) Europe (UK, Netherlands, Germany, Austria, Switzerland, etc) 2.5 million; (d) Africa (South Africa, Mauritius, East African Countries, etc) 2.5 million; (e) Middle East (UAE, Saudi Arabia, Kuwait, etc) 2.5 million; (f) Far East & Southeast Asia (Malaysia, Singapore, Myanmar, etc) 2.5 million; (g) Pacific Islands (Fiji, Australia, New Zealand) 0.7 million; and (h) Sri Lanka and Nepal 4.5 million (Thomas Abraham,Global NRI/PIO Community- A Perspective, Talk delivered at the Overseas Indian Conference organized by Indian Merchant Chamber , Mumbai, 7 January 2001) http://www.gopio.net/NRI_PIO_Mumbai.html

11. ibid

12. Bharat Gupt, n.9

13. *The Hindu,* 10 January 2003, p.1

14. The benchmarks for success, which the pravasi community has set, are a challenge for us in India. They make us examine why the Indian is so much more innovative, productive and successful abroad than in his own country. They prod us to create a business, investment and economic climate, which is conducive to success as anywhere in the world. Thomas Abraham, President, GOPIO, further stated that "we are prepared to respond to your expectations from India. We do not want your richness, we want the richness of your experience (Prime Minister Vajpayee's Inaugural Address at first PBD, *The Hindu*, 10 January 2003, p.1)

15. *The Hindu*, 9 January 2004,p.11

16. *The Hindu*, 8 January 2005,p.1

17. ibid

18. Dr. Manmohan Singh further emphasized that "the idea of 'Pravasa Bharatiya' has been in the making throughout the 19th and 20th Century. Today, at the dawn of the 21st Century it is an idea whose time has truly come. We speak different languages, we practise different religions our cuisine is varied and so is our costume. We are over a billion Indians and over 25 million overseas Indians, living in 110 different countries. Yet, there is a unifying idea that binds us all together. The economic policies, which the GOI had initiated a decade ago, have enabled India to connect with overseas Indian more vigorously and engaged them in meaningful ways in the reconstruction of Mother India. These policies have significantly contributed to the emergence of India as a major global player in the economic world and with the

tremendous strides. India has been making in the knowledge based sector. Dr. Manmohan Singh opined that "there is no doubt that the 21st century is going to be an Indian Century". (Manmohan Singh,n.2,p.7)

19. *The Hindu*, January 8, 2005, p.11
20. *The Hindu*, January 9, 2005,p.9
21. *The Hindu*, January 7, 2006,p.1
22. *The Hindu*, January 8, 2006.p.1
23. *The Hindu*, January 10, 2006, p.3
24. Indian government's nominee to UN Secretary- General post (*The Hindu*, June 20, 2006,p.11
25. *The Hindu*, January 30, 2005,M3
26. NRI from North America, The Hindu, February 1, 2005,p.17
27. ibid
28. 29.Bharat Gupt,n.9
29. 30.Sunil Prasad,n.5
30. J.C. Van leur as quoted in George Coedes, 1966,The Making of Southeast Asia, London, p.55 (English translation by H.M.Wright)
31. Tran Thi Ly, "Influence of Indian Culture on Southeast Asian Culture", paper presented in the Seminar- India- Vietnam Friendship: A 50 year Perspective, organized by the Indian Embassy in Vietnam, Honai on 2 October 1997.
32. 33.Nayan Chanda, " Indians in Indochina", K.S. Sandhu, and A.Mani(eds), *Indian communities in Southeast Asia*, Singapore, 1993 ,p.42
33. K.S.Sandhu, and A.Mani (eds), *Indian communities in Southeast Asia*, Singapore, 1993 p.XX
34. V. Suryanarayan, " Overseas Chinese and Overseas Indians in Southeast Asia: A Comparative Study", *Strategic Analysis*, Vol.XVIII No.9, December 1995,p.1217
35. n.34, p.XXI
36. 37.L.M.Singhvi, *Report of the High Level Committee on the Indian Diaspora*, Ministry of External Affairs, January 2002 http://www.indiaday.org/government_policy/singhvi-detail.asp#7
37. ibid
38. Bhagavan Singh, "Indians in the Pacific" in Vidya Sagar and Manohar Puri (eds), Mother India Children Abroad ,New Delhi, Year :nil, p.28
39. Sir Alan Burns, *Fiji*, London, 1963,p.205

40. P.Munirathnam Reddy, "The Changing Contours of Fijian Ethnicity," Indian Association for Asian & Pacific Studies, (Proceedings of the First Biennial Conference, 2002), Kolkata,2004 p.464

41. Michaiel Field, Fiji's future suddenly looking brighter, May 25, 2006 http://www.fijilive.com/news/show/news/2006/05/25/fijilive11.html

42. n.37

43. John Connell, "Neither Indian nor Australian? Contemporary Indian Migration to Sydney,"paper presented in the Seminar on *India& Australia: History, Culture and society*, organized by India International Centre (IIC-Asia Project), New Delhi, December 6-7,2002

44. ibid

45. http://www.teara.gov.nz/New Zealanders/ New Zealand pcoplcs/Indians/7/cn

46. Deccan Chronicle, April 4, 2006,p.11

20

Indo-Australian Relations in the Emerging World Order

Chandrakant Yatanoor

"Australia is an extraordinary accident of history", writes former Prime Minister of Australia Mr. Paul Keating in his political memoir. [1] Further, he says that "from the earliest years of European settlement, the island continental country has been redefining itself, shifting its image of what it means to be Australian in response to the changing world." [2] Admittedly, its image can no more be captured in such popular and somewhat derisive epithets as the "down under country" a drop in the centre" or "a dot nowhere." [3] Its sordid past as a cluster of penal colonies appended somewhat artificially to the British Empire acting as an outpost of the British monarch, has now been obliterated completely. Instead, the status of being an independent sovereign member of the British Commonwealth has been conferred on Australia. Behind these far reaching developments, at least until recently, it had even boasted of a relatively secure and prosperous economy and a society based on shared cultural values.

However, at the dawn of the new millennium, Australia has begun facing an uncertain economic future, an increasing social and cultural diversity and above all, the most challenging task of carving out for itself a secure niche in the fast-changing global order. To many in Australia, charting a new course in its historical evolution is doubtless necessary and exciting. By all means, the laying bare of opening up an inward looking society and sheltered economy, is imperative to meet the current challenges of international competition and cosmopolitan culture. At least until now, for the people of Australia defining themselves in the face of changes occurring all around the island country has been less daunting. With the retreat of British imperialism concomitant to Asia – Africa decolonisation movement, Australia could swiftly turn to the US for its strategic security as well as for its active participation in the emerging new world order. Australia could effect such of those changes in its identity from being an outpost of the British empire to that of an important link in the chain of the US-led western alliance system with efficacy in the 1950s. What perhaps facilitated its shift was its own "imagined" identity of being a nation of the European people, and therefore, could legitimately belong to the Western alliance system in the changing world order.

In line with its historical experience and past self-understanding of the liberal democratic tradition, Australian elite, therefore, opted for multiculturalism as a state policy since the beginning of 1970s. Commitment to multiculturalism as a state policy guaranteeing rights to individuals within a pluralist society undoubtedly called for a series of legislative measures to ensure equality before law and claimant social discrimination based on race, ethnicity or for that matter, even gender. At the same time, it also facilitated and even justified the liberal and non-discriminatory immigration laws. It may be argued that the decisive cultural break with Australia's past not came so much with the Asian immigration as with the events leading to the granting of the political rights to the aborigines. Such pronounced shift in identity obviously created for its elite, new anxieties both within and outside Australia. Australia's emerging socio-political architecture with its pronounced accent on multiculturalism has drawn the attention of a number of countries especially India. All said and done, in the fast changing international scenario, it is in India's interest only to discover areas of potential engagement with countries which embody prospects of a mutually beneficial relationship.

Indo-Australian Relations

Indo-Australian involvement has a long history. Although

India and Australia differed in their perspectives and postulate on various issues in post-second world war era, their economies have been moving closer to each other. Culturally, as well as in their faith in the democratic value system, both the countries were drawn to each other. However, their closeness has been more implicit than pronounced. Australia has been trying to get its relations with India, revitalized. India has been rapidly becoming a major economy of the world and a significant trading partner. Indian focus on Australia and Australian focus on India has been on mutuality of economic interests. Both are vigorous parliamentary democracies attached to democratic principles and values. Both speak a common language to forge business relations. As fellow members of the Commonwealth, India and Australia share common bonds of English language and similar legal, financial and governmental institutions. Both follow democratic political processes with federal structures for devolution of power.

Despite structural and normative commonalities, India and Australia found themselves on divergent perceptional parameters. While these were generated by cold war politics and prisms, they were aggravated by the absence of traditional linkages and exacerbated by vast distances, which were both geographical and psychological. Divergent perceptions date back to the pre-independence period with diverse views of Empire, wherein Australia tended to regard itself as an extension of the Empire and India became rapidly anti-imperialist. Further, the multi-cultural milieu of India was a stark contrast to the policy of multi-culturalism, dominated as it was, by white Australians. [4] While at a later stage, Australia lent support to the national liberation struggles, it remained vehemently part of the western ideological and psychological framework. Australia's perceived security needs and psychological orientations led to its joining the US sponsored military alliance viz., the ANZUS and SEATO. India's security and economic needs espoused independence in foreign affairs, which took the form of non-alignment. The Indo-Australian divergence became significant when Pakistan became an ally of the US; Pakistan a self-sworn enemy of India, thus became a co-ally of Australia. Australia began supporting Pakistan vis-à-vis India on issues crucial to India's basic security. [5]

A brief survey of Indo-Australian relations reveals a pendulum pattern. While there were periods which were marked by a higher degree of friendship and understanding, there were also periods which were marked by heightened tension and problems. These more or less, corresponded to the changes in domestic political regimes in Australia. Up to the end of cold war, Indo-Australian relations improved when the labour party headed the government, and deteriorated under conservative governments. In the post-cold war period, however, this has not been the case. The Whitlam years saw a greater understanding of India's position and of non-alignment. There was also an espousal of the Indian Ocean as a Zone of Peace. Bob Howke's endeavours to locate Australia as an Asia Pacific player rather than a far away Western outpost, proved conducive to the Indo-Australian relations. Prime minister, late Rajiv Gandhi's visit to Australia in 1986 and Bob Howke's return visit to India, were symptomatic of friendly ties. Concerted efforts resulting from the end of cold war and, more important, India's economic reform processes, led to an incipient awareness of India in Australia. [6]

The improvement in relations during Bob Hawke's period was taken forward by the Howard regime when several significant initiatives were undertaken to generate the impulses for a mutually co-operative and beneficial relationship. Even though this was a conservative government, relations between India and Australia did not deteriorate. This was largely the result of various global changes that were occurring, particularly, the end of cold war, followed by the dramatic collapse of the Soviet Union. This period also saw the initiation of economic reforms in India both in terms of liberalization and globalization of its economy. The Australian Senate's Committee on Foreign Affairs, Defense and Trade, published a report specifically on Indo-Australian relations. This detailed study underlined the growth in the awareness of India, among Australian decision makers. The opening of Indian markets to foreign goods and investments created a profound in Australia. There began the concerted efforts to enhance bilateral relations, particularly in trade and investments. The establishment of the Australia-India Council (AIC), the Indian Australian Council (IAC) and the New Horizons Programmes, created much optimism. [7]

Ever since the beginning of the 1990s, economic relations between India and Australia have shown a dramatic increase particularly, in areas of trade and investment. The gradual restructuring and liberalisation of India's economy have provided much of the impetus for the expanding bilateral trade relationship. Despite its status as a developing country, India has a huge potential as a market for trade in goods and services. In 1994, it was rated the fifth largest economy in the world in purchasing power parity terms. Now, this position has comedown to the third place. This is of immense commercial significance to Australia. Indo-Australian trade has grown almost 200 percent since 1991. The balance on trade is highly fovourable to Australia; whereas in 1998, the Australian exports constituted US$ 395 million. [8] India's exports to Australia are mainly cotton textiles and clothing, engineering goods, chemicals and related products, plantation and agricultural products and leather manufacture. India is a bulk importer of coal, wool and non-ferrous metal and also sophisticated plant and machinery, dry fruit and paper from Australia.

Indian economy has been one of the fastest growing economies of the world, since the last few years. As Indian economy is projected to grow by 6 to 7 percent, this is the time for Australian business to take advantage of the growing middle class Indian market. Also, India being the world's second most populated country, its market potential for Australian exports increased substantially in mid-1980s. India was Australia's fifteenth largest trading partner. Now, India has become one among Australia's top ten trading partners. Around eighty joint ventures have been established and thirty more are in the offing.

All these developments can be attributed to the far- reaching economic reforms ushered in by India. With favorable growth outlook, the burgeoning demands of a huge middle class, offering excellent prospects for the growth of Australian trade, the Commonwealth government of Australia has been making every effort to cash on these, since 1996.

Pokhran II Nuclear Test and Indo- Australian Relations

When India conducted nuclear test in May 1998, Australia reacted in a strong manner. On 11 May, the Prime Minister of Australia John Howard termed India's action as an" ill judged step". [10] On 14 May, the then Minister for Foreign Affairs, Alexander Downer, described them as" outrageous acts". [11] Further, Australia reacted strongly by;

- Suspending official visits to India;
- Suspending defence ties, joint naval/ military exercises and by recalling their defence representatives in Delhi;
- Suspending all kinds of aid except humanitarian one;
- Denouncing the actions of India at international forums and extending it to the international press.
- Speaking rudely to official representatives of India in Australia and else where; and
- Lobbying other nations in the Asia pacific to voice strong criticism.

The language and tenor were considered by India to be diplomatically intemperate. The immediate reaction in India was one of defiant questioning: "who is Australia to decide about India's security concerns?" It left an impression in India, of Australia as a country, which was much too eager to please the US with whom India always had strategic and perceptional differences. On May 28, 1998, India responded by suspending all bilateral military cooperation, by disallowing Australian naval ships from visiting Indian ports and territorial waters, and by cancelling all over flight facilities to Australian military aircraft. [12] On its part, India's political elite did not exhibit the diplomatic deftness that was required in the period immediately following the nuclear explosions, particularly in its intent projections which it did at a later stage only. This state of chill, which lasted for more than a year, manifested the deep misconceptions that existed between the two countries.

Later Developments

The first step towards normalisation of relations after the Pokhran II freeze was in February 1999, with the visit to India by Australia's the then Deputy Prime Ministers, Tim Fischer who was also Minister of Trade. The focus was on strengthening trade and investment. Apart from convening the Joint Ministerial Commission, Co-operation in three areas emerged with the signing of an Investment and Promotion Agreement, a sports MOU and two Agricultural Agreements. [13] In April 1999, bilateral trade got a further boost with the decision of Austrade India to restructure its operations to facilitate a Pan-India presence. An India - Business Center was established at New Delhi, which focusses on five sectors with parallel specialised offices in the related cities - Information Technology (Bangalore), mining (Kolkata), automotive components (Chennai), agri-business (Mumbai) and the infrastructure related development (New Delhi). [14] The arrival of the Secretary of the Australian Department of Foreign Affairs and Trade in February 2000, marked the resumption of bilateral senior official level talks. For the first time apart from trade, the scope for broader engagement in other areas was explored including WTO, Southeast Asia, Indian Ocean, Environment, the Commonwealth and CTBT. [15]

Prime Minister, John Howard's visit to India in July 2000 was remarkable for underlining the benefits of diplomatic positivism. The Howard –Vajpayee Summit was not only an exercise in managing strategic divergences but also an attempt at probing areas of commonalities as an avenue for channelising action. Above all, it manifested the transformation in Australia's perceptions of India. The nuclear issue, though not forgotten, was relegated to the background. It was realized that a single issue could not be allowed to "contaminate the entire relationship" and efforts were made to revitalise relations in multiple sphere. [16] Four broad areas of commonalities were emphasised for inspiring cooperative efforts. Priority was attached to augmenting the trade relations, an area where, it has been of advantage to Australia for a long time. Indo-Australian trade came down from Rs. 66,831 million in April 1998-99 to Rs. 54,581 million in April 1999-2000. The Australian investments in India stood at Rs. 50.5 billion. [17] India's commitment to economic reforms meant more markets for the Australians, whose economy is trade driven. India's lead in IT Sector is another potential factor with India possessing skill and Australia the markets.

The global and regional environment in the last 4 to 5 years saw changes in equations, perspectives and priorities of states. Various factors contributed to mutations in perceptions of the US and the west with regard to South Asia and in particular India. The recognition by the world and especially by the US, of international terrorism and its close nexus to narcotics and to fundamentalism, centred around Pakistan – Afghanistan, (with the Osama Bin Laden factor), Pakistan's insidious aggression on Kargil and its defeat by India, India's responsible behaviour within the context of nuclearised South Asia in not crossing the LOC despite grave provocation, the collapse of democracy in Pakistan and its reversion to military dictatorship highlighted the changes in South Asian stability. The geo-strategic dynamics in the Central Asian region together with the China factor, had led to the shedding of the cold war baggage in the perceptions of the US and the West towards India.

The processes of globalisation and liberalisation in India had already opened a vital channel with the Indian markets and its expanding middle class, being the favourable factors for better relations with India. The latter's emergence as a leading one in the IT sector, was important. Above all, there were India's credentials as a democracy. All this led to a dramatic upswing in Indo-US relations, manifested first in the highly successful visit of the then President Bill Clinton to India, followed by former Prime Minister A.B.Vajpayee's visit to the US, and also in India's relations with

Russia and other European states. These events enabled Australia also to reallocate its priorities Vis-à-vis India, shifting its focus from the nuclear tests and the CTBT to a more wide ranging perspectives and relationship.

Despite differences, what is of significance, is that India and Australia are now seriously engaged in the business of promoting bilateral relations. Reverting back to the earlier theme, the dire need was to continue with the often arduous task of managing divergent perceptions by low profile negative reactions and by focussing and building on commonalities. In view of the fast changing international scenario, it is in the interests of both India and Australia to shed their differences and to work towards the mutually beneficial relationship.

The year 2004 and 2005 are eventful in the history of the bilateral relations between India and Australia. The surprise results of 2004 elections in India, with the defeat of the BJP led ruling coalition and the formation of the Congress led coalition in the form of UPA at the centre, changed the equation. There were was some sort of panic in the minds of the public regarding the nature of the government and the policies to be followed in regard to other countries. Despite many short-term hiccups that have been thrown up by the political system, in the long run, India's democracy provided a positive influence on the countries economic prospects. About the survival of Indian democracy against all these odds like political instability and uncertainty, Edward Luce wrote in Financial Times that, "Every time India goes to the polls, it becomes the largest electoral exercise in history". [18] Observers of the 2004 general election campaign noted that for the first time since independence, economic prosperity has emerged as a key issue in a general election because, the NDA regime announced a series of reforms in the run up to the April 2004 election.

During the UPA regime, the economic rise of India, had significant implication for Australian international economic policy. The growing economic importance of India is good news for Australia. Historically, Australia's economy repeatedly benefited from the rise of Asian economic powers, with first Japan and then Korea and now India providing Australia with dynamic export markets that have provided an important stimulus to economic growth. India's growing strategic importance and continuing economic expansion mean, it is set to become one of Australia's key regional and bilateral partners. The total trade of goods and services between India and Australia was worth A$ 7.4 billion in 2004, conferring tenth place on India in the list of Australia's trading partners. The proposed Trade and economic Framework (TEF) would set the direction for the facilitation and future development policy dialogue and cooperation on issues of mutual interest. On May 19, 2005, the India-Australia Business Council hosted the successful 2005 Joint Business councils (JBC) meeting at the Four Seasons Hotel, Sydney.

The Australian Minister for Foreign Affairs, Mr. Alexander Downer, visited India from June 6 to 9, 2005. The visit comes at a time of keen interest, including the world's major powers, in engaging more closely with India. Australia has for some time, recognised India as an emerging power of increasing importance. The bilateral economic, governmental and people-to-people links between India and Australia are well established. Mr. Downer's visit provided an opportunity to raise Australia's profile in India and take forward key aspects of the relationship. The primary focus on the visit to India was the fourth round of the bilateral Foreign Minister's Framework Dialogue (FMFD). Mr. Downer met Indian Prime Minister Dr. Manmohan Singh, former MEA, Mr. Natwar Singh and Dy-Chairman of the Planning Commission. During his visit, he reiterated Australia's continuing support extended to India's candidature for a permanent seat in the UN Security Council. He also pursued interests across a broad range of areas including a proposed increase in high level ministerial visits, particularly in science and technology, energy, agricultural and defence, greater cooperation on counter – terrorism and cooperation between the Indian and Australian film industries.

In addition, both the countries are trying to expand cooperation in other fields, also. Australia is assisting India in meeting its energy demands and there was also a strong focus on the education sector. Both countries are agreed to jointly support a touring exhibition of Bradman memorabilia to India in the near future. Cultural exchange programmes are instituted in various fields. Those are Border-Gavaskar Scholarship, for young cricketers, cultural connection through ceramics, AIC Australian Studies Fellowships and Scholarships and the establishment of South Australian Chapter of the Australia - India Business Council on June 30, 2005. This has begun to support local businesses investment by Indian companies into South Australia and to promote South Australia and India as mutual tourist destinations.

Finally, the shifting balance of economic weight in the world, will lead to changes in the stricture of the international economic policymaking. This process of global reorientation will provide opportunities for India and Australia to work with each other. One can say that, there is a good case of considering the G-20 as an alternative to the G-8 as a forum for guiding the global economic management. This proposal would have interesting policy implications for India and Australia, as both are members. The proposition that India and Australia should work towards promoting a more enhanced role for the G-20 has some attractive features. For example, this will provide an opportunity to both the countries to work with growing powers such as China and Japan. This will provide an opportunity to both the countries to work together and secure a place in what would then become a much more important part of the international economic architecture of the new global economy. In this direction, the birth of another Asian economic giant in the form of the India economy, should be seen as yet more positive news for Australia's future economic wellbeing.

Notes

1. Paul Keating; *Engagement: Australia Faces the Asia-Pacific*, (Sydney, macmillan-2000), p-26.
2. *Ibid.*
3. D. Gopal, *Australia: In the Emerging Global Order*, (Shipra

Pub, Delhi, 2002) p-1.

4. *Ibid.* p.257.

5. N.Verma Shanta, "Australia and India Towards Managing Perceptional Divergence", *Educational Dialogue*, (Australian High Commission, New Delhi, July, 1999).

6. Marika Vicziany and Kenneth McPherson (Ed), *Australia and South Asia: A blue print for 2000*, (National Centre for South Asian Studies, Melbourne, 1994).

7. Government of India, MEA, *The Commonwealth of Australia*, September 1998. Internet document.

8. Hari Sharan Chabra; "Economic Cooperation in the India Ocean Rim", *World Focus*, April 1998.

9. *13th Australia – India Joint Business Council*, (Sydney), April 10-11, 2000.

10. Australian High Commission, *News Release*, "Indian Nuclear Tests", (New Delhi), May 12, 1998.

11. *Ibid*, May 15, 1998.

12. Government of India, *Press Information Bureau*, "India to withdraw Defence Attache from Australia", New Delhi, May 28, 1998.

13. *Australian High Commission, News Release*, Tim Fischer Concludes Successful visit to India", February 26, 1999.

14. *Ibid*, "As trade Strengthens Pan- Indian Presence", April 30, 1999.

15. *Ibid*, "Australia- India Senior Officials Talks", February 23, 2000.

16. *National Herald*, July 13, 2000.

17. *The Tribune*, (Chandigarh), July 13, 2000.

18. Ludward Luce, *Financial Times*, May 2004.

21

India and Australia in Strategic Partnership

S. Utham Kumar Jamadhagni

The current international system is dominated by economic globalization and the emergence of transnational security issues like weapons proliferation and more importantly, terrorism. These broader trends of post cold war world have forced many countries to draw new spatial lines of position in the international matrix. Confrontation is being replaced by cooperation in almost all spheres of inter-state interaction. With the end of ideological confrontation, new opportunities for closer cooperation with other states, have risen.

Regional powers, mechanisms for increased interaction, and regional issues and methods to counter challenges, have come to occupy centrality in world affairs. Loss of superpower balance and the absence of another potential great power necessitate a check over possible single power hegemony. Only joint regional efforts at strengthening economic and gradually political and ultimately military stakes can achieve this goal. The field of activity that has been neglected most is that of the oceans. The factor that would soon become the most indispensable source of physical, economic and even military welfare is, by all means, the ocean. The all-encompassing dimension namely, maritime security that not only deals with military naval security but also probes into a host of other areas of economic, social and cultural importance, thus warrants close attention. Besides, security from, and of the ocean waters, maritime security encompasses the safety of sea routes, prevention of illegal activity at sea and preservation and exploitation of marine based resources – that could soon replace the fast dwindling land-based sources – ensuring national interests and enhancing prosperity.

India and Australia are nations with a strong maritime tradition and an overt dependence on the sea for trade and security. India, as a peninsula and Australia, as an island continent/nation, are ocean dependent for their very survival as a territorial and economic entity. Indian Ocean as the lifeline, forms a common denominator that entails closer cooperation. Indian trade flourishes on its waters (97 per cent by volume) The Indian Ocean is the only all weather sea-lane. About half of the world's oil and other energy sources cross the Indian Ocean. Large reserves of hydrocarbons on the offshore of Indian Ocean littorals will shape the world's future energy flows. However, it is not just abundant in economic potential but is the stage for major problems of the world. According to the 1998 report of the Independent World Commission on the Oceans aptly named, *The Ocean: Our Future*, the inter-state territorial disputes, global climate change, illegal fishing, habitat destruction, pollution, drug smuggling, congested sea lanes, unlawful migration, and piracy, are prevalent. While problems are aplenty, regional arrangements are below satisfactory levels. [1]

The status in the global hierarchy of Australia as a middle power that is developed and positioned in a region of relative volatility and instability aiming to provide "leadership" in global issues, and that of India, as a great power aspirant also interestingly in an unstable neighbourhood assuming increasingly stronger roles in the world affairs, have a cumulative effect on identifying the converging interests and areas. While ties through the Ocean dates back to two centuries, the geopolitical linkages to first order powers, be it United States in the case of Australia and to a lesser extent Soviet Union for India, have often fielded them in opposing ranks. However, now the dynamism of South East Asian economies, their renewed significance in the politico-strategic calculus of both countries as well as fresh challenges to regional peace and order have brought back focus on the Indian Ocean. Problems like the rising militancy, coupled with the threat of terrorism, strike a common chord. Only changing global political architecture and the need for both countries to forge new markets and opportunities, have forced Australia and India to "look west" and "east" respectively. Thus, this paper points to the scope for cooperation between countries like India and Australia in the strategic area. Though this newfound enthusiasm is reflected in the visits of ministerial and trade delegations, strategic partnership is a cautious road to tread.

A historical update of Australia- India relations would help in identifying the general trends in bilateral relations, the external influences that have coloured them, and the current state of the ties. The Post Cold War paradigm shift [2] in International security, has had a "ripple effect" on regional security policy of individual nation states. India and its foreign policy are looking east. The Indian Prime Ministerial visit to the South East Asian countries has recognized this shift in focus "it was also a strategic shift in India's vision of the world and India's place in the evolving global economy". [3] This reorientation also entails greater interaction with a country that has similar interests in East Asia i.e., Australia. As a British colony and later as leader of the third world countries through the non-aligned movement, India had captured the western interest in the past. The economic potential and the emergence of India as a "software power house" has sharpened the interest in hitherto neglected areas like the Asian rim.

More than half a world apart, India and Australia stand as guardians of the Indian Ocean. Whether it be an East India Dutch ship *Zuytorp* that sailed to Australia in 18th century or the cavalry parade at the Commonwealth inauguration in 1901 or the migration of Indian labour to the plantations of Queensland in the early 19th century or the consignment of coal that left the shores of Australia for India, ties between the sentinels of Indian Ocean have been on the start-stop trajectory for long.

The first links established by the new colony of New South Wales, the first Australian settlement, were with India, which provided grain, foodstuffs, clothing and livestock when supplies in the new colony ran low and short. India, as historian of early Australia, David Walker explains, "was a lifeline for early NSW". [4] The earliest contact between India and Australia was through the British East India Company. According to Michael Nash, Australian marine heritage expert, Australia's trade with India goes back to 1791, when a government store ship, *Sydney Cove*, was sent to Calcutta in British India for providing additional food supply. While returning from India with rice, sugar, tobacco, salted meat, soap, candles, textiles, leather wear, livestock, etc., the ship sank off the coast of Tasmania in 1797. [5]

In the early 1800s, Coal Harbour (Newcastle) near Sydney, began to export coal to India under the governorship of Philip Ridley King. [6] Later muslin silk and camels figured in the top imports from India. [7] Newly unearthed research, points to the first Australian writer John Lang rendering services to India. He even appeared as a defence lawyer for an Indian against the British East India Company. He was the first foreigner to be invited to the court of Jhansi where he had a personal interaction with the warrior-maiden. [8] He also counselled Rani of Jhansi during the first Indian war of independence. His many works though mostly fiction, being now brought to light, reflect his deep attachment to India. [9]

On 1 June 1833, Brevet Captain J.G. Collins of the 13th Light Dragoons wrote to Henry Chamier, Chief Secretary of Madras, suggesting that he be given 18 months leave and half pay in advance to visit NSW and Van Dieman's Land, to buy horses for the Madras artillery and dragoons. Linked to this proposal, was the imaginative idea that a depot be set up at King George Sound in Western Australia, staffed by the retired to oversee the convalescing Indian army people, where remounts could be collected from the eastern Australian colonies, for eventual dispatch to Madras. [10] During 1835, the 13th dragoon obtained one hundred and fifteen remount horses, of which seven were Australian horses. These were known as "Walers". [11] A military department notification No. 594 of 2nd March 1887 refers to the Indian government's intent to purchase some 1222 Walers rated as Class 1 horses "suitable for army purposes" to be used in Madras. [12] The Australian Walers soon became a prized possession as their all-round skills and ability were greatly appreciated.

India also participated in the Federation inaugural celebrations in Sydney on January 1, 1901. They were a major attraction of the military parade. "The dark-skinned men crowned with turbans are the Indian Contingent". [13] The impressive Indian contingent symbolized the reach of the empire. Media reports like, "The vast extent of her majesty's dominions, to which yesterday we indissolubly bound this united Commonwealth, was typified not only by these representatives from the extreme ends of the Empire, but by the contingent of Indian soldiers who made so distinct and popular a feature in yesterday's demonstration", [14] greatly appreciated their presence .

Colonial Relations

While colonial trade brought the two closer, Britain remained the lynchpin of interactions. Having been drawn gradually into the global affairs, Australia first saw Britain as the guarantor of its security. The World War and the threat of Japanese invasion of Australian territory, witnessed an enhanced interference in world events. The end of the war and the waning of the British power left Australia with no alternative, but to join the American alliance. Due to this formalisation of US-Australian ties, India, like many other countries, often found itself in the opposing camp.

Within weeks of the outbreak of the war, two of Britain's key warships-the force, which had been expected to guarantee Australia's security - were sunk by the Japanese off the coast of erstwhile Malaya. Britain's naval presence in the Far East (as this region was known) was effectively destroyed. On December 27, 1941, the Australian Prime Minister John Curtain had published his landmark statement that Australia would look towards "America free of any pangs as to our traditional links or kinship with the United Kingdom". While relations with Britain would remain strong, America was now the great and powerful friend with which Australia would forge a long-standing alliance that would soon become the centerpiece of Australia's security calculus. [15] It became a voluntary apparatus of the United States' strategic policy in this region. In due course, Australia became a party to many international policy stances on issues with which India disagreed. The two countries have diverged on many international issues, e.g. on Korea, Vietnam etc. This in itself, did not sour the bilateral relations, as the two democracies otherwise held many values in common.

The respect for each other's sovereign rights to take foreign policy decisions in keeping with their own national interests, kept the relations warm and cordial politically throughout the fifty years of the Cold War despite the differences. [16] However, these differences have inevitably put a limit to the depth of the association on international political and security issues.

Fus(e) Logic

There is reason for being optimistic about the prospect of warmer relations in future with a number of common strategic realities and possibilities. India and Australia have the Indian Ocean as a common geographical and economic denominator. Being the only perennial warm water ocean, the Indian Ocean moves the bulk of the world's marine trade, through its waters. With an energy dependent economy, India has to depend on imported oil that plies through these waters. Australia, as a leading exporter of natural resources, depends heavily on the Indian Ocean. Hence the need to maintain secure sea-lanes is paramount to both the countries.

Also as a geo-strategic factor, the Indian Ocean holds great significance. The inter-lying region of East Asia evinces significant interest in both the countries. India once reigned over these countries and its cultural influence is pervasive to this day. [17] Australia as the regional big brother and a major trading partner has huge stakes in the region. While India, despite its recently reverted focus on the region, is yet to build on its past relations Australia has exhibited an active involvement in the political, security and economic issues of the East Asian region.

The security concerns of India in the wake of the Chinese naval expansion and the possibility of the Chinese acquisition of islands from Burma and the long-term Indian ambitions to ascribe a larger role to the Indian Ocean region, partly to checkmate China's influence, and the emerging threats to Australian security through terrorism, are reasons for closer cooperation. To India, to further those ambitions, the need to strengthen relations with two other major naval powers in the Indian Ocean region - South Africa and Australia - seems imperative. They are, in a sense, the two sentinels of the Indian Ocean. [18] Australia, like India, regards the idea of Indian Ocean as a zone of peace as an ideal and long-term objective for the regional stability. [19]

The Indian Diaspora is reaching Aussie waters too, not only as immigrants but also as students who hold immigration potential. With the information technology industry taking the world by storm, Indian computer talent could also seek greener pastures down under. The skilled and excellent manpower could be hoped to gain influence in the coming years.

Their individual contributions to the UN peacekeeping processes and other activities have been laudable. "Australia has a long and proud tradition of involvement with the UN, we have influenced its proceedings substantively, and often beyond the expectations of a country of our population size. It is our hope that in considering Australia's relationship to the UN we can build on our past achievements and ensure a strong and strategic empowerment with the UN in the future." [20]

For long India has faced neglect from Australia on various fronts. Small wonder then, that in 1989-90, Australia's exports to India amounted to only a little more than AUD 0.5 billion, while India's exports to Australia were lower, at a little more than AUD 0.25 billion. However, the balance of trade position has now tipped in Australia's favour. It is now projected that the trade would increase substantially, making India one of Australia's biggest export markets. [21]

Myth and Reality

The unsuccessful campaign in 1915 at the battle of Gallipoli, saw both Indian and Australian troops fighting for the allied cause. In fact, the 29th Indian Infantry Brigade was the only body of allied troops to reach the summit of the ridge and to gaze down on the waters of the Dardanelles. [22] Nearly 1358 Sikhs of the Indian mule cart corps perished in this campaign, compared to 8709 Australians. [23] An interesting aspect during the inter war years (1919-1939), is that the Australian officers served on full-time basis in the British units in India formed part-time units, upon their return. Under the White Australian policy, this practice of sending Australians to work besides Asian communities, is a never repeated occurrence. This was "a small but significant military relationship" [24] that precedes all claims of Australian relations with Asia.

The World War brought India and Australia closer. The World War II saw India figuring as the leading supplier. With great distances separating each of the active theaters of war from the main source of supply in the United States, there was a need to reach the remote theatres at the earliest. Instead of relying most heavily on water transport, the very nature of the war, made it imperative that a system of air supply be developed, supplementary to the older and slower methods of surface transport. The fastest and most economical method of moving combat aircraft from the factory to the front, was to ferry them under their own power. To keep them in battle at their highest efficiency, an air transport service for the rapid delivery of spare engines and parts an auxiliary equipment of all kinds, flight crews, and ground personnel were an absolute necessity.

The combined strategy devised by the British and American staff at the Washington conference of December 1941, had embodied, in addition to a long-range plan of action, certain immediate objectives to be attained in 1942. These were first, to make secure important areas of war production likely to be attacked, and second, to provide for the security of the principal sea routes and seven main air routes over which men and supplies could be moved to the battlefronts while the conference was still in session, it had become clear that the Philippines could not be held, principally because the Japanese had cut the only sea and air lanes over which available reinforcements, such as they were, could reach MacArthur. By the end of February 1942, the air connection between India and Australia was also cut, although some heavy bombers and other reinforcements from the United States were able to get through before the Japanese captured Singapore and overran the Netherlands East Indies. The Australia-Philippines and the Australia-India air routes, included in the seven, declared to be of the highest strategic importance, were thus lost in the first shock of the Japanese attack.

In the struggle to rebuild societies after the Second World War, the Commonwealth foreign ministers met in Colombo in January 1950 to draft an economic and technical assistance programme that came to be known as the Colombo Plan. In this manner, it was hoped to serve the twin purposes of development *as against poverty and destruction* as well as strategic *as alleviating poverty would bring about political stabilization.* Under this plan, Australia provided wheat and flour to India and Pakistan for on-selling to pay for dams and power plants. It is significant as it was the first important multilateral aid scheme, if not as an aid for poor nations. Under the plan Australia provided over a period of 4 years from 1951-54 a sum of 13.8 crore.

Together with an economic aid, Australia even suggested a NATO like military pact but this according to Nehru, amounts to getting the risk of Chinese communist aggression, aggravated, let alone adding any capacity to repel it. So, this dimension was ignored. Evatt, to the bitter end remained opposed to the idea of allowing India to remain in the Commonwealth as a full member, without the retention of some of the king's prerogatives. Newly independent India, in particular, seemed unlikely to be satisfied with dominion status; if it opted for a republican constitution, could it remain in the Commonwealth?

With the Australian federation, came the "White's only immigration policy", that restricted the people settling in

Australia, along racial lines. This drastically reduced the number of Indian immigrants, right until the 1960s. Almost all Indians settled in the Woolgolga region of New South Wales. However, Australia has travelled far from an exclusionist society in 1900s, to celebrating the multi-culturalism in the 21st century.

Past relations have also been coloured by misperceptions. Because of its close alliance with America, Australia has been termed a "lackey". [25] Australia openly acknowledges the close relations with the United States but her actions and reactions on the international arena, are designed more by Australia's national interests than by the fact that it has a security alliance with the US. Analysts are quick to point to her strong views regarding arms control and disarmament by way of an illustration. The restrictive immigration policy and the reported "racial bias", gave an impression of an "intolerant" Australia. Earlier, media had reported of the dropping of sonar buoys around the India destroyer, INS Chakra, in international waters. Though Australia deemed it normal practice, India felt offended. [26]

During the First World War, the Australian nurses served in India too. Some 320 of them worked in hospitals at Deolali and other places. There was even an unsavoury episode, involving the nurses in 1918. [27] In recent memory too, India has been in the eye of the storm. The gruesome murder of Australian missionary Graham Steines and the Pokharan explosion, have not augured well. The Australian Prime Minster termed it as an "ill-judged step" that affected the security situation of the region. [28] His foreign minister Downer announced some of the most stringent measures including the recall of High Commissioner, the withdrawal of the defence adviser at New Delhi, the total suspension of defence relations and the suspension of ministerial visits to India to reinforce the "strength of our condemnation of the outrageous acts perpetrated by India." [29] India held that this was stronger than the western reaction and inconsistent with Australia's reaction of the French nuclear tests in 1995. The exaggerated report of mistreatment of Indian army officers expelled from the Australian institutes after the Pokharan explosion had also left a bad taste.

The 1998, Pokharan explosion temporarily staggered the progress and stymied the start of a new relationship. Australia's reaction to the nuclear tests included the suspension of defence contracts, non-humanitarian aid and ministerial visits. However, the Australian government after two years broke the ice with the visit of Foreign Minister Alexander Downer from March 21-24, 2000. In preparation for this visit the Deputy Prime Minister Tim Fischer came to India in February 1999. However, Pokharan II has had a positive fall out too. Australia has accepted the new reality of India as a nuclear power. It now treats the bilateral relationship in a wider context of common political, strategic and economic interests and concerns and is in the process of institutionalising dialogue at all levels. It also recognises India as a rising regional power both politically and economically.

A New Sojourn

Australian policy perspective has travelled far from the 1990 report of the Senate Committee on Foreign Affairs and Trade that the relations with India "lacked substance" [30] to the plethora of high-level exchange of visits in the late 1990s. The "New beginning" with increased economic contact in the early 1990s, paved the way for a reassessment of India's importance in the eyes of Australia. The Australian foreign minister visited India from 19-23 October 1996, to launch the Australia-India New Horizons promotion of tourism and culture. Also the Deputy Prime Minister Tim Fischer designated 1997, as the year of South Asia.

Even before independence, India was highly critical of White Australian policy making it "one of the most hated countries in India". [31] Australian officials were also aware of the growing discontent due to specific cases involving Asians. Opposition to this policy, grew within Australia too. Some like Colin Moodie, even suggested a modification of the policy to secure the abiding goodwill of both India and Pakistan by not naming it "White

Australia policy" and by admitting any Indian with sufficient means and westernization. [32] However the recent governmental interaction in the form of high level exchange of visits in the post Pokharan II era has surely been encouraging.

The process of exchange of visits was set rolling and the series of visits by Shadow Foreign Minister Laurie Brereton in February 2000, Opposition Leader Kim Beazley in April 2000, Immigration and Multicultural Affairs Minister Philip Ruddock in July 2000, Trade Minister Mark Vaile in October 2000, Minister for Communications, Information Technology and the Arts Senator Richard Alston in December 2000, an Australian Parliamentary delegation led by Hon. Andrew Southcott, MP in November 2000, followed. Important visits from State Governments included that of Deputy Premier Hendy Cowan of Western Australia in February 2000 and Deputy Premier Jim Elder of Queensland in May 2000.

From the Indian side, the Minister of Information Technology and Parliamentary Affairs Pramod Mahajan visited Australia in April 2001 and later as leader of a goodwill Parliamentary delegation of whips of different political parties in May 2001. The goodwill delegation included Minister of State for Parliamentary Affairs and Petroleum & Natural Gas, Santosh Kumar Gangwar and Minister of State for Parliamentary Affairs and Railways, O. Rajagopal. A large delegation of Members of Parliament and Assembly Speakers from different states led by the Speaker of the Lok Sabha G.M.C. Balayogi and Deputy Speaker of the Lok Sabha P. M. Sayeed, attended the 47th Commonwealth Parliamentary Association Conference in September 2001. Minister of Health and Family Welfare Dr. C.P. Thakur led a 62-member delegation to the 6th International Conference on AIDS in Asia and Pacific held in Melbourne in October 2001. Other important visits included that of Governor of Andhra Pradesh, Dr. C. Rangarajan in October 2001, to render the Narayanan Oration at the Australian National University (ANU) and the Minister of Rural Development M. Venkayya Naidu in November 2001, to attend the Commonwealth Local Government Forum in Brisbane. [33]

Foreign Minister Downer's visit was reciprocated by the visit of the Joint Ministerial commission led by the Indian Commerce minister Murasoli Maran in April 2000. The Australia – India joint business council met in the following month. However, the Prime Ministerial visit by John Howard in July 2000, the first after a gap of 11 years, signified Australia's earnestness and was aimed to add "new vigour and activity" [34] into the relation. It was in search of a common "strategic outlook" on issues relating to the Indian Ocean region and its environs. [35] In a pre-departure press release, the Prime Minister acknowledged, that since India was an important player internationally and globally, "an enhanced dialogue on trade and strategic issues" was to be pursued. The emphasis on trade was highlighted. [36]

With the visit of the trade minister Mark Vaile in October of the same year, India witnessed an impetus to areas of cooperation in trade and business, as evident from the Memorandum of Understanding (MoU) signed on Information Technology. [37] In June 2001, Indian external affairs and defence minister Jaswant Singh visited Australia, leading to some important policy outcomes and identification of areas of cooperation. More importantly it was agreed to hold a strategic dialogue between the two countries. [38] Accordingly, the first Indo-Australian strategic dialogue was held on August 30, 2001.

The dialogue focused on issues concerning economic security, energy security and security of the Asia-Pacific region. The talks were said to be "open, constructive, wide-ranging and demonstrated shared perspectives and common interests". It was recognized that India and Australia were "factors for stability" in the Asia-Pacific region. [39] The second strategic dialogue has also been held and there seems to be ample opportunities to build on the relations. The 9/11 attacks could now open up another area of cooperation i.e., anti terrorism. Unfortunately, the visit of Prime Minister Vajpayee to attend the CHOGM meet in March

2002, was cancelled in the wake of communal riots in Godhra, Gujarat.

The foreign minister Alexander Downer, visited India again in 2005. He reiterated Australia's support for India's candidature for the permanent membership of UN Security Council. Both the sides expressed satisfaction at the rapid growth in bilateral trade and economic relations in recent years and reiterated their desire to enhance cooperation in this area. [40] Prior to this, there were a series of visits of business delegations from various states of Australia. South Australian Premier, Western Australia's head of executive, discussed trade relations with southern Indian states and Australia is now promoting itself as an alternate educational destination. The latest visit of John Howard to India in March 2006, emphasises the importance accorded to India in Australian calculus. Significantly, the Prime Ministers dealt with enhancing defence links, too.

Policy Place

The labour government was quite close to Nehru. Chiefly, the then Australian Prime Minister was even asked to mediate between India and Pakistan, which he refused. Strategically, India has been only recently recognized as an important player in the regional affairs. The Menzies government was on the other hand committed to the demands of bipolarity and the US policy of containment. This stood in complete contrast to Nehru's non-alignment vision. The tit for tat continued with India disapproving of ANZUS pact while India's pegging of the Chinese participation in the Korean War in the U.N. was turned down. At the Bandung conference, Nehru pointed that the geographical proximity of Australia and New Zealand would make them come "closer to us". [41] Some diplomatic and political figures were sympathetic and had a little understanding of perceptions. An Australian High Commissioner to India put it succinctly that "What we say is usually more important than what we do." [42] While the mention of India in this light might not be acceptable to

Indian officialdom, the fact that India now regularly figures in the policy pronouncement of Australia, is worth noticing.

Menzies in 1947, as opposition leader, argued that India was not yet ready for independence. [43] In the aftermath of Indian independence, the assumption of office by two contrasting personalities at the helm of affairs, namely, Menzies in Australia and Nehru in India one being an ardent follower of the crown, while the other being one who had spent most of his life fighting to free India from the yoke of colonialism, cast a long shadow on the bilateral ties. While the former was committed to the demands of bipolarity and the containment policy, the latter stood in sharp contrast, with non-alignment. The ANZUS and SEATO evoked Indian disapproval, whereas Australia criticized Indian stand on the Korean issue. Under the Colombo plan, Australia provided one of the largest aid packages to India, in 1952. The attention given to South Asia during the first decade of independence, waned after the inclusion of the trade dominated aid, in Australian foreign policy.

But the image of Australia as an adjunct to US and UK, steering clear of regional membership and more importantly, the "white Australia policy", made it highly unpopular in the eyes of the Indian elite. While the Cold War mostly placed the two in opposing camps, the end of it has proved promising. The political and military developments of the 1962 Sino-Indian war, the 1971 war of liberation of Bangladesh and the emergency of 1975, sparked interest in India occasionally. This waning curve received a boost only when India's economic development was taken cognizance of and found its mention in the foreign and defence policy white papers, and even in the national political party manifestoes. However, the movement from recognition to action, has been slow, but steady.

Strategically, India has been only recently recognized as an important player in regional affairs. In a run up to the publication of a new White paper on Australia's foreign and defence policy, the Foreign minister Alexander Downer, in a speech on May 7, 2002, pointed to "the world's three most volatile flashpoints",

[44] apart from the West Asian region – the Taiwan Strait, the Korean peninsula and Kashmir. While the mention of India in this light might not be acceptable to Indian officialdom, the fact that India now regularly figures in the policy pronouncement of Australia, is worth noticing.

The policy paper on defence published in 2000, recognizes, that it is India's growing role in the wider Asia Pacific strategic system that will have more influence on Australia's security. The paper noted that, "India is increasingly important to the wider regional strategic balance. This has not only increased Australia's interest in building contact on security issues with India; it has also made India more interested in Australia's distinctive approach and outlook on regional security affairs. The Government hopes that early progress can be made in setting up the kind of dialogue that will allow us to explore and better understand one another's perspectives". [45]

The 1997 Defence policy and the successive policy papers, have recognized that the future security and prosperity of Australia, arc increasingly dependent on that of the wider region. [46] Viewing India as a major player in this region, the 1997 Australian strategic policy document included the development of a strategic dialogue with India as one of its goals. This, perhaps after the Cold War, has been the first attempt to officially acknowledge India's position in Australian diplomatic horizon. It also indicates that in contrast to the popular belief, it was not the Pokharan II explosion but the trade and strategic potential of India, that warranted an increased focus of Australia's geopolitical radar.

In Australia, domestically too, India's role in the region has come to be recognized. This is evident from the Labor party pronouncements on its official website which state that "Australia must embrace India, a country of immense potential, an important participant in global and regional forums, and a trading partner of growing significance. Australia has long neglected India in our foreign relations. Labor will work energetically to remedy this deficiency and enhance our ties with the world's second most populous nation." [47]

At a time when much of the world is preoccupied with the issue of strategic uncertainty, it is noteworthy, that Australia and India recognise one another as factors for stability in the Asia-Pacific and Indian Ocean regions. This point was made formally in a joint statement issued after their inaugural bilateral strategic dialogue in August 2001. That dialogue was a significant step forward, substantive as well as symbolic, in a relationship, which had passed through a difficult period in the aftermath of India's 1998 nuclear tests. For the first time, the officials and uniformed officers from both the sides met, to share the perspectives on a full range of global and regional security issues.

The success of the very first formal dialogue, and an increasingly apparent convergence of security interests, including the addressing of the terrorism, helped to influence both the governments in extending the dialogue when it was held for a second time in March this year, by raising the level of representation and participation, with the addition of subgroups on defence, counter-terrorism and immigration. In the run up, to the publication of a new White paper on Australia's foreign and defence policy, the Foreign minister Alexander Downer, in a speech delivered on May 7, 2002, pointed out, that he was asked to mediate in India's dispute with Pakistan over Kashmir — one of the "the world's three most volatile flashpoints," [48] the others being the Taiwan Strait and the Korean peninsula. He however, declined with thanks. [49]

In conjunction with the enhancement of the strategic dialogue, the Australian and Indian Governments reached an agreement in March 2003, on the text of a Memorandum of Understanding on Counter-Terrorism, which will be a significant addition to the web of agreements both the countries have been developing with partners, against terrorism. The wider defence relationship, which includes staff college exchanges and ship visits, has grown quickly since the restoration of formal defence relations in 2000. This relationship, being built on a growing recognition of shared interests including the Indian Ocean and maritime and sea-lane security issues holds real promise and carries prospects of turning the corner.

This was underlined, when the frigate HMAS Adelaide visited Chennai on a dedicated goodwill visit, and took part in an exercise, using an Indian vessel. At the same time, Maritime Commander Rear Admiral Gates, was meeting the Indian counterparts to discuss next steps in developing an active relationship between the two navies. [50]

Crystal Gazing

Several developments in the international realm, seem to merit a main focus on the multilateral cooperation. The recent concern regarding the terrorist attacks and the Australian conception that the focus on the Asia-Pacific in both the economic and strategic terms and the possibility of use of Australia as an informed interlocutor for the Southeast Asian region and as an ally of the United States, by India on the other, has brought India and Australia closer. In setting up an anti-terrorist squad, in monitoring the political events of East Asia and in aiming at realizing a region of relative peace and security, both the countries have a lot to achieve, lest their national pride should be at stake.

Geopolitics is yet another factor in the convergent interests of our countries. The descriptions of Australia and India as Indian Ocean neighbours, are more than being just symbolic, when one sees the proximity of India's Andaman and Nicobar Islands, to Christmas Island. But there are the shifting global and geopolitical realities - such as the threat of international terrorism - point towards convergence of interests and the logic of engagement.

Concurrence of threat potential, is a point of mutual interest. But, the future of Australia's strategic partnership with India, depends on the strength of US- Australian alliance and several other factors. The possible scenarios that have to be considered before attempting to think of strategic partnerships, are Australia's aspirations with respect to this region and its threat perceptions. Also, the recognition of India as a potential superpower and a regional hegemon and its consequent fallout on bilateral relations, are enumerated and discussed below.

Scenario 1: Continuance of Australia-US Alliance

A strong, enduring and consolidated partnership with the United States, particularly one that is assertive and continues to dominate the world affairs, would certainly enlist Australia – as its most reliable ally outside the Western hemisphere – a willing defender of American interests. If there is a continuation of Australian and American alliance, which in all probability would, together with the scenario of a more powerful Indian Ocean power if China or India is posing a threat to US interests, Australia would be the ideal choice for forward deployment. The intelligence-gathering US-Australia 'joint facilities' in central Australia, have lost none of their importance after the end of the Cold War. On the contrary, they have been upgraded. Indeed, these facilities could have new roles in regional security if Japan and South Korea go ahead with the Theatre Missile Defenses. The Defence White Paper 2000, also mentions India as one among only three countries, including China and Indonesia that pose potential danger to Australia or would ever have a capacity to do so.

At least two states mentioned as potential enough, to pose such a threat in the next 10-20 years, namely, India and China, are also interestingly among the fastest growing economies, possessing huge armed forces equipped though, not with state-of-the-art but at least partially self developed arsenal, importantly nuclear too, entrenching their presence in the IOR. While the current American relations with these Asian giants exhibit *bonhomie*, tables could turn, in the next two decades. A possible China-Taiwan conflict might group Australia with US in an appropriate response. India as a global economic player, perceived as an aspirant of great power status, could face the containment tactics of the United States, where Australia could enact the role of a willing substitute. Indian or Chinese missile development, acquisition and deployment are watched with grave concern. in Australia. The reason beyond the stated one of regional stability of the Indian Ocean region, could even include "benchmarking" of the current Australian capabilities to get upgraded to a future role of confrontation as part of an extra regional coalition.

Australia contributed forces to the Korean, Vietnam and Gulf conflicts. In February 1998 crisis with Iraq, Australia sent SAS forces, and it endorsed the December 1998 US/UK punitive strikes against Saddam Hussein's regime. Australia was the only regional country willing openly to criticize China in early 1996, when China launched missiles across the Taiwan Strait in an effort to intimidate Taiwan during its first presidential elections. At that time, Australia's defence minister warned China that its minatory behaviour might incur dire consequences. In 1995, Australia entered into a new strategic alignment with Indonesia, prompted by both countries' determination to resist China's strategic pressure in the South China Sea. Australia welcomed the upgrading of the US-Japan alliance in 1996, recognizing the centrality of that alliance for regional stability and its own security. Australia's alliance with the United States was upgraded in the same year, with Australia expressing greater willingness to use the alliance to help shape the regional security environment. The US alliance continues to enjoy strong electoral and bipartisan support. [51]

While this is true, India's standing with the US also needs to be taken into consideration. An exchange of high level visits; the choice of USA as the most favoured higher education destination for Indian students; the increasing economic and political visibility of Indian immigrants in USA and the economic and strategic significance of India's development and the acknowledgement of India as a "strategic partner" could influence other permutations of international relations and diplomacy.

Scenario 2: Aspiration of great power status

Australia's role as a middle power – a state whose size, population, location, level of development and resource endowments and the contribution to the war effort on the side of the allied powers – demands a different status. Traditionally the middle powers were assumed to have neither military, material capabilities nor any inclination to provide the kind of leadership, a superpower possesses. But the involvement of Australia in the East Timor issue – forcing Indonesia to heed to democratic pressures so as to initiate the process for setting up a government belies this assumption. Australia provided complete financial, logistic support and even policing offers to the United Nations Mission for East Timor (UNAMET). She then successfully maintained pressure over Indonesia first to ensure peace and in the face of increased violence gained control using multilateral force, clearly exhibiting the extent to which intentions could play a significant part in strategic affairs.

The episode is seen as an assertion of principal power status and the ominous ring that Australia could turn out to be the strongman of Asia. Australia has an increasing involvement in the affairs of small states in the Oceania region for example Fiji, Bougainvillea, Solomon Islands, East Timor. Success rates in either quelling the rebellion or "establishing democracy" and in the use of force to fulfil part or whole of such mandate, certainly add feather in its cap. Australia continues to involve itself in the United Nations missions and increasingly contributes to multilateral force structures like those to Iraq to aid in rehabilitation, and leading a multi national stabilizing force to East Timor and to the Solomon Islands. The success in the East Timor venture could embolden Australia to attempt such efforts ostensibly far away from its borders to deal with the 'arc of instability' extending well into the Indian Ocean region.

As nation states still remain the basic building block of the international system, and the competition between them remains an underlying reality and the modern capable armed forces equipped for high-end warfare, remain indispensable. If Australia wants to become a more global player, then it should be prepared to possess a commensurate force with adequate budget to fulfil that role. Restructured defence forces for global operations on budgets that have been optimised for predominantly regional roles, will prove ineffective. East Timor underlined that reality. The military modernisation is still proceeding at a pace in the Asia Pacific, especially with respect to air and maritime capabilities. [52] This development must also been taken into reckoning by Australia.

Scenario 3: India as a Threat to Australia

Control over the resources of the Indian Ocean and the ensuing competition pose another challenge, where Australia might cross swords with India and even nations like South Africa. In a globalised economy and open market era, any race to capture new markets, could pitch the Indian Ocean powers against each other. Indian Ocean provides in abundance, living and non-living resources and renewable and non-polluting sources of energy. Tropical climate favours growth of marine animal life in the form of fish, plants and other marine animals useful for human consumption and for making drugs and pharmaceutical products. Exclusive economic zones of various coastal countries, have oil-natural gas and minerals in the form of polymetallic nodules and hypothermal vents.

The maritime interests of India manifest in the Indian Naval Doctrine, the first of its kind for this ocean state, aim at safeguarding the sea lanes of communication, maintaining stability in the Indian Ocean region and more importantly, power projection [53] into the littorals. The engagement of South East Asia including the prospect of joint training exercises, technology transfer, could improve India's presence in Australia's neighbourhood. Offer of low cost, high-end technologies, equipment to the relatively weak states against their stronger neighbours will ruffle feathers. Indian naval and coast guard shopping list includes subs, anti-ship missiles, aircraft carriers fitted with strike aircraft like the Russian Su-30.

Threat of terrorists using weapons of mass destruction is considered a possibility "more likely" than anytime in the past. While these scenarios point to the probable areas of concern, the

Australia's capability to mount such challenges needs scrutiny. The moderate economic successes could multiply with an increasing demand from external resource-dependent economies of the IOR. Use of aid, investment and assistance as tools of foreign policy is prevalent. The Australian Defence Force faces the imminent prospect of 'block obsolescence' – when major platforms such as the F/A-18 *Hornet* multi-role fighter aircraft, the F-111 strike fighters, the P-3C *Orion* long-range maritime patrol (LRMP) aircraft and all of the Navy's surface combatants will need to be replaced in the next 10-12 years. [54] The decision on possible replacements is pending. Contrast this with the acquisitions of the region especially those of China, India and Indonesia, which interestingly have all opted for the Russian made Soviet Sukoi Su-30 strike aircraft. Also Australia's maritime capability is severely limited with the ageing of platforms. There is a growing concern of the regional capabilities and acquisitions and the need to either increase defence expenditure from the current modest amounts of roughly 2 per cent of the GDP or lease or purchase foreign, mainly American equipment to replace existing platforms.

Conclusion

Futuristic estimates on oil dependence, prospecting newer export markets, deepening understanding and influence of the interlying Asian landmass, and the need to build a peaceful and secure Asia- Pacific region and in turn ensuring a safer global environment have forced India and Australia to extend a firmer handshake. This could lay the foundation for a more meaningful closer cooperation. The relations could now take off in a big way as security, economy and the sheer need for diversification of foci on the foreign policy front have brought both India and Australia closer than ever before. Identifying areas of mutual interest and concern in the realms of economy (like the issue of globalisation and its effect on nations), global security (like the importance of the Indian Ocean region, the scepter of terrorism, its causes and related concerns especially unique to this part of the world), and diplomacy (as in the need for bilateral understanding of foreign policy directions), will broaden the scope of the relationship. Strategic interests and similar geo political conditions could only facilitate such eventuality. How these factors are best utilised, will determine the future ties of two of the most important players in the Asia pacific region.

A strategic relationship between India and Australia will be influenced by the continuation of the alliance partnership with America and India's own relations with USA, the emergence of new and strong powers in the region as well as Australia's aspiration to achieve greater status in the ladder of state power. The engaging and of late triumphant military presence of Australia in its immediate neighbourhood as a policeman, strongman or as America's 'deputy' points to the capability of use of force to further interests including maritime ones. Though the current trends of defence spending and planning are at modest levels, with the changing regional (that may well extend to the IOR in the near future) strategic environment, and/or a radical national government and more importantly, perhaps an inclination to achieve greater power status, the logic for more effective defence spending could pave the way for a force with a "strategic edge". Lastly, growth of the regional players like India, China and even Indonesia in the economic, military and political sense could be treated as inimical to Australian interests and thus entail 'caliberated' response. West Asian security currency and the outcome of control of resources and states in the African littoral could also increase Australia's involvement in the world politics. Although the path towards a structured, more concrete strategic partnership with Australia is a remote possibility, it is fraught with issues and concerns. The road to full-fledged strategic partnership with Australia thus, has to be trodden with as much caution as enthusiasm.

Notes

1. For a detailed discussion of various aspects refer, Dennis Rumley, D.Gopal,eds.. India and Australia: Opportunities, (Aurthors press, New Delhi, 2004).

2. The transition away from bipolarity in International Relations has taken place and the debate on the system that has replaced it is ensuing. For an interesting discussion refer, B. Ramesh Babu, "Towards Non-Hegemonic Globalisation", in Bernard D'Sami, G.Gopa Kumar (eds.), In pursuit of American Studies Experience of South India, (South India American Studies Network, Chennai, 2002), pp. 240- 248.

3. C.S. Kuppusamy, India's Look East Policy: more aggressive, better dividends paper no.1663, 3.1.2006.

4. HON. AL GRASSBY, AM, Book review, Labour History, Volume 83, Nov 2002, pp 222.

5. Is the Australia-India relationship gaining momentum? An observer's view by Dillip Dutta Monday, 15 March 2004.

6. Marjorie Barnard, A History of Australia, (Frederick A. Praeger, New York, 1963). p.91.

7. Ibid., p.127.

8. http://www.atributetohinduism.com/Women_in_Hinduism.htm.

9. Australian with 19th century India links remembered: Plaque unveiled in Mussoorie, Australian High Commission, News Release, 12, August 2005. http://www.ausgovindia.com/public/news/2005/050812.htm.

10. A.T. Yarwood, Walers - Australian Horses Abroad, (Melbourne University Press, Melbourne, 1989), pp 40-41.

11. C.R.B. Barrett, History of XIII Hussars, 13th Light Dragoons history of H.M. 13th Light Dragoons, (William Blackwood & Sons, London 1911).

12. http://www.yarramalong.net/about_walers.htm.

13. The Leader (Melbourne) 5 January 1901, p. 23.

14. Grant McMurdo, Australian Foreign policy, Victorian Association for Social Science Teachers, Victorian Certification of Education (VASST VCE) Issue paper, February 2002, http://www.vasst.asn.au.

15. Ric Shand, Text of Basham 2000 lecture on "India: A New beginning", Faculty of Asian studies, Australian National University website, www.anu.edu.au/asianstudies/bash2.html.

16. The South Indian kings conquered parts of South East Asia and the influence is pronounced in the cultural realm to this day (as evident from the Indonesian traditional theatre form called Gamelan where the epic Ramayana is performed. See Peter Stack's East meets East in a Hindu Epic, San Francisco Chronicle, March 30, 1997), and also by the political and economic clout of the ethnic population settled there.

17. P.R.Chari, "Fiji and Indo Australian ties", The Hindu, 19 July 2000.

18. Lt. Col. Bhupinder Singh, Indian Ocean and Regional Security, (B.C. Publishers, Patiala, 1983), p. 63.

19. Caroline Lambert. 2000. Address to the Joint Committee on Foreign Affairs and Trade on Australia's role in the United Nations in the Post Cold war environment on Feb 21, 2000. Women's rights action network's website.

20. Ric Shand, n.16.

21. Khalid A-H Ansari, Lest we forget, Mid-day April 26, 2005 http://web.mid-day.com/news/world/2005/april/108163.htm.

22. The Gallipoli Campaign, Australian dept of Veterans' affairs,http://www.dva.gov.au/commem/commac/studies/anzacsk/aday4.htm.

23. Richard Gehrmann The Forgotten Indian Connection: Australian Soldiers of the Raj: 1919-1939abstract at the War, Society, And Culture: Approaches And Issues conference, Newcastle War Society and Culture Symposium, 2 November 2001, http://www.newcastle.edu.au/group/wsc/conference2001/symp2001abstracts.html.

24. Jcnnclle Bonnor, 2001. Australia - India Security Relations: Common interest or Disinterest? , Working Paper 67, Australian Defence Studies Centre, p.12.http://idun.itsc.adfa.edu.au/ADSC/pub-wp.htm

25. Ibid., p.13.

26. For a detailed discussion on the issue see, Ruth Rae, Reading between unwritten lines: Australian Army nurses in India, 1916-19, Journal of the Australian War Memorial, No36, May 2002 Source: http://www.awm.gov.au/journal/j36/nurses.htm.

27. John Howard, Media Release, 12, May 1998.

28. Alexander Downer, "Australian response to India's nuclear tests" Media Release, 14 May, 1998.

29. Ric Shand, n.16.

30. Christopher Waters', "War, Decolonization and Postwar Security " in David Goldsworthy (ed.), Facing North: A Century of Australian Engagement with Asia, Vol. 1, (Melbourne University Press, 2001), p. 130.

31. J.D. Legge, Australian Outlook: A history of Australian Institute of International Affairs, (Allen& Unwin, Sydney, 1999), pp 84-5.

32. Article on India-Australia Relations, www.abs.gov.au.

33. Howard's Indian overture, The Observer, 15, July 2000.

34. A voyage of renewal, The Hindu, 13, July, 2000.

35. Australian High commission, News Release, PA13/2000, June 20,2000 from www.ausgovindia.com.

36. "India and Australia," The Observer, 21, October 2000.

37. Huma Siddiqui, "Economic and regional security to figure in dialogue with Australia", Financial Express, July 6, 2001.

38. Ravi Tomar, "Australia India Relations: Strategic Convergence?," Research Note no 5, 200102, Department of Parliamentary Library, Commonwealth of Australia, Canberra, 2001, p.2, from www.aph.gov.au/library/pubs/rn/2001-0-/02rn05.pdf.

39. Official visit of the Australian Minister for Foreign Affairs, Mr. Alexander Downer to India on June 7 -10, 2005.

40. Ibid., p.207.

41. Memorandum Tange to Casey, Policy Critique, 22 June 1955, pp.6 & 8, Tange papers DFAT.

42. Alan Watt, Australian Diplomat: Memoirs of Sir Alan Watt, (Angus &Robertson, Sydney, 1972), Martin A, Robert, Menzies : A Life, Vol 2, 1944-1978, (Melbourne University Press, Melbourne 1999), pp.174-5

43. Alexander Downer, Text of Speech titled 'Advancing The National Interest: Australia's Foreign Policy Challenge' May 7,2002. p.5. www.australianpolitics.com.

44. White Paper on Defence Policy, Defence 2000-Our Future Defence Force, (Commonwealth of Australia, Canberra, 2000), p.33.

45. Australian Bureau of Statistics, Evolution of Australia's Strategic Defence Policy – special article on defence in Year book Australia 2001. www.abs.gov.au.

46. The policy pronouncement of the Labor party on its official websitewww.alp.org.au//policy/platform2000/chapter_15.html.

47. Alexander Downer, n.44.

48. David Galsworthy (ed.), Facing North: A Century of Engagement with Asia, Vol.1, (DFAT, Melbourne University Press, Melbourne, 2001), p.205.

49. H.E. Ms Penny Wensley Ao "India's Changing Regional and Global Outlook - and Emerging Opportunities for Australia as a Result of Shifting Policies" Speech to Asia Society And Australia-India Business Council, Hyde Park Room Sheraton On The Park, Sydney, Friday 27 June 2003.

50. Robyn Lim, "Australia and Maritime Security Okazaki Institute-special presentation", www.okazaki-inst/okazaki-eng.htm.

51. Aldo Borgu, Reshaping the ADF, ASPI,www.aspi.org.au/reshaping_ADF_AB.pdf.

52. Indian Maritime Doctrine, Integrated Headquarters, Ministry of Defence (Navy) June 2004, p.133.

53. Desmond Ball (ed.), Maintaining the Strategic Edge: The Defence of Australia in 2015, Canberra Papers on Strategy and Defence, No.133, Strategic and Defence Studies Centre, Research School of Pacific and Asian Studies, (ANU Canberra, 1999), p.2.

54. SIPRI data on Australia's military expenditure as percentage of GDP,1988-2001.

22

India-New Zealand: Economic Transaction and Cultural Swapping

G.Vijay Kumar Reddy and M. Prayaga

Discovered by the Dutch navigator Abel Tasman (1603-1659) in 1642, New Zealand was nominally annexed to Britain at the instance of James Cook (1728-1779), in 1769, but only in 1840, the islands were formally annexed by the home government. In the sequel, constant and increasing friction began to befall between the Maoris, the high-spirited and vigorous natives and the White population of traders and fugitive convicts from Australia and others. The Maoris, perhaps the most intelligent of semi-indigenous races of the world, having initially offered resistance, gradually emerged as a body of useful citizens of New Zealand, being cultured and interesting folks. Thus, besides preserving the Maoris, New Zealand in due course, chose to preserve the self-governing system that had been in force there, over years.

Right from the beginning, New Zealand's population, as in the case of Australia, has been enlarged by a net immigration which, being at once in excess and frequent, seems to have made New Zealand even more definitely a marginal land than Australia. In fact, with a more heavy and more reliable rainfall and with a more equable and more temperate climate than Australia, the islands have been more suited to a large population probably, than Australia and life has been, on the whole, less difficult for the individuals. New Zealand has been one of the pioneer states in matters of sincere attempts to secure the well-being of all its people. There, a comparative handful of Whites have managed in the mass, to live and prosper with some success in a land, which has many natural advantages.

The inception of Indian immigration to New Zealand dates back to late 18th century. The British East India Company ships having carried shipments to Australia, used to anchor in New Zealand 'to pickup homeward cargoes' and Indians working in the British East India Company most of whom being sepoys (Soldiers) and lascars (Indian Shipmen), [1] became so enamoured of New Zealand's beauty that they abruptly broke their voyage and abandoned the ships forthwith, to settle in the islands and thus, Indian immigration may be said to have had strange beginnings as far as New Zealand was concerned. Today, Indians readily recognize New Zealand as a cricket-loving and cricket-playing nation and as a country where Indian films are being shot frequently in view of the island's scenic splendour and spectacular scenery.

Prior to 1880, Indians were not enumerated in the New Zealand census records though the impact of their presence was felt. One of the records shows, that a Bengali man, having abandoned the British Naval vessel, had married a Maori woman in 1810. According to some other records a man of Indian origin had lived along with his Maori wife in the Bay of Islands in 1815 and another Indian had lived in Stewart Island, in 1814. For the first time, the 1881 census of New Zealand officially recorded the presence of six Indian men who had lived in Canterbury and worked as servants of a wealthy English family that had arrived from India. [2]

Indian immigration to New Zealand increased gradually, during the years 1890-1900. By 1896, the number of Indians increased to 46 and by 1916, the number was 181 including 14 females. Most of the Indians who had left for New Zealand during the early phase of immigration, were from the Navsari and Surat regions of Gujarat and also from Jalandhar and Hoshiarpur in Punjab.

During the early years of immigration, most of the Indians worked as cheap labourers, building roads, collecting bottles and selling vegetables and fruits. Most of them resided in Christchurch and Auckland. The Indian population by 1945, had numbered 1,554 and the Indian immigrants had to face racial attacks from the members of the 'White New Zealand league', established in 1926. The main aim of the league was to oppose the immigration of the Chinese and the Indians because the members of the league felt that both Indians and Chinese posed a threat to the racial purity, and the economic prosperity of the European New Zealanders. Because of the nefarious activities of this league, Indians were forbidden from entering barber shops, private bars and from occupying the balcony seats in theatres and were not allowed to join any association. [3]

Gradually, Indians became united and formed a united front to get their rights safeguarded and to promote and propagate Indian values and culture. The Auckland Indian Association was the first organisation of its kind. During 1950's and 60's, some of the Indian associations started conducting classes in Gujarati language and culture for the benefit of younger people. Many of the language classes continue even today. Formal teaching of Hindi began in Wellington in 1985. By the year 1921 itself, the Indians in the island nation, started a Gujarati monthly News Paper *Aryodaya*. This was followed by another periodical *Uday* which was published between the years 1933 and 1935. An English paper was published by the Indian community, known as *Indian Chronicle*, but was a short lived one in 1972. [4]

India and New Zealand have been enjoying friendly and cordial relations. In the early part of the 20th century, the common bonds as identified, between the two nations were commonwealth, parliamentary democracy, English language and sports. [5] Sports arena has been a common bond between the two countries since a long time. New Zealand made its Olympic hockey debut in Montreal in 1956. Indian Hockey team was the only team that played with New Zealand apart from Australia, before 1956. New Zealand and India share a special kind of relationship in the game of hockey. The first overseas tour of the Indian hockey team, to New Zealand was, in 1926. The tour of the Indian Army Hockey team in 1926 saw the emergence of the legendary hockey player Lance Naik Dhyan Chand, who scored 201 goals in just 43 matches in the three overseas tours that followed the 1926 tour to New Zealand. [6]

Ashok Kumar, the son of Dyan Chand, toured New Zealand, decades after the 1935 tour. On the tour, an old goalkeeper chanced to meet Ashok Kumar on a wheelchair and said:

Your father was a marvel. I saved his first shot at goal by diving full length to my right. The second shot at goal was far to my left. I dived and saved yet again. Then Dhyan Chand said - if you save my next shot, I will stop playing hockey. True to his word, on his next possession, Dhyan Chand hit a scorcher right over my head to the centre of the net. The gap between my head and the bar was very little but the ball went through into the goal [7]

Maoris, the original inhabitants of New Zealand, had the unique distinction of presenting a trophy for the national hockey championship of both India and Pakistan. During the 1935 Indian hockey tour of New Zealand, the Maoris presented the Indian hockey team with a shield in appreciation of the performance of the Indian team. This Maori shield, later on became the official trophy of Indian national hockey championship. But it is very unfortunate that today, the shield is in Pakistan because in 1946, the undivided Punjab had won the national hockey championship and in 1947, with the formation of Pakistan, West Punjab remained with Pakistan. The newly formed West Punjab Hockey Association refused to return the shield to India. Thus, today the Maori shield is the symbol of hockey supremacy in Pakistan. [8]

Apart from hockey, cricket is one of the major sporting events between the two nations. The cricket loving Indian community have started many sports associations and sports clubs, the important one being New Zealand Indian Sports Association established in 1960's. The important Indian migrants who represented New Zealand in the international events of the sports are, Ramesh and Mohan in hockey in 1976 Olympics, and Dipak Patel in cricket who had played for New Zealand recently. [9]

Although there are nearly 55,000 [10] of Indian migrants today in New Zealand, the relations between the two nations continued to be tenuous until 1990's. But after 1990, there had been an increase in the high level visits between New Zealand and India. The initiation of 'Look East Policy' by India in 1990's and India's active participation in the high profile regional organisations such as ASEAN, and ARF, brought India into a region wherein New Zealand has been trying to make deep inroads. India's profound interest in the Pacific Island states came to the fore when in 2003, India became a dialogue partner in the Pacific Forum. [11] The recently concluded East Asian Summit in which, both India and New Zealand are members, has provided a convenient platform for both the nations, to foster strong relations.

With regard to trade between the two countries, while 'services trade' has been growing substantially, the merchandise trade between the two nations, is yet to realise its full potential. To promote trade and business, to identify the areas of potential cooperation, and to develop the means of augmenting the trade turnover, both the nations had signed a Trade Agreement, during Prime Minister Rajiv Gandhi's visit to New Zealand in October 1986, in accordance with which a Joint Business Council (JBC) and a Joint Trade Committee (JTC), were established. The first meeting of India - New Zealand JTC was held in New Delhi on 4-5 June 1987, in which, both the sides agreed to create a conducive environment for trade expansion and to develop trade relations on a fast track. Since then, JTC has met 10 times, the tenth meeting having been held in Bombay, in 2005. [12]

In the present world of globalisation, the strength of economic relationships between the two nations, is often measured by the bilateral trade in goods. According to the indicator, the New-Zealand and India economic relationship has been steady, but has neither mustered its full strength nor gained momentum. There are indications that the trade ties between the two, are poised enough for prospective growth. India has become New Zealand's twenty seventh largest trading partner and twenty seventh most important destination for New Zealand's merchandise exports. [13] In fact, the balance of trade between the two nations, has improved from a negative $32.3 million in 1999-2000, to $6.19 million in 2003-2004 (Table 22.1). [14]

The data for 2004-05 on Australia was collected from the Ministry of Commerce and Industry, ***Annual Report, 2005-2006***, Govt. of India, New Delhi, 2006). These values, given in Indian currency (Rupees), were converted into US$ @ exchange rate of Rs. 44.9315 = 1 US $.

As displayed in the table, India's trade with Australia exposes fluctuation in the growth rates of imports and exports, whereas India's trade with New Zealand shows a trend distinguished by a consistent growth.

New Zealand has been exporting no cereals. Initially except for some gold and some coal that were imbedded in mines, the country used to depend almost entirely on its production of wool and meat with a later addition of the dairy products (which eventually took the first place among the exports from the islands) and others like fruits. The relative side of the annual wool clip has been an additional indication of the marginal character of the New Zealand's situation because the wool is the first product in the sequence of the exploited products of the great farming areas of the world and hence, the second place that New Zealand occupies today, in the export of wool. With regard to the wool exports New Zealand has to its credit, 30 per cent of the share in India-New Zealand trade worth US$ 57.5 million, compared to the share in India-Australia trade worth US$ 82.4 million by the end of 2004. [15] Therefore, India can concentrate on improving the trade relations with New Zealand in the Pacific region regarding other commodities like the dairy products and thus scrupulously avoid depending entirely on Australia. India has ample opportunities at its beck and call, to improve mutual trade and to realise full potential of the bilateral relations. A reference to a commodity like Timber which occupies 23.35 per cent in the New Zealand's imports to India, may not be out of place here.

The major items that are being exported to New Zealand from India, are readymade garments, linen, diamonds, pharmaceuticals, sports equipment, footwear and leather items. Apparel and

Table 22.1: Bilateral Trade between India and New Zealand

(Value in US $ million)

Sl. No.	EXPORTS	2000-01	2001-02	2002-03	2003-04	2004-05
1.	to New Zealand	**63.28** (405.87)	**62.21** (418.02)	**67.70** (504.18)	**85.97** (584.30)	**88.76** (450.35)
	per cent Growth	(0.64)	-1.69 (2.99)	8.82 (20.61)	27.00 (15.89)	3.25 (-29.74)
2.	India's Total Exports	44,560.29	43,826.73	52,719.43	63,842.97	80,540.19
	per cent Growth		-1.65	20.29	21.10	26.15
3.	per cent Share (1÷2)	0.14 (0.91)	0.14 (0.96)	0.13 (0.96)	0.13 (0.92)	0.11 (0.56)
	IMPORTS					
4	from New Zealand	**79.34** (1062.76)	**82.17** (1306.10)	**76.40** (1336.79)	**78.89** (2649.24)	**107.25** (2761.20)
	per cent Growth		3.57 (22.90)	-7.02 (2.30)	3.25 (98.18)	35.95 (4.23)
5.	India's Total Imports	50,536.46	51,413.29	61,412.13	78,149.61	109,173.23
	per cent Growth		1.74	19.45	27.25	39.70
6.	per cent Share (4÷6)	0.16 (2.10)	0.16 (2.54)	0.12 (2.18)	0.10 (3.39)	0.10 (2.52)
	TOTAL TRADE					

Contd...

7.	**with New Zealand**	**142.61** (1468.570)	**144.38** (1724.14)	**144.10** (1840.97)	**164.86** (3222.54)	**196.02** (3211.55)
8.	per cent Growth		1.24 (17.40)	-0.19 (6.78)	14.41 (75.64)	18.90 (-0.68)
9.	India's Total World Trade	95,096.75	95,240.01	114,131.56	141,992.58	189,713.42
	per cent Growth		0.15	19.84	24.41	33.61
10.	per cent Share (7÷9)	0.15 (1.54)	0.15 (1.81)	0.13 (1.61)	0.12 (2.28)	0.10 (1.69)
	TRADE BALANCE					
	India's Trade Balance with New Zealand	**-5,976.16** (-605.89)	**-7,586.56** (-888.06)	**-8,692.70** (-832.61)	**-14,306.65** (-2064.94)	**-28,633.04** (-2310.85)
	Exchange rate: (1US$ = Rs.)	45.6844	47.6919	48.3953	45.9513	44.9315

Note: Figures given in parentheses refer to Australia.
Source: www.ciionline.org/common/92/countryDetail.asp

footwear (21.5 per cent) continued to be the largest export commodities to New Zealand, Textiles (20.4 per cent) and others, being floor coverings, metal products, sports goods, and marine equipment. [16]

Dairy products is one of the important items of imports into India from New Zealand. 'Fonterra' one of the New Zealand's largest dairy products divisions, entered the Indian market as 'New Zealand Milk'. The consumer products division of Fonterra, established a joint venture with Britannia Industries, which form India's largest food products division. Craig Norgate the Chief Executive of Fonterra said, that the agreements with Britannia would provide the dairy industry of New Zealand a 'strategic point of entry' into world's fourth largest economy. He further said:

India's total dairy market, at NZ 50 bn, is one of the worlds biggest. Steady growth and liberalisation of India's economy has opened up attractive opportunities for investment in the country's dairy industry. [17]

Apart from other commodities, the agricultural products by themselves make a sector where there is a lot of potential to be tapped by both the nations. For all its high percentage dependence on agriculture, India's agricultural imports had remained very low, and this condition had been attributed to the levels of tariff and non tariff protection in the sector. High tariffs on items of New Zealand's interest, restricted India's exports to New Zealand. Moreover, the stringent New Zealand laws on agricultural products, stood in the way of imports and exports. New Zealand's economy is very much dependent on agriculture, horticulture and forest products and the laws of New Zealand strictly restrict the introduction of any agricultural products, due to pests. [18] In the words of Dr. Malcolm Cone, who headed a group of researchers from Asian Institute, the University of Otago, to study the potential Kiwi investment in India, has said:

Take the agricultural sector. In India food production is very large industry second only to China in the production, however up to 40 percent of perishable produce is wasted because there is inadequate storage and transporting facilities available in the more isolated agricultural producing regions. New Zealand has proven expertise in the transport and storage of agricultural products, which could be introduced to the Indian markets. Bio Technology is another area for economic partnerships. [19]

In recent times, the trade profile has been completely in for a change with the trade base getting diversified into differently specialised and manufactured products such as electric transformers, sorting machinery, transmission and telecommunications equipment, vehicles, plastic and plastic products and pharmaceuticals. [20] Yet another important area that has huge potential is, forestry. To meet the growing demand in the construction field and other industries, India, while protecting its forest wealth, seeks to import timber. With large reserves of harvested timber, New Zealand is a natural choice for the import of timber. [21]

Both the nations have been taking effective steps to improve bilateral trade. India and New Zealand have entered into an agreement in 1999, to avoid double taxation. [22] India New Zealand Joint Business Council was established in 1988, in order to bring together the business sectors of both the countries to look ahead for prospects in the field of Information Technology. On December 7, 2001 both the governments have entered into an agreement to promote ties in Information Technology. [23]

Tourism

In the services trade, both the nations have immense potential for cooperation. Especially in the tourism sector, New Zealand views India as an extremely potential market, in future. With nearly five million passengers travelling abroad from India in 2005, India has become one of the important tourism markets in the world. New Zealand is also one of the nations of scenic beauty in the world. Nearly 120 Indian films, have been shot in New Zealand. These Films served as an advertisement and publicity for the New Zealand Tourism. The number of Indian visitors to New Zealand, has been on the rise. Approximately, 17,300 visited New Zealand in 2002, 16,000 in 2003, 19,800 in 2004 and nearly

20,000 in 2005. The number of Indian tourists to New Zealand is expected to reach 40,000 to 50,000 by 2007. [24]

In 2003 itself, 'Tourism New Zealand' had opened its office in Mumbai. This office in India has launched a special programme in September 2004, to develop a group of well trained and educated travel agents, particularly to promote an awareness among the Indians about New Zealand and its tourist attractions. By May 2005, there were about 230 Kiwi Specialist Travel Agents, in India. [25]

Education

Education, a sacred institution that has come down to us from time immemorial, is one of the service sectors receiving a lot of attention from New Zealand government. Taking its cue from the UK, the US, Australia and other western countries, New Zealand has been trying to encourage the Indian students, to seek admission into colleges and universities in New Zealand. In fact, India and New Zealand have signed the Education Cooperation Agreement (ECA) on March 29, 2005. The ECA was signed by Shri Arjun Singh, Minister for Human Resource Development on behalf of India, and Mr. Trevor Mallard, Minister for Education, on behalf of New Zealand. The highlights of ECA are:

1. Exchange of research materials, publications, educational literature, teaching aids, demonstration material and information;
2. Organization of joint conferences, exhibitions and seminars;
3. Organization of joint research programmes and publications;
4. Organization of training programmes for educational administrators and teachers;
5. Exchange of academic and other administrative staff;
6. Exchange of scholars, teachers, experts and students;
7. Twinning arrangements between institutions of higher learning;
8. Setting up of educational/training programmes between institutions of educational excellence in technical, vocational and higher education;

9. Setting up of chairs on contemporary studies;
10. Providing scholarships for further education in recognized institutions of higher learning;
11. Providing mutual assistance in the fields of IT, computer, mathematics and science. [26]

New Zealand's education sector has succeeded in attracting a good number of Indian students. By January 2005, there were nearly 2500 Indian students pursing higher studies in New Zealand. Of these, 703 were in the universities, 579, at private training establishments, 590, at polytechnics 102 students in the state private primary or secondary schools and colleges of education whereas 439 did not have their education recorded. The New Zealand education network holds annual fairs in the important urban centres in India, to attract more and more students to New Zealand's universities and colleges. [27]

Information Technology

Information technology is one of the key areas of interest for the New Zealand business community. New Zealand is well aware of the growing IT market and the benefits that India's IT industry offers in 'high end skills'. New Zealand's Prime Minister who visited Bangalore in 2004 said: "We see enormous opportunity to collaborate with the Indian IT industry, which has achieved a global scale of operation." Clarke also expressed optimism to the reporters thus: "with large ideas from India's global firms, we too can incubate start ups. There is every possibility of cooperation." [28]

New Zealand is fast becoming one of the major outsourcing destinations for major IT projects. Independent analysts Gartner and A.T .Kearney have identified New Zealand in the pacific, as one of the world's most attractive centres for off shore IT development work. The consultancy firm A.T. Kearney, has ranked New Zealand as a 12th one among the 25 top outsourcing destinations in the world. In fact, in the IT circles, New Zealand is referred to, as 'new India'. In 2001 itself, India and New Zealand had entered into an agreement for Cooperation in the Area of

Information Technology and Services. As per the agreement, both the parties have agreed to identify the areas of common interest for potential cooperation. Some of the areas of common interest identified, are:

- General policy and regulatory approaches;
- Software and multi-media content development;
- Advanced communications technologies;
- Internet applications;
- E-commerce consumer protection policies;
- Cross-border issues such as cyber-crime, intellectual property rights, privacy and the security of applications of e-commerce and information industries.

Cooperation in the above areas will be promoted through the development of relations between business, research bodies, educational institutions, central and local government agencies and other organisations concerned with progress in the information industries. [29]

Conclusion

According to Peter Hobbs, the Trade Commissioner, for New Zealand Trade and Enterprise, based in New Delhi, "India is not a market for the faint hearted. But with the world's second largest population and a growing economy, exporters should seriously consider the opportunities this huge and dynamic country offers." [30] India with huge population and wide diversity of market segments (high, medium and low income, rural and urban) offers ample opportunity for consumer and industry products. India's focus on several new areas to boost economic growth, would offer more opportunities for Indian exporters. With the availability of cheap labour and low cost infrastructure, India has been contemplating an increase in its share of world's outsourced manufacturing. This development in a way, offers New Zealand companies, numerous opportunities in the field of consultancy and technology for food processing, education and also methods, to improve the low level of productivity. In recent years, there has been an increase in high level visits reflecting a paramount importance both the sides are now attaching to the taking of the bilateral ties to new heights. New Zealand's Prime Minister Helen Clarke visited India in October 2004, to promote business and to foster closer ties between Auckland and New Delhi, in the areas of trade and tourism. She was accompanied by a business delegation besides the representatives of Indian Community in New Zealand and senior officials. She is the first Prime Minister of New Zealand to visit India in almost two decades after the late Prime Minister David Lange's visit in 1985. Complimenting India on the efficacy of its Look East policy and its impact on the growing India-New Zealand partnership, Premier Clarke observed:

We are aware that India's 'Look East' Policy looks as far as New Zealand. India, like New Zealand, has well developed interest and partnerships with East Asia, especially through its dialogue partner status with ASEAN and participation in the ASEAN Regional Forum. As India looks east, its interests increasingly intersect with those of New Zealand and we see India's interest in East Asia and the Pacific as appropriate and in keeping with the role a country of India's size and stature will play in the 21st century. [31]

On tracing the evolution of India-New Zealand relations, one feels like concluding by remaining true to facts that, compared to India-Australia relations, the course of India-New Zealand relations, has run smooth, but for mild and short lived threats of strain enroute, as New Zealand gave the impression of impulsively recalling its ambassadors along with Australia, though scrupulously refrained from making anything like an adverse comment on India's nuclear tests.

Notes

1. www.teara.govt.nz/NewZealanders/NewZealandPeoples/indians.html.
2. *Ibid.*
3. www.tepapa.govt.nz/LEARNING/AAINA/cermonies/indians_nz.html.

4. www.teara.govt.nz/NewZealanders/NewZealandPeoples/indians.html.

5. www.hicomind.org.nz/indo_nz_relations.html

6. www.bharatiyahockey.org/olympics/2004/NewZealand.html

7. *Ibid.*

8. *Ibid.*

9. www.teara.govt.nz/NewZealanders/NewZealandPeoples/indians.html

10. L.M. Singhvi, *Report of the high Level Committee on the Indian Diaspora* Ministry of External Affairs Foreign Secretary's Office, Ministry of External Affairs, 2001.

11. www.mfat.govt.nz/Foreignregions/sea/countrypapers/indiapaper.com.

12. www.hicomind.org.nz/indo_nz_relations.html.

13. "Country Focus: New Zealand", *Bombay Chamber International Trade News*, Vol. vii, No. 10, October 2005.

14. *The Hindu*, 21-10-2004.

15. "Country Focus: New Zealand", *Bombay Chamber International Trade News*, October 2005.

16. www.prosperity4.com/information/news/viewarticles.html.

17. www.findarticles.com/p/articles/mi_mODQA/is_2001.html.

18. www.mfat.govt.nz/Foreignregions/sea/countrypapers/indiapaper.com.

19. www.otago.ac.nz/news/2005/21/10.html.

20. www.ficci.com/immage.

21. www.indianewslink.co.nz/march.2.2005.html

22. For full text of agreement see, www.incometaxindia.gov.in/doublepercent20agreement_in.html

23. For full text of agreement see, www.ecommerce.govt.nz/international.html

24. www.tourismnewzealand.com.

25. *Ibid.*

26. www.sarkaritel.com/news_and_features/apr2005/20indnzeducation.html.

27. www.listener.co.nz.html.

28. www.indiadaily.com/editorial/10-19e-04.asp.

29. www.ecommerce.govt.nz/international/ indianzagreement.html.

30. www.24X7updates.com/fullstory.news.html.

31. www.indiannewslink.co.nz/10_special_issue/opinion_2html.

23

Indian Community in Australia

Y. Yagama Reddy

Super Continent Connection, yet Culturally Disconnected

In recent times, Australia and India, the two Indian Ocean littoral states, have been underscoring the commonalities between them, as if they have discovered them, of late. Geological history points out, that the 'gondwana' super-continent encompassing Antarctica, Australia and the Indian subcontinent, remained a single landmass, until 160 million years ago. Having been separated from Antarctica, the other two components drifted away to the present geomatical location. This shared geological past is testified to, by the similarities in the mining conditions between Australia and India which have of late, begun adopting similar mining techniques.

Lest any attempt to understand the 'continental drift' mechanism should make us drift away from the main focus of this paper, the reference to the Quaternary geology which offers a fascinating account of early human contacts across this region need not be out of place here. The exposed vast stretch of sea bed following the fall of sea level by 100 meters during the last and fourth glaciation period around 20,000 years ago, obviously served as a land bridge to facilitate the migration of ancient (primitive) man along with plant and animal species as far east as Australia. Though the research in human genetics found no conclusive evidence of the blood group compatibility between the indigenous people in southern India and in Australia respectively, there are certain ethno-linguistic features which point to the prehistoric links between these indigenous people in both, during the late Stone Age. The post-glaciation period, marked by the rise of sea level to the present level, had witnessed the land bodies acquiring the present shape in the form of several thousands of islands straddling between the Indian sub-continent and Australia.

It is of much significance to note that the sea and climate were at the root of early cultural contacts between India and Southeast Asia for almost 1,500 years from the beginning of the Christian era - the period which forms a glorious chapter in the cultural history of India and Southeast Asia. Indian acculturation in Southeast Asia, had been so profound that the Indian cultural base had even endured the Western cultural influence, exerted under the European colonial rule. It is quite amazing to learn that the Indian culture did not reach the shores of Australia which thus remained in the moribund backwaters while Indianization process in Southeast Asia was rapid. As I have discussed in one of my research papers, [1] the turbulent monsoon winds getting deflected perpendicularly at the equator would have deterred the attempts of navigators to cross the equator, with the help of their rudimentary ship-craft which could sail all along the direction of monsoon winds across the Bay of Bengal. The argument that the non-availability of tropical produce in Australia would have discouraged the adventurers of navigation, is quite untenable in the absence of any kind of knowledge of the geography of this island-continent until and after the voyages of Captain Cook in late 18th Century.

Indian Migrations into Australia in 19th Century

For all the trading links between India and Australia established during the rule of British East India Company, these two countries remained apart. Geoffrey Blainey, Australia's renowned historian, remarked that "Australia seemed to be a satellite of India as well as a colony of England." [2] But Blainey's observation could not sustain in view of an official opposition to the attempts of Australian pastoralists to import the indentured labour from India. Though the recruitment of cheap Indian farm labour for Australia was proposed as early as 1779, the itinerant Indians seemed to have started migrating to Australia since 1792. [3] In the midst of immigration restrictions, and discrimination towards Indians, the pioneering Indian immigrants were known to have arrived in Queensland early in the modern history of Australia. [4]

By 1838, there were 250 Indians who were classified under the category of "and others"; and their number rose to 350 in 1850, [5] many of whom were Sikhs. It was during this formative phase, that the British settlement in Australia was not evenly carried out. When substantially large number of Europeans began to settle in other states of Australia, its population crossed the mark of 1.0 million by 1860s. In 1861, the Indian population in Australia was estimated at 2500. [6] Subsequently, a change in the attitude of Australian government towards Indian labour, was noticed. As a result, the increase in Indian-born people in Australia was largely on account of the movement of 'camel drivers' from northwestern India (now in Pakistan) and the agricultural workers who were drafted as indentured labour for the cultivation of sugarcane and banana in Queensland in late 19th century.

Australia's White Policy Restrictions

When Australia became a federated state in 1901, the Indian population stood at 7760. [7] The Immigration Restriction Act (1901), which came to be known as White Policy, halted the Indian immigration until 1920s when the Reciprocity Act officially removed the restrictions. The cattle industry in 1920s, served as a "pull" factor for another spell of Indian immigration. Nonetheless, there were restrictions imposed on the Indians seeking residential status, despite their being declared as the British subjects. Even then, by 1947, there were 8162 Indians including those Indians who were born in Australia; and their strength got almost doubled (15574) by 1966 when Australia abandoned its White Policy. [8]

The Onrush of Indian Immigration

The change of policy facilitated the settlement of about 6,400 Indian immigrants during the decade of 1961-71. According to Gwenda Tavan at the School of Social Sciences in La Trobe

University, this low volume of Indian immigrants was due mainly to the "unwillingness and indifference of Indians" to Australia. With the immigration of about 46,500 during the two consecutive decades (1971-91), the total of Indian population rose to 61,602 which included about 41,000 people settled in New South Wales, Victoria and Western Australia. [9] The 9,000 Sikh population, constituting 15 per cent of the total Indian population, is also largely concentrated in the above 3 states, particularly in the cities of Sydney (3,000) and Melbourne (3,000). [10] In the context of post-Cold War globalization scenario, the Indian population (95,455) in 2001 [11] was close to the mark of 1 lakh which, though accounted for just 0.5 per cent of the total Australian population (about 19 million), represented a decadal increase of more than 60 per cent over the 1991 population (61,602). It is interesting to note that at the turn of this century, as per the Australian Bureau of Statistics, there were 156,624 Australians of Indian ancestry, either by virtue of migration or by birth in Australia with at least one Indian parent. This proportion (0.73 per cent) of Australians in possession of Indian heritage-base, is now reckoned as a significant factor for developing people-to-people contacts and for promoting the understanding of India among the Australians. [12]

It is against this backdrop of demographic character (over space and time), that the immigration of Indians into Australia has become a debatable, though not disputable topic at various levels. Far beyond the academic exercise of probing into the 'push' and 'pull' factors for an international migration pattern, there are 3 Es lying at the base of Australia becoming a fascinating destination for Indians. The 3 Es include: Educational facilities, Employment opportunities and Entrepreneurship avenues, which need to be considered as 'pull' factors for the recent Indian migration to Australia on a large scale.

Australia a Preferred Destination for Indians

Enterprising Avenues for Investment: India had for long, pursued the 'inward-looking' policy characterized by an unwholesome obsession with the South Asian politics and protectionism towards its industry and service sectors. In the context of post-Cold War imperatives, India was forced to stir out of the fortress of its traditional inhibitions and embark on perusing the path of globalization. India's Look East Policy (LEP) launched in 1992, has been in pursuit of getting its ties with Southeast Asian neighbours resurrected, as well as getting its partnership with the other countries in the Asia-Pacific region forged and fortified. Australia's efforts at 'rediscovering' India, have also stimulated the process of the bilateral partnership mustering strength. On the basis of the recommendations of the 1990 Senate Standing Committee, Australian government established Australia-India Council (AIC) as a statutory body to get the bilateral relations strengthened through the 'track-II' initiatives.

As a part of its Look West strategy, Australia organized 'India Today 1994' festival to showcase the trade and investment opportunities for Australians, in India. Subsequently in 1996, 'Australia – India New Horizons' promotion campaign was held in 6 major Indian cities to promote Australian culture, technology and business. Thanks to the bipartisan support extended to the efforts of both the governments at developing a "dynamic and forward looking approach to the bilateral relationship", there have been visible positive trends as in the case of bilateral trade and investment flows. The quantum of bilateral trade has grown to A $ 5.6 billion in 2004 [13] from a meagre trade of A $ 0.9 billion in 1990 [14] making India, the Australia's 15th largest trading partner. About the same time, Australia ranked as India's 8th largest overseas investor with A $1.0 billion approved, for 140 joint ventures.

The major Indian investments in Australia are made by Oswal Group (ammonia plant in Western Australia), Sterelite Industries (copper mining in Tasmania and gold mining in Queensland), Aditya Birla Group (copper mining in Western Australia and Queensland), Asian Paints (Queensland), Tata Steel (Brisbane), Taj Group of Hotels (Sydney) and the Oberoi Hotels International

(Melbourne). The Government of India and other public sector undertakings, besides their involvement in tourism and in banking (SBI), have established respective branches, like New India Assurance Company, Air India and Engineers India Ltd. (Perth). Of much significance is the presence of all (some 25) major Indian IT companies in Australia, especially Infosys, Satyam, TCS and Birlasoft, which have their Software Development Centers established in Sydney and Melbourne. [15]

Australia is believed to be capable of promoting itself as an ideal base for Indian companies; and the "Indian Community in Australia is identified with inspiring ideas for promoting Australia than Australians do." [16] It will not be inappropriate to mention that the Indian Commerce & Industry Minister, Kamal Nath, while addressing the 9th meeting of Australia-India Joint Ministerial Commission (AIJMC) held on 19th May 2005 in Sydney, stated much against the general perception, that the "Indian investment in Australia is larger than Australia's investment in India." He also gave a call for taking bilateral partnership to new heights in the form of "Australian natural resources using India's human resources." [17]

Employment Opportunities: The other 'pull' factor pertains to the gainful employment and improved career prospects in Australia for the Indian trained/skilled personnel. Even as these two nations were trying to come out of the shackles of their traditional inhibitions, there were about 10,000 Indian IT professionals employed in Australia in 1991. In the context of Asianization of Australia, the Indian settlers with a share of 3.7 per cent of the total moved up to the 5th rank from the 10th position (2.3 per cent) during 1986-1996. The strength of ICT professionals in 1960s and 1970s was such a minuscule thing that they could not figure in the top-ten source-countries. [18] The increase in the volume of Indian immigrants is due predominantly to ICT professionals (accounting for 64 per cent of the total), followed by those in other professional occupations. As per the salary levels of 1991, the Indian skilled migrants were considered to be of higher income group with an average annual per capita income of more than A $ 40,000. [19]

Interestingly, as per the 1996 salary levels, the median annual income (A $19,500) of the Indian immigrants was much higher than that of the other immigrant groups and even exceedingly higher than that of the Australians' average earnings (A $15,300). [20] Yet, these 'elite migrant workers' have been subjected to exploitation by those who are colloquially known as 'head hunters' or 'body-shoppers'. This 'extra-legal exploitative relationship', though considered to be part of 'complex system of agent chains', has often branded the ICT professionals as 'bonded labour' or 'indentured servitude." [21] As per the 1996 and 2001 Australian Census of Population and Housing, the highest proportion (36 per cent) of Indians were in the higher positions (as managers or administrators), thanks to the highest qualifications they possessed when compared to the other overseas-born Australians. Curiously enough, the preponderantly higher proportion (more than 96 per cent) of Indians is far more proficient in English language, than the other Asian immigrants and even those from the European countries like Greece, Italy and Poland. [22] As regards the spatial distribution, about 90 per cent of Indians are concentrated in the capital cities of the states of Australia, of which 40 per cent are found in New South Wales followed by Victoria (32 per cent).

About 2/3 of them own a house, indicating their permanent settlement in Australia. [23] In late 1990s, many Indians were found seeking better prospects in occupations such as trade, engineering and accountancy which have implicit linkages with the Indian investment in Australia. As a result, there has been an increase in the Indian immigrants who have gained lucrative employment as managers or administrative staff. Equally commendable, is the dynamism of some Indians who have been involved in catering (hotels/restaurants) in almost all the cities of Australia which I have had the good opportunity of visiting recently, as part of the AIC Australia Studies Fellowship programme.

The increase in skilled migration was mainly due to "strong interest from Indians in migrating to Australia", to quote the Australian High Commission spokes man, John Fisher (First Secretary), who further observed that "Indians are attracted to Australia for its dynamic economy, stable government, secure environment and welcoming multicultural society." Fisher's view was shared by other scholars like Prof. Raghabendra Jha of Research School of Pacific and Asian Studies at Australian National University who termed the Australian society as 'balanced and quite open', and thus, very much conducive to immigration. The upsurge in the Indian settlements in Australia, as remarked by Graemo Hugo in his analysis of the trends in Indian immigration, has its positive impact on the strength and spread of social networks linking India and Australia. This trend, as Hugo further elaborates, will continue further, inasmuch as the Indians readily conform to the criteria currently adopted in Australia for the selection of settlers. In fact, the new regulations, introduced by the Australian government in response to the demand of Australian business lobby, served as a stimulation "for a rapid increase in the skilled migrants particularly ICT migrants to Australia under 457 visa category." [24] In the light of these developments, as Prof. Raghabendra Jha of ANU envisioned, any kind of outsourcing may not have anything like a direct bearing on the Indian migration.

Better Career Prospects Luring the Indian Students

In addition to the potential avenues for the enterprising investors and employment opportunities for the skilled ICT personnel, Australia has of late become the much-sought-after destination for the Indian students who are in pursuit of higher education - masters (2years), doctorate (more than 2 years), vocational/technical training courses in TAFE (Technical and Further Education) mostly in ICT, business administration, accountancy and engineering. From a meagre enrollment of 378 in 1990, the number of Indian students in 1999 rose exactly to 9,362. [25] Mark Vaile, the Australian Trade Minister, noted in his statement at the 9th AIJMC meeting (Sydney: 19 May 2005), that "there are currently 21,000 Indian students studying in Australia." [26] This represents an increase of 83 per cent over the figure of 11,400 in 2002, or 50 per cent over the enrolled strength of 14,000 in 2003. The Indian students who ranked ninth and fourth in 2003 and 2004 respectively, moved up to the second place among the total number of international students. From the ninth rank source of international students in 2003 and fourth rank in 2004, the Indian students community in 2005 moves up to the second place; and Australia is the third most popular overseas destination of Indian students. Thanks to the liberalization of Indian economy during the post-Cold War period, Australia has become the home of 80,000 Indian students, which accounted for 26 per cent of Indians studying abroad, next only to the USA (44 per cent) over the past decade. [27]

Indian students have formed an ideal target group of Australian programme of international marketing of educational services, from which Australia has benefited, as in 2,000, to a tune of A$ 3.7 billion. [28] This prompted Australian government to initiate measures to sustain the flow of Indian students into Australian institutions. Further, Australia's legislation (1999) has been facilitating the overseas students to secure permanent residence in Australia. Recently (May 2005), Australian High Commission (AHC) in India has introduced "new streamlined procedures" which testify to its commitment to enhancing "the service to the students wishing to study in Australia" and to extending "practical benefits to applicants", [29] in the form of part-time jobs. The key factors attracting the Indian students to Australia include: the growing awareness of Australian quality-education, affordable fees and living costs, safe environment (as AHC First Secretary mentioned), shared information on a wide range of academic programmes (facilitated by an MOU signed by the Australian Vice-Chancellors' Committee with its Indian counterpart in 1999), involvement of AEII (Australia Education International-India) at AHC in processing the applications, and the Indian newspaper advertisements. Interestingly, as a recent study indicates, Indian primary applicant arrivals were accompanied by approximately the same number of dependents mostly in the age group of 20-30 years.

Despite certain controversies surrounding the Indian student migration and the related concerns of genuine students, and the limited number of scholarship for Indian students, Australia remains an attractive country for students who entertain the idea of staying permanently. Many Indian students - whom I met at various universities in Perth, Brisbane, Canberra, Melbourne, Sydney and Wollongong during my visits to Australia in November 2003 and later during September-November 2005 as part of Australia-India Council Fellowship Programme - were confident of finding employment befitting their expertise gained through Australian system of education; and they have also indicated their strong desire to settle in Australia. Indian students are at variance with other Asian students - particularly the Chinese, Koreans, Japanese and Indonesians - because of their (Indians') sense of familiarity with Australia through shared commonalities based on colonial heritage (like English language, legal jurisprudence, democratic pattern, business accountancy and cricket). Surprisingly, I have found a good number of students pursuing Masters/Doctorate courses in humanities and social sciences besides pure sciences, business administration, medicine and engineering.

Irrespective of the level of competency they had gained earlier in their respective fields from the Indian universities, they got themselves adapted to the requirements of the Australian education system. These products of Australian Universities - such as software engineers, academics in the Universities, MBA degree holders settled in various administrative set-ups and the medical professionals to mention a few - are now well-contended with the placements and well-settled as permanent residents. Unlike their counterparts in the Indian Universities, the Indian students in Australia are absolutely and blissfully free from the sense of false prestige; and many of them are seriously and sincerely subscribing to the concept of "earn while learning", so that they are able to derive a sense of supreme satisfaction from their 'self-supporting' nature that prevents them from taxing their parents. Indian students pursuing MBA and ICT, are successful in securing part-time employment in various establishments which are far away from their respective university campuses.

Role of Indian Community in Bilateral Partnership

For all the diversity based on language, religion, customs and traditions reflecting the complexity of the Indian identity, the Indian community is flourishing, getting themselves adapted to the native (Australian) environment and integrated with the host community. Yet, Indian community in Australia - as Deepa Balakrishnan, Research Development Coordinator in Monash University, points out - suffers from lack of bond among themselves, unlike the Chinese and the American Indians. She further laments that the poor and improper understanding of the Australian society by the Indian community has been impinging on the prospects of bilateral relations. Indian community has to transcend the barriers of language, religion and region which they had inherited whilst they were in India. Various socio-cultural organizations in almost all the Australian cities and the big Hindu temple-complexes as in Perth, Sydney and Canberra are testifying to the sense of Indian belongingness. Worth mentioning are the Indian Cultural Association of Queensland (estd: 1995), Brisbane Times and Radio Brisvaani (estd: 1998).

Committing themselves to serve Australia's developmental needs, the emerging Indian community is in an admirable position to contribute to the development of links between Indians and Australians and the strengthening of the India-Australia partnership. What is furthermore required, is the need for evolving an organizational framework of people-to-people contacts as part of track-II mechanism supplementing the efforts of the Indian government at moving bilateral partnership onto the flank of complementarity. It is true that Australia's official relationship with India, which Mark P. Thirlwell of Lowy Institute of International Policy (LIIP) (Sydney) considered an "economic giant" is "fairly a narrow front" one. In any case, it is hard to disagree with the observation of Alan Dupont that it is time the relations at the political level were reinforced to strengthen the India- Australia bilateral partnership for mutual benefit.

Notes

1. For a detailed discussion on this aspect, see Y. Yagama Reddy, "India – Australia Relations: Opportunities and Challenges," in Sonthosh Sareen, Sheel Nuna and Malathi Mathur (eds.), *Cultural Interfaces*, (Indialog Publications, New Delhi, 2004), pp. 214-226.
2. This was quoted by David J. Twine, in his "Keynote Address…." at *Seminar on Indo Australian Business and Economic Relations,* University of Delhi and Australian High Commission in India, February 19, 2002. Blainey's work, *The Tyranny of Distance,* (Melbourne, 1996: p. 61), was quoted by Meg Gurry, "A Tale of Missed Opportunities Australia's Relations with Indian since 1947," in Marika Vicziany (ed.) *Australia – India Economic Relations: Past, Present and Future,* Indian Ocean Centre for Peace Studies, the University of Western Australia, Nedlands (WA), 1993, pp.11-12.
3. Manjit – Singh Sekhon, "Sikhs in Australia and their religion," pp. 120-135 and Purusothama Bilimoria, "The Hindu Identity and Ethnicity in Australia", pp. 46-57; both in Abe W. Ata (ed.), *Religion and Ethnic Identity: An Australian Study*, (Spectrum Publishers, Richmond (Victoria), 1989).
4. Sarva Daman Singh, "Indians (History of Queensland Indian Community)', Maximilian Brande·(ed.), *Multicultural Queensland 2001: 100 years, 100 Communities, a Century of Contributions*, Dept. of Premier and Cabinet Multicultural Affairs Queensland, Brisbane, 2001, pp. 184-188.
5. R.S. Gabbi, *Sikhs in Australia*, (Aristoc Offset Pvt. Ltd., Glen Waverley (Victoria), 1998), pp. 178-190.
6. See Graeme Hugo, "Recent Population Movements between India and Australia: Trends and Implications", in D. Gopal and Dennis Rumley (eds.) *India and Australia: Issues and Opportunities*, (Author press, New Delhi, 2004), pp.229-298.
7. Graemo Hugo, n. 6, p.233.
8. *Ibid*, pp. 229-298
9. R.S. Gabbi, n. 5.
10. Manjit-Singh Sekhon, n.3

11. Graemo Hugo, n.6. While discussing the ethnic composition of total Australian population (in 1998), Charles A. Price has put the Indians (in Australia) at the mark of 110,300. See Charles A. Price, "Post-Ware Immigration: 1947-98", *Journal of Australian Population Association*, 15(2), 1998, pp. 115-129.

12. See Mark P. Thirlwell, *Indian: The Economic Giant*, (Lowy Institute for International Policy), Longueville Media, Double Bay (NSW), 2004.

13. ICFDC, *Indo-Asian News Service*, June 9, 2005, at http://www.icfdc-External_20050609_b.html.

14. See Mark P.Thrilwell, n. 12.

15. See FICCI, India-Australia Economic and Commercial Relations.

16. Mark P. Thirlwell, n.12. Also see Milissa Butcher, "India isn't quite perfect but has good opportunities for Australia," *Online Opinion* (Australia's e-journal of social and political debate), 1 March 2004.

17. ICFDC, India-Australia: Enhancing Economic Relations, May 25, 2005.

18. Laksiri Jayasuriya and Kee Pookong, *The Asianization of Australia: Some Facts about the Myths*, (Melbourne University Press, Carlton South (Victoria), 1999), p.95.

19. Salim Lakha, "Indian Computer Professionals in Australia", Bureau of *Immigration Research (BIR) Bulletin*, No.5, Dec. 1991, pp. 32-33.

20. Laksiri Jayasurya and Kee Pookong, n. 18, p.62. See also *Australian Census of Population and Housing*, quoted in Graemo Hugo, n.6, p.279.

21. Carmen Voigt - Greft and Siew - Ean Khoo,"Temporary Migration of Indian ICT Workers to Australia", *Asian and Pacific Migration Journal*, 13(2), 2004, pp.137-154.

22. For more details, see Laksire Jayasuriya Kee Pookong, n. 18.

23. Quoted in Graemo Hugo, n.6, pp. 278 (especially Tables No: 10.16, 10.17 and 10.18).

24. Carmen Voigt – Graft and Siew-Ean Khoo, n.21, p.152.

25. Carmen Voigt-Graft and Siew-Ean Khoo,"Indian Student Migration to Australia", *Asian and Pacific Migration Journal*, 13(4), 2004, pp.423-443.

26. ICFDC, "India-Australia: Enhancing Economic Relations," n.17.

27. ICFDC, "India – Australia: An Emerging Partnership", n.9. Also see Mark P.Thirlwell, n.12, p. 116.

28. Department of Immigration and Multicultural and Indigenous Affairs (DIMIA), *Combined Onshore and Offshore Visa Grants, Immigration Update*

29. ICFDC, *India – Australia News,* May 25, 2005.